Flightpath

AVIATION ENGLISH FOR PILOTS AND ATCOs

TEACHER'S BOOK

Philip Shawcross

CAMBRIDGE
UNIVERSITY PRESS

CAMBRIDGE
UNIVERSITY PRESS

University Printing House, Cambridge CB2 8BS, United Kingdom

Cambridge University Press is part of the University of Cambridge.

It furthers the University's mission by disseminating knowledge in the pursuit of education, learning and research at the highest international levels of excellence.

www.cambridge.org
Information on this title: www.cambridge.org/9780521178709

© Cambridge University Press 2011

First published 2011

A catalogue record for this publication is available from the British Library

ISBN 978-0521-178709 Teacher's Book
ISBN 978-0521-178716 Student's Book with Audio CDs (3) and DVD

Additional resources for this publication at www.cambridge.org/elt/flightpath

Contents

Preface

Aviation English is unique in English for Specific Purposes due to the high stakes of its outcomes which directly affect the safety of the travelling public. Aviation students are set apart by the immediacy and individual responsibility of their decision-making, the demands imposed by the precision of their language, the voice-only character of their communication, and the fact that the lives of so many people are suspended in mid-air.

In the *Flightpath Teacher's Book* we have tried to meet this exciting and daunting challenge by providing teachers with the strongest support possible, not only in terms of appropriate teaching strategies but also in terms of information about the operational background and the functional relevance of the content and exercises. This is not just a Teacher's Book to accompany a coursebook, but can also be used as a self-training manual and reference source for Aviation English teachers at many different levels of experience.

The pedagogical principles you will find here are based upon the 2010 edition of ICAO Document 9835, the holistic descriptors of the rating scale, and ICAO Circular 323. We have tried to build on and exemplify these in specific operational situations, but we cannot encourage you strongly enough to return regularly to these sources.

We hope that the safety and operational content which is the basis of *Flightpath* will not only fire your students' motivation and enhance their learning, but also provide the means to extend their professional skills after the course by directing them to the full range of media and documentation on aviation language and safety which is available in English.

For pilots and controllers, achieving and maintaining communicative proficiency in English is a life-long process and an integral part of their professional lives. As teachers, few commitments can be as stimulating and rewarding as supporting them effectively in this process: certainly, I feel deeply privileged to have been involved in the aviation community.

I am extremely grateful to Jeremy Day for all the expertise, experience and innovation he has brought to this project: with his work on the Teacher's Book, he has also greatly extended the scope of the activities in the Student's Book. You can find further material on the course website, **www.cambridge.org/elt/flightpath/**. This contains a substantial aviation glossary and regularly updated articles, case studies, media links, classroom resources and activities.

This book is dedicated to the unsung heroines, and a few heroes, of aviation English: teachers working over the years for air navigation service providers, aviation training centres, airlines and technical universities, many of whom gathered together for the first time around Fiona Robertson in March 1984 in what was to become the International Civil Aviation English Association. They have been the pioneers and the guarantors of good practice in Aviation English.

Philip Shawcross

To the teacher

What do pilots and air traffic control officers (ATCOs) need?

For the vast majority of their work, pilots and ATCOs need to be able to use and understand standard phraseology, the simplified and highly structured version of English that they use to communicate with each other. But they also need to be ready to cope with unexpected and non-routine situations of all sorts. For such cases, they need to understand and be able to use plain English.

The purpose of this book is not to teach standard phraseology, which pilots and ATCOs will have learned as part of their initial training courses. Nor is it to persuade pilots and ATCOs to replace standard phraseology with plain English. The strongest message one hears from pilots and ATCOs is that 'we don't want English teachers coming in and telling us how to do our job'. Rather, we need to provide them with an additional resource that may, in exceptional situations, save many lives.

Can I teach Aviation English if I don't understand standard phraseology?

In principle, yes, you can use your expertise in plain English, as well as your knowledge of clear pronunciation, to provide a useful service to pilots and ATCOs. In this Teacher's Book, we have been careful to include explanations (**Background notes**) of all the standard phraseology and technical language used in the course. We have also provided detailed sample answers to all open-ended questions, role-plays and discussions in the course (**Suggested answers, Possible answers**), again so that you can provide expertise without being an expert yourself. If you are an experienced teacher of Aviation English, some of this guidance may seem rather obvious, but we wanted to provide maximum support for less experienced teachers. Note that Unit 1 includes a lot of phraseology, so it could well be the easiest unit for your students, and the most difficult one for you to teach.

However, the more you know about your students' work and needs, the more useful your teaching will be. For this reason, we strongly advise you to study standard phraseology (for example, ICAO document 4444). There is a list of relevant **sources** near the beginning of each unit, which we recommend that you study. Aviation English is a very serious business, so you need to take your preparation seriously. We also recommend that Aviation English teachers are trained by reputable training providers, and that they continue to regard their professional development seriously throughout their careers, dedicating time to refresher courses and to self-study in their field.

One very basic component of phraseology that less experienced teachers will need to make sure they know is the International ICAO Radiotelephony Alphabet, and also the internationally agreed pronunciation of numerals in aviation radiotelephony.

A further support for all teachers that we have provided is an extensive **Aviation English Glossary**, which you can download at **www.cambridge.org/elt/flightpath/**. You may want to print this out for your own use and also for the use of your students.

What is the level of the course?

Flightpath is designed first and foremost to help learners reach ICAO Level 4. ICAO Level 4 is an internationally agreed standard of English – above that required to carry out standard radiotelephony – that all pilots and Air Traffic Control Officers need in order to work in the industry, and to fly planes or control traffic in international airspace. Within some organisations, a Level 5 standard may be desirable. The ICAO descriptors for levels 3, 4 and 5 are on page 8 and 9 of this *Teacher's Book*. The material in the course is designed to stretch and to challenge students, and with higher level learners, *Flightpath* can also be used to support learners aiming at a Level 5 standard of competence. It is also suitable for learners doing recurrent training after achieving Level 4 in the past.

Flightpath is designed to focus on the core professional skills rather than prepare learners for any particular test. There are many different tests of ICAO Level 4 worldwide, and it may be that your learners are preparing for one of them. Naturally, the best way to prepare for a sound test of language competence is to ensure that you work on the competence, rather than just 'teach to the test' – and this is particularly true in a safety-critical field such as aviation. However, it will still be useful for teachers to familiarise themselves with any test that their learners are preparing for.

What is the main priority of Aviation English learners?

ICAO regard the components of Aviation English competence as a 'pyramid' (see page 8) with all the skills building up to support the most important one: **the ability to interact fluently and effectively in aviation communication**. The syllabus of *Flightpath* is built on the same principle of 'interaction above all': the core interactions of Aviation English, especially those that take place between pilots and ATCOs, are at the heart of the course.

How is *Flightpath* structured?

Each of the ten units of *Flightpath* is built around a particular operational issue in aviation. There is an introductory unit which deals with general issues in aviation language. The remaining nine units fall into three sections corresponding to all the phases of flight: ground movements, en-route threats, and approach and landing incidents.

The units are divided into sections reflecting operational and communication issues in aviation. The unit starts with a **Lead-in**, usually based on discussion of an extract from safety-related material, which is designed to get students talking about the subject-matter of the unit and to help teachers get a feel for their students' awareness of the topic and ability to talk about it in English.

Each unit contains **Language Focus** sections, dealing with particular points of English grammar and vocabulary within the aviation context, and **ICAO Focus** sections which draw on ICAO and other industry publications to encourage a deeper understanding of issues in aviation communication.

The main part of the unit closes with a longer communication task, under the title **Putting it together.** This draws together the material in the unit and provides opportunities for students to put together the skills and language they have practised. See *How do I use the* Putting it together *sections?* below.

Most of the units also then have a task using the **DVD** which accompanies the course. See *How can I use the DVD?* below.

Each of the three sections of the course ends with a **Review**, which provides quick practice and a reminder of the language encountered in the preceding three units. The activities in the Review sections focus in turn on the six different competencies of the ICAO scales: Pronunciation, Structure, Vocabulary, Fluency, Comprehension and Interaction.

How do I use the *Putting it together* sections?

The main part of each unit ends with a major communication task, where students practise the language and skills they have learnt during the unit. It is vital that you monitor these carefully to make sure that all students really have mastered the relevant language and skills. You should also analyse their performance carefully and openly during the **Debriefing.** The **Progress check** at the end of each unit is a tool for checking systematically for remaining problems. It is worth devoting plenty of time to discussing both of these sections with the class.

If problems remain, you will need to set up revision work, either for individual students or for the whole class. This could mean simply repeating exercises that you have already done from the coursebook, or using the glossary to make quizzes and tests. Alternatively, you may need to create your own exercises tailored to your students' specific needs. Remember that you can use your students' expertise and experience to generate situations for role-plays. They can also create exercises and tests for each other; the process of making a test is often the best way of learning. Make sure you follow up any problem areas in later units, and keep working on them until your students have mastered them.

Why is there a lot of pairwork in the course?

Since Aviation English is driven so much by the efficient exchange of information, it is natural that *Flightpath* makes extensive use of pairwork activities built on the principle of the 'information gap', where two students have different sets of information and need to communicate effectively in order to transfer this to each other.

These are signposted through the course in two ways, depending on the emphasis of the activity. You will see references to *Pilots* and *ATCOs* for activities which are role-plays of pilot–ATCO communication, and *Student A* and *Student B* for more generic pairwork activities where students are not necessarily playing these two different roles.

In pilot-only classes, some students will often be expected to play the role of ATCOs. Likewise, in ATCO-only classes, you will find yourself asking students to play the role of pilots. We think this is a sound pedagogical approach: in order to speak a common language, it is essential that each of the two professional groups understand the culture of the other group and the particular difficulties they face. By putting themselves into the others' shoes in the language classroom, they may acclimatise themselves better to the other group's particular needs and difficulties, and be able to apply this in their professional practice.

In addition, we also recognise that there are some areas where ATCOs and pilots will have different priorities, and so we have provided different activity options and prompts to be used with ATCO-only classes or pilot-only classes. These are Unit 5, ex. 4; Unit 8, ex. 10 and 20; Unit 9, ex. 6 and 7a; and Unit 10, ex. 8c and d, 27a, and 34.

What do I do if I have an odd number of students?

For every activity which is designed for pairs (or groups of three or four), this *Teacher's Book* provides guidance on how to adapt the activity for different class sizes.

How can I use the audio CDs?

Many training centres for pilots or ATCOs are equipped with language labs, which allow students to complete listening tasks individually (e.g. listen and repeat, listen and respond). If you are lucky enough to have access to a language lab, we recommend that you use it for many of the listening tasks in *Flightpath*. In this Teacher's Book, however, we have provided guidance for teachers without language labs.

Since the students have the audio material from the course packaged with their *Student's Books*, they are likely to also derive a great deal of benefit from using the CD material for additional practice outside the class.

So that the tracks on the three CDs can be found easily by the teacher, the icons in the *Student's Book* refer directly to the CD and the track number: for example, ○ **2.14** means CD 2, Track 14, not Unit 2, Track 14.

The tasks which accompany the audio material in the course are aimed both at developing listening comprehension and also as models of, and cues for, spoken production.

How can I use the DVD?

The *Flightpath DVD* contains eight extracts from authentic aviation industry training video materials, based on real incidents, produced by airlines and industry bodies such as Eurocontrol and the UK National Air Traffic Services. The original purpose for which it was designed in the industry training context was as thought-provoking material for discussion of more general safety issues and human factors in aviation during training workshops, and to encourage best practice for both pilots and Air Traffic Control Officers.

The DVD-based tasks in the *Student's Book* are designed both to foster this kind of professional discussion in class, and also for more specific focus on features of Aviation English.

The DVD has English-language subtitles which can be switched on and off depending on whether you want to focus on comprehension or on more detailed language study, and photocopiable transcripts of the DVD material are also available on the course website (**www.cambridge.org/elt/flightpath/**).

Where can I find the answers?

For activities which have clear and unambiguous answers there is an **Answer Key** in the *Student's Book* (pages 166–173). This is to help the teacher save time in class, and will also support the self-study learner.

For the freer, more open-ended and more discursive activities in the course, answers are provided in the *Teacher's Book* and can be identified quickly by the grey shaded boxes. Depending on how open-ended the activity is, these keys have one of three headings:

Answers: if the activity demands a single, unambiguous answer. For easy reference, answers in the *Student's Book* key are also repeated in the *Teacher's Book*.

Suggested answers: where different answers are possible, but best practice makes certain answers very likely. Where students' answers differ from those provided here, teachers may find it very interesting to explore with the whole class why the answers differ and what reasons their students give for their answers, which may be just as valid as those in the *Teacher's Book*.

Possible answers: for more open-ended and discursive activities, especially where answers draw on the student's working contexts and experiences. There is no 'right' answer in these cases, but the keys will help the teacher understand the background and issues behind the answers their students may produce.

Page references

Page references in the *Teacher's Book* refer to the *Student's Book* unless otherwise stated.

Are you sure I can teach Aviation English?

There is nothing to be ashamed of in being an inexperienced teacher: all teachers have to start somewhere. As long as you take your work seriously, prepare carefully for your lessons, read as many of the background texts as you can and learn from your students and more experienced colleagues, you can be proud that you are doing a job that could help save hundreds of lives.

General resources

The Teacher's Brief at the beginning of each unit contains a detailed list of resources specific to the topics of that unit. However, the titles and websites below will be of constant benefit throughout your use of *Flightpath*.

Airbus: *Flight Operations Briefing Notes* (www.airbus.com)

Aviation English Services (www.aeservices.net)

Boeing: *Aero* online magazine (www.boeing.com)

Eurocontrol: *Preventing runway incursions*, 2008 (www.eurocontrol.int)

Eurocontrol: *Reducing Level Bust* (www.eurocontrol.int)

Flightpath website: (www.cambridge.org/elt/flightpath)

Flight Safety Foundation: *ALAR Tool Kit* (www.flightsafety.org)

Flight Safety Foundation: *AeroSafety World* online magazine (www.flightsafety.org)

Godwin, T. and Thom, T.: *The Air Pilot's Manual,* vols. 3–7

Gunston, B.: *The Cambridge Aerospace Dictionary*, 2004

International Civil Aviation English Association (www.icaea.pansa.pl)

ICAO: *Document 4444 – Air Traffic Management* (www.icao.int)

ICAO: *Document 9835 – Manual on the Implementation of ICAO Language Proficiency Requirements*, 2nd edition, 2010 (www.icao.int)

ICAO: *Circular 323 – Guidelines for Aviation English Training Programmes*, 2009 (www.icao.int)

Live ATC: Live air traffic (www.liveatc.net)

National Transportation Safety Board (www.ntsb.gov/aviation/aviation.htm)

Robertson, Fiona: *Airspeak*, 2nd edition, 2008

Skybrary (www.skybrary.aero)

Smart Cockpit (www.smartcockpit.com)

ICAO Language Proficiency Rating Scale Levels 3, 4 and 5

Proficient speakers shall:

a) communicate effectively in voice-only (telephone/radiotelephone) and in face-to-face situations;

b) communicate on common, concrete and work-related topics with accuracy and clarity;

c) use appropriate communicative strategies to exchange messages and to recognise and resolve misunderstandings (e.g. to check, confirm or clarify information) in a general or work-related context;

d) handle successfully and with relative ease the linguistic challenges presented by a complication or unexpected turn of events that occurs within the context of a routine work situation or communicative task with which they are otherwise familiar; and

e) use a dialect or accent which is intelligible to the aeronautical community.

For the full text of the ICAO Holistic Descriptors, which define the context in which language is used, see *Doc. 9835 4.5: Annex 1: Descriptors of ICAO Language Proficiency requirements*.

The ICAO Rating Scale contains six language skills; proficiency in all of these skills must be at least at Operational Level 4. However, as ICAO Doc. 9835, pages 2–10, emphasises, these proficiency skills form a pyramid in which the foundation skills support the aim of communication: interaction.

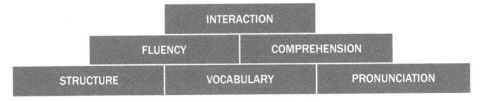

For a full explanation of the ICAO Rating Scale, see ICAO *Doc. 9835 4.6: Explanation of Rating Scale Descriptors*.

THE ICAO RATING SCALES: LEVELS 3, 4 and 5

PRONUNCIATION	STRUCTURE	VOCABULARY	FLUENCY	COMPREHENSION	INTERACTIONS
Level 5: Extended					
Pronunciation, stress, rhythm and intonation, though influenced by the first language or regional variation, rarely interfere with ease of understanding.	Basic grammatical structures and sentence patterns are consistently well controlled. Complex structures are attempted but with errors which sometimes interfere with meaning.	Vocabulary range and accuracy are sufficient to communicate effectively on common, concrete and work-related topics. Paraphrases consistently and successfully. Vocabulary is sometimes idiomatic.	Able to speak at length with relative ease on familiar topics but may not vary speech flow as a stylistic device. Can make use of appropriate discourse markers or connectors.	Comprehension is accurate on common, concrete and work-related topics and mostly accurate when the speaker is confronted with a linguistic or situational complication or an unexpected turn of events. Is able to comprehend a range of speech varieties (dialect and/or accent) or registers.	Responses are immediate, appropriate and informative. Manages the speaker/listener relationship effectively.
Level 4: Operational					
Pronunciation, stress, rhythm and intonation are influenced by the first language or regional variation but only sometimes interfere with ease of understanding.	Basic grammatical structures and sentence patterns are used creatively and are usually well controlled. Errors may occur, particularly in unusual or unexpected circumstances, but rarely interfere with meaning.	Vocabulary range and accuracy are usually sufficient to communicate effectively on common, concrete, and work-related topics. Can often paraphrase successfully when lacking vocabulary in unusual or unexpected circumstances.	Produces stretches of language at an appropriate tempo. There may be occasional loss of fluency on transition from rehearsed or formulaic speech to spontaneous interaction, but this does not prevent effective communication. Can make limited use of discourse markers or connectors. Fillers are not distracting.	Comprehension is mostly accurate on common, concrete and work-related topics when the accent or variety used is sufficiently intelligible for an international community of users. When the speaker is confronted with a linguistic or situational complication or an unexpected turn of events, comprehension may be slower or require clarification strategies.	Responses are usually immediate, appropriate and informative. Initiates and maintains exchanges even when dealing with an unexpected turn of events. Deals adequately with apparent misunderstandings by checking, confirming or clarifying.
Level 3: Pre-operational					
Pronunciation, stress, rhythm and intonation are influenced by the first language or regional variation and frequently interfere with ease of understanding.	Basic grammatical structures and sentence patterns associated with predictable situations are not always well controlled. Errors frequently interfere with meaning.	Vocabulary range and accuracy are often sufficient to communicate on common, concrete, or work-related topics, but range is limited and the word choice often inappropriate. Is often unable to paraphrase successfully when lacking vocabulary.	Produces stretches of language, but phrasing and pausing are often inappropriate. Hesitations or slowness in language processing may prevent effective communication. Fillers are sometimes distracting.	Comprehension is often accurate on common, concrete and work-related topics when the accent or variety used is sufficiently intelligible for an international community of users. May fail to understand a linguistic or situational complication, or an unexpected turn of events.	Responses are sometimes immediate, appropriate and informative. Can initiate and maintain exchanges with reasonable ease on familiar topics and in predictable situations. Generally inadequate when dealing with an unexpected turn of events.

UNIT 1
Language and communication in aviation

Operational topics	Types of RT communication situations; Call signs; Instructions; Abbreviations and acronyms; Examples of miscommunication; Managing communication
Communication functions	Misinterpretation; Giving instructions and readback; Communication errors: omitted or incorrect call sign; Requesting clarification and making requests; Switching from standard phraseology to plain language; Saying why unable; Checking understanding
Language content	Confusable meanings; Confusable sounds; Word endings; Interrogative words and phrases; Requests; American and British usage; Explanations of non-compliance

Unit 1 Teacher's brief

Unlike Units 2 to 10, Unit 1 has not got an operational focus (e.g. on the ground, en-route, and approach and landing). The purpose of Unit 1 is to:

- explore the various linguistic and communicative considerations which are at the foundation of the **ICAO Language Proficiency Requirements** (LPRs) and which the students will apply in different operational situations throughout *Flightpath*;
- define and raise awareness about the scope of the book, its **training objectives** and activities;
- highlight the potential **hazards of poor communication** and inadequate language proficiency;
- clarify the distinction between **standard phraseology** and **plain language**;
- draw attention to some of the **differences** in aviation English usage around the world; and
- provide teachers and students with an opportunity to establish a **working relationship**.

In this unit of the Teacher's Book, we have explained many phrases in standard phraseology. Note that this is for you, the teacher, to enable you to discuss the extracts in an informed way with your students, who should already be very familiar with this language. Note that in other units, the emphasis will be much more on plain language, which students are likely to find more difficult but that teachers should find much easier.

Although you are *not* expected to teach standard phraseology in this course, you should make it a priority to learn as much about it as possible for yourself, using the sources listed below. ICAO Documents 4444 and 9835 are a good starting point.

The standard phraseology in *Flightpath* has three purposes only:

- create the communicative context within which aviation plain English is used;

- offer realistic cues for transition from phraseology to plain language; and
- provide familiar matter for enhancing pronunciation, intonation and fluency.

Unit 1 Sources

- *Air Pilot's Manual*: Volume 7, *Radiotelephony*, 2009*
- Flight Safety Foundation: *ALAR Tool Kit – ALAR Briefing Note 2.3: Pilot–Controller Communication*: (ICAO focus with Exercise 6)
- ICAO: *Document 4444 – Air Traffic Management**
- ICAO: *Document 9835 – Manual on the Implementation of ICAO Language Proficiency Requirements*, 2nd edition, 2010*
- ICAO Journal: *Volume 56, No. 3; Volume 57, No. 3; Volume 58, No. 4; Volume 59, No. 1; Volume 63, No. 1; Volume 64, No. 3* on Language Proficiency*
- National Technical Information Service: *United States Airline Transport Pilot International Flight Language Experiences – Report No. 2: word meaning and pronunciation* (ICAO focus with Exercises 4a and 14a)
- Trémaud, M.: *Erasing Confusion, AeroSafety World*, May 2010 (Exercise 5a)
- UVE Aviation: A glossary of common acronyms and abbreviations used in civil aviation*
- Werfelman, L.: *Speaking the same language, AeroSafety World*, November 2007
- Werfelman, L.: *Speak Up, AeroSafety World*, December 2010–January 2011*

*these documents will be of value to teachers throughout *Flightpath*

Lead-in

Each unit, as well as certain sections within a unit, starts with a lead-in quotation from a safety or operational expert. The quotes are to be used as a means of generating a general discussion about some of the topics addressed in the exercises in order to place them in a broader context. Brian Day, formerly an Australian air traffic controller, and currently a world expert in search and rescue, was the Secretary of the ICAO Proficiency Requirements in Common English Study Group (PRICESG). As such, he is very conscious of the safety repercussions of good communication.

Students who are professional pilots or air traffic controllers should all be very familiar with standard ICAO phraseology. Standard phraseology is a formulaic language code which prescribes concise, unambiguous and universally accepted utterances to be used in specific situations as defined in Chapter 12 of ICAO Document 4444: Air Traffic Management. It consists typically of controller instructions and transmissions of information (*Report reaching Flight Level 250*, *Expect climb at 28*) and pilot requests, confirmations or transmissions of information (*Request right turn*, *Runway vacated*, *Airborne 35*).

ICAO Annex 10, volume II, 5.1.1.1 states that 'ICAO standard phraseology shall be used in all situations for which it has been specified. Only when standardised phraseology cannot serve an intended transmission, plain language shall be used.'

Standard phraseology is used in this book, but *Flightpath* is <u>not</u> designed to teach standard phraseology, nor are aviation English teachers qualified to teach it unless they are also qualified operational instructors. On the other hand, *Flightpath* is designed to develop plain English skills.

The first two questions are an opportunity to make sure that students are clear about the course objectives, i.e. attaining proficiency in plain language when standard phraseology is insufficient.

Examples of situations where recourse to plain language is necessary are: sick passengers or crew, damage to the aircraft or system failures, severe or unexpected weather, delays, obstacles on the ground, unserviceable navigation or ground equipment, terrorist threats or bomb scares, re-routeing etc.

Quote: **Tell students to read the quote and find (a) two things that need to be understood and (b) two reasons why it is important to understand them.**

> Answers:
> a that language is an imperfect medium; that language is easily misunderstood
> b in order to be accurate; to make the airways safer

1a **Discuss the question with the class.**

> Suggested answer:
> See Teacher's brief for an explanation of standard phraseology. The plain language used by pilots and ATCOs is still much more formal and formulaic than everyday English. For example, words tend to be pronounced in full, without contractions. Longer (and more precise) words are often used (e.g. *What is the condition of your passenger?* vs *How's your passenger?*; *The cabin crew are administering first aid.* vs *The crew are treating his injuries.*).
>
> Plain language will be a major focus throughout the rest of the book.

b **Students discuss the question in pairs and then share their best stories with the class.**

> Possible answers:
> Basically, plain language is required in many unexpected, non-routine communicative situations such as enquiring about and giving reasons for delays, describing and giving the consequences of technical failures and malfunctions, reporting cases of illness among the crew or passengers, describing weather conditions, talking about conditional situations, cause and effect, unusual behaviour, threats to safety and security etc.

c **Discuss the question with the class, eliciting both problems with language in general and specific language problems with radiotelephony. Refer back to stories from exercise 1b where appropriate.**

> Suggested answers:
> ◆ Language is linear (i.e. one thing must follow another), whereas real-life events happen simultaneously.
> ◆ Language may be too slow to communicate fast events.
> ◆ Language can be too digital (e.g. a shape could be described as circular or square), but the real world is analogue (e.g. shapes can be something between a circle or a square, but this requires much more language to explain).
> ◆ Language is ambiguous – one word may have several meanings (e.g. *the paper is very <u>light</u>*).
> ◆ For most pilots and ATCOs, their working language (English) is not their first language, so the problems are multiplied.
> ◆ The speaker or listener may not know the word for a particular thing or action, or may struggle to communicate it.
> ◆ A speaker's accent may be unfamiliar.
> ◆ The communication channel (radio) can be of low quality.
> ◆ The risks associated with mistakes are much higher than in most other situations of language use.

Standard phraseology and plain language

This listening and responding exercise will certainly illustrate some of the examples provided by students in the Lead-in section, and then make them more aware that in certain cases standard phraseology is appropriate, while in others plain language is required. The exercise also highlights the range of lexical domains which they must call upon: cargo, weather, health, safety, security, time, materials, geography, topography, malfunctions, physical and sensory descriptions, causes, rules etc.

2a **●1.01 Go through the two examples with the class. Elicit how it is possible to tell the difference. [Suggested answer: In terms of language, standard phraseology can contain much simpler vocabulary and grammar. The situations described are also more common – things that pilots and ATCOs talk about every day. Plain language is needed for non-typical situations.]**

Tell students to write the numbers 1–10 in their notebooks. Then play the recording for students to write *S* (standard phraseology) or *P* (plain English) next to each number. Students then compare their answers in pairs.

Answers:		
1 Standard	5 Plain	9 Standard
2 Plain	6 Plain	10 Plain
3 Plain	7 Plain	
4 Standard	8 Plain	

Background notes:

◆ *ATC* means Air Traffic Control.

◆ *ATCO* means Air Traffic Control Officer.

◆ '*Request taxi for departure*' means '*I am requesting permission to move the aircraft from the apron [at the terminal] along the taxiways to the runway holding point for departure*'. Pilots often say *requesting taxi for departure* in this situation, but this does not comply with strict phraseology rules.

◆ '*Report your level*' is an instruction to inform ATC about the aircraft's flight level, i.e. standardised altitude at a universal atmospheric pressure of 1013 hectoPascal or millibars.

◆ A *missed approach* is when an aircraft approaches an airport in order to land, but does not actually land, typically because of low visibility, an obstacle on the runway etc. and goes around to make another approach.

◆ *ILS* stands for Instrument Landing System, which uses radio transmitter signals to guide an aircraft down, typically when visibility is poor. ILS consists of the glideslope (G/S), localizer (LLZ, LOC) and Locator (LOC). See www.pilotfriend.com, www.flightsimaviation.com

◆ *Manoeuvrability* /mənuːvrəˈbɪlɪtɪ/ refers to the extent to which an aircraft can manoeuvre /məˈnuːvər/, i.e. move around, get into the right position.

Extension activity:

When you check with the class, elicit the situation that each transmission comes from. In some cases, this will involve speculating possible reasons.

Suggested answers:
1 The pilot is requesting taxi instructions to taxi to the departure runway.
2 An ATCO is asking about an injured passenger in order to predict and be prepared for the crew's subsequent decisions.
3 The pilot has seen an obstacle on the runway while preparing to take off or land.
4 An ATCO is asking about the aircraft's flight level.
5 The crew have reported damage to the aircraft, and the ATCO is trying to assess how serious the incident was and what its consequences might be.
6 An ATCO is briefing a pilot before a tricky landing attempt in case he has to perform a missed approach. If the pilot has to go around, i.e. discontinue his approach, he must climb on an extension of the runway centreline axis and contact the Tower for instructions as he is currently on another frequency, perhaps Approach.
7 An ATCO is asking about a hijacking. During such a situation, ATC needs to monitor events constantly in order to deal with sudden dangers and coordinate with security services.
8 An ATCO is asking whether the pilot will need the fire service, an ambulance, a tow vehicle, technicians, security services or police on arrival.
9 A pilot wishes to make an Instrument Landing System approach.
10 An ATCO is asking a pilot for information about aircraft damage or malfunction which may affect how the pilot can control the flight.

b **●1.01 Play the recording again for students to think about how they might respond. They mark a tick (✓) if it is possible to reply using standard phraseology and a cross (✗) if it is not possible. Afterwards, they discuss their reasons in pairs and then feed back to the class.**

c **●1.01 Go through the examples with the class. You may want to check some of the plain English vocabulary (e.g. *concussed*, *severe bruising* /ˈbruːzɪŋ/, *to administer first aid*). Then play the recording, pausing after each transmission, and ask volunteers to suggest a suitable response. Discuss each response with the class to generate plenty of ideas** before moving on to the next transmission. In questions 2, 3, 5, 7, 8 and 10, you may wish to draw the students' attention to verbs used to express impressions or reported information.

> **Suggested answers:**
> 1 Taxi to holding point Bravo 3 Runway 27 Right via Delta. Hold short of Runway 27 Right.
> 2 He appears to be concussed and have severe bruising. The cabin crew are administering first aid, but he requires urgent medical attention.
> 3 I can see what looks like pieces of tyre on the right-hand side of the runway about 500 metres after the touchdown zone.
> 4 We are passing through Flight Level 260.
> 5 A catering truck has impacted our rear right-hand door and the purser has reported that the lower door hinge looks twisted.
> 6 Climb straight ahead on extended runway centreline to 2,500 feet and contact Tower 119.75.
> 7 The cabin service manager has reported that two men carrying knives are holding a group of passengers hostage in the forward cabin on the main deck.
> 8 Will you have the fire brigade standing by at the far end of the runway to check that there are no signs of fire from our left-hand engine?
> 9 Cleared ILS approach Runway 28 Right.
> 10 Our ailerons seem to be responding a bit slowly, but the response from the other flight controls feels normal.

Background notes:

- *Ailerons* are flight control surfaces on the outer trailing (rear) edges of the wings which enable the pilot to control the aircraft about the roll axis, i.e. raising one wing and lowering the other, or *banking*, as during a turn.
- A *holding point* is a place indicated by painted ground markings, illuminated signage and (often) stop bars where aircraft stop until they are authorised to enter the runway.
- *Via* can be pronounced /ˈvaɪə/ or /ˈviːə/, but in radiotelephony, /ˈvaɪə/ is preferred.
- *Hold short of* means stop and wait just before you get to a particular place.

Extension activity:

Students test each other in pairs. One reads a transmission from audioscript 1.01 on page 174 to elicit a suitable response from his/her partner. They then swap roles.

Misunderstanding

No aircraft accident or incident has ever had a single cause; however, poor communication has been a contributing factor in some of the worst accidents in aviation history. Language is inherently ambiguous. Without the visual cues, facial expressions and body language we rely on heavily in everyday communication, radiotelephony has a considerable potential for generating misunderstanding. This is one of the factors which explain the emphasis on the use of standard phraseology wherever possible. In this section, the various forms which misunderstanding can take are explored.

The short recordings in this section which illustrate different types of misunderstanding should also draw attention to the 'fragility' of oral communication: how a small deviation can have significant consequences in an operational context.

These three exercises exemplify three characteristics of many activities in *Flightpath*: drawing on the students' own experience to make the communication relevant (a, d), developing analytical listening skills (b), and combining speech production with any 'passive' skills (c). Examples of how misunderstanding can affect safety might be:
a vocabulary confusion: e.g. the use of *actual* when *current* is meant
b readback error: e.g. '*Descend Flight Level 190*' read back as '*Descend Flight Level 150*'
c non-standard phraseology: e.g. '*Maintain 160*' instead of '*Maintain heading 160*' (*160* could be a flight level, a heading or an airspeed.)
d incorrect or imprecise use of English: e.g. '*We extinguish the fire.*'; '*We are extinguishing / will extinguish / have extinguished the fire.*'?
e garbled message / an inaudible or missing word or phrase: e.g. '*We'll need a chtndpk on arrival.*'
f incorrect pronunciation: e.g. '*There is a problem with the service.*' instead of '*There is a problem with the surface.*'

3a **Students discuss the six causes of misunderstandings in pairs. You may need to check the meaning of *garbled* (= unclear, inaudible, typically because of technical problems). Where possible, they should think of examples from their own experience or anecdotes they have heard. Then elicit examples of each from the class.**

> **Suggested answers:**
> **Vocabulary confusion:** '*We have controlled all our instruments and the readings seem correct.*' *control* means *to command or give an order* not *to check*
> **Readback error:** '*Egyptair 465, turn right heading 230.*' – '*Turn right heading 320, Egyptair 465.*'
> **Non-standard phraseology:** '*How far are you from TEH?*' rather than '*Report distance from TEH.*' When standard phraseology exists for a given task, it should be used. *TEH* is a waypoint or navigation beacon.
> **Incorrect or imprecise English:** '*We lose communication.*' Is this past or present? Is it still the case?

> Garbled message: '*Climb Flight Level 250. xxxxx 350 in 20 miles.*'
>
> Incorrect pronunciation: '*We are making a steep climb.*' when in fact the speaker means a *step climb.*

b **○1.02** Play the first transmission to elicit why it is described as a readback error and what might have caused the error. Then play the rest of the recording for students to complete the exercise. They compare their answers with a partner before checking with the class. When you check the answers, elicit exactly what went wrong with each transmission and a possible cause of the problem. Afterwards, students test each other in pairs. One reads a transmission from audioscript 1.02 on page 174 to elicit a suitable response from his/her partner. They then swap roles.

> Suggested answers:
> 1 b – The pilot repeats the instruction but with the wrong number. *Five* and *nine* are easy to mix up, as they contain the same vowel. For this reason, *nine* should be pronounced *niner*.
> 2 e – The word after *large* is impossible to make out.
> 3 a – The pilot uses *previous* when he means *scheduled* or *estimated*.
> 4 c – The pilot uses non-standard phraseology. The correct form should be *line up and wait*. (See answer to exercise 14d for an explanation.)
> 5 d – '*At take-off*' can be interpreted as *ready for take-off, lined up for take-off* or *taking off*.
> 6 f – The pilot mispronounces *wheel* as '*well*'.

Background notes:

◆ Note the structure of the exchange in transmission 1. The ATCO gives the call sign of the aircraft (Delta 357) first to make it clear who he/she is talking to. The pilot gives the same identification code at the end of the transmission, to make it clear who is talking.

◆ The *threshold* of a runway is the beginning of the usable portion of a runway (downwind end).

◆ Transmission 5 is one of the most famous examples of a misunderstanding caused by ambiguous language since it was one of the causal factors which contributed to the aviation accident in Tenerife in 1977. See Unit 3, exercise 16a.

c **○1.02** Play the recording again, pausing after each transmission to elicit suitable responses from volunteers. Discuss the best response with the class before moving on to the next transmission.

Background note:

When dealing with misunderstandings, the word *Correction* is used to indicate that an error has been made by the person making the transmission; *Negative* contradicts a previous statement by the other speaker; *Say again* is used when a transmission has not been heard or understood or the listener is not sure of the content; *I say again* announces a repetition or a rephrasing; *Read back* is an instruction to make the interlocutor acknowledge specific instructions or information.

d Students work in pairs to describe their experiences of, or anecdotes they have heard about, misunderstandings. They then share their best (or worst) stories with the class.

e Discuss the question with the class, focusing on the examples from the audioscript and students' own stories.

> Suggested answers:
> The misunderstandings can be classified into two categories: where the listener fails to understand the message at all, because the message doesn't make sense; and where the listener understands the wrong thing (e.g. *9,000 feet / 5,000 feet*). The former situation is dangerous because it slows down communication and may be distracting. There is a danger that the listener could give up trying to understand and simply pretend to understand (a common phenomenon for non-native speakers of a language). The latter situation is potentially much more dangerous, as both sides believe they have communicated successfully. This is why it is so important to read back key information such as altitudes.

Language confusion

The use of non-standard phraseology and dealing with *garbled* (= unclear) messages are beyond the remit of this book, but being able to deal with their consequences is not. Using correct vocabulary, grammar, syntax and pronunciation, however, correspond to three of the six language skills and criteria in the ICAO rating scale.

This section pursues the exploration and awareness-raising of how miscommunication can occur from a more linguistic standpoint through lexical confusion (exercise 4a), mispronunciation (exercise 4b) and word endings (exercise 4c).

ICAO FOCUS

Look at the quote with the class, focusing on the three problems cited. Discuss the question with the class.

Language note:

The speaker uses *won't* to refer to a typical present situation, not a future prediction or plan.

Possible answer:
The answers to this question will depend very much on cultural and linguistic backgrounds and how students have been taught general English. Pronunciation, especially pronunciation by speakers of unfamiliar language backgrounds, is a commonly reported difficulty. Students also often complain of speed of delivery and vocabulary.

Pronunciation is probably the most frequently quoted cause of incomprehension, especially when pilots fly into regions of the world they are not familiar with or into very busy airports like Chicago O'Hare or Los Angeles, where the density of traffic in an English-speaking environment means that delivery rates are quite high. It is important to remember how much easier it is to understand someone speaking English when one is familiar with the cultural and linguistic background of their mother tongue.

Other causes of misunderstanding, or of needing more time to understand, are: the use of non-standard phraseology, the inability to paraphrase if the initial utterance is not understood, a failure to adjust one's own speech to the level of proficiency of one's interlocutor.

Background notes:

♦ The report referred to in the quote is excellent background reading for this unit. It can be found and downloaded online by conducting a simple search for its title or by using this URL: http://www.faa.gov/library/reports/medical/ oamtechreports/2010s/media/201007.pdf. Report 1 is also available to download, and is also extremely useful for teachers of aviation English.

♦ A *frequency change* refers to radio frequencies. If the frequency that the pilot and ATCO are using becomes too weak or distorted, they may agree to switch to a different frequency.

♦ A *fix* is a radio beacon that a pilot can use to identify the aircraft's position and direction.

♦ A *waypoint* is a point on the journey to the final destination (e.g. a pilot may fly from Warsaw to London by flying first towards Berlin and then Amsterdam). *Off-route waypoints* are used when a plane is diverted (e.g. if there is a heavy storm over Berlin, the pilot may be instructed to head for Copenhagen).

4a Students complete the exercise in pairs and then feed back to the class. When you go through the answers, elicit the cause of confusion and any similar examples students can think of. You may need to check the following plain English expressions: *unruly* (= noisy, argumentative, causing trouble), *fumes* (= unpleasant or harmful gases emitted from a fire or chemical reaction), a *stroke* (= a very dangerous medical

condition caused by a lack of oxygen supply to the brain), *severe concussion* (= injuries to the brain after a heavy blow) and *bruises* (= discoloration of the skin caused by a blow).

Answers:
1 after/aft
2 security/safety
3 alternative/alternate
4 strangers/foreigners
5 request/require
6 hardly/hard
7 controlling/monitoring
8 meat/meal

Background notes:

♦ *Aft* is an adjective referring to the back part of a plane. *Rear* is also used with the same meaning. It contrasts with *forward*. The words *before* and *after* should only be used to talk about time relationships.

♦ An *alternate* /ˈɔːltənət/ is an airport along or near the scheduled route to which the aircraft can divert and where it can land in case of an incident during the flight. An *alternative* is an option and it can be related to any aspect of the flight: routeing, level, heading, timing etc.

♦ Passengers are required to fill in *immigration cards* before landing in some countries. This saves a lot of time at passport control.

♦ A *stand* is the place where the aircraft parks, where passengers board and disembark.

♦ The *gear* refers to the landing gear, i.e. the wheels and the mechanisms connected to them.

♦ If an engine *ingests* a bird, the bird is sucked into the engine.

♦ *Climb-out* refers to the initial climb from the airport of departure.

♦ *Indications* are the readings on the various flight instruments. In this case of a bird ingestion, the pilots would monitor the main engine parameters, which are N1 (fan and low pressure compressor rotation speed), N2 (high pressure compressor rotation speed), Engine Pressure Ratio (EPR) and Exhaust Gas Temperature (EGT) as well as engine vibrations.

b ○1.03 Play the first transmission for students to identify the problem. If they are able, you could see if they can identify the incorrect words and the intended words without referring to them on the page. Discuss the incorrect and correct pronunciations with the class. Then play the rest of the recording for students to choose the intended words. They compare their ideas with a partner before checking with the class. When you go through the answers, elicit the correct pronunciation.

Answers:
1 ~~quite~~ quiet
2 ~~lose~~ loose
3 ~~services~~ surfaces
4 ~~well~~ wheel
5 ~~array~~ area
6 ~~feed~~ feet
7 ~~rich~~ ridge
8 ~~eyes~~ ice
9 ~~washing~~ watching
10 ~~heat~~ hit

Extension activity:

Students take turns to read one of the transmissions aloud, using audioscript 1.03 on page 174. They change the transmissions to make sure they pronounce the problematic word correctly. You may need to check the following plain English expressions: *overcast* (= very cloudy) and *intoxicated* (= under the effect of alcohol or drugs; drunk).

Background notes:

♦ *Quiet hours* refers to the time (e.g. 23:00–06:00) when aircraft movements to and from the airport are restricted or prohibited to avoid disturbance by noise.

♦ *Cowling* refers to the panels (cowls) surrounding the engine. It is the main part of the engine nacelle (the structure which encloses each engine).

♦ A *walk-around inspection* is made by the First Officer at the stand between two flights; he makes sure that there is no apparent damage.

♦ *De-icing* is performed by the airport services in cold weather either by aircraft passing under a gantry or by special tankers with hydraulic platforms which spray de-icing fluid onto the wings, flight control surfaces, empennage (the horizontal and vertical stabilisers on the tail of the aircraft) and fuselage.

♦ The *main gear* refers to the main landing gear which is located under the inner wing and, in very large aircraft, under the centre fuselage (the body of the aircraft). It consists of wheels mounted on axles forming a bogie (the assembly of several wheels, axles and the horizontal linking structure, as on a train) which is attached to the gear leg through a shock absorber. The gear is maintained rigid, retracted and extended by a series of struts, braces and actuators.

♦ A *dew point* is the temperature at which condensation, and so precipitation, begins in cooling air.

♦ The *field* or *airfield* is another term for the *aerodrome* or *airport.*

♦ A *purser* is the chief cabin attendant on medium-sized narrow-body aircraft.

c **⊙1.04 Check students understand the instructions by playing the first transmission. Then play the rest of the recording for students to complete the exercise. When they have checked with a partner, go through the answers with the class. Note that speakers of some languages have particular problems pronouncing word endings. If your students have such problems, you may need to go through the pronunciations several times.**

Answers:	
1 lifting	6 clear
2 disconnect	7 slowly
3 services	8 checked
4 cleared	9 disconnected
5 turning	10 reduced

Background notes:

♦ An *instinctive disconnect push button* is a small red pushbutton on the control wheel or sidestick used to disconnect the autopilot quickly.

♦ A *yoke* is another word for the control wheel which controls the ailerons on a conventional aircraft.

♦ *Cleared* (= given permission)

♦ *Heading 130 degrees* is a direction, roughly south-east.

♦ *Autopilot* and *autothrust* are two computerised systems which provide the flight controls and engines with orders.

♦ *Pushing back* means that a tractor, tug or tow vehicle moves the aircraft back away from its parking stand so that the crew can start the engines and taxi to the runway.

♦ *Visual separation* is the separation between two aircraft based on the pilots' visual contact rather than a distance imposed by ATC.

♦ *11 o'clock* is a direction, *not* a time (which would be pronounced 'eleven hundred hours'). *12 o'clock* means straight ahead, so *11 o'clock* means a little to the left.

Extension activity:

Students work in pairs to remember what each transmission was about, using only the words in exercise 4c (and possibly the terms from the background notes above) to remind them.

d **⊙1.04 If your students have problems pronouncing the endings of words, pause the recording after each transmission for them to repeat as many times as necessary until they can pronounce the words properly. If your students don't have major problems with word endings, play the recording all the way through again for students to remind themselves of the sentences. They then work in pairs to say the whole sentences from memory, paying particular attention to the endings.**

Readback

Readback is one of the most basic and fundamental safety nets in radiotelephony communication. The practice of the recipient of a message reading back the key items of information received from his/her interlocutor is the first way in which both parties are sure of sharing identical information. This explicit acknowledgement also has the psychological function of reassuring both parties. For example:

ATCO: *Finnair 356, descend to Flight Level 150. Cross Umea at Flight Level 170 or above.*

Pilot: *Descend Flight Level 150. Cross Umea Flight Level 170 or above, Finnair 356.*

In *Flightpath*, readback is used as it is such a fundamental part of RT communications, but not for operational or phraseology purposes, rather as a form of repetition activity to monitor comprehension and practise pronunciation, intonation and phrasing.

For professional pilots and controllers, these are basically warm-up activities which should not present a considerable challenge. These activities are, however, an opportunity for the teacher to focus on individual pronunciation in an environment without semantic complication at the very beginning of the course.

ICAO FOCUS

Students read the quote to identify issues with readback. They then discuss the questions in pairs, including stories from their own experience, before feeding back to the class.

Suggested answers:
Good readback discipline is one of the pillars of aviation safety. By reading back the instruction, clearance or information received, the pilot demonstrates to the controller (or vice versa) that the contents of the original transmission have been correctly and fully understood. This reassures both parties, avoids action based on incorrect or incomplete information, and avoids time wasted on the radio frequency by requesting clarification or confirmation.

Background notes:

Pilots and ATCOs are supposed to read back clearances (e.g. take-off, route and landing), approvals (e.g. pushback and engine start) and instructions (e.g. taxiing and change of frequency).

The following types of ATC message should always be read back: taxi/towing instructions; level, heading and speed instructions; airways or route clearances; approach clearances; runway-in-use information; clearances to enter, land on, take off from, backtrack on, cross or hold short of any active runway; SSR (Secondary Surveillance Radar) operating instructions; altimeter settings; frequency changes; types of radar service; transition levels. For example:

ATCO: *Air France 592, hold position.*
Pilot: *Holding position, Air France 592.*

ATCO: *Malaysian 2836, contact Ground 118.350.*

Pilot: *Ground 118.350, Malaysian 2836.*

ATCO: *Tam Express 287, cleared to Santos via Charlie 1, São Paulo 3 departure, squawk 4561.*

Pilot: *Cleared to Santos via Charlie 1, São Paulo 3 departure. Squawk 4561, Tam Express 287.*

ATCO: *China Eastern 197, after departure, cleared to zone boundary route Golf. Climb to altitude 2,000 feet QNH 1019, squawk 6344.*

Pilot: *After departure, cleared to zone boundary via route Golf. Climb to altitude 2,000 feet, QNH 1019, squawk 6344, China Eastern 197.*

For more detailed instructions, pilots will and should take notes. Therefore, the note-taking activities within *Flightpath* are operationally relevant.

For a full account of standard phraseology, refer to ICAO Document 4444.

5a ○**1.05** Go through the first example with the class, making sure everyone understands the need for good *pronunciation* (i.e. correct pronunciation of sounds), *clarity* (i.e. sounds pronounced clearly and distinctly) and *delivery* (i.e. sounds pronounced loudly and slowly enough to be understood). Then play the recording to elicit suitable responses from volunteers. Remember that the focus is on pronunciation, clarity and fluency not on correct phraseology, which is not the aim of this book. Afterwards, students test each other in pairs. One reads a transmission from audioscript 1.05 on page 174 to elicit a suitable response from his/her partner. They then swap roles.

Background notes:

◆ *Give way* means to let another aircraft pass first during ground movements.

◆ *Squawk* is a transponder identifier code which enables an ATCO to identify each aircraft on radar screens. '*Squawk 6722*' means '*select transmission code 6722*'. Pilots may sometimes use the expression '*Squawking 6722*', with squawk as a verb (= *I am squawking*), but it is normally treated as a noun (= *Our squawk is …*).

◆ If you *expedite a climb*, you perform it as quickly as possible.

◆ *Orbit* means to perform a 360° circuit usually in order to delay. For safety reasons, ATC will tell the pilot whether to orbit left or right.

◆ A *minimum approach speed* refers to the fact that each aircraft type (B737, A320 etc.) will have a minimum speed at which it can safely fly in a given configuration, i.e. clean configuration (all flaps and gear retracted) and then with flaps and slats extended to different degrees (5°, 15°, 25° etc.) and the gear extended. This speed will decrease as the flaps, slats and gear are extended.

♦ *Controlled airspace* is an airspace of defined dimensions within which air traffic control service is provided to controlled flights. It is divided into different classes according to altitude. See www.nats.co.uk

♦ *Vectoring* means issuing headings to aircraft to provide navigation guidance.

♦ A *visual approach* means an approach to a given runway where the pilot relies on visual references such as VASI (Visual Approach Slope Indicator), PAPI (Precision Approach Path Indicator) and topography rather than using the Instrument Landing System.

b **Make sure students know what to do and know how to request clarification. Requesting and providing clarification is a key skill which will be practised throughout the course since it enables misunderstandings and communication gridlocks to be lifted. Students then take turns to read one of their transmissions aloud to elicit a suitable readback response from their partner. When they have finished, go through the transmissions with the class to elicit the best responses to each. Afterwards, students could swap roles and repeat the exercise.**

If you have an odd number of students you could have one group of three, where the third student reads transmissions from audioscript 1.05 on page 174.

Background notes:

♦ *118.375* is a radio frequency.

♦ *Report short final* means that the pilot advises ATC when he/she is on the last section of the approach.

♦ *On runway heading* means flying on a heading which is an extension of the runway centreline.

♦ An *autoland* is an autopilot function which enables the aircraft to be landed automatically.

♦ *Information Lima* identifies a specific ATIS (Automatic Terminal Information Service) in a series A, B, C, D etc. giving up-to-date information about conditions at the airport.

♦ A *foreign object* is the general name for something which should not be there. In this case, it could be a bird, a plastic bag, etc.

♦ The *apron* is the paved area around the terminal buildings, hangars and cargo terminals where aircraft park.

♦ '*Pan-pan, pan-pan, pan-pan*' indicates an urgency call which concerns the safety of the aircraft, but does not require immediate assistance. It is a lesser degree of urgency than the distress call 'Mayday'.

♦ A *flame-out* is a loss of engine combustion.

♦ A *precautionary landing* is an anticipated landing decided on by the crew in order to manage an abnormal situation (e.g. technical failure, illness etc.), but which is not an emergency.

Communication errors: Omitted or incorrect call sign

Each unit contains a short *Communication errors* section based on various quotations from Flight Safety Foundation ALAR (Approach and Landing Reduction) Briefing Note 2.3. These quotations are ways of relating the aviation English content of *Flightpath* to good communication practice and also encouraging students to pursue their personal reading of safety documents in English.

The topic in Unit 1 is an appropriately simple one: the use of call signs. In general, numerals are the aspect of the language with which pilots and controllers are most familiar. Numerals are spelled and pronounced in a distinctive way to avoid confusion: '*zero*', '*wun*', '*too*', '*tree*', '*fower*', '*fife*', '*six*', '*seven*', '*ait*', '*niner*', '*dayseemal*', '*hun dred*', '*tousand*'. Note that *fower* rhymes with *flower*. *Wun*, *too* and *ait* are pronounced as normal numbers – the spelling changes are intended to discourage speakers from trying to pronounce them the way they are normally spelled.

Nonetheless, there are cases when similar call signs (e.g. Dragonair 2594 / Dragonair 2954) being used in the same airspace may be confused. When controllers are aware of this, they may assign a different call sign to one of the aircraft.

The purpose of this section is not training for or correcting standard phraseology – students should self-correct – but rather recycling basic numerical call sign, heading, runway and wind speed data with the emphasis on pronunciation and delivery. Generally, students will find all numerical and alphabetical data to be the easiest to handle, but their pronunciation may require attention.

ICAO FOCUS

Read the quote aloud to check students understand all the terms. Then discuss the two questions with the class, eliciting examples from students' own experience where possible.

Suggested answers:

♦ An omitted or incorrect call sign could result in a flight crew acting on an instruction, clearance or piece of information which was not intended for them, as well as causing confusion for other flight crews. At best, the clarification required would waste time on the radio frequency. At worst, this could result in the wrong aircraft turning, climbing, descending, departing etc. and so increasing the risk of a conflict.

♦ Readback is repeating the key items from an instruction, clearance or piece of information received, so that both parties are sure the transmission has been correctly and fully understood. Hearback is listening to the other party's readback to make sure that the original message was correctly understood.

Background note:

- If you *jeopardise* /ˈdʒepədaɪz/ something, you place it at risk.

6 ●1.06 Make sure students know what to do by playing the first two communications. Note that in communication 1 there is no readback, so students need to provide it; in communication 2 there is an incorrect readback, so students need to correct it. Play the rest of the recording to elicit appropriate responses from volunteers. Discuss the best response to each communication with the class. Afterwards, students test each other in pairs. One student reads a communication from audioscript 1.06 on page 174 to elicit the correct response from their partner.

Suggested answers:
1 **Pilot:** Cleared (to land) Runway 26 Right, wind 220 degrees, six knots, Aeroflot 238.
2 **ATCO:** Gulfair 4752, I say again 4752, negative: turn left heading two niner zero, I say again two niner zero, intercept ILS 26 Left.
3 **Pilot:** Runway 21 Right, QNH 987 hectoPascal, Silkair 3925.
4 **ATCO:** Air Madagascar 376, negative: descend to Flight Level 160, cross Habsheim above Flight Level 180, I say again, above 180.
5 **ATCO:** China Eastern four six niner, I say again four six niner, contact Ground 124.365.
6 **Pilot:** Runway 17 Left vacated, Taca 559.
7 **Pilot:** Runway 08 Left, intersection Delta 1, behind Boeing 737, intersection Delta 2, Air France 3784.
8 **Pilot:** Join downwind Runway 21 Right, wind 190 degrees, six knots, QNH 1017, Turk Air 575.

Background notes:

- *Intercept ILS* means capturing the localizer and glideslope radio transmitter beams which guide the aircraft during an ILS approach.
- *QNH* means an atmospheric pressure setting altitude above mean sea level within a certain defined region.
- *hectoPascal* (millibars) is the most common unit of atmospheric pressure. Inches of mercury (in. Hg) is used in the United States.
- *Level 160* refers to a flight level, corresponding approximately to a height of 16,000 feet. Flight levels are calculated based on atmospheric pressure read by a barometer at ISA (International Standard Atmosphere), i.e. 1013 hectoPascal, rather than actual distance above the ground or sea.
- Communication 4 may cause some confusion (especially for teachers), when the pilot is cleared to descend to Level 160 but then told to cross Habsheim above Level 180. The aircraft is perhaps at FL 350 and has been cleared to descend to FL 160. In the course of its descent it must be above FL 180 when it flies over Habsheim.

- *'Report vacating'* means please report that you are *vacating* (= leaving or exiting), or have vacated a runway or parking stand.
- *Downwind* means in a direction away from the source of the wind, 180° from the landing direction.
- *'Join downwind Runway 21'* means make an approach to Runway 21 facing the wind. Aircraft always take off into the wind, so start at the downwind end of the runway.

Communication situations

Throughout *Flightpath* we try and develop skills which will reinforce the students' situational awareness, i.e. their ability to build a mental picture of their environment from combining different sensory inputs: direct communications with ATC; monitoring communications with other flights in their airspace; radar displays; external vision; instrument readings etc.

Another complementary skill which we seek to develop is the ability to grasp the 'bigger picture' in listening comprehension, i.e. not only to focus on detail or individual words, but to be able to identify the type of discourse: requests; instructions; acknowledgements; questions; providing information; clarifying etc.

This section contains activities with both these objectives.

7a ●1.07 Before you listen, ask students to work in pairs to describe what they can see in the eight pictures and to predict what the transmissions might be. Then play the recording for them to complete the task.

Answers:
1 f	3 a	5 e	7 d
2 c	4 h	6 b	8 g

Background notes:

- *'Go around'* means to discontinue an approach.
- *'Request emergency vehicles standing by'* is used to ask for the fire service, ambulance etc. *to stand by* (= be prepared) to handle an emergency.
- *RVR* (Runway Visual Range) is a value representing the horizontal distance from which a pilot will see the centreline and edge lights or runway markings down the runway measured automatically at three points.

b **01.07** Elicit from the class the difference between an *instruction* (= telling sb to do sth), a *request* (= asking sb to do sth) and *information* (= telling sb about sth). Then play the recording again for them to complete the task.

> Answers:
> 1 Instruction   5 Information
> 2 Request   6 Information
> 3 Instruction   7 Instruction
> 4 Instruction   8 Information

Extension activity:

Students work in pairs to reconstruct the eight transmissions word-for-word, using the pictures and their answers to exercise 7b to help them. When you go through the answers, elicit which of the eight transmissions are in plain English.

Answer: Transmissions 6 and 8 are in plain English. The others are in standard phraseology. Note that in transmission 6, the use of '*you are*' turns the transmission into plain English.

c **Students discuss the transmissions in pairs and then feed back to the class.**

> Answers:
> 1 Standard   4 Standard
> 2 Standard   5 Standard
> 3 Plain   6 Plain

Background notes:

- *Due* is used as a preposition meaning *due to / because of*.
- *ATIS* (Automatic Terminal Information Service) is a continuous broadcast of recorded non-control information in selected high-activity terminal areas.
- A *glide path* is the flight path of an aircraft during approach, especially when making an ILS landing.

d **01.08** Check students understand the words in the six categories (especially *amending, acknowledging* and *feasibility*) by asking for simple examples of each. Then play the recording for students to complete the task. They check in pairs before feeding back to the class.

> Answers:
> a 1, 11   c 5   e 3, 4
> b 6   d 7, 8, 9 f 2, 10, 12

Background notes:

- *Windshear* is a large local wind gradient, i.e. sudden changes in wind speed and direction which are especially dangerous close to the ground during approach and landing.

- *Debris* /ˈdebriː/ is the general name for rubbish which is where it shouldn't be. Foreign objects on the ground can be extremely dangerous for aircraft.
- If you have *visual contact*, you are able to see it. The expression '*We are visual*' is also used.
- *Backtrack* means having landed on the runway in use, to turn 180° and proceed along the runway in the opposite direction in order to exit it.

Extension activity:

Play the recording again, pausing after each transmission, for volunteers to respond appropriately. Students could then test each other in pairs using audioscript 1.08 on page 174.

8 **Students work in pairs or groups of three to create at least six short dialogues. Point out that they can use the transmissions in audioscript 1.08 as guidance, but that they should try to make their transmissions relevant to their own working contexts. Afterwards, ask volunteers to perform their transmissions for the class. Give and elicit feedback on the clarity and accuracy of students' transmissions.**

Requesting clarification and making requests

Clarifying and requesting are language functions identified in Appendix B of ICAO Doc. 9835 which will be practised throughout the course as they are such essential skills in resolving misunderstanding and uncertainty in radiotelephony and especially in unexpected or abnormal situations.

Given their functional importance, and also their role in confidence building, we have chosen to introduce them in a simple form from the start of the book indicating that these language skills are the tools which very often will enable a confusing situation or a deadlock to be resolved. Clarification will often involve paraphrasing, i.e. finding simpler or more appropriate language for a given situation and with a given interlocutor. It will also be necessary when students are faced with incomplete or ambiguous information which may be the result of their interlocutor's inadequate language proficiency.

In standard phraseology, direct questions are rarely used. Instead of saying *How far are you from …?*, a controller will say *Report distance from …*. A pilot will say *Request start-up* rather than *Can we have start-up approval?* However, in more complex communicative situations where plain language is used, or when the workload is light, pilots and controllers will revert to the use of conventional interrogative forms.

ICAO FOCUS

Elicit from the class what exactly *Say again* means in standard phraseology, and when to use it. They read the quote to compare it with their ideas. Then discuss the three questions with the class.

Suggested answers:
Say again may not actually be a call for the initial utterance to be repeated word for word, but to be paraphrased either using standard phraseology, where possible, or in other words in plain language. The second question refers to the importance of picking up other oral cues such as tone of voice, pronunciation, rate of delivery and fluency and the context in which the transmission is taking place. In question three, students could suggest phrases such as *I mean*; *that's to say*; *in other words*; *I want to say*; *that is*, etc. to introduce a paraphrase.

9a Make sure students understand the task (i.e. that they have just made the statement, and the listener has told them to say again). Students discuss the task in pairs.

Suggested answers:
1 We are having difficulty remaining on the glideslope and localizer.
2 There is a lot of turbulence at our present level.
3 Our hydraulic pressure is decreasing.
4 There is no turbulence.
5 We cannot see anything. / The sky is clear.
6 All the landing gear are extended and locked down. / downlocked.
7 Stop and let the B777 pass.
8 Orbit (to the right or the left). / Make a 360° turn.
9 I will call you back. / I will get in touch again.
10 Have you understood? / Do you read me?

Background notes:

◆ *Stabilising* means to be on the glidepath at the correct airspeed, in the correct configuration (flaps, slats, gear) and to have completed the checklists.
◆ *Bumpy* means turbulent.
◆ *Three greens* refers to the three green arrows or indicator lights on the landing gear display which indicate that the landing gear is extended and correctly locked down.
◆ A *triple 7* is a Boeing 777.
◆ *Perform a 360* means to make a complete turn or traffic pattern, to orbit, usually as a delaying action.

b Discuss the best clarifications with the class.

10a ◐1.09 Tell students to make brief notes as they listen. They then compare their notes with a partner to explain the misunderstandings. Then discuss the answers with the class.

Suggested answers:
1 310 could be a heading (310 degrees) or a Flight Level (FL 310).
2 This is not very informative and requires the controller to ask for more precise information thus occupying the frequency and wasting time.
3 The lights may be approach or runway lights or simply lights in the surrounding countryside.
4 Below 1000 hectoPascal, the unit of measure should always be used to avoid possible confusion with the inches of mercury scale, e.g. 29.98.
5 Horizontal visibility should be expressed in metres.
6 The controller cannot be expected to know the maximum capacity of a given aircraft configuration, and the number of passengers on board may be significant for evacuation or ground transportation purposes.
7 The unit of measurement of altitude should be given; in Russia, CIS (Commonwealth of Independent States: the former Soviet Union republics) and China, altitude is measured in metres, whereas feet are used in most of the rest of the world.
8 Expectations or estimates of time should be expressed precisely.
9 '*A bit*' is much too vague in an operational context.
10 The controller will need a precise description for the information to be useful; it may be a dog, a car, a piece of metal debris, a person etc.

Language focus: Asking questions

Tell students to close their books. Elicit on the board as many ways of starting questions as possible. This should include (a) yes/no questions; (b) questions with question words; and (c) ways of asking questions in standard phraseology. As you go through, elicit ways that each question could continue. Then students compare the list on the board with the ideas in the book to see if they missed anything.

Extension activity:

If you think your students have problems forming questions in English, draw this grid on the board to elicit how most of the questions listed in the book fit into this system:

Question word	Auxiliary verb	Subject	Main verb	Rest of question
-	Do	you	need	more time?
What	is	the problem?	-	-
How much fuel	have	you	got?	-
How far	are	you	-	from the threshold?

Note that the only exceptions are the standard phraseology questions and subject questions (= questions about the subject, e.g. **Which runway** *is in use?* **Who** *signed the weight and balance?*).

For extra practice, tell students to cover the right-hand column of the Language Focus box in order to think of good questions for each prompt in the left-hand column.

Background notes:

* *TCAS advisory* means a message given by the Traffic Collision Avoidance System warning the crew of the presence of another aircraft with which there may be conflict.
* The *weight and balance* refers to the recording and checking of the aircraft weight, load distribution and centre of gravity.
* *Speedbird* is the call sign for British Airways.
* *CAM* is the identifier for Cambridge (UK).

b ●1.09 Play the recording again, pausing after each communication for volunteers to ask a suitable question.

> **Suggested answers:**
> 1 Confirm heading or flight level.
> 2 What exactly is the problem? / Say your problem.
> 3 Describe the lights. / Where are these lights?
> 4 Confirm hectoPascal (millibars) or inches of mercury. / Do you mean hectoPascal or inches of mercury?
> 5 Say RVR. / What is the horizontal visibility?
> 6 How many passengers do you have on board?
> 7 Confirm altitude 3,000 feet.
> 8 How much time do you need?
> 9 How long do you expect to be delayed?
> 10 What exactly can you see? / What does it look like?

Extension activity:

Students test each other using audioscript 1.09 on page 174 to elicit a suitable question.

c Go through the example with the class to make sure students all know what to do. Students then work in pairs to ask and answer questions. Afterwards, you could go through the questions and answers with the class, eliciting the correct forms.

If you have an odd number of students you could have one group of three, where the third student takes the last four Student A questions and the first four Student B questions.

Background notes:

* *ETD* stands for Estimated Time of Departure.
* *F/O* stands for First Officer.
* The *threshold* is the end of the runway where the aircraft touches down.
* The *mid point* is the central section of the runway.
* The *stop end* is the opposite end of the runway from which the aircraft touched down on.
* *kt / kts* is an abbreviation of knot/knots (1 kt = 1.852 km/h).
* *RVR* stands for Runway Visual Range.
* *TWY* is an abbreviation for *taxiway*.

Language focus: Making requests

Tell students to cover their books and then elicit from the class different ways of making requests. Students read the information in the box to check their ideas. Elicit the differences between *can*, *could*, *may* and *would* in requests.

Language note:

May is only used in requests for permission, typically with *I* (e.g. *May I …?*), while *would* is only used in requests for action, typically with *you* (e.g. *Would you …?*). *Can* and *could* are used in both types of request, but *could* is more polite.

11a Students discuss the question in pairs and then feed back to the class.

> **Answers:**
> '*Request higher level*' and '*Say again*' are in standard phraseology; the others are in plain language. The other questions might be used in more extended or detailed exchanges or when time is less of an issue.

b ●1.10 Go through the example with the class. Then play the recording, pausing after each situation to elicit suitable requests from volunteers. Students then test each other in pairs by reading one of the situations from audioscript 1.10 on page 174 to elicit suitable requests.

Suggested answers:
1 Can we use the longer runway? Request emergency services standing by. Request instructions to jettison three tonnes of fuel.
2 Pan-pan, Pan-pan, Pan-pan. Request precautionary landing.
3 Minimum fuel advisory; request immediate vectors to nearest suitable airport.
4 Request maximum landing distance and towing on arrival.
5 We are unable to depart for another 30 minutes due (to) a sick cabin attendant. Request a later departure slot. / Can you give us a later departure slot?
6 The active runway is unserviceable due (to) snow clearance/removal. Are you able to hold for a further 20 minutes?
7 Are you able to / Can you accept a more southerly route?
8 Taxiway Delta 3 is closed/blocked. Taxi via Charlie and Delta 2.

Background notes:

♦ An *in-flight turnback* occurs when the crew decides to return to their airport of departure. This may be problematic because the aircraft is likely to be full of fuel and therefore over its *maximum landing weight* (= certified value above which fuel must be jettisoned or burnt off if landing becomes urgently necessary and structural damage is to be avoided).
♦ If you *jettison* fuel, you dump it in order to reduce weight.
♦ A *holding pattern* (or *holding circuit*) is a manoeuvre used to delay and wait for clearance to make an approach and land.
♦ *Roll-out* means the landing phase after touchdown when the aircraft is decelerating along the runway.
♦ A *turboprop* is an aircraft with propellers which are driven by a gas turbine (e.g. ATR, Dash 8, Fokker 50, Saab 2000, C–135, A400M).

Abbreviations

Many abbreviations are used in operational English. Some are said as acronyms (e.g. ATIS, ETOPS, PAPI), others letter by letter as abbreviations (ILS, RVR, VOR). In operational documents, many contractions are used but said as whole words (BKN – broken, SCT – scattered, ALTN – alternate). In all cases, students will have to know how these acronyms, abbreviations and contractions are said using the conventional rather than the phonetic alphabet and recognise their meaning and the context in which they are used.

A glossary of abbreviations can be found at the back of the Student's book on page 191. Exercise 13 is designed simply to give students practice using a glossary to develop their vocabulary. It can be extended by using aviation, aeronautical or general purpose dictionaries in class or the online *Flightpath* glossary.

Both students and teachers should be aware that there are several different categories of aviation or aeronautical dictionary and that the context in which they have been written will determine both their content and the nature of the definitions which they contain. Dictionaries are written in different professional environments and with particular end-users in mind. So there are dictionaries for aeronautical engineering and design, aircraft manufacture, general aviation, aircraft maintenance, avionics, military aviation, airline marketing, flight and structural tests etc. Although there are points at which they overlap, no one dictionary will cover the whole field of aviation. Also, it is important to remember that there may be as many as ten meanings (or translations) for a single entry. Dictionaries and glossaries are invaluable learning tools which should be handled with caution and expertise.

12a **Students work alone to match as many abbreviations as they can. Encourage them to refer to the glossary in the Student's Book to check their answers. When you check the answers with the class, elicit what each abbreviation stands for and how to pronounce each one.**

Answers:
1 ILS	5 RVSM	9 ETOPS
2 RVR	6 AIRPROX	10 MSA
3 LDA	7 IAF	11 ATIS
4 TCAS	8 EGPWS	12 in.Hg

Background notes:

♦ *AIRPROX* is pronounced /ˈeəprɒks/
♦ *ALAR* is pronounced /ˈeɪlɑː(r)/
♦ *ATIS* is pronounced /ˈeɪtɪs/
♦ *ETOPS* is pronounced /ˈiːtɒps/
♦ *in.Hg* is pronounced in full as *inches of mercury* (1 in.Hg = 3.386 hPa)

Extension activity:

Use the following questions to generate discussion around the 12 abbreviations. Then tell students to test each other in pairs by reading the definitions to elicit the correct abbreviation from their partner (or vice versa).

1 What is the function of a localizer and a glideslope? [**Answer:** The localizer and glideslope are part of the Instrument Landing System which enables aircraft to make most of their approach

automatically by using horizontal and vertical guidance signals from radio transmitters on the ground.]

2 What is RVR measured in? [**Answer:** metres]

3 Why can't some parts of the runway be used during touchdown and landing? [**Answer:** The touchdown zone is located some distance from the threshold level with the glideslope transmitter so that the aircraft has a safety margin and does not land too short.]

4 Which system alerts the crew of risk of collision with the terrain? [**Answer:** GPWS (Ground Proximity Warning System)]

5 How do the RVSM rules work? [**Answer:** At altitude, vertical separation is reduced from 2,000 to 1,000 feet.]

6 How close is 'dangerously close'? [**Answer:** There are four categories of airprox; in Category A, a serious incident, the safety of the aircraft may have been endangered.]

7 What other points are there in an instrument approach? [**Answer:** outer marker, inner marker, final approach fix]

8 In what situations might the EGPWS be especially useful? [**Answer:** When making an approach in Instrument Meteorological Conditions (IMC) to an aerodrome located near high terrain.]

9 Where is the ICAO head office? [**Answer:** Montreal, Canada]

10 What is a typical MSA for airports? [**Answer:** It depends greatly on the surrounding terrain and may vary from 800 feet to 5,000 feet.]

11 How does ATIS work? [**Answer:** ATIS information is recorded, broadcast and updated on a regular basis to provide crews with information about the conditions at the aerodrome.]

12 What is the equivalent in in.Hg of 1000 hectoPascal? [**Answer:** 29.53]

b ●1.11 Make sure students know how to complete the table (i.e. that the number 1 goes with *IRS*). Then play the recording for them to complete the exercise.

Answers:			
1 IRS	4 ACC	7 IAS	10 ACARS
2 ETA	5 INS	8 OAT	
3 EFIS	6 ASI	9 AAL	

Language note:

These abbreviations have been chosen because they contain letters that many learners of English confuse (*A, E, I, R*, etc.), both while listening and when speaking.

c **Students discuss the meanings of the abbreviations in pairs and then feed back to the class.**

Answers:	
AAL above aerodrome / airport level	
ACARS Aircraft Communications (Communicating), Addressing and Reporting System	
ACC Area Control Centre	
ASI Airspeed Indicator	
EFIS Electronic Flight Instrument System	
ETA Estimated Time of Arrival	
IAS Indicated Airspeed	
INS Inertial Navigation System	
IRS Inertial Reference System	
OAT Outside Air Temperature	

d ●1.11 Play the recording again for students to repeat the abbreviations. Make sure they all pronounce the letters correctly.

Extension activity:

Students test each other in pairs by reading one of the abbreviations aloud to elicit its meaning from their partners or vice versa. They could include the abbreviations from exercise 12a for added difficulty. Make sure they pay attention to correct pronunciation of the letters.

e **Students work in groups to spot the abbreviations used in the Aomori, Japan VOR Z Runway 24 approach chart and then explain what each one means in full, what it refers to and why this information is necessary for pilots. Further information on each of these items can be found in the online glossary.**

Answers:	
RWY Runway	
VOR VHF Omnidirectional Range	
Crs course	
Alt altitude	
MDA Minimum Descent Altitude	
MDH Minimum Descent Height	
Apt elev airport elevation	
Alt Set: IN (hPa): altitude setting – inches (hectoPascal)	
FL Flight Level	
R radial	
DME Distance Measuring Equipment	
IAS Indicated AirSpeed	
IAF Initial Approach Fix	
MAP Missed Approach Point	
NM nautical miles	
APCH approach	

13 **Students work alone to match the words and definitions and then check with a partner. When you have gone through the answers with the class, students can test each other in pairs by reading a definition to elicit the correct word from their partner.**

Answers:

1 h	4 k	7 l	10 i
2 c	5 b	8 e	11 f
3 g	6 j	9 a	12 d

Background notes:

♦ A *heading* is a horizontal direction while a *trajectory* is a direction in three dimensions. Specifically, *heading* means the angle between the horizontal point of reference (e.g. compass north, magnetic north or true north) and the longitudinal axis of the aircraft (i.e. the line from nose to tail around which the aircraft rotates). It is not to be confused with the *track* which is either: 1) the path of the aircraft over the Earth's surface from take-off to touchdown; or 2) the angle between a horizontal point of reference and the actual flight path.

♦ *Flare* is final nose-up pitch of a landing aeroplane to reduce the rate of descent approximately to zero on touchdown.

♦ *Paving* includes all parts of the apron, runways and taxiways except those covered in grass, earth or sand.

♦ A *strip* is a piece of paper or cardboard, or an electronic equivalent, which enables a controller to record basic data about a flight and manage flow control. Before the development of hi-tech visual displays, these strips were the main source of information for ATCOs. They are still used as a backup system in case the electronic systems fail.

♦ The difference between a *go-around* and an *orbit* is a go-around is a missed approach when the pilot decides to discontinue the approach and go around to make another approach. An orbit is a delaying action by which a crew flies a circuit of 360°.

American and British English

The introductory quote (from United States Airline Transport Pilot International Flight Language Experiences – Report 2: word meaning and pronunciation) allows the teacher to discuss with the students other, less immediate and obvious, consequences of poor communication / language proficiency than those seen at the beginning of the unit (e.g. loss of time, distraction, loss of anticipation and having one's control of the situation threatened). Good flying skills depend on the pilot being 'ahead of the aircraft', i.e. being aware of what will happen and being able to anticipate and integrate all the different sources of information into situational awareness.

The various considerations raised in Unit 1 are designed to broaden the students' awareness of the different operational factors which are involved in a proficient use of aviation English and hopefully give a greater relevance to all the exercises in *Flightpath*.

In the fifties, sixties and seventies of the last century, the United States dominated both aircraft manufacturing and the civil aviation industry; general aviation is still more widespread and accessible in the US than anywhere else. As a result American English aviation terminology, idioms and phraseology tended to be the most widely used worldwide. The development of a strong aircraft manufacturing industry in Europe, Brazil and Asia and the fact that some large regulatory bodies (ICAO, EASA, IATA) tend to use a British or 'mid-Atlantic' English mean that aviation professionals will be regularly confronted with both variants of English. This section briefly attracts students' attention to this fact and to some of the more common differences in spelling and lexis which they will encounter and should be able to take in their stride.

They should of course be reminded that aviation English is a language of international communication and also that all the variants of the English language have much more in common than they have specific features.

ICAO FOCUS

Students read the quote to find out what is the most typical result of a breakdown in communication. Elicit from the class what is meant by being 'behind the aircraft'. Students then discuss the two questions in pairs and then feed back to the class.

Suggested answers:
Deciphering an unclear transmission takes effort and time and may distract the crew from flying the aircraft. If you are 'behind the aircraft', you are no longer able to anticipate what the aircraft is going to be doing in a few seconds or more. Given the speed at which aircraft travel, and their natural inertia, it is extremely important for pilots to be able to know what to expect.

14a **Students work alone to complete the task and then check with a partner. When you go through the answers, elicit from the class more general rules for British and American spelling, and ask which they think is most common in international communication.**

Answers:
American spelling center, color, downdraft, gage, leveled, program, stabilizer, tire
British spelling centre, colour, downdraught, gauge, levelled, programme, stabiliser, tyre

Language note:

- The *-re/-er* distinction is also found in *theatre/ theater, manoeuvre/maneuver*, etc.
- The *-our/-or* distinction is found in many words, e.g. *favour/favor, odour/odor, behaviour/behavior*, etc.
- In British English, it is normal to double a final *-l* when adding a suffix (e.g. *traveller, signalled*). In American English, a final *-l* is only doubled in stressed syllables (e.g. *fulfilled, controller*).
- In British English, *program* is used to refer to computer programs. All other uses of the word are spelled *programme*.
- The suffix *-ize* is becoming more widely used by speakers of British English.
- In British English, a *tyre* is a noun but *tire* is a verb (= to get tired).

Background notes:

- A *downdraught/downdraft* is a downward movement of air caused by a descending body of cool air.
- A *stabiliser/stabilizer* is also called a *tailplane* or *empennage*.

b Students work alone to complete the exercise and then compare their answers in pairs. When you go through the answers with the class, elicit which version students would use. Note that there is no right or wrong way.

Answers:
American English handoff, traffic pattern, stack, airplane, jetway, in.Hg, ramp, visibility: miles, clear the runway, deplane
British English handover, traffic circuit, hold, aircraft, airbridge, hPa, apron, visibility: kilometres, vacate the runway, disembark

Background notes:

- A *handoff/handover* is a transfer of a flight from one controller or area to another.
- A *traffic pattern* or *circuit* refers to a predefined flight movement used either for holding or to prepare an approach.
- A *jetway/airbridge* is a walkway for passengers from the terminal building directly onto the aircraft.

c, d Discuss the questions with the class.

Answer:
d In September 2010, the United States FAA finally adopted the standard ICAO phraseology '*Line up and wait.*' in place of '*Taxi into position and hold.*', which had been current in the United States to give pilots authorisation to enter the active runway and place the aircraft on the centreline ready for their take-off clearance. This was part of an overall movement to improve runway and taxiing safety (see Flight Safety Foundation, *AeroSafety World*, March 2010 and September 2010). There had long been concerns about the risk of confusing '*Taxi to holding position*' and '*Taxi into position and hold.*' For this reason also many civil aviation authorities prescribe the term '*holding point*' rather than '*holding position*'.
It is also common practice in the US for numerals to be said in a non-standard way, i.e. '*two ten*' rather than '*too wun zero*', '*eleven thousand feet*' rather than '*wun wun thousand feet*', '*Runway seven*' rather than '*Runway zero seven*'. There are many documented cases of altitudes being confused, especially 10,000 and 11,000 feet, or runways being confused due to frequency congestion or interference.

15a **○1.12** Play the recording and pause after each speaker to elicit where each one might be from.

Answers:
1 the Gulf	4 South East Asia
2 Britain	5 North America
3 Russia	6 South America

Extension activity:

Discuss with the class reasons whether native or non-native speakers of English are more difficult to understand and why.

b Discuss the question with the class.

Putting it together: Standard phraseology and plain language

The principle behind the lead-in quote should stand in golden letters behind all the aviation English which is taught and should be understood by students. However, there are many situations in which pilots and controllers need to rely on plain language to resolve unexpected situations. Students will be able to give other examples and you should explore and analyse with them the sort of language required in each case in terms of both lexis and grammar.

The theme of *Putting it together* is therefore 'code switching', i.e. the ability to move from phraseology to plain language (and ultimately vice versa) when circumstances require it. In the present case, plain language is required to explain why one is unable to comply with an instruction or a request and check proper understanding by paraphrasing.

This final section practises several of the points explored previously in this unit: recognizing different types of language (exercise 16a); use of vocabulary associated with the inability to comply, which is a common reason for reverting to plain language (exercise 16b); practising saying that one is unable to comply and explaining why in pairs from both a pilot's and a controller's standpoint (exercises 17a and b); and making sure of correct comprehension and paraphrasing (exercise 18).

ICAO FOCUS

Read the quote aloud and then discuss the question with the class. If students have limited experience, get them to imagine situations where they would need to switch to plain language.

Preparation

16a Students discuss the ten transmissions in pairs and then feed back to the class.

Answers:
1 standard	6 non-standard
2 standard	7 standard
3 standard	8 plain
4 non-standard	9 standard
5 plain	10 plain

Background notes:

- Transmission 4 is non-standard because while a reference is made to other aircraft lining up first, the aircraft which precedes this one is not identified. As a result, this aircraft could line up too early.
- For transmission 6, see answer to exercise 14d.
- Transmission 9 means *'fly parallel to the runway on which you are going to land in the direction the wind is blowing before turning and flying into the wind to land behind the 737 which is now three miles from touch-down'*.

b Students work alone to complete the transmissions and then check with a partner. When you go through the answers with the class, elicit which transmissions are in standard phraseology, which are in plain language and which include a mixture.

Answers:
1 heavy	5 direct
2 failure	6 IMC
3 minimum	7 turn-off
4 visibility	8 blind

Background notes:

- A *clean speed* is the aircraft airspeed with flaps, slats and landing gear retracted.
- *Direct Madras* means flying directly to Madras or towards the Madras beacon without passing via another waypoint.
- *IMC* means weather conditions (cloud, fog) which make it impossible to fly visually (VMC) and so which require the crew to use their instruments to fly.
- A *flaps-up landing* occurs when the crew is not able to extend the high-lift flaps. This results in the minimum speed of the aircraft being higher and so the aircraft landing at a higher speed and probably requiring a longer stopping distance.
- A *blind spot* is a point on a radar screen where information is not displayed or an area outside the aircraft hidden from the pilot by the airframe.

ICAO FOCUS

The quote from Dr Jeremy Mell highlights the issues involved. Jeremy Mell was one of the key members of the ICAO PRICESG, was head of language at the French Ecole Nationale de l'Aviation Civile in Toulouse and the author of a doctoral thesis studying verbal communications between pilots and controllers in standard and non-standard situations.

Elicit a definition of language proficiency (in the context of aviation English). Then tell students to read the quote to compare it with their ideas. Elicit from the class examples of checking mechanisms both from standard phraseology and from plain language situations. Then discuss the question with the class.

Suggested answer:
- Conventional checking mechanisms used in phraseology are, *confirm* and *say again*. In plain language, expressions such as *Did you mean…?*; *Are you sure…?*; *Can you repeat that…?*; *What/Where/When exactly is/are …?*; *Which … did you mean/say?* etc. can be used.
- Checking mechanisms are essential to remove the ambiguity, uncertainty, confusion and misunderstanding which reduce situational awareness, i.e. the pilot's and the controller's vision of the operational environment derived from radio communication and visual displays.

Background notes:

Fluency and interaction are two of the six ICAO Rating Scale language skills.

Code switching is something we all do when we use language: we do not talk to a friend in the same register as we use when speaking to a university professor or a politician. Pilots and controllers recognize immediately when standard phraseology is being used and respond accordingly. However, when they hear language containing expressions such as '*We have a problem with our electrical generation.*' or '*How long do you expect to be delayed?*' they also recognize that the discourse has switched to plain language and they will also respond accordingly.

Students should be trained to react immediately to any uncertainty by requesting clarification or confirmation. This is one of the characteristics of the operational proficiency defined by ICAO. This proficiency is based upon self-confidence just as much as linguistic knowledge.

Communication

17a **◐1.13** Play the recording, pausing after each request to elicit a suitable response from volunteers. Encourage students to be creative (i.e. not simply to agree to all the requests).

Background notes:

- A *slot* is a short period of time during which a given aircraft has approval for departure.
- *Start-up* refers to starting the aircraft engines usually immediately after push-back.
- An *ATR* is a twin-engine turboprop regional transport.
- *VOR* means VHF Omnidirectional Range and is a type of ground-based navigation transmitter which sends signals in all directions to enable aircraft to identify their position. The intersection of two VOR radials provides the aircraft's position.
- *Higher* means a higher flight level.

b **◐1.14** Again, play the recording to elicit suitable and creative responses from volunteers.

Background notes:

- *Spacing* is a safe distance between aircraft. A key role of an ATCO is to maintain spacing at all times.
- A *high-speed turn-off* is a runway exit which is at an angle that allows the aircraft which has just landed to leave the runway without decelerating completely and so vacate the runway for other traffic and reach the terminal more quickly.

Extension activity:

Students repeat exercises 17a and b in small groups. One student reads requests from audioscripts 1.13 and 1.14 on page 175 to elicit suitable responses from his/her partners. They then swap roles.

18 Go through the example with the class to elicit a range of ways of checking information (e.g. *Do you mean …? So …? You mean …?*). Then students work in pairs to role-play the interactions. Afterwards, elicit from the class examples of checking each piece of information.

If you have an odd number of students you could have one group of three. The third student can take the last three of Student A's statements and the last three of Student B's.

Background notes:

- *Zulu* means UTC or Universal Time, Coordinated, formerly GMT.
- *Broken up* refers to an interrupted transmission.
- '*Please give us five miles behind the heavy.*' means the pilot is requesting a horizontal separation of five miles between himself and the preceding wide-body aircraft in order to avoid the effects of wake turbulence.
- If somebody is *incapacitated*, they are unconscious or too ill to function properly.
- A *fast landing* is a landing made above the usual landing speed of the aircraft either because of adverse wind conditions or because the flaps are not fully extended. This will probably result in a *hard landing*.
- A *hard landing* occurs when an aircraft has a high rate of descent (or *sink rate*) during the last few seconds of approach due either to a high airspeed or to turbulent wind conditions (*windshear*).

Debriefing

19 Discuss the question with the class. Give and elicit feedback on the strengths and weaknesses of the role-plays, and elicit suggestions as to how to overcome the weaknesses.

Progress check

Students work alone to complete the progress check and then compare their answers with a partner. Then discuss with the class, and discuss what they need to work more on, both in class and during self-study.

UNIT 2
Ground movements

Operational topics	Markings and signs; Airport areas; Ground equipment; Abbreviations; Turnaround incidents; Obstacles; Hot spots
Communication functions	Confirming and clarifying; Taxi clearances; Call signs; Requesting start-up and pushback approval; Handling turnaround incidents; Giving advice and resolving problems; Detailed taxi instructions; Communication errors: failure to acknowledge correctly
Language content	Adjectives; Location and movement; Alphabet and numerals; Physical characteristics (colours, shapes, sizes); Damage and problem vocabulary; Adverbs; Word endings

Unit 2 Teacher's brief

Unit 2 opens the first part of the book devoted to **hazards on the ground**. It is an opportunity to explore and use all the terminology and activities related to the use of **airport layout** and **infrastructure**, **ground equipment**, **ground staff**, **servicing**, **incidents** and **damage**, **parking**, **pushback** and **taxiing** with which both flight crew and controllers should be familiar.

The purpose of this unit is to provide students with the language they need to describe the complex physical and operational environment of the airport and so to be able to handle any **unforeseen situation** during turnaround and taxiing successfully. It also prepares the framework for a more in-depth treatment of **communications on the ground** and **runway incursions** in Units 3 and 4.

Turnaround, the time between the arrival of a flight at its parking stand and its departure for the next flight, is a period when the flight crew's attention is turned to a whole series of activities where the airport ground staff is involved and contact with Air Traffic Control is limited. The flight crew communicate with different categories of ground staff both by radio/ interphone and face to face, in situations where safety is an ongoing concern and the operational time constraints to depart on time create what is a potentially stressful environment.

The flight crew communicate with:
* *aircraft maintenance technicians / mechanics / engineers*, who inspect and service the aircraft (engine oil levels, tyre pressure and wear, signs of fuel or hydraulic leaks, impact damage to the engine air intakes and wing leading edges etc.), perform any small repairs and make entries in the aircraft technical logbook. This is line maintenance.
* the *ramp supervisor / loadmaster*, who is in charge of a team of handlers loading and unloading cargo and baggage. Baggage loading devices are one of the main causes of damage to the aircraft during turnaround.

* the *fuelling agent*, whom the captain informs about the amount of fuel required for the next flight.
* the *duty officer / station manager* who handles any administrative or financial questions.
* the *dispatcher / red cap*, who provides the weight and balance sheet which must be checked and signed by the captain. The weight and balance sheet contains updated information about the aircraft payload (passengers, baggage, cargo and fuel) and its location. This allows the aircraft's centre of gravity, which must be within certain limits for safe take-off and flight, to be calculated.
* *ground handlers*, who usually install and remove wheel chocks and supervise the pushback of the aircraft with a tractor / tow vehicle / tug.

In the meantime, the aircraft is also attended by caterers, cabin cleaners and water and toilet servicing trucks. These activities tend to be managed by the cabin crew.

With so many simultaneous actions, the potential for damage or injury is high. An incident is likely to affect the departure of the aircraft. In this case the flight crew will have to contact Air Traffic Control (Ground or Apron) to inform them of the situation and possibly negotiate a change in their departure slot (see *Handling turnaround incidents* key terms).

Cold weather or poor visibility (see Unit 5) may further complicate operations and require the intervention of de-icing and snow clearance teams.

Before take-off and after landing, routine communications between the flight deck and ATC involve **pushback and start-up approval**, **taxi instructions** to and from the terminal and the **identification of the parking stand or gate** (see *Start-up approval and taxi instructions* key terms). These communications can be complicated by (and thus require excursions from standard phraseology to plain language) delays, poor visibility, aircraft technical problems, absence or failure of ground equipment, brake overheat, obstacles on the taxiways or apron, smoke or fire, collisions with vehicles or other aircraft, unwell or belligerent passengers, crews losing their way, suspicious individuals, obscured or faulty signs and markings (see *Lead-in* and *Airport layout* key terms), building or maintenance works on the airport, changes to routine taxi routes, damaged or icy paving, bomb scares, other aircraft blocking the way, misunderstanding etc.

Communicating in order to handle routine and non-routine situations safely is the subject of this unit.

Unit 2 Sources

◆ www.eurocontrol.int The Airport Research Area
◆ www.flightglobal.com Ramp Safety
◆ www.fsinfo.org Special edition, August 2003
◆ ICAO *Runway incursion* video (Unit lead-in)
◆ ICAO Circular 323: *Guidelines for Aviation English Training Programmes,* 2009 (ICAO focus with Exercise 19b)
◆ www.interairports.co.uk Airport Ground Movements
◆ Skybrary: All articles under *Ground Operations*, www.skybrary.aero
◆ Transport Canada: *Danger on the runway* DVD (Exercise 24a–27b)
◆ Trémaud, M.: *Erasing confusion*, AeroSafety World, May 2010 (Exercise 19b)

Lead-in

The lead-in quotation is by a former, very long-standing president of ICAO (International Civil Aviation Organisation). The role of ICAO, the UN aviation agency and aviation's international regulatory body, is itself a subject of discussion. His commentary on a safety video evokes common sources of error on the ground which could result in a runway incursion, a topic we explore in Units 3 and 4.

An airport is an extremely busy place with many types of vehicle moving around; some of them are listed in the answers for exercise 1a below.

Quote: **Tell students to read the quote and find three examples of problems and the general name for this type of problem. Then ask students about their own experience and whether they think the examples are realistic. Ask students to talk about some of the incidents, collisions, accidents, damage and injuries which may happen during turnaround.**

Answers:
a pilot who is arriving at an unfamiliar field; a poorly trained vehicle driver who takes a short cut across a seemingly inactive runway; a busy air traffic controller who momentarily forgets a particular aircraft.

All are examples of runway incursions.

Background notes:

◆ The word *aerodrome* is more general than *airport* or *airfield*, and covers any place from which aircraft flight operations take place.
◆ Note the use of *transit* as a verb (= to pass across or through sth).
◆ A *runway incursion* occurs when an aircraft, a vehicle, a person or an animal enters an active runway.

1a **Students brainstorm a list in small groups and then feed back to the class.**

Possible answers:
Airports are indeed busy places and, in addition to aircraft, one encounters: passenger buses and coaches, mobile lounges, fuel tankers and bowsers, de-icing vehicles, cargo loaders and mobile conveyor belts, fire engines, water servicing trucks and catering trucks, follow-me cars, friction-testing cars, crew minibuses, snow ploughs and snow blowers, technicians' vans and dispatchers' cars, tugs or tow vehicles with tow-bars, ground power units and air start units etc. as well as all the various categories of servicing staff around the aircraft during turnaround.

b **Discuss the question with the class.**

Suggested answer:
An airport is a noisy place; many people wear ear protection and so may not be aware of what they cannot see. There are a lot of people and machines working and moving simultaneously in a relatively confined space around the aircraft on the ramp. Ramp staff use corrosive, sharp and explosive materials. Aircraft engines are able to ingest people and large objects and their thrust can blow over a car or van.

c **Students discuss the question in small groups and then feed back to the class.**

Possible answers:
Pilots and marshallers can misjudge the distance between the wing tips of their aircraft and another aircraft or vehicle during docking and pushback; any damage to an aircraft is very costly. Servicing vehicle drivers can collide with aircraft or other vehicles. Refuelling agents can fail to stop refuelling and cause a fuel spillage. Pilots can misunderstand taxi instructions and gate numbers and enter an active runway without clearance. Controllers can confuse aircraft, give incorrect taxi instructions or fail to monitor aircraft movements.

Airport layout

Communicative and operational issues:

This first section addresses the basic but important question of the physical layout of the airport (areas, signs and markings, buildings, locations) so that pilots and controllers can describe where they are and give precise instructions about where to go.

Exercise 3 contains opportunities, through brainstorming and description of purpose, to cover many areas, buildings and equipment and to prepare for exercises 4 and 5.

2a Students complete the matching exercise in pairs and then feed back to the class. Then discuss the difference between a marking and a sign with the class.

> Answers:
>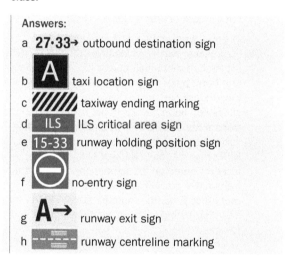
> a 27·33→ outbound destination sign
> b A taxi location sign
> c ////// taxiway ending marking
> d ILS ILS critical area sign
> e 15-33 runway holding position sign
> f ⊖ no-entry sign
> g A→ runway exit sign
> h runway centreline marking

Background notes:

Moving around the airport is facilitated by a large number of distinctive (vertical, illuminated) signs and (horizontal, painted) markings. These vary somewhat from country to country. Recognizing and respecting them is a key safety factor. These activities raise awareness about just a few of these signs and markings and develop the students' ability to describe physical objects (colours, shapes). The listening task is a simple example of deductive skills, rather than straight description, which pilots and controllers are constantly called upon to use.

◆ A *marking* is painted horizontally onto the runway while a *sign* is mounted vertically on a signpost.
◆ An *outbound destination sign* indicates the direction to common taxi routes.
◆ A *taxi location sign* indicates the taxiway that an aircraft is currently on.
◆ A *taxiway ending marking* consists of striped lines on the far end of an intersection indicating the end of a taxiway.

◆ An *ILS critical area* is an area which an ATCO may instruct aircraft to hold short of in order to avoid interference with an ILS signal.
◆ A *runway holding position sign* indicates where aircraft must hold until cleared onto a runway.
◆ A *no-entry sign* indicates that a taxiway etc. is closed or unserviceable.
◆ A *runway exit sign* indicates an approaching taxiway to vacate a runway.
◆ A *runway centreline marking* is a series of painted marks materialising the runway centreline. Note that the centreline is a reference axis, not the painted line itself.

Extension activity:

Students test each other in pairs by pointing to a sign to elicit its definition from their partner. You could also elicit from the class other examples of markings and signs.

b Discuss the questions with the class.

> Possible answers:
> There are regional or national differences in colour and shape, but common characteristics should be recognizable.

c ◉1.15 Play the recording for students to complete the exercise. They discuss their answers in pairs; encourage them to try to remember exactly what each ATCO instruction was.

> Answers:
> 1 f   3 g   5 a   7 d
> 2 e   4 b   6 h   8 c

Background notes:

◆ *hold short* (= to stop before)
◆ *line up and wait* (= enter the runway and stop on the centreline awaiting take-off clearance)
◆ *hold* or *hold position* (= wait)
◆ Taxiways are identified alphabetically (Alpha, Bravo, Charlie etc.) and runways according to their approximate orientation and relative position if there is more than one runway with the same orientation at a given airport (27R: 27 Right is oriented approximately 270 degrees, i.e. west. The exact orientation, e.g. 272°, will be indicated in small characters as it is on the Seattle chart, page 26).
◆ *CAT III conditions* means that visibility is very poor and that aircraft ILS automation is being used for take-off and landing.

Extension activity:

Students test each other in pairs by pointing to a marking or sign to elicit from their partner the correct ATCO instruction from the recording.

3a Students work in pairs to brainstorm their lists. When you go through the answers with the class, write students' answers on the board, as this will be useful for later exercises. You could also use the list in the answer key below to generate more ideas (e.g. *What about the area around the airport buildings? What's that called?*).

Possible answers:
Airport areas
apron: area around airport buildings used for aircraft movement and parking
de-icing station: designated location where aircraft are de-iced in cold weather before departure
engine run-up area/pad: remote location where aircraft engines can be tested
gate: parking stand directly connected to the airport terminal by an airbridge
high speed exit: angled taxiway allowing aircraft to vacate runway without decelerating completely
holding point: position where aircraft must stop before entering runway
hot spot: intersection indicated on the chart where the risk of collisions and incursions is high
INS check point: remote location with well-defined geographical coordinates where aircraft's inertial navigation system (INS) can be reset
intersection: crossing of taxiways, runways or taxiways and runways
maintenance area: area, usually with hangars and workshops, where aircraft are maintained and repaired
outer taxiway: continuous taxiway between apron and inner taxiways and runways
ramp: area around terminal buildings where aircraft are parked and serviced
remote/outlying stand: parking position which is not directly connected to terminal
runway: paved surface available and suitable for aircraft take-off and landing
runway exit: short taxiway which allows aircraft to leave runway
stand: parking position
stopway: additional paved area beyond the normal end of the runway to allow for aircraft overrunning in an emergency
taxiway: paved way for aircraft to move between the terminals and the runways etc.
threshold: serviceable beginning of the runway (*serviceable* here means the length and width of the runway which can actually be used by aircraft; maintenance may be being carried out on some parts of the runway or snow may not have been cleared from the entire width)
touchdown aim-point: painted marking on runway to indicate touchdown zone
touchdown zone: area after threshold where aircraft usually touch down initially on landing

Airport buildings
cargo/freight terminal: building used for storage and handling of containers, pallets etc.
control tower: tall ATC building with overall visibility of airport
finger: extension from main terminal building jutting out into the apron and containing gates
fire station: base for fire service and their fire-fighting equipment
general aviation terminal: terminal for private, business and leisure aviation
hangar: shelter for housing aircraft on the ground
passenger terminal: building for passenger check-in, security, immigration etc.
pier: corridor connecting the airport terminal with gates
satellite: sub-terminal at airport to bring passengers nearer to gates

Airport infrastructure and equipment
blast fence: barrier which diverts efflux (engine exhaust gases) behind parked or taxiing aircraft
fuel farm: place where fuel tanks are located and tankers are parked
glideslope antenna: ILS aerial connected to the transmitter of a radio beam (signal) providing vertical flight path guidance
HIRL: High Intensity Runway Lighting
localizer antenna: ILS aerial connected to the transmitter providing directional guidance
met office / weather bureau: station gathering and distributing updated weather reports and forecasts
paving: hard surface of runways, taxiways and aprons
perimeter fencing: security barrier around the outer limit of the airport
radar antenna (aerial): portion of the radar system used to radiate and intercept signals
runway centreline lighting: lighting along the longitudinal axis of the runway
runway edge lighting: white lights on each side of the runways
wind sock: traditional fabric sleeve hung from mast to give rough indication of local wind velocity (strength/direction)

Extension activity:

You could turn exercise 3a into a simple game. Ask each pair in turn to give one answer and write it on the board. Keep the three columns separate. They may not repeat a word that another pair has already given. Keep going until some pairs run out of ideas. The last pair to add a word to the list is the winner.

You could use the list of possible answers above to extend the lists, by asking questions (e.g. *What is the name for the area around airport buildings used for aircraft movement and parking?*). Again, you could award points for correct answers.

Afterwards, students could test each other by asking similar questions to elicit the correct term from their partner.

b **Students work in pairs to discuss the questions. They should make sure their partners know the meaning of each word from the board. Point out that if there are any words that neither of them know / can explain, there will be a chance to discuss them with the class at the end. Then go through the answers with the class and deal with any remaining questions.**

> Suggested answers:
>
> The *apron* is the large open paved space around the various terminal (and maintenance) buildings where aircraft are parked and from which they are taxied towards the runways and other parts of the airport. It is the essential area of concern during turnaround, pushback and start-up. Both pilots and controllers need to be very familiar with the apron layout to avoid errors and collision.
>
> A *hangar* is a large building to shelter aircraft during maintenance and repair. Hangars are usually located towards the periphery of the airport. While their location is known, they are not usually involved in ATC instructions and usually it is maintenance staff who oversee towing the aircraft to and from the hangars.
>
> The *glideslope antenna* is located to the left or right of the runway near the touchdown zone. It transmits signals which guide aircraft on a correct rate of descent so that they touch down a few hundred metres after the runway threshold. The glideslope is one of the two essential parts of the ILS (Instrument Landing System); the other is the Localizer. Both pilots and controllers depend on its accuracy.

Extension activity:

Students test each other in small groups by asking questions about the words on the board (e.g. *What do you call the place where you …? What's the name of the equipment you use to …?*).

c **Students complete the exercise alone and check with a partner.**

> Answers:
>
> | | | | | |
> |---|---|---|---|---|
> | 1 e | 3 j | 5 i | 7 f | 9 g |
> | 2 h | 4 a | 6 b | 8 c | 10 d |

Background notes:

- A *gantry* is a metal framework shaped like a bridge. In addition to de-icing gantries at an airport, other well-known examples include gantries holding overhead road signs, shipbuilding cranes or automated carwashes.

- *Dispatch* is the name of the service which is responsible for planning and monitoring the flight of an aircraft. A *flight dispatcher*, also known as a *red cap*, acts as an intermediary between Dispatch and the flight crew, bringing them weight and balance and cargo documentation for approval.

4 **○1.16 Before you listen, discuss with the class why the four marked points are likely to be runway incursion hot spots (e.g. HS 1 could be a hot spot because vehicles from the Maintenance Centre cross Runway 1R 19L at this point). Then play the recording for students to complete the exercise. They discuss their answers with a partner before feeding back to the class.**

> Answers:
> 1 T
> 2 F – Runway 09–27 intersects Runway 1 Right–19 Left.
> 3 F – Taxiway Alpha gives access to Runway 19 Right.
> 4 F – The control tower is 1,283 feet above sea level.
> 5 F – Taxiway Delta does not intersect the runway.
> 6 T
> 7 F – Runway 01 Left–19 Right is longer.
> 8 T

Background notes:

- Combining audio and graphic inputs is a fundamental technique for both pilots and controllers which will be developed in different forms throughout the course. Pilots use (typically Jeppesen) airport charts like this to find their way around the various airports they fly to.

- A *hot spot* is an intersection indicated on the chart where the risk of collisions and incursions is high.

Extension activity:

Play the recording again and pause after each sentence. Elicit from the class a correction for each false sentence.

5a **Students work alone to complete the exercise and then compare their answers with a partner. Remind students that they are using these words in an aviation context.**

> Answers:
> along – across; aft – forward; ahead – behind; back to – out from; incoming – outgoing; left – right; near – far; on – off; out of – into; outbound – inbound; over – under; to – from
>
> **Note:** The opposite of *around* is *across* if we are talking about an object moving in relation to a space or an obstacle. *Through* would also be an opposite.

Background notes:

• Prepositions, and words of location and movement generally, are constantly being used in operational communication to give information about direction (*to the holding point*), position (*at the gate*) or time (*in ten minutes*) and in many phrasal verbs (*to turn back*) and technical terms (*turnaround, nose-in*).

• *Forward* here is used as an adjective (e.g. *the forward part of the plane*), so the opposite is *aft* or *rear*. As an adverb, the opposite is *backward(s)*.

Extension activity:

Students test each other in pairs by saying one of the words to elicit the opposite from their partner.

b **Students work alone to complete the sentences and then check in pairs.**

Answers:	
1 on	6 back
2 ahead	7 far
3 incoming	8 right
4 to	9 over
5 along	

c **Go through the example with the class, getting students to follow the directions with a finger. Elicit why the pilot needs to hold short of the two runways, and why he needs to request permission later to cross the runway. [Answer: The pilot needs to hold short and request permission because otherwise there is a serious risk of accidents. The ATCO is giving instructions and directions, not a clearance.] Students then work in pairs to request and give directions. Afterwards, go through any problematic directions with the class.**

If you have an odd number of students you will need to have one group of three, where the third student takes points 1 and 4 from Student A and points 2 and 5 from Student B.

Extension activity:

You could repeat the activity with a map of an airport your students know well. You could even use the classroom as an airport, where students (ATCOs) give their partners (planes) directions between tables and chairs, ideally with several 'planes' following different directions at the same time. Of course you will need to be sensitive: some students may be more receptive to such games than others.

Communication errors: Failure to acknowledge correctly

Communicative and operational issues:

Misunderstanding can occur if a generic term like *Roger* or *Wilco* is used instead of a full readback or acknowledgement. *Roger* and *Wico* can be used correctly in communicative situations where there is no possible ambiguity and a full readback is not required.

Pilot:	*Going around.*
ATCO:	*Roger.*
ATCO:	*Report ready for departure.*
Pilot:	*Wilco.*

ICAO FOCUS

Tell students to read the quote to identify the mistake and how it should be corrected. [**Answer:** The controller uses *Roger* when he should provide a new instruction.] Then discuss the question with the class.

Suggested answer:
The use of *Roger* is dangerous when specific confirmation of a clearance, instruction, altimeter setting etc. is required. It does not allow the other speaker to be sure that the message or instruction has been correctly understood.

6 ○1.17 **The purpose of this exercise is to emphasise the importance of providing unambiguous information through a specific acknowledgement, which leaves the interlocutor in no doubt that his/her instruction or request has been fully understood. It is both a habit-forming activity of good practice and a confidence-building activity.**

Go through the example with the class, eliciting why it would be wrong to use *Roger* in response. [**Answer:** Because the pilot needs to read back the ATCO's instruction. *Roger* would be redundant in a standard situation like this.] Play the recording, pausing after each transmission for volunteers to provide suitable responses. Discuss the best responses with the class.

Extension activity:

Students could test each other in pairs using audioscript 1.17 on page 175.

Background notes:

- *Final* is often used as a noun, meaning *final approach*, typically four nautical miles (nm) from the threshold. It is often used in the plural (to be '*on finals*'), referring to the last couple of minutes of flight.
- *Reset Squawk ident* refers to the fact that the pilot enters a specific four-digit code which a transponder on the aircraft transmits throughout the flight and which enables the aircraft to be identified on the controllers' radar screens.
- *Ice patches* are intermittent ice cover on the ground.
- A *no-show* is a passenger who is booked on a flight but who does not check in or board.

Confirming and clarifying

Communicative and operational issues:

Confirming and clarifying follows on from acknowledging in exercise 6. It is also intended to build good practice and focus on improving communicative fluency rather than acquiring new content.

This section contains a large amount of alphanumerical information. This is very common in radiotelephonic communication; it conveys key information (headings, flight levels, radio frequencies, flight numbers etc.) and also is usually the easiest type of language for pilots and controllers to use.

7a ○1.18 The purpose of exercises 7a, b and c is not to teach students to use alphanumerical language at this relatively advanced stage in their study, but rather to offer a well-known medium to allow the teacher to focus on the students' pronunciation and fluency without being distracted by content. It is equally an opportunity to grasp units of measurement and to discuss what they refer to.

Elicit from the class how they would pronounce each reference, etc., then play the recording to check. With weaker classes, you could ask the whole class to repeat after each item. You could also discuss with the class what each reference, etc., might refer to (see Background notes).

Suggested answers:
(responses)
1 wun too fower decimal tree too fife MegaHertz
2 wun zero wun niner hectoPascal
3 Part Number four six seven two niner one seven eight Echo
4 too fower fife degrees
5 Condor wun fower tree ait
6 tree wun too knots / three hundred (and) twelve knots

7 one thousand two hundred feet per minute
8 Mach zero point seven niner
9 a three / tree degree slope
10 two niner niner ait inches of mercury
11 one hundred (and) nine tonnes
12 ETD wun seven fife ait / seventeen fifty eight

NOTE: Point out that it is common practice in the US not to insert *and* between the hundreds and tens. '*tree*' is the correct pronunciation of 3, '*fower*' of 4, '*fife*' of 5 and '*niner*' of 9 in RT, but often these numbers are said in a conventional way.

Background notes:

- *MHz* (*MegaHertz*) is a unit of measurement for radio frequency.
- *P/N* stands for *part number*.
- *fpm* stands for *feet per minute*, a unit of measurement for rate of climb or descent.
- A *Mach number* is the ratio of the speed of the aircraft to the speed of sound.
- A *slope* is a gradient, i.e. an angle to the horizontal.
- *ETD* stands for Estimated Time of Departure.

b Students test each other in pairs and take turns to point to a number for their partner to pronounce it.

c Students discuss the question in pairs and then feed back to the class.

Answers:
1 124.325 MHz is a radio frequency
2 1009 hPa is an atmospheric pressure
3 P/N 46729178E is the number of a spare part
4 245° is a heading, a course, a bearing or a radial (a *radial* is a magnetic bearing or angle from a navigation aid on the ground which allows the crew to know their position and capture the approach path)
5 Condor 1438 is a flight number
6 312 knots is an airspeed
7 1,200 fpm is a rate of descent or climb
8 Mach 0.79 is a Mach number
9 3° slope is a typical glideslope gradient, or rate of descent
10 29.98 in.Hg is an atmospheric pressure or altimeter setting
11 109 tonnes could be a relatively small aircraft weight, or the payload or the fuel load of a large aircraft
12 ETD 17.58 is the time a flight is expected to depart
NOTE: Metric tonnes are generally used for aircraft, payload and fuel weights

Extension activity:

Students could write another list of ten more references, etc., for their partners to pronounce.

8a **◐1.19** This exercise takes the precise listening activity in exercise 7 a step further by requiring students to request confirmation of what they have heard. This listening exercise should also be used as a situational awareness activity to ask the students to describe the situation from the transmission they hear.

Go through the example with the class. Then play the recording, pausing after each transmission for a volunteer to correct the data. Afterwards, students can test each other in pairs using audioscript 1.19 on page 175.

Answers:
1 Austral 283 / 15
2 RWY 25 / Lufthansa **37**
3 Avianca **357** / 45
4 second / F 14
5 **767** / RWY 17
6 BHQ / 18 / M
7 AA 757
8 **25** / Thai **607**
9 A320 / **39**
10 China Eastern 295 / S15 / L

Background notes:

◆ '*At your discretion*' means timing or navigation is to be decided by the pilot.
◆ *Slot times* are allocated take-off times for flights. See *Start-up approval and taxi instructions* below.
◆ If a plane is '*bogged down*', it is stuck in the mud, damp earth or sand.
◆ '*BHQ*' refers to an aircraft registration rather than a flight number.

b **◐1.19** Discuss with the class why the pilot is requesting confirmation [**Possible answer:** Either because there was a mistake in the data or simply that the transmission was not clear]. Then play the recording, pausing after each transmission for a volunteer to request confirmation, using word stress to attract attention to key information. Students can repeat the exercise in pairs using audioscript 1.19 on page 175.

Language focus: Adverbs

Elicit from the class what adverbs are and when they are used, with examples. Students then read the two example sentences to find four adverbs. They then read the rules to see how the four adverbs from the examples function. Check why *hard* doesn't end in *-ly*. [**Answer:** Because *hard* (= in a hard way) and *hardly* (= almost not) have very different meanings.]

Point out that all the adverbs in the Language focus box play a significant role in making information more precise and thus creating a more accurate mental picture.

Answers:
Adverb qualifying an adjective: *severely* (*concussed*)
Adverbs qualifying verbs: *slightly* (*scratched*); (*braked*) *hard*
Adverb qualifying other adverbs: *only* (*slightly*)
Adverbs ending in *-ly*: *severely, slightly, only*
Adverb making meaning stronger: *severely*
Adverbs making meaning weaker: *slightly; only*
Adverbs as common words: *only; very; well*

Language note:

Quite has two meanings. When used with a normal adjective (e.g. far, dangerous), it means *rather, somewhat* (e.g. it's quite far away). But when used with extreme adjectives (e.g. impossible) it can mean *completely*. For this reason, it may be safer to avoid it in most situations.

Extension activity:

Students work in teams. Read one of the definitions below for teams to write down the correct adverb. At the end, go through the answers. The team with the most correct answers is the winner.

Which adverb from the Language focus box:

1 means *little by little*, *step by step*? (gradually)
2 means the same as *hardly*? (scarcely)
3 means the same as *immediately*? (straight away)
4 often comes before *injured, burnt,* etc.? (severely)
5 is the opposite of *on purpose / deliberately*? (accidentally)
6 means the same as *nearly*? (almost)
7 tells somebody to try to be quick and not to wait? (as soon as possible)
8 means *a little*? (slightly)
9 qualifies adjectives, but not as strongly as *very*? (quite)
10 is the adverb equivalent of the adjective *good*? (well)

9a Students work alone to complete the sentences and then check in pairs.

> **Answers:**
>
> | | |
> |---|---|
> | 1 very | 5 just |
> | 2 almost | 6 severely |
> | 3 hard | 7 only |
> | 4 a little | 8 soon |

Background note:

RH simply means right-hand. *Right-hand / Left-hand* are generally used to avoid confusion with *right* meaning *correct* and *left* meaning *remaining*.

b ○**1.20** Make sure students realise the sentences are those from exercise 9a. Play the recording once without pausing and ask students to underline the stressed words. Then check with the class which words they underlined. Play the recording again, pausing after each sentence for a volunteer to repeat. With weaker classes, you could get the whole class to repeat.

10 This activity combines the steps from the previous sections in short clarification scenarios using adverbs to qualify information. Go through the examples with the class, drawing attention to the + and – signs. Point out also that the ATCO will need to make a question with *how*. Students then work in pairs to make conversations using their prompts. Afterwards, go through some of the conversations with the class.

If you have an odd number of students you will need to have one group of three, where the third student takes conversations 2 and 4 from Student A and conversations 3 and 6 from Student B.

Background note:

The *nose gear* refers to the wheels, leg, steering system etc. at the front of the aircraft.

11 In this second pairwork activity the amount of information handled is greater and students request and provide the cause of various typical ground situations. Go through the example with the class, pointing out how the cues are transformed into the conversations. Practise the first set of cues with the students. The cues are fairly extensive and little improvisation is required. Students then work in pairs to make conversations using their cues. Afterwards, go through some of the conversations with the class.

If you have an odd number of students you will need to have one group of three, where the third student takes the first three problems from Student A and the last six problems from Student B.

Background notes:

* *Pax* is a common abbreviation for *passengers*.
* A *suspect packet* is any parcel or object which is not clearly identified and whose presence in a particular place is not justified.
* A *tractor* is a towing vehicle, used especially during pushback, i.e. moving a plane backwards from the stand. It is also referred to as a *tug* or *tow vehicle*. See www.skybrary.com: Pushback.
* *CG* means centre of gravity.
* *F/O* means first officer.
* *FOD* means foreign object damage, i.e. damage to the aircraft from stray objects on the ground or birds in flight.
* *Legal working time* refers to the maximum number of hours that a crew may work without a break. This is an important safety issue, as tired crews are much more likely to make mistakes. In the event of long delays, a crew may exceed its legal working time and be unable to ensure a flight.

12a The abbreviations in this exercise are very common and are usually said using the conventional rather than the phonetic alphabet. Students work in pairs to discuss what the abbreviations mean. When you go through the answers with the class, elicit when each abbreviation might be used.

> **Answers:**
>
> a **ATC** Air Traffic Control
> b **FOD** Foreign Object Damage
> c **NDB** Non-Directional Beacon
> d **UTC** Universal Time (Coordinated)
> e **ATD** Actual Time of Departure
> f **GPU** Ground Power Unit
> g **QFE** altimeter setting to indicate height above aerodrome
> h **VHF** Very High Frequency
> i **ETD** Estimated Time of Departure
> j **ILS** Instrument Landing System
> k **RVR** Runway Visual Range
> l **VOR** VHF Omnidirectional Range

b ○**1.21** Make sure students know to write a number (1–12) beside each abbreviation as they hear it. Then play the recording. When they check in pairs, make sure they know to pronounce the letters properly, as this is part of the exercise. Finally, check the answers carefully with the class.

c The pair work in this exercise takes the form of a freer and more far-ranging discussion. Students work in pairs to ask and answer questions about the abbreviations. Point out that the aim is to practise pronunciation of letters, not just to focus on these particular abbreviations. Finally, go through the answers with the class, again focusing on when each abbreviation might be used.

Answers:
ACC Area Control Centre
AFIS Automatic Flight Information Service
amsl above mean sea level
ATIS Automatic Terminal Information Service
DME Distance Measuring Equipment
ETD Estimated Time of Departure
IMC Instrument Meteorological Conditions
NDB Non-Directional Beacon
PAPI Precision Approach Path Indicator
RVR Runway Visual Range
SID Standard Instrument Departure
VFR Visual Flight Rules

Start-up and taxi instructions

Communicative and operational issues:

After communicating using the terminology of the airport environment, we turn to the first actions involving aircraft movement and routine ATC communication. The flight crew contacts the Ground Controller to request approval for pushback from the stand and engine start-up, and to receive taxi instructions to go from the apron to the active departure runway. Each flight has a departure 'slot' during which it must depart: if there is any delay at the stand, they may miss their slot and have to negotiate a new one. Alternatively, there may be traffic congestion or environmental conditions which delay their departure. Times expressed are often only the minutes of a given hour (e.g. slot 45).

13a **○1.22** The transmissions in these exercises are routine and in standard phraseology. They should be used to focus on pronunciation, recognising numerical information (flight and gate numbers) and discussing airline call signs and destinations. Students listen to write down the call signs and destinations. They then check in pairs before feeding back to the class. You may need to check the meaning of *bound for* (= going to).

Answers:
1 **C24**: Thai 236 / New Delhi
2 **C28**: Croatia 792 / Zagreb
3 **C21**: Austrian 517 / Frankfurt
4 **C26**: Air Berlin 209 / Warsaw
5 **C25**: Scandinavian 651 / Bergen
6 **C22**: Ice Air 432 / Luxembourg
7 **C27**: China Southern 569 / Shanghai
8 **C23**: Japan Air 773 / Tokyo

b **○1.22** In this activity students use textual data to respond to the previous requests and give specific start-up times, Standard Instrument Departures, which pilots find in their charts and documentation, and 4-digit transponder squawk identifiers, which enable the aircraft to be identified on the controller's screen. Go through the example with the class. Then

play the recording, pausing after each transmission for a volunteer to deliver approval and departure information. Students can repeat the exercise in pairs using audioscript 1.22 on page 175.

Background note:

SID stands for *Standard Instrument Departure*, a pre-planned, coded ATC IFR (Instrument Flight Rules, i.e. using flight instruments to control the aircraft rather than visual references outside the aircraft) departure routeing.

c **○1.22** Go through the example with the class. Point out that students have to respond to the initial requests and explain why start-up approval cannot be given immediately. This is a common occurrence and can be caused by a great variety of reasons. Then play the recording, pausing after each transmission for a volunteer to say why approval cannot be given. Students can repeat the exercise in pairs using audioscript 1.22 on page 175.

Background notes:

- If a plane is *on hold*, it is waiting, stopped, standing by.
- If a plane is *in line*, it is queuing.

Physical characteristics

Communicative and operational issues:

The airport represents the most complex visual environment pilots and controllers are faced with. Moreover, there are a greater number of unforeseen occurrences and specific vehicles and equipment than in flight. Especially during taxiing and in poor visibility when the controllers are less able to monitor the airport, the flight crew may have to describe and interpret phenomena, objects and persons they encounter. Precise descriptions can enhance not only safety but security.

14a Students work in small teams to come up with as many words as possible for each category. Use this as an opportunity to explore, organise and practise all the students' existing descriptive lexis. When you collect the answers on the board, award a point for each good answer. The team with the most points at the end is the winner.

Possible answers:
Condition: damaged; injured; clear; damp; closed; serviceable; flashing; running; obstructed
Colour: (light/pale/dark) red; green; yellow; brown; white; grey; purple; pink; orange; magenta; cyan
Size: narrow; small; long; short; deep; shallow; high; wide; thick; thin; deep

Shape: circular; triangular; semi-circular; spherical; square; rectangular; round; pointed; tapered
Feature: pale; light; shiny; rotating; intermittent; heavy; matt; smooth; rough
Material: wooden; metallic; concrete; plastic; rubber; steel; aluminium; glass; composite; carbon

Extension activity:

Students work in pairs to come up with at least one object/situation/event for each word on the board.

b ⊙1.23 Before you play the recording, discuss briefly with the class what they can see in each picture. Then play the recording while students match the communications to the pictures. They then check in pairs before feeding back to the class. You may need to check the meaning of *disabled*, *in the vicinity* (= nearby) and *get under way* (= start).

Note that all the activities which require students to correlate audio and visual inputs reinforce the fundamental cognitive processes in which pilots and controllers are constantly engaged.

Answers:			
1 d	3 c	5 e	7 h
2 f	4 a	6 g	8 b

Background notes:

♦ A *blow-out* is a tyre burst.
♦ A *tug* is another name for a *pushback tractor*.
♦ *ULD* is an abbreviation for unit load device, a pallet or container which can be loaded onto a plane as a single unit. *The hold* is the series of underfloor cargo compartments in a plane.

c Students work in pairs or small groups and describe the pictures. Make sure they understand that they should use the descriptive language from exercise 14a.

d Tell students to close their books. Read the example aloud, pausing for students to guess what you are describing. Once they have guessed correctly, continue the description, pausing before key words to elicit them from the class (e.g. Inside there's a … *motor* which drives a … *generator*.) Finally, elicit what the description included. [**Answer:** dimensions, external parts and functions, internal parts, where it is normally seen.] Students then work in pairs to describe their objects and guess what their partners are describing. When they have finished, elicit the best descriptions from the class.

If you have an odd number of students you will need to have one group of three, where the third student takes description 3 and 5 from Student A and descriptions 4, 6 and 8 from Student B.

Handling turnaround incidents

Communicative and operational issues:

Incidents during turnaround are numerous and affect operational safety and punctuality. Both flight crews and Apron Coordinators / Ground Controllers are called upon to describe situations and provide appropriate responses or solutions.

15a Go through the example with the class, eliciting if anything else can be bogged down. Students then work in pairs to think of examples for each description. Then go through the answers with the class. Point out that being able to describe incidents, damage and malfunctions correctly facilitates rapid and appropriate responses. Encourage students to refer to their own experience, which is often extensive and rich.

Possible answers:
bogged down: landing gear; aircraft
cut: a cable; a connection; a tyre
flat: tyre
scratched: fuselage; panel; skin
broken: glass; link; cover; pen
damaged: landing gear; wing tip; door
frozen: water; flight control surfaces; leading edge
smoking: engines; cargo compartment; broken-down vehicle; GPU
defective: part
inoperative: GPU; ASU; lighting; radio
seeping: oil; fuel; tank; union; connection; pipe
burst: tyre; bottle
deflated: tyre; escape slide
jammed: flaps; linkage
snowbound: airport; aircraft
cancelled: flight; departure; leave
delayed: flight; departure; arrival
leaking: oil; fuel; tank; union; connection; pipe
spilled: fuel; oil; water; hydraulic fluid
collapsed: landing gear; building
dented: leading edge; air intake; fuselage; skin
lost: baggage; cargo; passenger; aircraft
stuck: valve; aircraft; passenger
congested: apron; airport; taxiway
failed: system; computer; part; attempt
missing: passenger; static discharger
twisted: fairing; fuselage skin; ankle
contaminated: fuel; water; runway surface
faulty: connection; system; part; unit
overflowing: tank; fuel; water
unserviceable: GPU; ASU; lighting; radio
cracked: windshield; glass; cargo
overheated: air conditioning duct; oil; computers
worn: surface; tyre; markings

Background notes:

- *Inoperative* is a general term meaning that a system or part cannot operate correctly and covering all reasons why something may be out of action, for example because it is *broken down*, *defective* (= with a malfunction), *jammed* (= stuck, unable to move), etc.
- The difference between *seeping* and *leaking* is that seepage is a very slow leakage, whereas a leak can be measured in drops per minute.
- A tyre may be partially *deflated*, but is only described as *flat* when most of the gas (aircraft tyres are inflated with nitrogen) has escaped.
- There is no significant difference between *defective* and *faulty*.
- If something is *unserviceable* (*U/S*), it cannot be used on the aircraft and must be replaced or repaired; it is *inoperative* (inop).

b **Students discuss their experiences in small groups and then share their best (or worst) stories with the class. Remind students to use the language from the Language box in their discussions.**

16 **Students work in pairs to complete the sentences and then feed back to the class. You may need to check** *food poisoning.*

Answers:
1 cancelled, delayed
2 leaking, seeping, unserviceable
3 bogged down, stuck
4 inoperative, broken down, unserviceable
5 frozen
6 dented, damaged, twisted, scratched, cracked
7 deflated, flat
8 missing, damaged

Background notes:

- *Unions* are connectors or fittings which attach one piece of piping to another. Here they are used to join *hydraulic lines* (i.e. the lines which power the flight controls and braking system). A *seal* is part of a union which prevents water leaking out.
- *Embraer* here refers to a type of aircraft (made by Embraer, a Brazilian aircraft manufacturer).
- The *fuselage* /ˈfjuːzəˌlɑːʒ/ is the main body of a plane (i.e. excluding the wings, tail, landing gear, etc.). It is also referred to as the *airframe* or *hull*, as in the expressions 'airframe and powerplant' and 'hull loss'.
- A *sill* is the lower edge of a doorway.
- Tyre pressure is measured in *psi* (= pounds per square inch).
- A *static discharger* or *wick* is a device on trailing edges for dissipating static electricity.

17a ○1.24 **Before you listen, go through the ten incidents with the class to discuss which are the most serious [Suggested answer: damage to the wing tip and running off the taxiway are probably the most serious problems as they will immobilise the aircraft and delay the flight for longer]. Make sure they know to write a number (1–10) beside each letter, as in the example. Then play the recording for students to complete the matching exercise. Students check their answers with a partner before feeding back to the class.**

Answers:				
1 f	3 e	5 a	7 b	9 i
2 c	4 g	6 j	8 h	10 d

Background notes:

- Operational staff are always being required to visualise situations from audio inputs and make inferences even when the specific vocabulary is not used.
- A *navigation light cover* refers to the transparent protective cover on each wing tip which houses a red light on the left-hand wing and a green light on the right-hand wing, like on ships, in order to show the direction the aircraft is moving in.
- *APU* stands for Auxiliary Power Unit. It is a small gas turbine engine, usually located in the tail cone, which is used on the ground when the engines are shut down to generate electricity, provide air conditioning and high-pressure air to start the engines.
- An *AGNIS docking system* is one of the most common forms of stand guidance, i.e. ways of guiding a plane to its correct position in the stand. AGNIS stands for Azimuth Guidance for Nose-In Stand.

b ○1.24 **In this exercise, students do what they have to do in the real world: provide appropriate solutions.** *Will* **is used here to express intention and reassure the interlocutor. Make sure students know to take notes in their notebooks. Then play the recording. Afterwards, students discuss the situations and their solutions with a partner. When you go through the answers with the class, elicit the best ways of phrasing the solutions. The suggested answers are not necessarily what you should expect of the students; they may express themselves effectively in fewer words and with the same vocabulary and phrasing as in the recording. As throughout** *Flightpath*, **the suggested answers are also designed to provide the teacher with additional and alternative lexis and structures which you may wish to feed back into the course.**

Suggested answers:
(phrasing the solutions)

1

Pilot: We are unable to push back because a servicing truck is blocking the inner taxiway.

ATCO: I will have the driver instructed to leave the area as soon as possible.

2

Pilot: Turkair 288, Maintenance are changing a worn tyre, but we should be ready for pushback soon. Request a new departure slot.

ATCO: When do you expect to be ready?

Pilot: Maintenance says we will be ready for pushback at 35.

ATCO: Expect a departure slot at 55.

3

Pilot: Argentina 356, Baggage handling has delivered the wrong baggage. We won't be able to make the 55 slot. I think we'll be delayed for some time.

ATCO: Call back when you are ready to depart.

4

Pilot: The tow vehicle at our gate has broken down. They have called for a new tractor. We'll advise you when we are ready for pushback.

ATCO: Roger. Call me when you are ready.

…

Extension activity: Adverbs

Students look at the ten transmissions in audioscript 1.24 on page 175 to find and underline all the adverbs. Note that some phrases (e.g. *when ready*) fulfil the same role as adverbs and are given here in brackets.

Answers:
1 yet, straight away
2 soon
3 still, considerably
4 (when ready)
5 quickly
6 expeditiously (= quickly and efficiently)
7 slightly, probably, fully
8 incorrectly
9 currently, still, approximately
10 now, (with caution)

Putting it together: Detailed taxi instructions

Communicative and operational issues:

We strongly recommend ICAO Circular 323 as basic reading for all aviation English teachers. In the follow-on questions from the quotation in the ICAO Focus box, many of the most common types of issue encountered during turnaround and taxiing are referred to: abnormal situations, system failures, health, obstacles, readback and clarification. This section draws together the lexis and functions introduced and practised throughout the unit.

Preparation

18 This bird's-eye view of an unusual airport is similar to the vision which pilots have and they are trained to notice particularities: surrounding terrain, runway length, width, orientation and exits, taxiway layout etc. and the precautions which these may entail. Students discuss the question in pairs and then feed back to the class.

Suggested answer:
This illustration is of Santos Dumont airport in Rio de Janeiro, Brazil. Its particularity is the fact that it is built on reclaimed land jutting out into the sea; originally, it was a sea-plane terminal. There are two parallel runways 02R/20L and 02L/20R: 20L and 20R are visible on the illustration. 02R/20L is wider. The terminal buildings are located on the landward side, which is on the right of the illustration. The runways occupy the full width of the land and the thresholds are next to the water at both ends. Pilots must be sure to have enough stopping distance if they wish to abandon (abort) a take-off or if they land long, i.e. too far down the runway from the touchdown zone.

19a ○1.25 Use the example to make sure students know what to do. Then play the recording. Students complete the words with the correct endings. They then check in pairs before feeding back to the class.

Answers:	
1 safely	6 spilled
2 completed	7 slightly
3 failed	8 differences
4 stronger	9 cracked
5 missing	10 correctly

b ○1.25 Play the recording again, pausing after each word for students to repeat it. Make sure they pronounce the endings clearly.

ICAO FOCUS

Michel Trémaud is a former Safety Director at Airbus and a member of the Flight Safety Foundation. The quotation from his article highlights the safety impact of different airport layouts which pilots should be able to notice and describe and controllers describe for pilots who are unfamiliar with them.

Airbus is a European consortium of aircraft manufacturers which produces aircraft such as the A300, A310, A320, A318, A319, A321, A330, A340, A380 and A350. The *Flight Safety Foundation* is an American-based international, non-profit association which promotes safety and safety awareness in aviation by its publications, studies, research, journals, conferences and website (http://flightsafety.org).

Tell students to read the quote and find three reasons for using plain language [**Answer:** to clarify, paraphrase and provide additional information]. Students then discuss the questions in pairs before feeding back to the class.

Possible answers:
Non-routine situations on the ground: collision with ground handling vehicles and other aircraft; fuel and oil spillage; adverse weather conditions; industrial action preventing certain services; loading incorrect baggage or cargo; misdirected passengers causing delays; de-icing queues causing delays; bad weather causing flights to be diverted and causing congestion; bomb threats; heightened security measures; unscheduled aircraft maintenance; aircraft directed to an incorrect stand; flight crew misunderstanding their taxiing or stand instructions; inappropriate ground equipment for a particular aircraft type; relief crew being delayed; crew members being ill; crew exceeding their legal duty times; flights running into quiet hours when movements are restricted; delayed boarding due to cleaners not having been available; departure delayed due to incomplete catering; baggage being unloaded due to a missing passenger; need to return to de-icing because of a delay in departure; power, lighting or equipment failures on the ground etc. In fact, the potential list is almost endless.
ATC system failures: power cuts; radar antennas; radio navigation transmitters; VHF communication; mainframe computer

Aircraft system failures on the ground: hydraulic and fuel leaks; low engine oil level; deflated, worn or damaged tyres; missing static dischargers; damaged wing and engine air intake leading edges; engine foreign object damage; APU unserviceable; computer failures and line replaceable unit (LRU) removal and installation; spurious fault messages; incorrect inertial navigation system coordinates; all Minimum Equipment List (MEL) no-go items; impact damage to the fuselage; inadvertent escape slide deployment; short circuits etc. Again, the list is endless.
Health problems: cuts; bruises; fractures; sprains; broken or cracked ribs; concussion; heart attack; asthmatic attack; epileptic fit; food poisoning; stroke; intoxication; loss of consciousness; dizziness; headache; ear ache; bleeding; rashes; burns etc.
Obstacles on the runway: vehicles; pedestrians; unauthorized aircraft; towed aircraft; animals (dogs, buffalo, crocodiles, cows have all been encountered); metal debris from other aircraft due to tail skidding or incorrectly attached parts (Continental was found liable and guilty of defective maintenance due to a metal part which fell from one of its aircraft at Paris Charles de Gaulle airport causing a tyre blow-out, perforation of a wing fuel tank and the subsequent crash of an Air France Concorde on 25th July 2000); rubber debris from aircraft tyres which have been detreaded; fuel or oil spills etc. Pilots should report any such obstacles because the potential impacts on safety are so great.

Quote: **Elicit from the class how airport layout can increase difficulties for flight crews. Students then read the quote to compare it with their ideas. Elicit from the class any examples they know of the situation described in the quote or similar situations.**

Background note:

A *runway threshold* is the beginning or end of a runway.

20 **Students look at the airport chart of Seattle, Washington State, International Airport and discuss the questions in pairs and then feed back to the class.**

Suggested answers:
1 Taxiways Charlie and Quebec serve several runway thresholds.
2 The risk factor is increased by the fact that the holding points for Runways 34C and 34R are very close together and this is identified as a hot spot.

3 Other factors which could make operations from Seattle problematic are: the number of transversal taxiways; three parallel runways which could be confused; Taxiway Tango which is very wide and could be confused with a runway; Taxiway Alpha, which is restricted to aircraft with a limited wingspan given the proximity of airport buildings; the need to change frequency when crossing the 'non-movement boundary' on Taxiway Whisky; and glideslope fluctuations on approaches to Runway 16L.

Communication

21 This exercise provides practice in giving and receiving detailed taxi instructions. When receiving instructions, pilots do actually take notes which they use during taxiing. Notice the importance of saying '*hold short*' of active runways, i.e. waiting for specific authorisation to cross. Go through the example with the class, reading the ATCO's directions aloud with students following on the chart. Students then work in pairs to request and give directions.

If you have an **odd number of students** you will need one group of three students, where the third student takes instruction 3 from Student A and instruction 4 from Student B.

> **Background note:**
>
> *Transient parking* is a place for planes to park temporarily.

22 This exercise reflects a frequent situation in which controllers must solve common taxiing problems without necessarily having the aircraft in sight. Go through the example with the class, eliciting any other possible ATCO instructions for this situation. You may need to check the meaning/pronunciation of *dust*, *ploughing* (/ˈplaʊɪŋ/), *prior to* (= before), *debris* (/ˈdebriː/) and *torrential rain*. Students then work in pairs to describe situations and provide instructions.

> Suggested answers:
> **Student A**
> 1
> **Pilot:** There is a 737 approaching from our right on Taxiway Kilo.
> **ATCO:** Give way to 737 from right to left.
> 2
> **Pilot:** Tunisair 435, we are on Taxiway Bravo 2. An elderly passenger is experiencing severe chest pains.
> **ATCO:** Tunisair 435, taxi to Stand 38 via Charlie and Echo.

3
Pilot: There is a lot of dust due (to) tractor ploughing a field next to Taxiway Hotel. Request deviation.
ATCO: Taxi via Foxtrot and Lima and hold short of Runway 16 Left.
4
Pilot: There seems to be a dog on Runway 31 Left.
ATCO: Roger. I will advise the airport authorities.
...
Student B
1
Pilot: Speedbird 376, due thunderstorm overhead, request delay departure.
ATCO: Speedbird 376, affirm. I will call you when the weather improves.
2
Pilot: Oman 076, there is an MD81 stopped ahead of us on Taxiway Tango 2.
ATCO: Oman 076, roger. I will contact him. Taxi to Runway 21 via Romeo.
3
Pilot: Northwest 2439, we have a flight attendant who has food poisoning. Request return to apron.
ATCO: Northwest 2439, roger. Taxi via Lima and Kilo.
4
Pilot: Slovakia 385, we are unable to cross Runway 29 Left. An Aeroflot Ilyushin 86 has stopped at the holding point on Taxiway Golf.
ATCO: Hold position.
...

If you have an **odd number of students** you will need one group of three students, where the third student takes instructions 1 to 3 from Student A and instructions 8 to 10 from Student B.

> **Background notes:**
> ◆ Note that the pilot in Student A transmission 2 describes *chest pains*. In general, symptoms rather than diagnoses are given when describing a medical incident over the radio.
> ◆ *Poor braking surface* refers to a runway surface which may be 'contaminated' by ice, snow or water, all of which will reduce the friction coefficient of the surface, i.e. make it more slippery, and mean that the tyres will not adhere as well to the runway. Therefore, longer distances will be required to stop the aircraft.
> ◆ Note that airport land is often used for agricultural purposes, hence the reference to *ploughing*.
> ◆ *Torching* refers to flames coming from the exhaust nozzle, usually caused by fuel ignited aft of the core engine.

- *INS coordinates* are precise geographical coordinates for the aircraft's inertial navigation system at a well-defined and remote spot on the airport.
- If a plane *backtracks*, it does a 180° turn at the end of the runway and taxis back to a runway exit or lines up for departure.
- *Engine blast* is the fast-moving exhaust gases from the engines which can cause considerable damage.
- *Short final* means the last minutes of flight when the aircraft is stabilised in its landing configuration and has probably less than four nautical miles to touchdown on the runway.
- A *radio check* is a request to a ground station to transmit in order to confirm audibility (readability). Readability is measured on a scale from 1 (*wun*) unreadable to 5 (*fife*) perfectly readable.
- Debris and unattached materials such as *loose plastic* can be sucked into the aircraft engines on the ground and cause Foreign Object Damage (FOD) which may be severe.

Debriefing

23 Students discuss the questions in groups and feed back to the class. This is also an opportunity for you to remind students of their strengths and weaknesses from this unit.

Progress check

Students then work alone to complete the progress check. They can then compare their notes with a partner to offer each other advice. Finally, discuss with the class and elicit what areas they need to do more work on.

DVD: *Danger on the runway*

Communicative and operational issues:

The clip was made at a regional airport in Canada. The small size of the airport makes it easier to focus on the safety issues in uncluttered situations. It is a training film produced by Transport Canada, the civil aviation authority.

Point out specific differences between North American and European usage (e.g. inches of mercury instead of hectoPascal to measure atmospheric pressure), and non-standard phraseology (e.g. '*Runway six Left*' instead of '*Runway zero six Left*'; '*Taxi to position Runway six Left*' instead of '*Taxi to holding point/position Runway six Left*'; '*Tan Air 79, pull up and go around*' instead of '*Tan Air 79, go around. I say again, go around. Acknowledge*')

24a Go through the questions with the class. Point out that in order to answer them, students will need to use their eyes, their ears and their background knowledge. Play the first part of the DVD for students to answer the three questions. They discuss the questions in pairs before feeding back to the class.

Note that in a small airport, the tower controller will manage all aircraft and vehicle movements. Impress on students how their interlocutor's mood can be revealed through tone of voice and delivery.

Answers:
1 there is a low ceiling; it has been raining; the atmosphere is a bit misty
2 a runway incursion
3 the driver is uncertain of his route, but does not read back and check his instructions adequately.

Background notes:

- '*Two miles on final for 14*' means 'on final approach two nautical miles from touchdown on Runway 14'.
- If a vehicle *rolls through* a hold line, it fails to stop and taxis past it.

b Discuss the questions with the whole class. Note that question 2 contains difficult grammar (*could have been avoided*), which you may need to explain.

Answers:
1 because he is a bit confused, was not entirely sure about the instructions given him, and was probably a bit embarrassed and did not wish to ask the controller to repeat again.
2 The incident could have been avoided if the truck driver had been trained better, if the driver had stopped systematically short of the runway and if the controller had checked that the driver had understood correctly when he heard his hesitation.

25a Students read through the transcript to guess/try to remember what information could go in each gap. Then play the DVD again, pausing frequently to check students have fully understood all the communications, especially if they had a problem with question 1 in exercise 24a. Afterwards, go through the answers with the class.

Answers:
1 Bravo, Charlie, Echo
2 Bravo, Echo, Charlie
3 Charlie, Echo

b Students discuss the questions in pairs and then feed back to the class.

Answers:

1 The driver was embarrassed and did not want to be seen to make another mistake so just said, '*Roger*'.

2 *Roger* is dangerous in cases where a full readback is required because the controller who gave the instruction cannot know whether his/her interlocutor (the other speaker) has correctly understood the transmission.

Extension activity:

At the end of the clip, the narrator says that 'it could be a different story at night or in poor visibility'. Discuss briefly with the class what might have happened in such conditions.

26a **Students read the six sentence endings. Elicit from the class some predictions of what the incident will involve. Then play the second part of the DVD for students to complete the exercise. Afterwards, students discuss the answers with a partner and feed back to the class, including any additional information they can provide about the three aircraft (e.g. that Express 3525 is a regional aircraft in the process of taking off, and the Citation is a business jet taxiing on the ground. The third aircraft, Tan Air 79, is on approach. The Citation crew seems inexperienced and uncertain).**

Answers:

◆ Express 3525 is (a) able to clear the other aircraft when taking off and (e) cleared for take-off on Runway 6L.

◆ Citation B77 (c) is running late and (f) mishears an instruction and taxis across the active runway.

◆ Tannair 79 (b) is on final approach and (d) has to pull up and go around.

Extension activity:

You may want to check students' understanding of the grammar in the narrator's final sentence: '*Had it not, … the outcome could have been deadly.*' This is an example of a third conditional to talk about the unreal past. Pilots and ATCOs may not necessarily need to be able to use this grammar accurately, but they do need to understand it, especially in the context of imagining potential outcomes of past mistakes.

Write the sentence on the board and elicit from the class another way of saying it, using *if*:

◆ *If Express 3525 had not managed to clear the Citation, there is a good chance that there would have been fatalities.*

Use the following questions to check students understand:

◆ Is this sentence about the past, present or future? [**Answer:** past]

◆ Is it about something that really happened, or something from the imaginary past? [**Answer:** imaginary past]

◆ What actually happened? [**Answer:** Express 3525 managed to clear the Citation so there were no casualties.]

◆ What tense structures are used in the *if*-sentence? [**Answer:** *if* + past perfect, *would/could/might have* + past participle]

◆ Why are different tenses used in the two parts of the sentence? [**Answer:** Because we don't normally use *would* after *if*.]

You could then use some of the sentences from exercise 26a to elicit more examples of the same structure, for example:

◆ *If Citation B77 hadn't been running late, the crew might not have made so many mistakes.*

◆ *If Citation B77 hadn't misheard the instruction, it wouldn't have taxied across the active runway.*

You could also ask students to make similar sentences about other runway incursions.

b **Tell students to discuss the question in small groups before they watch again. They should then watch and make notes of the mistakes. Finally, discuss the questions with the class. If students cannot detect the non-standard phraseology by themselves, give them clues. Discuss the ambiguity of 'Taxi to position Runway six left'. Does it mean 'Line up and wait on Runway six Left' or 'Hold short of Runway six Left'?**

Suggested answers:

1 The phraseology used by the controller and pilots is non-standard on several occasions: '*taxi to position*' is not standard phraseology and could be interpreted as either '*taxi to holding position*' or '*line up and wait*' / '*taxi into position and hold*' (on the runway). The controller says '*six*' instead of '*zero six*' which would avoid confusion with *wun six, too six* or *tree six*. The correct phraseology is *contact Tower 118.9*. The phrase '*traffic on the roll*' used when speaking to Tan Air 79 is not clear; it could refer to either departing or arriving traffic. The standard instruction for a go-around is *Tan Air 79, go around. I say again, go around. Acknowledge.* Standard phraseology for leaving a runway is *vacate* rather than *exit*.

2 The key mistakes are: a) a lack of coordination between the two ATC frequencies so that the controller we hear initially is not aware of the instructions given to Citation Bravo 77 by the Tower; b) the Citation Bravo 77 crew being in a hurry and misunderstanding their taxi instructions; c) the Citation Bravo 77 crew starting to cross a runway (06L) without authorisation from ATC; d) insufficient monitoring of Citation Bravo 77's movements when the controller should have been aware that the crew were not familiar with the airport layout; e) the controller not taking sufficient precautions about making sure that Runway 06L was clear before clearing Tan Air 79 to land.

3 The incident could have been avoided by: a) better coordination between the controllers so that they were aware of each other's instructions; b) greater sensitivity to the obvious lack of familiarity with the aerodrome by the Citation crew; c) clearly given and read-back taxi instructions; d) the Citation crew requesting confirmation if they were not sure of their position and taxi routeing; e) the Citation crew holding short of the active runway and requesting permission to cross; f) the Citation crew being aware of their own uncertainty, haste and lack of attention and using proper crew resource management to handle the situation; g) ATC showing greater discipline in phraseology, the monitoring of aircraft ground movements and making sure that the active runway was clear and that there would be sufficient spacing between arriving and departing aircraft.

Several causes of runway incursion (by the truck and the Citation) are demonstrated in the video: lack of familiarity with the airport; failure to request clarification; fear of annoying the controller; being in a hurry; ambiguous instructions in non-standard phraseology; readback and hearback errors; failure to react when one is uncertain about one's interlocutor's understanding; handling several aircraft simultaneously; poor visibility; darkness. Most of these causes, or contributing factors, can be addressed by better communication.

27a **Go through the task with the class, eliciting as many suggestions as possible and writing them on the board. See answers to exercise 27b for a list of possible causes and recommendations.**

b **Play the third part of the DVD for students to compare it with their ideas from the board. You may need to play the DVD twice, as some of the information is presented quite quickly. Afterwards, discuss any differences with the class. You could also take this opportunity to check some of the vocabulary from the DVD (e.g. *vigilant, ambiguous, assumptions, keep your cool, courteous*).**

Answers:
Causes: distractions; uncertainty; poor visibility; miscommunication (including poor language proficiency) and working under pressure
Recommendations: basic training on runway safety for all staff using the airport; good RT discipline (readback/hearback); always hold short of a runway until specifically instructed to cross; always question if in doubt; recognise when one is working under pressure such as time constraints; familiarise yourself with airport layouts and any changes to airport infrastructure; use up-to-date charts; note down any complex taxi instructions; verbalise instructions with the other crew member; use standard phraseology

Extension activity:

For each of the recommendations, discuss with the class: 1) why exactly it is important; 2) what can go wrong if the recommendation is not followed.

UNIT 3
Communication on the ground

Operational topics	Turnaround activities; Ramp Safety; Handling incidents; 'We are at take-off'; Managing a fire emergency; Problem solving on the ground
Communication functions	Responding to instructions; Communication errors: failure to acknowledge correctly (pilots); Reporting anomalies; Describing what you can see, hear, feel etc.; Asking for clarification; Responding to problems; Describing an action in progress; Describing a completed action; Managing a departure
Language content	Pronunciation: verbs ending in *-ing*; Ground equipment vocabulary; Current actions and activities; Word groups; Perception: describing what you think is happening; Stress in statements and questions; Completed actions; Having something done; ICAO communicative tasks

Unit 3 Teacher's brief

Unit 3 builds on the lexis and structures introduced and practised in the previous unit with respect to the airport environment in more or less routine situations. We now look more closely at some specific operations which occur while the aircraft is on the ground and also focus on ambiguity in communication, handling an emergency (fire) and solving problems which may occur. Therefore much of the lexis and background information in the Teacher's Book relating to Unit 2 remains valid and useful in Units 3 and 4.

We have already seen in Unit 2 how the airport can be a dangerous place to work. In Unit 3, we look more closely at ground operations, the various steps of a **turnaround**, the different types of **ground support equipment (GSE)** and the activities associated with them, describing **unusual phenomena** in the airport area (odours, stray animals, unauthorised personnel, debris, deteriorated airport infrastructure, obstacles, the effects of bad weather conditions etc.), how **imprecise and non-standard language** can have dramatic consequences, liaising with the **fire service** and what happens during **pushback**.

Unit 3 also prepares for what is the major safety concern in this first part of the course, **runway incursions**, particularly in the section 'We're at take-off'.

Unit 3 Sources

- www.airlinepost.com: Tenerife 1977 (Exercises 16a–e)
- Airports Council International: *Airport Safety*, 2009
- www.airport-technology.com: Ground Equipment
- Bjelkerud, M. and Funnemark, E.: *Under New Management*, *AeroSafety World*, July 2008 (Unit lead-in; Exercise 4)

- www.faa.gov: Airport Safety
- Flight Safety Foundation: *Best Practices for General Ramp Safety* video (Exercises 25a–27d)
- www.omegaaviation.com: Airport Ground Equipment
- www.skybrary.aero: Ground Operations; Los Rodeos, Tenerife, 1977 (Exercises 16a–e)

Lead-in

The lead-in quote, from the Flight Safety Foundation *AeroSafety World*, is very short, but sufficient to spark a class discussion about operational pressures and hazards, the vocabulary of safety/security equipment and measures, and the resulting communication situations while the aircraft is on the ground.

Communicative and operational issues:

Although not the prime focus of the ICAO Language Proficiency Requirements, the communications which the flight crew and controllers may be engaged in on the ground cover a very wide and unpredictable range of topics and situations and often have safety implications. As, in most cases, standard phraseology is not provided for these situations, plain language and familiarity with a great variety of lexical domains are required (see ICAO Doc. 9835, 2010 issue, Appendix B Part II.1 and III).

Quote: **Read the quote aloud. Elicit from the class a range of turnaround activities and possible ground hazards, as well as safety and security measures and safety equipment.**

Suggested answers:

Turnaround activities: See exercise 2a.

Hazards: injury to ground staff from aircraft, vehicles, equipment and substances; vehicles damaging aircraft; vehicles colliding; fuel, oil and hydraulic fluid spillage and contamination; damage to cargo and baggage; terrorist threats etc.

Safety/security measures: personnel screening; passes and identity; safety management systems; procedures and protocols

Safety equipment: high-visibility safety vests; protective clothing (gloves, goggles, masks etc.); safety barriers and cordons; safety perimeter around the aircraft; ground markings; REMOVE-BEFORE-FLIGHT safety flags; probe and inlet covers; wheel chocks; apron lighting; anti-collision beacons (on aircraft) and strobe lights (on vehicles); safety cones and cordons

1a, b, c Students discuss the three questions in pairs and then feed back to the class.

Suggested answers:

1b See **Safety/security measures** and **Safety equipment** above

1c Ultimately, the flight crew is the most affected by delays in the ground handling activities. Any delay in a flight departure is analysed and the responsibility is assigned to a given service.

Ground operations

The emphasis in this section is on identifying the main turnaround activities and the personnel involved in them. We focus more on the equipment used in the next section (Ground Equipment, exercises 11 and 12).

2a Students discuss the pictures in pairs and then feed back to the class. Discuss exactly what each picture shows.

Answers:

a containers being loaded into an aircraft hold from a scissor/hydraulic platform loader by ground handlers

b the First Officer performing the 'walkaround' or external inspection of the aircraft

c meals, drinks and newspapers being brought to the aircraft by caterers

d a mechanic or ground handler putting wheel chocks in place to stop the aircraft from moving

e the aircraft being pushed back from its stand by the tug driver and ground handler / mechanic

f the fuel agent refuelling the aircraft

g the marshaller/'batman' guiding the aircraft to its stand

h the passengers boarding the aircraft along the walkway/airbridge

b, c, d, e Students discuss the four questions in pairs and then feed back to the class. Note that exercise b has no correct answers, but should produce some good discussion.

Suggested answers:

b Some of these activities will be simultaneous or vary from one turnaround situation to another, but the first activities will always be *g* (marshalling) and *d* (wheel chocking) and the last *h* (passenger boarding) and *e* (pushback). The external inspection is usually early on in the turnaround in case there are any signs of damage or failure which need repairing.

c Potential communication with: **dispatchers** (cargo and baggage, hazardous cargo, aircraft weight and centre of gravity); **loadmaster / ramp supervisor** (loading operations); **aircraft maintenance technician / mechanic / engineer** (all technical issues, walkaround inspection with First Officer, engine servicing, update of aircraft logbook); **ground/tower controllers** (any circumstances impacting operations, stand number, departure slot time, weather and operational conditions, start-up and pushback approval, taxi instructions, flight plan amendments); **fuelling agent** (fuel uplift); **passenger service agents** (situations affecting boarding); **ground handlers** (pushback); **airport security guards and police** (security threats, prisoners, valuables etc.); **airport station manager** (higher-level operational issues such as scheduling of flights, diversions, health and safety, security etc.); **airport office** (airport fees for each landing and take-off and the parking and ramp services); **fire service** (fire fighting, fuel or corrosive fluid spillage, brake overheat etc.); **paramedics** (sick or injured passengers or crew); and even passengers in difficulty or being difficult.

d The flight crew interface the most with the **dispatchers** or 'red caps' for all the flight documentation, weight and balance information, cargo documents, cargo loading etc. and with the **line maintenance technicians** for any outstanding technical problems, making entries in the aircraft technical log and for the external inspection, which may be conducted in cooperation with the First Officer.

e The answer to this question depends very much on the size of the airport. In small aerodromes, controllers will liaise directly with more categories of personnel; in large airports, communications will probably be divided among apron coordinators and ground, departure or tower controllers.

Extension activity:

Students work in pairs and test each other on the questions from exercises 2a–e (e.g. *What happens first? Who is involved in this stage? Who do they have contact with?* etc.).

3a, b **This is an opportunity to discover the hazards related to different steps in the turnaround process. Discuss the questions with the class.**

> **Suggested answer:**
> a ATC is directly involved in communicating the stand number, in any delays about incoming aircraft being able to enter their stand, in any ramp activities which will affect departure times, start-up, pushback approval and taxi instructions.

> **Answer:**
> b Handling the departing flight was found to be the most dangerous phase of turnaround, probably for two main reasons: it lasts longer than the other phases and involves more personnel, equipment and vehicles simultaneously than any other phase.

Extension activity:

You could generate additional discussion by arguing that each of the procedures in exercise 2a has an impact on ATC activity and eliciting examples (e.g. by affecting turnaround times and keeping to, or disrupting flight schedules). You can do the same by arguing that each of the activities in exercise 3b can be dangerous and eliciting possible examples.

> **Possible answers:**
> **Preparing the stand** can be dangerous because servicing vehicles are being put into place for the arrival of the aircraft. If the stand is vacant, there is much more space to work in. However, if one flight follows another immediately, there may be interference between the staff and equipment servicing the two aircraft.
>
> **Parking the aircraft** can be dangerous because care must be taken to stop the aircraft at exactly the correct position, the engines are running and a body which can weigh several hundred tonnes is moving.
>
> **Handling the arriving flight** can be dangerous because several different vehicles are being moved into position simultaneously.
>
> **Handling the departing flight** can be dangerous because this is the longest and most complex phase in turnaround and all the staff are under pressure to work quickly and get the flight away on time. Refuelling, water servicing, walkaround inspection, catering, cleaning, cargo loading, boarding are all taking place either simultaneously or in quick succession.

Pushback / taxi out can be dangerous: the aircraft is moving again and is moving backwards without the crew having any visibility; on the ground wingmen often accompany the aircraft to make sure the wing tips have proper clearance. It is during pushback that most aircraft collisions occur.

De-icing can be dangerous because the de-icing agents are working in extreme cold on high hydraulic platforms and with toxic chemicals.

4 ○**1.26** Make sure students understand that they should write a number next to each picture. Then play the recording for students to complete the exercise. Students check in pairs before feeding back to the class.

> **Answers:**
> | | | | |
> |---|---|---|---|
> | 1 a | 3 g | 5 h | 7 d |
> | 2 b | 4 f | 6 e | 8 c |

Background notes:

♦ The *lower cargo deck* is divided into a forward and aft cargo hold, which on larger aircraft may be subdivided into compartments. The holds/compartments are subdivided into bays each one of which corresponds to the size of a ULD (Unit Load Device) or container.

♦ An *external walk-around check* involves the First Officer, and often the line mechanic, making a complete tour of the outside of the aircraft and inspecting critical points to make sure that no parts of the aircraft are damaged, missing or incorrectly positioned. These points include: the air data probes on the forward fuselage; the radome and leading edges of the wings; engine cowls and empennage for impact damage; the external lights (landing, take-off, taxiing, runway turnoff, navigation, anti-collision, logo); the landing gear mechanisms; the tyres; the belly; the fan and compressor blades (hence the need for a torch); the hydraulic bays (usually in the main landing gear bay) for leaks; the crew oxygen cylinder blow-out disks (green disks on both sides of the forward fuselage which are ejected and show red if the crew's oxygen cylinders are subject to overpressure and discharge); the drain masts (aerodynamically faired drains along the lower fuselage to drain overboard any leaked water or condensation. The drain masts are heated electrically to avoid icing up and the word HOT is painted on them in red); the static dischargers; the primary (elevators, ailerons, rudder, trimmable horizontal stabiliser) and secondary (flaps, slats, spoilers, airbrakes) flight control surfaces; the discharge valves (which regulate cabin pressurisation); the passenger and cargo door areas etc. The aircraft maintenance technician (engineer or mechanic) will also check the engine oil levels and replenish them if necessary and enter any observations or action taken in the logbook.

- At *nose-in* stands, i.e. those directly in contact with the airport passenger terminal, parking or docking is usually assisted by an automatic system. If this is unserviceable (*U/S*) or incorrectly set for the arriving aircraft, then a marshaller needs to guide the aircraft manually.

- If a plane *uplifts* fuel, it takes it on board, i.e. it refuels. *Uplift* can also be used as a noun, to refer to the amount of fuel uplifted.

- A *leg* is a part of a long-haul journey, where the plane stops to refuel one or more times on the way.

- Transmission 6 is a frequent type of communication from the flight deck to the handler or mechanic with a headset, saying that they can start pushback and indicating the direction the aircraft should be *facing* (i.e. have its nose pointing) to start taxiing.

- The *ground* refers to the ground crew (i.e. the ground handlers or mechanics whose job it is to set and remove the chocks, to prevent the aircraft from moving).

- *Chocks* are rubber or wooden blocks to prevent aircraft movement while parked.

Extension activity 1:

Write the following words and numbers on the board:

chocks	east	external	forward
U/S	vegetarian	ten	107

Students work in pairs to discuss which transmission they came from (using the pictures in exercise 2a to remind themselves) and what they referred to. Then they listen again to check.

> **Answers:**
> 1 forward (hold); 2 external (walkaround); 3 (the nose-in parking is) U/S; 4 (uplift) 107 (tonnes); 5 (under way in about) ten (minutes); 6 (push back to face) east; 7 chocks (are in place); 8 vegetarian (meal trays)

Extension activity 2:

You could use the audioscripts for a brief revision and contextualisation of some important grammar structures. Tell students to look at audioscript 1.26 on page 176 and underline examples of the following structures:

- infinitive with *to*
- present continuous
- *will* and *should*

When you go through the answers with the class, elicit the reasons for using these structures.

> **Answers:**
> - **infinitive with *to*:** *containers to be loaded* (= something exists which needs to be done); *need a marshaller to guide us / need to uplift* (= *need* + (object) + *to*); *ready to get under way / unable to push back* (= adjectives + *to*); *push back to face east* (= in order to)
> - **present continuous:** *he's just doing the external walkaround / the passengers are boarding / catering is delivering* (= activities at the moment of speaking)
> - ***will*** and ***should*:** *I'll ask* (= spontaneous decision or offer); *we'll need a marshaller / we'll need to uplift* (= predictions based on opinion); *we should be ready* (= an expectation)

Quote: **Students read the quote to identify the problem and its cause. This short quotation from the Norwegian risk analysis picks up on the unit's initial lead-in.**

> **Answer:**
> The problem – safety was put at risk. The cause – time pressures during turnaround.

5a **This is essentially an opportunity to discuss in more detail the time pressures to which staff are subjected and talk about the working environment of these different categories of personnel. Students discuss the question in pairs, focusing on what each group of people have to do during turnaround and why they are under pressure.**

> **Suggested answers:**
> Operational pressures: being on schedule (commercial); respecting the departure slot (operational); shortened turnaround times (economic); growing volume of traffic: growing size and complexity of airports; large number of simultaneous ground servicing actions, vehicles and staff; security restrictions; increased volume of paperwork (traceability); new technologies; labour legislation etc.
> **Pilots** are under pressure because ultimately they are responsible for the safe and timely departure of the aircraft and may have to liaise with all the different professions involved in the turnaround.
> **ATCOs** are subject to any delays which may be caused during turnaround, but which they do not control. Delays in departures or arrivals will always have a knock-on effect on the traffic flow as a whole.
> **Dispatchers** spend their life running between the ground and the flight deck. They are responsible for bringing updated documents for the captain to check and sign at the last minute and interfacing with the loadmaster if there are any changes in the nature, quantity or positioning of the cargo and baggage.

Engineers may have only routine checks to make, or they may have to deal with technical failures, troubleshooting and repairs, often in the cramped and crowded environment of the cockpit, where they increasingly interface with the aircraft's computers through the MCDU (Multipurpose Control and Display Unit). With modern technology, and notably ACARS (Aircraft Communication Addressing and Reporting System), line maintenance will be informed by a downlink of any aircraft malfunctions in real time while the aircraft is still in flight and so have time to prepare troubleshooting procedures and spare parts, if required.

Ground crews are basically in charge of unloading and loading cargo and baggage under the authority of a loadmaster. It is a relatively lengthy business even though loading is automated. The late delivery of cargo, the delivery of incorrect baggage due to a gate change, for example, or a passenger who fails to board and whose baggage must be offloaded make their work more stressful.

Cabin crews supervise cleaning operations, check the cabin for missing or unserviceable equipment, liaise with line maintenance about cabin items (lighting, communications, passenger entertainment, toilets, galleys, emergency equipment etc.) and deal with the caterers. They come under stress and will be faced with time pressures if any of these things are missing or if there are unwell, missing or belligerent passengers.

Passenger handling agents: Passenger service/handling agents are basically in charge of boarding. They are faced with time-related pressures if passengers are late or missing.

b Discuss the questions with the class.

Extension activity:

You could extend the discussion by asking whether it is safe/sensible for so many people to be under such pressure, and if it is possible for these pressures to be reduced.

6a **⊙1.27** Play the recording for students to complete the task. They discuss their answers in pairs, trying to remember as much as they can about each transmission, before feeding back to the class.

Answers:
1 loading
2 servicing
3 refuelling
4 towing
5 de-icing
6 taxiing
7 docking
8 cleaning

Background notes:

♦ *Perishable goods* are items such as fresh food which must be kept under specific conditions to protect them from spoiling too soon. Perishable goods have priority and may even result in other cargo, or even service passengers, from being offloaded.
♦ The engine oil is always checked ('*dipped*') during turnaround.
♦ Aircraft are refuelled using either independent tankers or fuel *bowsers* which pump fuel from an underground fuel distribution system.
♦ If the aircraft has a serious hydraulic failure, braking and steering may be lost.
♦ *Advanced Visual Docking Guidance System* is another term for the Nose-in Guidance System or PAPA (Parallel Aircraft Parking Aid). Different technologies are used, but basically they all use a system of lights to guide the crew to the correct position for their aircraft type.

Extension activity:

You could use audioscript 1.27 on page 176 to revise and contextualise the use of the present perfect. Tell students to read and/or listen and make notes on what has happened and what hasn't happened yet. They should include all the examples they can think of, not only those given in the present perfect in the script. Students discuss their answers in pairs before feeding back to the class. Note that all of the examples illustrate the use of the present perfect to describe a past event with present results, so you could also elicit the present result of each event.

Suggested answers:
1 two pallets have arrived (result: we can complete loading); they haven't finished cargo loading (result: it's still happening)
2 the engineer has finished (result: the plane is ready)
3 I have requested a tanker (result: it is on its way)
4 the hydraulic power has failed (result: we have no power and we will need to be towed)
5 we haven't been de-iced yet (result: we can't depart yet)
6 the pilot has requested taxi instructions (result: he is waiting for the instructions)
7 Advanced Visual Docking Guidance Systems have been installed (result: the crew can park without a marshaller)
8 the company has not arrived (result: the plane cannot be cleaned).

b Discuss the question briefly with the class.

Answer:
They all end in *-ing*.

7a ◐**1.28** Students listen to complete the answers. They discuss their answers in pairs, trying to remember as much as they can about each transmission, before feeding back to the class.

Answers:
1 starting
2 closing
3 approaching/taxiing/moving
4 giving way
5 vacating
6 waiting

Background notes:

◆ Flight crews often confirm that they are in the process of doing something using the present continuous either in an abbreviated, phraseology-compliant ('*Starting Number 2.*') or in the full form ('*We are closing the doors now.*')

◆ The difference between a *gate* and a *stand* is that a gate is an aircraft parking position which is 'nose in', i.e. where passengers can board and disembark via a mobile airbridge directly to and from the terminal building. A stand may be 'nose in' or it may be 'outlying' or 'remote', i.e. away from the terminal building, and require the passengers to be transported by bus or mobile lounge.

b **Discuss the question with the class.**

Language focus: -*Ing*

Elicit from the class a) two different reasons for using -*ing* in RTF (radiotelephony) communications, and b) differences compared with general English. They then read the information in the box and compare it with their ideas.

Answers: a) The two main uses are as a verb to describe an ongoing action and as a noun to describe an activity.

b) A difference compared with general English is the frequent simplification of present continuous by omitting the subject and the verb *be*. There are also, of course, many situations in which pilots and controllers use plain language with extended range and grammatical sentence structure.

Language note:

The final element in a compound noun almost always states the general category. For example, a *loading procedure* is a type of *procedure*, *incoming flights* are *flights*. When an -*ing* form is the final element, the first element is often the object of the related verb. For example, *cargo loading* means that people load (verb) cargo (object). In *incident reporting*, people report (verb) incidents (object). Note that plurals are not normally used for the first element, which is why we don't say *incidents reporting*.

Extension activity:

Write the following words on slips of paper, so that each group has a complete set.

cargo	loading	loading	procedure	cabin
cleaning	cleaning	materials	aircraft	towing
oil	servicing	docking	guidance system	incident
reporting	holding	point	converging	traffic
incoming	flights			

Students close their books. They sort the slips into eleven compound nouns, each including one -*ing* word. Note that there is a list of correct combinations in *Language focus* point 2, but other correct combinations are also possible (e.g. incoming traffic, aircraft servicing). The first group to make eleven good compound nouns is the winner. When you go through the answers, elicit rules for deciding which element comes first (see *Language note* above).

8a ◐**1.29** Go through the example with the class. Then play the recording, pausing after each transmission for a volunteer to respond. Discuss with the class whether other responses would also be suitable/acceptable. As a follow-up, students could test each other in pairs, using audioscript 1.29 on page 176.

Suggested answers:
1 Standing by
2 Holding short
3 Pushing back
4 Crossing Taxiway Romeo
5 Checking altimeter setting
6 Contacting frequency 121 decimal 95
7 Slowing down
8 Overtaking Star Alliance Boeing 737
9 Holding short
10 Expediting crossing

Background note:

The altimeter setting, i.e. standard pressure attitude with reference to sea level (QNH) or to the airport elevation (QFE) is critical, especially during descent and approach.

b Students work in pairs to find more examples, either by looking through the parts of the book covered so far or using their own knowledge and experience. Make sure they understand that they need to include only activities and compounds containing *-ing* forms. When they have finished, go round the class, asking for one example from each pair and writing it on the board. Keep going until all pairs have run out of examples. The last pair to give an example is the winner. You may need to check the meaning of some of the examples.

> **Possible answers:**
> **Activities:** preparing (the stand); parking (the aircraft); handling (the arriving/departing flight); de-icing; catering; refuelling; taxiing; lining up; holding short; starting up; turning; vacating; servicing; fire fighting; towing; shutting down; boarding; disembarking/deplaning; landing; braking; cleaning; opening; closing; vacating; clearing; reading back; pushing back; requesting (clearance/permission), etc.
>
> **Compound nouns:** nose-in parking; passenger handling agents, etc.

9 Students work alone to make compound nouns. When they check in pairs, students discuss what each compound means and what it refers to. Then go through the answers with the class.

> **Answers:**
>
> | | | | |
> |---|---|---|---|
> | 1 d | 3 f | 5 a | 7 b |
> | 2 g | 4 h | 6 c | 8 e |

Background notes:

- *Braking action* is a measure of likely adhesion of tyres to the runway.
- The *leading edge* of a wing is the front edge.
- An *outgoing flight* is departing.
- *Ground handling personnel* include the dispatcher, the loadmaster, baggage handlers, mechanics or engineers, the tug driver, caterers, water servicing staff, waste water staff, refuelling agent, cleaners etc.

10 Discuss with the class what an apron coordinator does [**Suggested answer**: The apron coordinator is in touch with the flight crew about any requests or unexpected situations during the turnaround and relays information to and from the ground servicing personnel and Ground Control, if this is going to affect traffic movements.]

Go through the example carefully with the class, focusing on how the cues are changed into the transmissions. You may need to check what tenses are used in the dialogue and why [**Answer**: Present simple for states (is, expect); present continuous for present temporary actions (what is the engineer doing?); present perfect for news with important present results (have called)]. Students then work in pairs to role play the situations. The role-plays will naturally require the use of different verb tenses. Note that they should repeat the four situations when they swap roles. Afterwards, ask some pairs to act out their situations for the class and pay attention to correct use of tenses, articles and prepositions (in bold below) and to clear pronunciation.

> **Suggested answers:**
> 1
> **Pilot:** Our cargo loading system is unserviceable. We have called Engineering.
> **Apron:** What is the engineer doing now?
> **Pilot:** He's replacing the drive motor.
> **Apron:** When do you expect to be ready to push back?
> **Pilot:** We expect to be ready to push back **in** 30 minutes.
> 2
> **Pilot:** Our departure is delayed because a cabin attendant is ill.
> **Apron:** What are you doing now?
> **Pilot:** We are waiting **for** a replacement crew member.
> **Apron:** When will she arrive?
> **Pilot:** She will arrive **in** 15 minutes.
> 3
> **Pilot:** We have received 25 additional passengers from a cancelled flight.
> **Apron:** What are you doing as a result?
> **Pilot:** We are uplifting an additional 3 tonnes of fuel.
> **Apron:** When will you be ready to get away?
> **Pilot:** We will be ready to get away **in** ten minutes.
> 4
> **Pilot:** The mechanic has found a deflated tyre.
> **Apron:** What is he doing now?
> **Pilot:** He is changing the tyre.
> **Apron:** How long will it take to complete the wheel change?
> **Pilot:** We will have completed the wheel change **in** five minutes.
> …

If you have **an odd number of students** you will need to have one group of three, where each student is the pilot for three situations and the ATCO for another three. This means this group will have a total of nine dialogues, compared to eight in the other groups.

Background notes:

- On large aircraft the cargo holds are provided with mechanised cargo loading systems consisting of rollers, tracks and a 'ball mat' opposite the door to move the containers and pallets into position. A *drive motor* is an electrical motor which moves containers into position.
- An incapacitated cabin attendant will prevent the flight's departure since safety regulations require a minimum of one cabin attendant for every 49 passengers.
- Receiving additional passengers (or cargo) increases the weight of the aircraft and so more fuel will often be required to cover the same distance.

Language note:

Situation 4 includes a verb in the future perfect (*will have completed*). If you think this will cause problems/confusion, point out that future simple (*will complete*) is just as effective here. The former structure describes the maximum time required (*it will take no more than five minutes*), while the latter predicts the actual time required (*it will take five minutes*).

Ground equipment

Communicative and operational issues:

During turnaround, much of the communication involves problems with ground equipment being absent, inoperative or inappropriate for a particular aircraft type. This section briefly reviews some of these situations and the lexis used.

11a This exercise is devoted to extending the students' knowledge of the vocabulary of ground support equipment and the variants which are commonly used. For example, the telescopic passageway which enables passengers to board from and disembark directly to the airport terminal may be referred to as an airbridge, a jetty, a jetway or a gangway, probably depending on the terminology used by the local manufacturer. Students work alone to match the pictures with their names and then check their answers in pairs. When you feed back with the class, elicit the meaning and use of each piece of equipment.

Answers:
a de-icing vehicle
b fire truck / fire engine
c airbridge/jetty/jetway/walkway
d GPU / ground cart
e tractor / tug / tow vehicle
f snow plough / sanding or gritting vehicle
g follow-me car
h nose-in docking system
i baggage cart / trolley / dolly

access platform: a platform mounted on wheels with steps which allows technicians to gain access to the higher parts of the aircraft
airbridge / jetway / boarding bridge: mobile walkway connecting the gate to the aircraft
airstairs: mobile stairs used at outlying stands
ASU: pneumatic Air Start Unit; on most modern jet aircraft, the APU is used to provide high-pressure air to start rotating the first engine. If the APU is inoperative, the crew will probably request an air start unit in order to fulfil this function.
baggage cart: small towed vehicle for transporting baggage
catering truck: elevator truck for delivering meal trays, drinks, newspapers etc.
chocks: rubber or wooden blocks to prevent aircraft movement when parked
conveyor belt loader: rotating rubber belt for loading bulk cargo
crew minibus: small bus to take crew to and from aircraft
de-icing gantry: large metallic structure under which aircraft pass to be sprayed with de-icing fluid prior to departure
de-icing truck: vehicle with tank and hydraulic platform for spraying aircraft with de-icing fluid
fire engine: vehicle for spraying an extinguishing agent or water
foam crash tender: vehicle for spraying fire-extinguishing foam
follow-me car: car used to guide aircraft
friction tester: vehicle which can measure braking coefficient of runway
fuel bowser: vehicle fitted with a pump for refuelling aircraft from an underground supply
fuel hydrant: underground fuel supply point
fuel tanker: vehicle containing aircraft fuel
GPU: Ground Power Unit; small gas turbine to provide electrical power
high-speed tug: tow vehicle used to tow aircraft over long distances, e.g. to and from a hangar
mobile lounge: telescopic vehicle able to transport passengers and enable them to board directly at outlying stands
nose-in docking system: visual guidance system designed to position aircraft at their stand
passenger coach: bus for transporting passengers to and from aircraft
passenger steps: mobile stairs used at outlying stands

run-up area: area used for engine run-up. See *Background notes* in exercise 11b below.

scissor lift loader: telescopic loader for containers and pallets

snow blower: vehicle which clears runways of snow by blowing

snow plough: vehicle which removes snow from runways with a large blade

steps: stairs used by technicians

stretcher: a collapsible canvas bed for carrying an injured person

sweeper: vehicle with rotary brush for removing dirt and debris

toilet servicing truck: truck with tank for emptying aircraft waste

tow bar: bar connecting the aircraft nose gear to a tow vehicle for pushback and towing

tug / towing truck / tractor: vehicle used to tow and push back aircraft

ULD: Unit Load Device, standard cargo container

water servicing truck: truck for replenishing aircraft's potable water supply. Potable /ˈpɒtəbl/ water is the clean water used in the lavatory wash basins and galleys, but not used as drinking water.

Background note:

Sanding or gritting trucks are used for melting ice which has formed on the paving.

Extension activity:

Students work in pairs and take turns to say the first part of a name from the table in order to elicit the complete name from their partner (e.g. A: Friction ..., B: ... tester; A: Lavatory ..., B: ... service truck). Where there are several possible endings, students should try to remember them all. Students could also test each other by asking *'What's another name for ...?'* or *'What do you call the thing you use to ...?'*.

b ○ **1.30** Make sure students know to write a letter (a–g), although they may find it easier to write a number (1–8) beside each photograph in exercise 11a. Then play the recording for students to complete the task. They check in pairs before feeding back to the class.

Answers:
1 c	3 f	5 e	7 d
2 h	4 a	6 b	8 g

Background notes:

♦ Large aircraft such as B747 and A380 require more than one door to be used for boarding and disembarking in order to move over 500 passengers in time.

♦ The docking system in transmission 2 is set for a B737-200 and not a B767. The correct setting of the docking system is important because it will determine the position in which a particular aircraft is parked, so that it does not impact the terminal building and so that the passenger doors are accessible for the telescopic jetways.

♦ Normally in R/T *due* is used rather than the more linguistically correct *due to*.

♦ The effectiveness of de-icing fluid is limited in time; if an aircraft is delayed, it may have to be de-iced again.

♦ After an engine change or repair, the engine must undergo an *engine run-up* at a specially designated protected location in order to test acceleration and maximum thrust. A *high-speed tug* is used to tow aircraft long distances across the airport, typically to and from the maintenance areas or remote parking. The nose wheels of the aircraft are actually positioned on the back of the tug.

♦ Leaking chemicals in the hold represent both a fire hazard and a risk of corrosion.

♦ If something is done *as a precautionary measure*, it is done to avoid a possible danger.

♦ The *APU* (Auxiliary Power Unit) is often used to provide electrical power and air conditioning when the engines are shut down and also air for engine starting.

♦ In poor visibility or when the airport is unfamiliar, flight crew may miss their turning.

Extension activity:

Students listen again to identify why the ground equipment is required.

Answers:
1 In order to disembark the passengers in time.
2 Because the nose-in parking system is set for the wrong aircraft type.
3 Because the pilot is waiting, perhaps for departure.
4 Because the plane has been waiting a long time.
5 Because they need an engine run-up.
6 As a precautionary measure – there has been a spillage.
7 Because the APU is unserviceable.
8 Because the pilot may have missed a turning.

12 Go through the example with the class, paying attention to the way the cues have been changed. Point out that the apron controller has no cue, so must think of an appropriate response. Check students know that the hash symbol (#) is said as 'number'. Students then work in pairs to describe their situations and give advice. Note that the 20 situations are all common. They are designed to allow students to describe situations and provide appropriate responses spontaneously.

Suggested answers:
Student A
1
Pilot: Apron Control, Air France 396. We are an Airbus 321 at Stand Tango 18. Our APU is inoperative. Request GPU before engine shut-down.
Apron: Air France 396, Roger. Dispatching GPU immediately to Stand Tango 18.
2
Pilot: Vietnam Airlines 571. We are at outlying stand Mike 08; there are no airstairs or coaches to meet us.
Apron: The coaches are on their way and the handlers are bringing airstairs from Mike 09.
3
Pilot: Avianca 746 at Gate 29. We have a prisoner and his escort on board. Confirm police escort at the gate.
Apron: Affirm. Police standing by at Gate 29.
4
Pilot: New Zealand 222, we are waiting for vegetarian meals from Catering for five additional passengers. We expect ten minutes' delay.
Apron: Roger. Call back when you are ready.
…

Student B
1
Pilot: Apron Control, Southwest 3284. We're waiting to enter Stand 23. There is a baggage cart blocking access to the stand.
Apron: Roger. Will advise Ground Handling immediately. Sorry.
2
Pilot: Finnair 593. We are at Gate 47. The jetty is unserviceable. Request airstairs to disembark our passengers.
Apron: I'll have airstairs put in place immediately, sir. Stand by.
3
Pilot: Iberia 850. We are at Stand Charlie 15 waiting to push back, but they have sent the wrong tractor. We are an A320. Please dispatch a new tractor to Gate Charlie 15 as soon as possible.
Apron: Wilco.
4
Pilot: Apron Control, Air Canada 819. We are an Airbus A330 showing one main gear tyre low pressure. Request maintenance and a later slot.
Apron: Air Canada 819, sending maintenance. Will request a later slot.
…

If you have an odd number of students you will need to have one group of three, where the third student takes the first three requests from Student A and the last three from Student B.

Background notes:

◆ A *stretcher case* refers to a case (= a person) requiring a stretcher (= a way of carrying a person who is lying flat, typically because of an injury or unconsciousness).

◆ *Line maintenance* or ramp maintenance is the aircraft engineering service which is provided at the ramp during turnaround for routine technical servicing (tyres, engines etc.) and small repairs or replacements.

Communication errors: Failure to acknowledge correctly (pilots)

Communicative and operational issues:

The quotation from the Flight Safety Foundation ALAR Briefing Note on Pilot–Controller Communication raises an apparently simple issue: the potential for misunderstanding in the use of the word *Roger*. It is nonetheless a reminder of the need for precision and transparency in communication either through proper standard phraseology or, when necessary, plain language. If a pilot replies *Roger* to a controller's instruction, the controller is unable to know whether the pilot has actually understood correctly or not.

ICAO FOCUS

Students read the quote to decide if it describes good or bad practice [**Answer:** bad]. Discuss why this practice could be dangerous [**Suggested answer:** because there is no opportunity to check or correct errors]. Discuss the question with the class.

Answer:
The differences between pilot and controller readbacks reflect the reciprocity of their functions: if a pilot does not give a correct readback, the controller cannot be sure that the pilot has understood his/her instruction; if a controller does not read back a pilot transmission, the pilot cannot be sure that the controller has understood his/her request or information.

13 ○1.31 This is a simple readback activity where accuracy, pronunciation and fluency are the main focus areas. Go through the example with the class, eliciting how students could request confirmation or clarification [**Answer:** 'Confirm holding point Echo 2' or 'Say again holding point']. Then play the recording,

pausing after each transmission for a volunteer to give a readback. If the volunteer requests clarification, play the transmission again. If the volunteer requests confirmation, you could provide this yourself, by saying 'Confirm' and repeating the relevant information. Afterwards, students test each other in pairs by taking turns to read the controller transmissions from audioscript 1.31 on page 176.

Background notes:

◆ The controller gives altimeter pressure settings (QNH) so that the crew can set their altimeter to the correct barometric pressure with respect to sea level before departure.
◆ *Report vacated* means 'report when you have left it'.
◆ The *upwind end* of a runway is the opposite end from where an aircraft starts its take-off roll.

Reporting anomalies

Communicative and operational issues:

In the more varied environment on the ground, (mainly) pilots often need to report anomalies and provide physical descriptions of phenomena. In this section we explore the language of sensory perception. With what is often limited visibility, it is important to be able to describe and interpret any physical phenomena.

14a The ten examples in this exercise are just a few of the many things which can occur on the ground and have serious consequences. Check students understand what an *anomaly* [/əˈnɒməlɪ/] is, and elicit some examples. Students then work alone to match the phenomena to the explanations. When they have checked in pairs, discuss the answers with the class. You may need to check the pronunciation of *severe* [/səˈvɪə/]. Elicit any stories they know of these or similar anomalies.

Answers:
1 i	3 h	5 c	7 j	9 e
2 d	4 f	6 g	8 a	10 b

Background notes:

◆ An anomaly is something unusual, unexpected or unexplained. Examples include those in exercise 14a.
◆ *Metal debris* from aircraft parts on the runway can have devastating effects as was shown by the Air France Concorde accident at Charles de Gaulle.
◆ The *airframe* is another word for the aircraft structure or fuselage and wings. The word *hull* is also used.

b ●1.32 With the class, discuss briefly what each picture shows. Then play the recording for students to match the pictures with the reports. Afterwards, students check in pairs before feeding back to the class.

Answers:
1 g	3 d	5 h	7 c
2 e	4 f	6 b	8 a

Background notes:

◆ During pushback the flight crew has no visibility of where the aircraft is going.
◆ Bird ingestion is a major threat, especially to aircraft engines, especially during take-off.
◆ The area around aircraft doors is vulnerable to damage from loaders, catering trucks and airstairs.
◆ A *thud* is a deep, dull noise caused by an impact (e.g. hitting a table with your fist).
◆ When doors are closed and locked, the handles/levers should be *flush* (= forming a continuous plane surface) with the fuselage skin.
◆ Only authorised personnel should be on foot at the airport and then only in designated areas and with security passes for that particular zone. Staff are made more and more aware of security threats.

Extension activity:

Students look at audioscript 1.32 on page 176. They read and listen to underline the phrases for asking about and describing what you can see/hear etc. They check in pairs. Then go through the answers with the class.

Suggested answers:
(*Be advised that*) we can see ...; ... it looks like ...; I can see ...; we have just heard ...; (and we have just) felt ...; Can you see if ...?; ... we noticed what looked like ...; From here, it seems that ...; There appears to be ...

c Students work in pairs or groups of three to describe the situations and prepare transmissions. These could be the same as those in audioscript 1.32 or they could be adapted.

d ●1.33 Go through the phrases in the Perception box briefly with the class, making sure everyone knows the differences between similar structures, e.g. *We noticed* (by accident); *We observed* (more carefully). You could also elicit some endings to the structures (e.g. *We are experiencing turbulence*). Then go through the example with the class. Play the recording, pausing after each transmission for a volunteer to make a sentence. Afterwards, students can test each other using audioscript 1.33 on page 176.

Background notes:

♦ A *cowl panel* is one part of the engine cowling: the fairing which surrounds and protects the engine and provides an optimum aerodynamic profile.

♦ A *crosswind* blows in a direction perpendicular to the direction of travel.

Extension activity:

Elicit from the class the pronunciations of '*I can see the vehicle*' and '*I can't see the vehicle*' and ways to avoid confusion.

Language note:

The difference between *can* and *can't* is of course crucial, but unfortunately the two words are not always easy to tell apart in some accents, especially when the speaker and listener have different language backgrounds. *Can* tends to be short and unstressed (/aɪ kn ˈsiː/) while *can't* is longer and stressed in full (/aɪ ˈkɑːnt ˈsiː/). A simple solution is to omit *can* (*I see the vehicle* rather than *I can see the vehicle*) and to say *cannot* in full (*I cannot see the vehicle*). It is also essential to use readback to check whether the other person has said *can* or *can't*.

15a **☉1.34 Pilots often take notes to help them memorise more complex instructions and input. Note-taking is a useful technique for both listening and memorising. This exercise develops listening skills with more complex information in plain language. Make sure students have their notebooks open to take notes. Go through the example with the class, focusing on the type of information that is noted. Then play the recording for students to take notes. They compare notes with a partner before listening again to check. Then go through the answers with the class.**

	Location	Aircraft/ Vehicle	Anomaly
1	Taxiway E2	United B 777	dark smoke, flames in tailpipe
2	Intersection taxiways R and N	Fokker 50	skidded, nose gear in snow drift
3	RWY 14, 200 m before exit B, RH side	Fedex Airbus	metal debris
4	Runway 21L	Air Berlin 259	hard landing, possible landing gear damage
5	Stand 16	LH A330 / Turkish A310	collision during pushback, A330 damaged wing tip
6	Taxiway G near intersection with Q	USAir 1587	stray dog

Answers:

Background notes:

♦ The *tailpipe* is the exhaust section of the engine aft of the turbine.

♦ Slippery (due to oil, ice, etc.) or because it was going too fast to grip the surface.

♦ A *freighter* /ˈfreɪtə/ is a plane for carrying heavy *freight* /freɪt/, such as industrial equipment, raw materials, livestock, food, parcels and goods.

♦ In *gusty* conditions, the wind speed changes suddenly, with strong gusts interspersed with calmer periods.

b **Students work in small groups to plan transmissions based on their notes. Note that a single incident may require several transmissions, as in the example. Make sure students know to invent any additional details that are necessary for the role-play, such as call signs. Afterwards, ask volunteers to read their transmissions and discuss the best versions with the class.**

Suggested answers:

1 ***Tower:*** United 483, you appear to have a tailpipe fire on your Number 1 engine. Turn left onto Taxiway Foxtrot and stop 300 metres from the intersection with Echo. The fire crew are being turned out.

Tower: Fire service, a United triple seven with what appears to be a tailpipe fire on Taxiway Foxtrot, 300 metres from the intersection with Echo.

2 ***Tower:*** An Air Iceland Fokker 50 has skidded off Taxiway November and has its nose gear in a snow drift. Send a tow vehicle and assistance for passengers in case of an evacuation.

3 ***Tower:*** Ground, have someone inspect the right-hand side of Runway 14, 200 metres before exit Bravo. An incoming flight has reported metal debris.

Tower: Fedex 607, the traffic which landed immediately after you reported metal debris on the right-hand side of Runway 14. You may want to carry out a detailed external inspection.

4 ***Tower:*** Air Berlin 259, Roger. I will advise line maintenance and have them standing by.

Tower: Be advised that an incoming flight has reported very gusty conditions on short final.

5 ***Tower:*** Lufthansa 448, hold position. We will instruct the tractor to tow you back to the gate and maintenance to inspect your wing tip for any damage. Advise us of the delay.

Tower: Turk Air 583, hold position. Say intentions.

6 ***Tower:*** Ground, a stray dog has been reported near the threshold of Runway 25 Right. Please take action now.

…

'We're now at take-off'

Communicative and operational issues:

This section focuses mainly on what has been the most deadly accident in aviation history: a runway incursion in which two B747s collided with each other on a foggy runway on the island of Tenerife in 1977. As in all accidents, there were several causal factors: poor visibility; a congested airport due to diverted flights; a break in transmissions; crew impatience due to the fact that, if they were delayed any more, the KLM crew would exceed their duty time; hierarchical dynamics between the Captain and First Officer, a failure to actually request clearance, but the assumption that they had; but also the use of non-standard phraseology; a failure to request readback; an ambiguous phrase and less than adequate language skills.

In the context of this course, it is an opportunity to draw students' attention to the potential ambiguity of language and how a single word can change meaning.

The recording in exercise 16b is based on the actual transcript of the transmissions leading up to the crash. It is a good idea to familiarise yourself with the background to the disaster.

16a Discuss with the class what they know about the phrase 'We're now at take-off', but avoid providing too much information or confirmation at this stage. Note that they could well know the story of the Tenerife crash, as it was so important in leading to improved standards in communication. Then refer students to the two diagrams. Students describe the events in pairs and then feed back to the class.

> Suggested answers:
> The two illustrations show two stages preceding the collision. Pan Am 1736 has just landed on Runway 30, but due to other aircraft already occupying the first three exits at the far end of the runway (holding point to Runway 12 and exits C1 and C2), the controller has instructed the Pan Am crew to backtrack and exit via C3. In the meantime KLM 4805 has lined up for take-off on Runway 30. Due to the fog, and the fact that C3 is angled for aircraft landing on Runway 30, the Pan Am crew misses C3 and taxis on to vacate via C4. Believing they have received clearance, the KLM crew start their take-off roll and collide with the Pan Am 747 before it is able to vacate the runway.

b ⊙1.35 Make sure all students have their notebooks open to take notes, and they understand what type of notes to take. You may need to check they understand the word *ambiguity* (= when a message may have more than one possible meaning, e.g. '*We're now at take-off*'). Then play the recording. Afterwards, students compare notes with a partner and listen again to check.

> Suggested answers:
> ♦ The controller makes an erroneous readback of the KLM call sign.
> ♦ The KLM crew take the controller's departure instructions for a take-off clearance.
> ♦ The KLM First Officer's expression '*We're now at take-off*' is ambiguous.
> ♦ The controller's transmission '*Stand by for take-off ... I will call you*' is interrupted.
> ♦ The Pan Am crew state that they have not vacated the runway.
> ♦ The KLM First Officer doubts that the runway is clear, but neither he nor the captain check to confirm this is the case.
> ♦ The KLM captain overrides the First Officer.

Background notes:

♦ The pilot's use of '*go ahead*' is another example of ambiguity, as it may mean *proceed/continue*, or it may mean *move forward*.
♦ *Clipper* was the call sign for Pan Am.
♦ *Papa beacon* refers to the navaid used by aircraft for that particular departure flightpath.
♦ The *325 radial* refers to a magnetic bearing from a navaid transmitter: VOR, Tacan etc. En-route navaid transmitters send out identifiable radio signals at different frequencies which are captured by aircraft. The bearing (i.e. the angle, between the transmitter, whose location is known, and the aircraft) allows a radial to be plotted between the navaid transmitter and the aircraft. The intersection of two radials from two different transmitters gives the aircraft's position.
♦ *Thrust* is the propulsive force generated by an aircraft engine. The other three forces which act on an aircraft are lift, weight and drag.

c Discuss the exchanges and the errors with the class.

The quote is from Dr Jeremy Mell, long-time head of languages at the Ecole Nationale de l'Aviation Civile in Toulouse, France, and also one of the leading members of the ICAO PRICESG. The questions which follow are language and communication awareness raisers with 'at take-off' as their starting point.

Elicit from the class two possible interpretations of the phrase 'We're now at take-off'. Students then read the quote to compare it with their ideas and discuss the questions in small groups. Point out that the third question refers to the ATCO's line from the dialogue in 16a ('OK ... Stand by for take-off'). Finally, open up the discussions to include the whole class, making sure everyone knows exactly what happened in the accident. Note that the second and third questions include some difficult grammar (could have said; should have said; might have done). It is important that students understand this is used to describe past mistakes and ways of avoiding them, but you may decide not to focus on these structures or to insist on grammatical accuracy with them at this stage.

Suggested answers:
• at take-off is not standard phraseology and not even usual idiomatic plain English. It is open to several interpretations: to be lined up; to be ready for take-off; to be in the process of taking off.
• The First Officer could have used correct standard phraseology: Ready for departure, or if he thought that they had been cleared 'Cleared for take-off Runway 30.'
• The ATCO at no time actually issued a take-off clearance nor was one requested by the KLM crew, so he did not expect the KLM 747 to be starting to take off. However, he also uses non-standard phraseology ('Stand by for take-off ... I will call you'). To be unambiguous, if he had a doubt, he should have used standard phraseologies such as Hold position or Line up and wait or Cancel take-off.
• at home, at work, at night, at your discretion, at the airport, at 12 o'clock
• The need to use standard phraseology when it is applicable, especially at critical phases of flight when clearances are involved. The fragility of plain language and how so much can rest on a single common word. The need to request confirmation or clarification if there is the slightest doubt in your mind.

Background note:
The take-off roll is the process of accelerating down the runway in order to take off. In the Tenerife crash, due to overcrowding at the airport, planes were forced to taxi up the runway and then turn around in order to take off. The ATCO thought the KLM flight was waiting, whereas in fact it was accelerating along the runway, where the Pan Am flight was still taxiing.

d, e **Students discuss the two questions in pairs and then feed back to the class. Ask for anecdotes from students' own experience: What went wrong? What happened? What could/should have happened?**

Possible answers:
d External factors such as bad weather, congested airports, diverted flights and delays can all threaten good communication because they tend to saturate the frequency, increase the controllers' workload and may cause a deterioration in the quality of the transmissions.
e Hierarchical relations, and the way these vary in different cultures, are something all flight crew have been faced with and something which many controllers may have witnessed or even experienced in their workplace. The captain, in the left-hand seat, is invested with huge experience and authority; the First Officer, in the right-hand seat, will have fewer flight hours, but often better computer and communication skills. However, because of their relative lack of experience and more recent basic training, First Officers sometimes have a lesser degree of certainty. The effectiveness of the crew is based on continuous crosschecking and monitoring and for good Crew Resource Management the more experienced captain should always take advantage of the First Officer's second pair of eyes and ears.

17a **⊙1.36 Word stress, phrasing and rising and falling pitch are as important as pronunciation in ensuring clarity in radiotelephony. While this exercise is designed specifically for this purpose, there are many written and audio materials in the course which can be used to practise these skills.**

Read the introduction aloud and check students understand what interrogative words are, using examples (e.g. *why, how much, what sort of*, etc.). Students then work in pairs to mark the stress. After playing the recording, discuss the answers with the class, and get volunteers to read the statements aloud with the correct stress pattern.

> **Answers:**
> 1 traffic, right; identify 2 gate; which 3 noise; sort 4 holding; where 5 see, something; what

b These free pairwork exchanges require improvisation although the subject matter is fairly conventional. The overall purpose here is to make students comfortable with requesting clarification and challenging by acquiring fluency in the phrases they require to do so. This also contributes to general discourse management skills. Students work in pairs to practise the dialogues, paying particular attention to stress. You could repeat the exercise by writing key words on the board (e.g. *traffic, right, identify*), and having students practise the dialogues with their books closed, using only the key words from the board.

c Go through the example with the class. Point out that the cues are very short, so they will have to invent most of the information. You may need to check the pronunciation and/or meaning of *obstacle* /ˈɒbstəkəl/ and *deteriorating* /dɪˈtɪərɪəreɪt/ (= getting worse). Students then work in pairs to act out the dialogues. Afterwards, ask volunteers to perform their dialogues for the class.

> **Possible answers:**
> **Pilots**
> 1
> **A:** I think we're near Runway 17.
> **B:** Which taxiway are you on?
> **A:** I think we're on Taxiway November.
> **B:** Are you at the holding point of Runway 17?
> **A:** Negative. We are approaching the intersection of November and Tango.
> 2
> **A:** I can hear a noise.
> **B:** What sort of noise?
> **A:** It sounds like a turboprop engine.
> 3
> **A:** I can see something in the fog ahead.
> **B:** What does it look like?
> **A:** It looks like a van.
> 4
> **A:** There seems to be a problem in the cabin.
> **B:** What kind of problem have you got?
> **A:** There are people shouting.
> ...

> **ATCOs**
> 1
> **B:** There are some delays.
> **A:** How long do you expect the delays to be?
> **B:** We expect delays of up to 40 minutes.
> 2
> **B:** The weather is deteriorating.
> **A:** What is the present RVR?
> **B:** RVR 600 metres.
> 3
> **B:** We have limited radar coverage.
> **A:** Can you provide us with SSR for a Runway 31 approach?
> **B:** Affirm.
> 4
> **B:** There aren't a lot of service vehicles available.
> **A:** Have you got a more powerful tow vehicle?
> **B:** Negative. There is some industrial action and most of the drivers are not available.
> ...

If you have an odd number of students you will need to have a group of three, where the third student takes the last two cues from Student A and the first three from Student B.

> **Background note:**
> *Radar coverage* is the area or scope reached by radar.

Extension activity:

Discuss with the class their experiences of ground movements in poor visibility.

Note that poor visibility considerably slows down ground movements. Many airports, but not all, are equipped with different types of ground movement radar which assists controllers. Some aircraft are equipped with various systems, such as global positioning, which can be of assistance in low visibility, and Head-up Displays or Navigation Displays which assist the crew. Failing all else, progressive taxi instructions and follow-me cars are still used.

A fire emergency

Communicative and operational issues:

This section explores the handling of a spectacular but controlled situation on the ground: an engine on fire. It uses a real-life example.

Language focus: *have something done*

Write the following four sentences on the board and elicit the differences between them:

a *We'll check our engines.*
b *Our engines will be checked.*
c *We'll have/get our engines checked.*
d *We'll get the engineers to check the engines.*

Suggested answer: In sentence **a** (active voice), the pilot (or his crew) is checking the engines. In **b** (passive voice), the focus is on the engines, and it is not important who is checking them. The pilot (and crew) may not be involved in this process. In **c** (*have/get something done* = causative passive), the pilot is taking responsibility for the process, although he will not conduct it himself. He will arrange for somebody to do it. There is no difference in meaning between *have* and *get*, although *have* is more formal and suggests a more deliberate action. In **d** (*get somebody to do something*), the pilot's role in arranging the process is more explicit, as is the agent (= the person who will perform the action).

18 **This exercise introduces some of the lexis and complete sentences which will be heard in the recording in exercise 20a. Students work alone to complete the sentences and then check with a partner. When you go through the answers with the class, check which sentence(s) include the structure *have something done* [Answer: sentence 2].**

Answers:
1 flame	5 shut
2 maintenance	6 shutting
3 exhaust	7 121.85
4 way	8 disembark

Background note:

The *exhaust* is the rear engine section which expels engine gases.

Extension activity:

With the class, discuss the situation in question 1 in order to make sentences with *have something done*.

Possible answer: I'll have it checked by our engineers.

19 **1.37 Neither pilots nor controllers can do everything themselves, so have to be able to say that they will have/get something done. In addition to practising these phrases, this exercise elicits practical and appropriate responses to specific situations.**

Play the recording, pausing after the first transmission to look at the example. Elicit other possible responses, using the structure *have something done*. Then play the rest of the recording, pausing after each transmission for volunteers to respond appropriately. You may need to check *unruly* (= loud and aggressive), *inebriated* (= drunk or under the influence of drugs) and *acute* (= serious, very strong).

Afterwards, students work in pairs to test each other using audioscript 1.37 on page 177.

Possible answers:
1 I'll get it replaced by the mechanics / the engineers / maintenance / Engineering.
2 I'll get the IT technician to repair it.
3 I'll get Catering to deliver some more.
4 I'll have the cleaners come back.
5 I'll get the firemen to cool them.
6 I'll get the dispatcher to print out a new one.
7 I'll have a tug sent to your stand.
8 I'll have the police escort him off the plane.
9 I'll have the ramp staff remove it.
10 I'll get an ambulance to meet you at the gate.

Background notes:

♦ A *weight and balance printout* is a document recording distribution of weight and CG (centre of gravity) at departure.
♦ A *hangar* is a very large building for sheltering aircraft in which maintenance and overhaul work is carried out.

Extension activity:

You could repeat the exercise, this time eliciting sentences with the structure *get somebody to do something*, e.g. *I'll get maintenance to replace it.*

20a **1.38 Go through the table with the class to elicit what type of information is required for each section (e.g. a number, a phrase). Point out that they may want to write the information in their notebooks, where there is more space to write. Then play the recording for students to take notes. They check in pairs before listening again to check their notes. Finally, go through the answers with the class and discuss how common this situation is and how well the people handled it.**

Answers:
1	Call sign	Hijet 451
2	Taxi instructions	Taxi via outer taxiway to Stand 17
3	Problem observed	flame from right engine during landing
4	1st instruction	Stop
5	2nd instruction	Shut down all engines
6	New frequency	121.85
7	Firefighters' action	checked and cooled right-hand engine
8	Crew action on engines	shut down both engines and discharged both fire extinguisher agents
9	Means of disembarkation	stairs
10	Number of passengers injured	0

Background notes:

◆ As the flight crew's outside vision is severely restricted, they are often reliant on controllers, ground staff or other aircraft for knowing what is happening on the exterior of their own aircraft, especially in the case of the landing gear, engines and the tail section. In this scenario, the controller has noticed flames escaping from the engine exhaust during landing. The aircraft is instructed to stop away from the terminal buildings in order to allow the fire service to intervene. The First Officer liaises with the Fire Chief and confirms that they have discharged both agents, i.e. have used both fire-extinguishing bottles on the engine on fire. The fire-extinguishing agent is sprayed inside the core engine and so has no effect on a tailpipe fire, which seems to be the case here. The crew plans to disembark the passengers by airstairs on the left-hand side, but the Fire Chief asks them to keep the emergency escape slides armed on the right-hand side as a precautionary measure.

◆ 'That's copied' means 'That is understood'.
◆ Quebec Oscar Kilo is the aircraft's call sign. Alphabetical call signs, usually the aircraft's registration, are used as well as numerical ones. The Fire Chief can see the aircraft's registration, but does not know their call sign.
◆ A *fire agent* is a fire-extinguishing chemical.
◆ The Fire Chief advises the pilot to stand by to *disembark by the slide* as a precaution, while the stairs are being put in place. A *slide* is a rapid-inflation pneumatic channel to enable passengers and crew to evacuate quickly.
◆ If the slide is *armed*, it will be deployed and inflated if the door is opened.
◆ 'Will do' simply means 'I'll do that'.
◆ A *degradation of the situation* means that the situation is worsening.

b Students work alone to write their summaries, using simple language (e.g. mainly past simple) and short sentences. Offer support while students are writing. Students then work in pairs to improve their summaries. Then ask volunteers to read their summaries aloud to the class.

Background note:

Writing tasks are quite frequent; they go from aircraft technical log entries, which are fairly concise (e.g. *Replace first-officer-seat drive motor*; *Monitor Engine No. 3 oil consumption*; *Bleed-Duct-Overheat message during climb-out from Cairo*) to a full report of an incident in an aviation context, which is increasingly international and even non-English-speaking airlines correspond with English-speaking manufacturers and authorities on a daily basis.

Example: During our take-off roll on Runway 21 Left, we experienced severe wheel vibrations, which seemed to come from the right-hand gear. As a result, we abandoned our take-off at 80 knots and returned to the ramp for an inspection by local line maintenance.

c This pairwork activity is a very short role-play using the main exchanges of the recorded scenario. The emphasis here should be on fluency. Go through the first two lines together. Then have students work in pairs to act out the situation. When they finish, they should swap roles and repeat the role-play. Finally, ask volunteers to act out their role-plays for the class.

Suggested answers:
ATCO: Hijet 451, taxi via outer taxiway to Stand 1.
Pilot: Outer taxiway to Stand 1, Hijet 451.
ATCO: Hijet 451, be advised that during landing we saw a flame coming from your right-hand engine.
Pilot: Copied. We have had problems with that engine. Request check from maintenance. Can you see anything?
ATCO: Affirm. We can see smoke and flames coming from your exhaust. The fire service is coming on your left-hand side.
Pilot: Thanks, Hijet 451.
ATCO: Hijet 451, hold position.
Pilot: Stopping. We have shut down our right-hand engine. Is it still on fire?
ATCO: Affirm. Shut down all engines.
Pilot: Both engines shut down.
ATCO: Contact fire service 121.85.
Pilot: 121.85, Hijet 451.

If you have an **odd number of students** you will need to have one group of three, where one student listens during each role-play. Use these students to perform the role-play for the rest of the class at the end.

Putting it together: Responding to situations

Communicative and operational issues:

The list of communicative language functions in Appendix B of ICAO Doc. 9835 from which the ICAO focus extract is taken should be a constant reference and source of guidance and validation for aviation English teachers. It has guided the activities in *Flightpath*. The culminating activities in this unit are responding spontaneously to various ground situations and managing a departure using communicative functions and a variety of verb tenses.

Purpose and relevance of activities:

The recording in exercise 22 contains transmissions for pilots and controllers to respond to spontaneously. The responses are not scripted and cues are not provided: both pilots and controllers are commonly faced with unexpected situations and must respond promptly in an appropriate way using the information in the original transmission.

In exercise 23, the pilot initiates the exchange with a controller, who responds using the cues. The scenario deals with a standard pushback and taxiing which becomes complicated first by a blocked taxiway requiring a re-routeing and then by a hydraulic failure which makes it necessary for the aircraft to return to the gate for maintenance.

ICAO FOCUS

Go through the excerpt with the class, eliciting one example of each task. Students then work in pairs to come up with more examples. Go through the examples with the class.

Possible answers:

- The windshield is cracked; the weight and balance sheet is missing.
- Set the anti-collision beacon switch to ON and advise Ground that the brakes are released.
- The windspeed has increased to 16 knots.
- Release the park brake before pushback.
- The last few passengers are boarding.
- The delay was caused by a damaged microswitch which had to be replaced.
- The aircraft is unloaded, refuelled, cleaned, provided with catering, loaded with cargo and baggage and serviced during turnaround.
- The wing tip seems to be very close to the B777 parked at the next stand.

Preparation

21a Look at the example with the class. Students work in pairs and take turns to make sentences using the cues. Then go through the answers with the class.

Answers:
- We are approaching Taxiway Delta.
- I am shutting down Engine 2.
- We are vacating Runway 28 Left.
- We are waiting for a tanker at Stand 19.
- We are holding short of Runway 04.
- I am trying to repair the VHF.
- We are following the A320.
- Visibility is decreasing. The fire is spreading.
- The passengers are evacuating.
- The fire service is coming.
- The light is flashing.

b Look at the example with the class. You may need to check the difference between *is vacated* and *has been vacated* (see *Language note* below). Students then work in pairs and take turns to make sentences using the cues. Afterwards, go through the answers with the class.

Language note:

For most of the examples in this exercise, two forms are possible: present simple + adjective (to describe a state, e.g. *the doors are closed*) and present perfect (to describe a process, e.g. *the doors have been closed*). In everyday English, these two forms may be treated as synonymous, but in aviation English, the distinction may have important consequences. For example, if the door *is closed*, perhaps it has not yet been opened, whereas if the door *has been closed*, somebody has closed it.

Sometimes only one form is possible, e.g. *cross taxiway H*, where the taxiway undergoes no change in state, so only present perfect is suitable (*Taxiway H has been crossed*).

Communication

22 ○1.39 Play the first two transmissions and go through the examples with the class. Discuss other possible responses with the class. Then play the rest of the recording, pausing after each transmission for volunteers to respond. Discuss other suitable responses before moving on to the next transmission. Afterwards, students test each other in pairs, using audioscript 1.39 on page 177.

Possible answers:

1 Iberia 287, the 767 on your stand had a tyre change. They will be pushing back in five minutes.
2 We will disembark the passengers from the right-hand side.
3 Japan Air 084, taxi 300 metres straight ahead, turn left onto Lima. At the intersection of Lima and Mike, turn left.
4 We have two passengers with head injuries, bleeding and severe bruising. We suspect broken ribs. The cabin attendants have performed first aid and bandaged their open wounds, Air France 219.
5 We are not sure whether to turn left or right at the intersection between Taxiway Juliet and Taxiway Oscar, Korean 793.
6 We will instruct the driver to vacate the area immediately. Thank you for the information, Transat 047.
7 Fedex 375, expect start-up approval in 15 minutes.
8 Affirm, Runway 21 Left vacated; we are taxiing on Taxiway Lima, China Eastern 888.

Background notes:

♦ The *extended threshold* is the end of the runway beyond the operational threshold which is usually only used for additional stopping distance in an emergency.
♦ The *manoeuvring surface* is an area where aircraft move on the ground and which should be clear of all obstacles and other vehicles.

Language note:

Transmission 3 contains some difficult but useful grammar: '*We are at what we thought was our stand ...*'. Note the use of past simple (*was*) to show a false assumption (using the same rules as reported speech). For simplicity, you could teach this phrase (*what I/we thought was ...*) as a single chunk of language to describe false assumptions.

Extension activity:

Play the recording again for students to write around four key words from each transmission (e.g. *waiting*, *stand*, *vacated*, *update*) in their notebooks.
They should not focus on call signs, stand numbers, etc., which you could write on the board for reference. Students then work in pairs to use the key words to reconstruct the original transmissions. This will focus their attention on the grammar structures in the transmissions, e.g. present perfect continuous (transmission 1), question forms (1, 3, 4, 5 and 7), present continuous (5, 7), etc. Elicit the correct versions from the class and then play the recording to check.

23 Make sure students read the information about the call sign, stand and runway on page 37, as this will help them during the role-play. You could write it on the board as a reference. Students then role-play the situation in pairs, and then swap roles. Afterwards, ask one pair to act out their dialogue for the class, to deal with any difficulties.

If you have an odd number of students you will need to have a group of three, where Student C listens during the first role-play and Student A during the second. These two students should be chosen to perform for the whole class.

Possible answers:

Pilot:	Air New Zealand 415, request pushback and start-up clearance from Stand Charlie 21.
ATCO:	Air New Zealand 415, all departures (are) on hold due (to) Runway 39 Left (being) closed.
Pilot:	What is our Estimated Time of Departure?
ATCO:	Expect 15 hundred.
Pilot:	Roger 15:00, Air New Zealand 415.
...	
Pilot:	Air New Zealand 415, request pushback and start-up.
ATCO:	Air New Zealand 415, pushback and start-up approved. Push back facing east.
Pilot:	Push back facing east, Air New Zealand 415.
ATCO:	Taxi Runway 36 Right via Golf and India. Hold short of Runway 36 Right at holding point Charlie.
Pilot:	Holding point Charlie, Runway 36 Right via Golf and India, Air New Zealand 415.
...	

Debriefing

24 Discuss the question with the class. Give and elicit feedback on the strengths and weaknesses of the role-plays, and elicit suggestions as to how to overcome the weaknesses.

Progress check

Students complete the progress check alone and then discuss their notes with a partner. Discuss with the class anything they still lack confidence in, and plan together how you can work on these areas.

UNIT 4
Runway incursions

Operational topics	The causes of runway incursions; Confusion; Precursors and best practice; ICAO recommendations for avoiding runway incursions (ATC); Low-visibility operations; Cases of runway incursion; Sterile cockpit; Distractions; Situational awareness
Communication functions	Call signs; Readback; Communication errors: failure to seek confirmation; Conditional clearances; Dealing with garbled messages; Reporting past actions; From phraseology to plain language: expressing inability to comply
Language content	Numbers; Modal verbs; Pronunciation and phrasing; Past tense: active and passive; Location

Unit 4 Teacher's brief

Runway incursion, aircraft or vehicles entering an active runway erroneously, and so running the risk of collision with arriving or departing aircraft, has been the cause of some of the most deadly accidents and serious incidents in recent aviation history (Tenerife 1977, Omsk 1984, Los Angeles 1991, Paris Charles de Gaulle 2000, Milan Linate 2001, Boston Logan 2005, San Francisco 2007). For this reason, organisations such as ICAO, Eurocontrol, Airbus and the Flight Safety Foundation have made considerable efforts to raise awareness and improve practices which would enhance safety in this area.

In terms of the airport environment, taxiing and departure language, Unit 4 draws heavily on the lexis and language functions already introduced and practised in Units 2 and 3. However, it explores in more depth the communicative aspects of some safety concerns and studies the circumstances of one particular runway incursion: Milan, Linate 2001.

The notion of **precursors** to an incident or accident, referred to in the lead-in quote, is developed in this unit. It is an opportunity to think about the 'anatomy' of an accident, i.e. all the different **contributing factors** which combine to make that accident possible. As such, it is an opportunity for the teacher to practise and recycle a wide range of topics and lexis with the students: communication failures, **insufficient language proficiency**, poor state of airport markings, technical failures, **distractions**, use of different frequencies, **use of two languages** on the frequency, absence of updated charts and information, **fatigue**, weather conditions, stress, **expectation bias**, failure to request confirmation or clarification etc.

Unit 4 Sources

- Agenzia Nazionale per la Sicurezza del Volo: *Final report on Milan, Linate, accident on 8th October 2001*, 2004 (Exercises 15a–e)

- Aviation Safety Network: *Milan, Linate, accident on 8th October 2001* (Exercises 15a–e)
- Darby, R.: *Keeping it on the runway, AeroSafety World*, August 2009
- Eurocontrol: *Preventing runway incursions*, 2008 (Exercises 1a, b; 17a–b)
- Eurocontrol: *When attention is diverted*, DVD (Exercises 24a–28)
- Flight Safety Foundation: ALAR Tool Kit (Exercise 7a)
- ICAO: Document 9870, Manual on the Prevention of Runway Incursions, Appendix A – *Communications Best Practice*, 2007 (Exercises 10a; 11; ICAO focus with Exercise 16)
- Lacagnina, M.: *Two's too many, AeroSafety World*, August 2008 (ICAO focus with Exercise 2a)
- Thomas, D.: *Sliding away, AeroSafety World*, November 2010
- Trémaud, M.: *Erasing confusion, AeroSafety World*, May 2010 (Unit lead-in; Exercises 4; 5a–c; 6
- UK Aeronautical Information Circular 11/2005: *European action plan for the prevention of runway incursions*, 2005

Lead-in

The lead-in to Unit 4 is fairly long because we are dealing with rather more abstract or conceptual factors that need to be brainstormed and discussed, then provided with real examples from the students' experience, before moving on into the core of the unit.

The idea of 'confusion' mentioned by Michel Trémaud in the lead-in quote is a significant one. While confusion can be caused by purely sensory inputs (in the case of Linate by faded taxiway markings), it is often the result of misunderstood communication. Whatever its origin, it is by requesting clarification or confirmation, and an accurate use of language, that confusion can be resolved.

The table in exercise 1b, taken from a Eurocontrol source, is to be used as a starting point to generate discussion about eleven factors which can lead to a risk of runway incursion. Both pilots and controllers will be able to relate to all these factors and should be able to give examples from their own experience. The point of exercise 1b is to draw attention to the fact that communication is the area in which there are the most contributing and causal factors. Each of these eleven factors has much potential for interesting discussion.

Quote: **Elicit from the class examples of taxiway or runway confusion events and their consequences [Suggested answers: Pilots confusing left and right parallel runways or confusing a large taxiway for a runway or confusing an inactive runway for an active runway or a departure runway for an arrival runway]. Students then read the quote and compare it with their ideas. Discuss with the class any anecdotes of such events, and what can be done to avoid them.**

1a **Check students understand the meaning of *precursor* (= an event which occurs before an incident, accident etc. and which is one of the contributing factors). Brainstorm a list of such precursors from the class and write them on the board. Students then discuss their responses to each one in pairs. Then discuss the best answers with the class.**

Suggested answers:
See Student Book exercise 5a for a list of precursors and exercise 7a for ways of responding.

b **Discuss the question with the class. You may need to check the meaning of *deficiency* (= inadequacy).**

Answer:
The green items are all related to inadequate training (of controllers, drivers and pilots); the orange items relate to airport infrastructure and logistics; the blue items all relate to communication. By far the largest number of contributing and causal factors relate to communication.

Background notes:

- A *contributory factor* is one of several factors that lead to an event. A *causal factor* is usually one of the main ones.
- *Driver training*, for drivers of service vehicles, etc., involves making drivers familiar with the airport layout, aircraft movements; taxiway and apron signage; protocols for the surfaces upon which they can drive and where they must stop and request permission to proceed; relevant radiotelephony practice; best practice in safety, security requirements and precautions, dangerous substances etc.

- *Frequency congestion* occurs when there are too many transmissions on the same radio frequency.
- *Conditional clearance* is when a clearance is given by a controller conditional upon another traffic movement (departure or arrival) occurring first. For example:
'*Cathay Pacific 396, behind Boeing 777 on short final, line up behind*' – See ICAO *Doc 4444 – PANS-ATM*: Chapter 12, para 12.2.7

c **Discuss the question with the class.**

Suggested answer:
The diagram shows very clearly just how safety-critical all the various factors related to RT communication are.

d **Remind students that they must each choose one of the causal factors to explain. Students work in small groups to explain the factors. Afterwards, go through all the factors with the class, eliciting as many practical examples as you can.**

Confusion

Communicative and operational issues:

This section looks at a simple, but common, case of communication confusion: numbers. The emphasis here is on pronunciation and fluency and an introduction to one aspect of the runway incursion topic which students should be at ease with.

ICAO FOCUS

Students read the quote to find what problems it describes. [**Answer**: incorrect pronunciation of numbers; two easily confused numbers]. Write on the board the numbers 71 and 79 and elicit why they might be confused. [**Answer**: Because *seven* ends with the sound /n/, and that sound may be incorrectly perceived as part of the next number (/nwʌn/), which, when spoken quickly, sounds like /naɪn/].

Students then discuss the question in pairs before feeding back to the class.

Possible answers:
5 and 9 can be easily confused if not pronounced correctly ('fife' and 'nin-er'). '2' and 'to' (and 'too') can also be confused, as can '4' and 'for' if '4' is not pronounced 'fow-er'. Therefore developing students' use of context is so important. Flight levels and headings can be confused if the units are not specified.

The emphasis in exercises 2a and b is on easily confused numbers (e.g. 5 and 9) and similar groups of numbers in a call sign (e.g. 569; 659). In exercise 3a, there are larger batches of information to be retained and reproduced.

2a ⦿**1.40** Play the recording, pausing after the first transmission to make sure students know what to do. Then play the rest of the recording for students to complete the exercise. They check in pairs before feeding back to the class.

Answers:		
1 b (979)	5 a (4213)	9 c (6833)
2 b (429)	6 b (5797)	10 a (1255)
3 b (868)	7 b (4031)	
4 b (6393)	8 a (7951)	

b Play the recording again, pausing after each call sign for a volunteer to repeat it. Go round the class asking each student to repeat one or two call signs. Have the other students decide if each student says it clearly enough. With stronger classes, it may not be necessary to play the recording for this exercise. Students then work in pairs to practise pronouncing the call signs, using audioscript 1.40. Their partners listen carefully to their pronunciation and suggest corrections.

3a ⦿**1.41** Go through the example with the class. Note that remembering and reading back large quantities of information is an important skill that pilots use regularly in their work. If you think this will be too challenging, you could allow them to take notes as they listen. Then play the recording, pausing after each instruction for a volunteer to read it back. Afterwards, students test each other in pairs using audioscript 1.41 on page 177.

Answers:
1 Lining up Runway 21 Left, intersection Charlie, Finnair 482.
2 Taxiing to holding point Alpha 1, Runway 12 Right, Gulf Air 2351.
3 Backtracking Runway 18 Left, Air India 1658.
4 Crossing Runway 09 Left, Korean Air 3738.
5 Line/Lining up behind Dragonair A320 on short final, Runway 23 Right, China Southern 2664.
6 Expediting crossing Runway 31 Left, Emirates 5315.
7 Taxiing to holding position Bravo 2, Runway 07 Left, Lan 338.
8 Lining up Runway 29 Right. Ready for immediate departure, Midland 6478.
9 Holding position, cancelled take-off, Egyptair 173.
10 Turn first left and contact Ground 121 decimal 35, Etihad 7481.

Background note:

Short final means the last part of the approach before touchdown, typically from the inner marker, or some two nautical miles, to the threshold.

b Students discuss the question in pairs and feed back to the class. Make a list on the board.

Suggested answers:
taxiways (Romeo 5; Romeo 9)
gates/stands (Alpha 27; Bravo 27)
runways (RWY 15; RWY 19)
wind velocity (210 degrees, 10 kts; 120 degrees, 10 kts)
time (15:35; 13:55)
altitude (5,000 ft; 9,000 ft)
flight level (FL 100; FL 110)
headings (250°; 290°)

Background note:

RTF stands for radiotelephony. *RT* is also used.

c Students work in pairs to practise saying their examples, using the list on the board as a reference.

Precursors

Communicative and operational issues:

This section on precursors has dense content and offers a lot of material for discussion. Over and beyond the exercises of matching, classifying and performing pair work, it is an opportunity for students to discuss, elaborate on and find examples of a whole range of safety considerations and situations where communication skills can remove confusion on the ground. It is a section which will benefit from being drawn out and having its content explored in some depth.

4 This exercise prepares the more abstract concepts used when talking about precursors and safety generally. Briefly check students remember the meaning of *precursor* (covered in exercise 1a). Students then work alone to match the words and phrases to their definitions. They check in pairs before feeding back to the class. You may need to check the pronunciation of *bias* /ˈbaɪəs/.

Answers:			
1 d	3 g	5 h	7 e
2 f	4 a	6 c	8 b

Background note:

Expectation bias is a particularly dangerous feature of the work of pilots and ATCOs, where so much of their work is formulaic and routine and it is very easy to assume that things are happening as they usually do.

Extension activity:

1 Students test each other in pairs by reading one of the safety-related words to elicit the correct definition from their partner.

2 Students could also read a definition to elicit the correct word from their partner.

3 Discuss with the class how to use each word (e.g. **there is a** *lack of* something; something happened **due to** somebody's unawareness **of** something; something was obscured **by** something; there was **a** *failure* **to** do something).

4 Elicit from the class how each word or phrase may relate to an actual precursor of a runway incursion (e.g. *there is a lack of awareness/signage/training*).

5a **Students work alone to put the precursors in the correct categories. They then discuss their answers in pairs. When you go through the answers with the class, make sure everyone fully understands the situations, and elicit examples from students' own experience. You may need to check the following words:** oversight **(= monitoring);** configuration **(= layout);** wear **(= damage caused by use over a long period of time); and** uncertainty **(= the situation when somebody isn't 100 per cent sure).**

> **Answers:**
> **Flight crew-related: a** – lack of readback (both pilots and ATCOs); **b** – ATIS message received, but relevant information overlooked; **d** – expectation bias at a familiar airport; **e** – not asking for confirmation of instructions from ATC; **j** – inadequate taxi briefing; **m** – failure to verbalise crew actions; **p** – changeover of function from pilot not flying to pilot flying just before line-up; **q** – uncertainty whether ATC instruction is directed to the correct aircraft (both pilots and ATCOs)
>
> **ATC-related: a** – lack of readback (both pilots and ATCOs); **c** – lack of oversight of taxiing aircraft; **h** – NOTAM prepared, but not issued; **i** – controller's hearback was ineffective; **k** – a non-standard taxi routine; **o** – issuing take-off clearance without confirming the aircraft's position; **q** – uncertainty whether ATC instruction is directed to the correct aircraft (both pilots and ATCOs)
>
> **Airport infrastructure-related: f** – misleading taxiway signage; **g** – current airport diagrams not showing the actual airport configuration; **l** – markings obscured by wear or patches of snow; **n** – taxiway lighting brighter than runway lighting.

Background note:

NOTAMs means Notices for Airmen. NOTAMs are notices about the condition or change to any airport, equipment, service or procedure notified within the Aeronautical Information Publication (AIP). NOTAMs are available in the form of Pre-Flight Information Bulletins (PIB) using a live database.

Language notes:

♦ *Oversight* has two very different meanings, each related to different verbs. As an uncountable noun, *oversight* means supervision, from the verb *to oversee*. As a countable noun, *an oversight* is something that has been forgotten or missed, from the verb *to overlook*.

♦ *Wear* can be a noun (commonly used in the phrase *wear and tear* [= damage from being used regularly, as in runway markings that gradually deteriorate as they get older]), or a verb (typically used in phrasal verbs such as *wear away/off*: e.g. *The markings are starting to wear away/off*). The related adjective is *worn*: e.g. *The paint is worn*.

b **◐1.42 Go through the example with the class. Tell students to make notes of the precursors as they listen (they could simply write a letter, a–q, from exercise 5a). Play the recording for the students to complete the exercise. Students discuss their answers in pairs and then feed back and discuss with the class. You may need to check the meaning of** worn **(see** Language note **above).**

> **Answers:**
> 1 q   2 l   3 k   4 e   5 a   6 n

Background note:

The *far end* of a runway is the opposite end from where the aircraft touches down or starts its take-off run.

c **◐1.42 Go through the example with the class. Then play the recording again, pausing after each transmission for a volunteer to respond appropriately. Discuss the best responses with the class. You could also discuss with the class how common or realistic these situations are. Afterwards, students work in pairs to test each other using audioscript 1.42 on page 178.**

Suggested answers:
1 Tower, Speedbird 5831, was that take-off clearance meant for us?
2 Tango Bravo November, turn right Taxiway Romeo 6.
3 Tower, Air Canada 428, we are in front of the General Aviation terminal. Confirm (that this is) correct routeing to Runway 28 Left.
4 Tower, Vietnam Airlines 288, confirm taxi instructions.
5 Air Austral 491, request fire service. Confirm.
6 Tower, Air Algérie 4921, confirm we are on the active runway.

6 Students discuss the question in small groups and then feed back to the class.

Suggested answers:
a **lack of readback by pilot or controller:** If the pilot does not read back a controller instruction, the controller has no way of detecting a misunderstanding which may lead to an incorrect action; if the controller does not acknowledge a pilot request, the pilot does not know whether the request has been taken into account.
b **ATIS message received, but relevant information overlooked:** The crew do not have up-to-date information about conditions at the airport.
c **lack of monitoring of taxiing aircraft:** ATC may not detect a pilot taxiing error and a possible incursion.
d **expectation bias at a familiar airport:** The crew may follow an incorrect taxi routine out of habit.
e **not asking for confirmation of instructions from ATC:** The crew may have misunderstood an instruction.
f **misleading taxiway signage:** The crew may take a wrong turning (see Linate).
g **current airport diagrams not showing the actual airport configuration:** The crew may not be aware of changes to the airport layout and the appearance of obstacles or restrictions.
h **NOTAMs prepared, but not issued:** The crew will be unaware of changes to operations, airport facilities and work in progress etc.
i **controller's hearback was ineffective:** The controller will not pick up a pilot error.
j **inadequate taxi briefing:** The crew may become confused and distracted during taxiing and enter an active runway.
k **a non-standard taxi route:** The crew will have their attention distracted by a more complex taxi routeing.
l **markings obscured by wear or patches of snow:** The crew may take the wrong turning.
m **failure to verbalise crew actions, instructions and clearances:** The crew may fail to pick up misunderstandings or understand different things.

n **taxiway lighting brighter than runway lighting:** This may lead the crew to line up on a taxiway rather than a runway, or to taxi on a runway.
o **issuing take-off clearance without confirming the aircraft's position:** The clearance may be given prematurely, cause confusion among the crew and the crews of other aircraft.
p **changeover of function from pilot monitoring to pilot flying just before line-up:** The pilots will not have time to assimilate their new functions and will be distracted at a critical moment.
q **uncertainty whether ATC instruction is directed to the correct aircraft:** An instruction may be taken by another aircraft leading to the wrong aircraft lining up.

7a The situations in this exercise are worthwhile as discussion activities for students to match situations and precursors, but also the six situations are of interest and should provoke comments in their own right. Elicit from the class what they know about the Flight Safety Foundation and the ALAR Tool Kit. Students then work in pairs to match the precursors in exercise 5a with the safety measures, and explain briefly how each one enhances safety. You may need to check the meaning of *enhance* (= improve something which is already good) and *conform to* (= agree with, follow). Afterwards, go through the answers with the class.

Answers:
| 1 d, g, j, k, m | 3 a, e | 5 n |
| 2 a, j, k, m | 4 g, j, k, l, n | 6 l, m |

♦ Using the airport diagram allows pilots to visualise the information they have received from ATC and agree on the taxi route together; they will be able to anticipate and monitor their progress. Any uncertainty or misunderstanding will then probably be revealed and they will be able to get confirmation or clarification from ATC.
♦ Taking notes is good practice; with a lot of information being received and heard on the frequency, it is useful to have a record of key data and as taxiing may be a long and complex process at a large airport, having a written reminder may be necessary and avoids increasing ATC's workload unnecessarily by requesting confirmation.
♦ If the crew is unfamiliar with the airport, if the controller is not sure of their language proficiency or if taxiing requires multiple taxiways and runways to be crossed, it is safer to give progressive taxi instructions, i.e. proceed step by step so that the crew does not have to remember too much at once and holds at points which may represent a safety risk.

- The airline's SOPs (Standard Operating Procedures) embody most of the best practices which the crew should apply in all phases and conditions of flight. These include methodical ways of obtaining and maintaining situational awareness by using all the inputs and data at the crew's disposal and sharing and crosschecking this awareness.
- There have been cases of flight crews entering an incorrect runway or mistaking a taxiway for a runway. If signage, location, dimensions and lighting do not correspond to what they know about the active runway, they should request confirmation from ATC.
- Saying things aloud in the cockpit is an excellent way of making sure that no uncertainty goes unchallenged and that both pilots are in agreement.

Background notes:

- *ALAR* stands for Approach and Landing Accident Reduction. The full toolkit is available from http://flightsafety.org
- If instructions are *hard-copied*, they are noted down on paper by the flight crew.
- *Progressive taxi instructions* are step-by-step instructions.
- The *line-up check* involves checking the identity of the runway and the departure clearance.
- A *challenge–response call* involves a request for confirmation and a response. See Rick Darby: *Keeping it on the runway*, *AeroSafety World*, August 2009.

b **Students discuss the questions in pairs and then feed back to the class.**

Extension activity:

You could repeat exercise 7a with other safety measures from the tool-kit section on Runway Incursions. See *The Standard Operating Procedures Template* in the *Flight Safety Foundation ALAR Tool Kit*.

Note that other parts of the tool-kit will be used in Units 8, 9 and 10.

8 **This pairwork exercise gives practice using plain language in one of the most vital functions where phraseology is not sufficient: asking for clarification or confirmation when the situation or the information which has been given is confusing. Go through the example with the class. Make sure students realise there are 20 dialogues: both students will request ten pieces of information and give ten pieces. Point out also that sometimes the requester will need to respond to the information. You may need to check the meaning and pronunciation of *quieten* /ˈkwaɪətən/ (= to calm somebody down). Students then work in pairs to make dialogues. Afterwards, ask volunteers to act out their dialogues for the class.**

If you have an odd number of students you will need to have a group of three, where Student C takes numbers 1 to 3 from Student A and numbers 8 to 10 from Student B. You can use the same system for both sets of cues (requesting information and giving information).

Suggested answers:
Pilot initiating (Pilots requesting information)
1
Pilot: Iberia 7455, we are at the end of Taxiway Echo heading north. The painted markings to the taxiways to the left and right are not clear / faded / worn. Can you assist us please? / Request assistance.
ATCO: Iberia 7455, Golf 3 is to the left and Golf 4 to the right. Turn right and taxi via Taxiway Golf 4. Hold short of Runway 27 Right.

2
Pilot: Giant 2375, the last transmission was garbled. Please say again.
ATCO: Giant 2375, taxi to holding point/position Bravo 4, Runway 15, via Taxiway Delta.
Pilot (readback): Taxi to holding point Bravo 4, Runway 15, via Delta, Giant 2375.

3
Pilot: Astana Line 268, confirm Runway 23 active; both 23 Right and 23 Left have high-intensity lighting.
ATCO: Affirm. Runway 23 Right (is the) active runway. They are performing lighting maintenance on Runway 23 Left.

4
Pilot: Air France 4396, we are at the east end of Taxiway Romeo. The access to Taxiway Sierra 2 is closed. Request instructions.
ATCO: Taxiway Sierra 2 is closed for drainage work. Turn left, taxi via Taxiway Tango 3; turn right Sierra 3. Hold short of Runway 13 Right.

...
ATCO initiating (ATCOs requesting information)
1
ATCO: Say reason stopped on Taxiway Kilo. / Why have you stopped on Taxiway Kilo?
Pilot: We crossed over the intersection of Kilo and Romeo and missed our left turn and are unsure of our taxi routeing. Request instructions.
ATCO: Turn first left and taxi via Tango to the intersection of Tango and Sierra. Turn left and taxi via Sierra to Romeo.

2
ATCO: Say the aircraft type and airline of the traffic ahead.
Pilot: It is a Singapore Airlines A380.

3

ATCO: Say reason (for) returning to gate. / Why are you returning to the gate?

Pilot: We have an engine lubrication / oil problem and require maintenance.

4

ATCO: Say nature and location of obstacle on taxiway. / What is the nature and location of the obstacle on the taxiway?

Pilot: Earth and stones from a (building) contractor's truck have spilled on to the paving of Taxiway India, 200 metres south of the intersection between Taxiways India and November. We are afraid of ingestion and request an alternative routeing.

ATCO: Roger. Take first right and taxi via Mike and Papa.

...

Background notes:

- # *1 T/O* means the first aircraft to take off.
- *Departures seem A1* means that departing flights are lining up on the runway from holding point/position Alpha 1.
- The *galley* is the part of the aircraft where the cabin attendants store and prepare food and drinks.
- A *circuit breaker* is an electrical protecting safety device which opens a circuit in case of an excessive flow of current. Most circuit breakers are located on the cockpit overhead panel and rear cockpit bulkhead.
- *ATR* is an Alenia Aeronautica and EADS consortium which manufactures short/medium-range turboprop aircraft: the ATR 42 and the larger ATR 72.
- An *axle* is a shaft on which landing gear wheels are mounted.
- A *stop bar* is a series of lights indicating whether access to a runway is authorised or not – see exercise 11.
- *a/c* stands for aircraft.

Communication errors: Failure to seek confirmation

Communicative and operational issues:

Frequency saturation, interference and garbled or clipped messages often hamper communication. It is important that students know how, and especially have the self-confidence, to challenge a transmission and ask for repetition, clarification, explanation or confirmation. Key words such as *not* or *right* may be inaudible without the recipient of the message necessarily realising it. It is bad practice to assume or guess at what was said: the correct reflex should be to request clarification.

ICAO FOCUS

Read the quote aloud and discuss the three questions with the class.

Suggested answers:
- A word may be misheard because there is a break or interference in the transmission, because it is incorrectly pronounced or because the person expects to hear something else.
- When people start guessing, i.e. filling in what they did not hear properly, they usually base their guess on what they expected to hear, which may not be what was actually said.
- If there is the slightest doubt about what you heard, you must request confirmation.

9 ◐1.43 Like many of the linguistically simpler exercises in *Flightpath*, exercise 9 is as much about confidence and reflex building as it is about language. The purpose of this exercise is less to identify the type of poor transmission than to respond correctly whatever the reason for incomplete understanding.

Go through the instructions carefully with the class. Elicit the differences between *clipped* (= cut short), *garbled* (= unclear because of radio interference); *unclear* (= not clear, possibly due to poor communication skills); *interrupted* (= having a break in the middle) and *incomplete* (= having some information missing). Make sure students have their books open on the correct Pairwork Activity pages (Student A: page 132 / Student B: page 140). Then play the recording, pausing after the first transmission to go through the example. For simplicity, it might be best to do the whole activity with the class first, pausing after each transmission and getting volunteers to respond using their cues, etc. When you are happy that everyone knows how the exercise works, you could repeat it with students working in pairs, again pausing after each transmission for them to continue each conversation with their partners.

If you have an odd number of students you will need to have a group of three, where Student C takes Student A transmissions 1–3 and Student B transmissions 6–8.

Background note:

- If an aircraft *maintains the runway heading* it climbs straight ahead, i.e. it takes off and climbs on the extended axis of the runway centreline.
- *Holding point* is not standard ICAO terminology, but was widely adopted by States in place of *holding position* to avoid confusion with the US phraseology *Taxi into position and hold*. Since September 2010, the US has adopted the standard ICAO phraseology *Line up and wait*.

Good practice

Communicative and operational issues:

The eight principles of good practice taken from the ICAO *Manual on the Prevention of Runway Incursions* (Doc. 9870) are defined largely from a controller's point of view, but all are immediately understandable to pilots. The reasons behind them will be apparent, and refer to concerns both populations can comment on. To gloss these eight points:

- Controllers use strips in front of them to monitor and control flights and as colour-coded memos to remind them of operating restrictions such as a closed runway or taxiway.
- The rationale for giving departure instructions prior to taxiing is that the crew have fewer things to focus on when the aircraft is at a standstill.
- The red lights of stop bars at holding points should be used systematically to prevent aircraft from entering an active runway inadvertently.
- Flight crews should not be given contradictory and confusing signals, e.g. told to enter the runway when the stop bar lights are still red.
- It is easier for flight crews if they use taxi routes they are familiar with.
- Flight crews should not have to memorise long and complex taxi instructions; if, for example, several taxiways have to be used, it is better to give a few instructions at a time.
- Holding on the active runway should be limited, as it immobilises the runway for other traffic and causes confusion and frustration for the crew involved.
- Visibility is diminished when holding at an oblique taxiway.

10a **As in the section on precursors, the recommendations in exercises 10a and b are designed to spark discussion, elicit the students' personal experiences and practise the lexis and grammar (modal verbs) used prior to the communication tasks in exercises 12 and 13. Students read the text to choose the three factors which they think have the most positive impact. Note that no answers are provided, as the choice will depend on students. Note also that the difficult words are explained in exercise 11, so avoid explaining vocabulary at this stage.**

b **Students discuss their choices with a partner. Then open up the discussion to include the whole class. You could play Devil's Advocate by disagreeing with their choices, in order to provoke more discussion.**

Language note:

Oblique and *angled* are used here as synonyms. The only difference is the direction the aircraft is coming from: if the aircraft enters or leaves the runway from an exit/taxiway which has a convenient angle facilitating a quick manoeuvre, it is angled; if the aircraft has to turn back, as it were, more than 90 degrees, it is oblique.

Background note:

Oblique exits/taxiways/turn-offs are designed to facilitate aircraft vacating the runway at speed, hence the term *high-speed turn-off*, and performing a *rolling start* for take-off.

11 **Students work alone to match the words with the definitions, and then check in pairs.**

Answers:
1 f	3 g	5 d	7 a
2 e	4 b	6 h	8 c

Language focus: Modal verbs

Elicit from the class the meaning and use of modal verbs in English (see *Language note* below). Then go through the examples in the box with the class, eliciting the function of the modal verb in each sentence. You may need to point out that modal verbs each have several functions, so it is important to understand which function is used in each particular case.

Suggested answers:
We can see ... (ability)
The passengers cannot board ... (inability)
Flights may be delayed ... (possibility)
We could exceed ... (possibility in conditional structure)
We must return ... (necessity)
You must not cross ... (prohibition)
All traffic shall stop. (statement of rules)
ATC should give ... *clearance* ... (strong recommendation)

Language note:

There are nine full modal verbs in English (*must, can, could, will, would, may, might, shall* and *should*), plus several verbs which share some features with modal verbs (e.g. *ought to, need, had better*) and many structures which have a modal meaning but are otherwise grammatically the same as normal verbs (e.g. *have to, be able to, be supposed to*, etc.).

The features of full modal verbs are:
1 no third person s (he may not ~~he mays~~)
2 can be negated with not/n't (mustn't not ~~don't must~~)
3 serve as auxiliary verb in questions (Shall we go? not ~~Do we shall go?~~)
4 followed by another verb in the infinitive without to (I can see not ~~I can to see~~)

Background note:

Duty time is the time during which a crew is scheduled and authorised to work.

12a **◎1.44** In this exercise, students will call upon their own experience and knowledge of what happens in common operational and everyday circumstances and respond using modal verbs. Go through the example with the class. Then play the recording, pausing after each transmission for volunteers to respond. Afterwards, students can test each other in pairs using audioscript 1.44 on page 178. Sentence 8 may cause some confusion: in this case, it means *I arrived at work late*, not *I've got to work late*.

> **Suggested answers:**
> 1 We must switch over to the standby power supply.
> 2 All the flights will be delayed.
> 3 Flights may be delayed.
> 4 You should use your glasses.
> 5 Yes, I can see them.
> 6 All traffic must use November and Papa.
> 7 They will be with them in 90 seconds.
> 8 You should be on time tomorrow.

Background notes:

◆ The *main generator* refers to a local electrical generator to supply the needs of the airport and ATC equipment.
◆ The *field* refers to the airfield.

b **◎1.45** Play the recording to compare it with students' own responses. Discuss any differences with the class and decide with the class which response was better in each case and why. Pause after each response for students to repeat, focusing especially on stress and intonation. Note that modal verbs tend not to be stressed in positive sentences.

13a **◎1.46** Refer students to the airport chart. Then play the recording for students to make notes. Afterwards, they compare their notes with a partner and listen again to check.

Answers:

	Location	Aircraft / vehicle	Details of incident
1	e	Dash 8 / A319	Dash 8 leaving holding point N4; A319 lined up RWY 09 from N5
2	g	car / LH 375	Rwy maintenance car parked on 36C between W3 and W4, LH 375 lining up
3	a	A320 / tractor	Air India A320 ready on RWY 09; tractor crossing N2
4	c	Citation / Beechcraft	Executive 444 RWY 22; Beechcraft TWY G2
5	f	Mexicana 388 / ATR 72	Mexicana 388 only just cleared ATR 72 vacating RWY 24 on S1
6	d	KLM 189 / MD–90	KLM 189 go around; MD–90 vacating RWY 18C
7	b	Falcon 483 / tug, Embraer	Falcon 483 cancelled take-off; tug towing Embraer on G4
8	h	Tunisair 045 / Hercules	Tunisair 045 lining up RWY 24; Hercules entering RWY from S4

Background notes:

◆ A *Dash 8* is a twin-engine turboprop regional transport aircraft.
◆ The *A319* is a slightly shorter version of Airbus' main short- and medium-range narrow-body jet the *A320*.
◆ *Hawker Beechcraft*, an American manufacturer of business and general aviation turboprop and jet aircraft, has produced many models of which the Baron, Bonanza, 1900 and King are amongst the best known.
◆ A *Citation* is an American twin-engine business jet.
◆ A *Hercules* is a Lockheed C-130, four-engine turboprop military transport plane.

b Go through the examples with the class. Make sure students understand that they need to produce both the transmissions for the necessary instructions and a report for Flight Ops / their supervisor for each incident. Students then work in pairs or small groups to plan the transmission and report for each incursion incident. Go through the best answers with the class.

Suggested answers:
1 – Dash 8, stop immediately. Dash 8, stop immediately. Traffic on active runway.
  Report: A Dash 8 was leaving holding point N4 while an A319 was already lined up on Runway 09 from holding point N5.
2 – Maintenance car, vacate the area near Runway 36 Centre immediately; this is the active runway.
  Report: A maintenance car was parked near exit W3 or W4 from Runway 36 Centre.
3 – Air India, hold position. Cancel take-off.
  – Tractor, vacate Runway 09 immediately; this is the active runway.
  Report: A tractor crossed Runway 09 from November 2 while an Air India A320 was lined up ready for departure.
4 – Executive 44, hold position. Cancel take-off.
  – Beechcraft, vacate Runway 22.
  Report: A Beechcraft entered the active runway, Runway 22, after a Citation had already been cleared for take-off.
  ...

Low-visibility operations

Communicative and operational issues:

Poor visibility is obviously one of the factors which makes ground operations more difficult and slower and increases the potential for errors and runway incursions. In the absence of shared visual references, reliance on oral communication becomes greater. This section is built around a serious runway incursion accident which occurred in poor visibility at Milan Linate airport in 2001.

Language focus: Passive (past tense)

Elicit from the class the structure and use of the passive in English (see *Language note* below).
Go through the examples with the class, eliciting whether the active sentences could become passive and vice versa. You could also use this opportunity to predict what happened, using only the six sentences as guidance.

Language note: The passive

The passive is used for two very different reasons in English.
1 To avoid referring to the agent (= usually the person who performed the action), typically because the agent is obvious, unknown, irrelevant or very general (e.g. people).
  Active: *The crew made the decision to go around at 19:00 UTC.*
  Passive: *The decision to go around was made at 19:00 UTC* (the agent, the crew, is obvious).
2 To place the agent away from the beginning of the sentence, typically to draw special attention to it, or because it is a long phrase that would sound strange at the beginning of the sentence.
  Active: *The highly experienced captain together with his crew made the decision to go around.*
  Passive: *The decision to go around was made by the highly experienced captain together with his crew.*

This second reason is important because English word order is fairly fixed, unlike many other languages, which allow a subject simply to be moved to a later position in a sentence with no grammatical transformation. For this reason, the passive is used much more in English than in many other languages.

The passive is formed from a form of the verb *to be* (or sometimes *to get*) plus the past participle of the main verb. The verb *to be* in the passive sentence is in the same tense form as the main verb in the active sentence: *The crew made* [past simple] *the decision. – The decision was* [past simple] *made.*

Extension activity:

Tell students that the sentences in the Language focus box are all from the reading text about the runway incursion at Milan, Linate in 2001. Students work in groups or pairs to predict what happened. Then they discuss their predictions as a class before deciding on the best / most likely prediction.

Suggested answers:
1 Sentence 1 cannot be transformed into the passive in the normal way because there is no object of the verb. However, passive is possible (*The aerodrome was operated* [*by the controllers*]) with a slight change of meaning. The active and passive versions relate to ways of thinking of an aerodrome, whether as something that operates by itself or something that is operated by people.
2 Sentence 2 has two passive forms, because the verb *give* has two objects: *Start-up clearance was given; The plane was given start-up clearance.*

> 3 Sentence 3: passive is possible but not very natural: *The throttles were advanced and the clearance was acknowledged.*
> 4 Sentence 4: active is possible: *The pilots and controllers used both English and Italian.*
> 5 Sentence 5: active is possible: *The controller cleared Flight 686 to taxi to Runway 36R.*

14 **Students discuss the question in groups and then feed back to the class.**

> **Possible answer:**
> Using two languages on the frequency, as was the case in Linate (English and Italian), and also in another runway incursion accident in Paris CDG the previous year (English and French), deprives those pilots who do not speak the local language of some of their situational awareness, i.e. knowledge of what other aircraft are doing simultaneously. However, using the national language for national flights is very common practice. Students will undoubtedly have experience of this and may also have views on whether only English should be used on the frequency, as has been suggested by some specialists. Opinions are divided.

15a **Students work alone to read the two texts to find out what happened and why. Allow at least three minutes for students to read. They then discuss their answers in pairs before feeding back to the class. Deal with any vocabulary issues, but encourage students to work out meaning from context rather than explaining all the words. Problematic words may include *range from … to …* (= including many values between two points), *split* (= divide in two), *diverging* (= moving or heading in two different directions away from each other) and *erroneously* (= by mistake).**

> **Answer:**
> As always, there were many causal and contributing factors which led to this accident: the poor visibility; the worn taxiway markings; the fact that the two flights were communicating on different frequencies; the use of two languages on the frequency (English and Italian); the Cessna pilot's failure to see or respect the stop bar; and probably the Cessna pilot's lack of familiarity with the airport layout.

Background notes:

◆ The difference between the *visibility* and the *RVR* (Runway Visual Range) is that visibility refers to overall horizontal visibility in any direction whereas RVR refers to an automatically measured visibility of runway lights and markings at three points along the length of the runway.

◆ *UTC* (Co-ordinated Universal Time) is (for most purposes) the same as GMT (Greenwich Mean Time), also referred to as *Zulu* in radiotelephony.

◆ The *throttles* are levers on the centre pedestal, located between the two pilot stations, which control engine thrust.

◆ A *nose-up elevator* means that the pilot pulls on the control wheel or stick in order to raise the nose of the aircraft by acting on the elevators. The elevators are the primary flight control surfaces hinged on the trailing edge of the horizontal stabiliser, which control the longitudinal movement of the aircraft.

b **Students work in pairs to answer the questions and then feed back to the class. You may need to check the meaning of the structure *should have taken*, as a way of describing a past mistake (= the right thing to do, which wasn't done).**

> **Answers:**
> 1 b   3 c   5 b   7 c
> 2 c   4 a   6 a   8 b

Background notes:

◆ If a pilot *retracts the gear*, he/she sets the landing gear lever on the right centre part of the instrument panel to 'UP' and the landing gear is unlocked, folds and enters the landing gear bays.

◆ *Thrust* is a force providing propulsion.

c **Exercises 15c, d and e give students an opportunity to resource the information about precursors they used earlier in this unit. Students discuss the question in pairs and then feed back to the class. Write a list of factors on the board, as this will be useful for exercise 15e.**

> **Answers:**
> The precursors and causal factors include: lack of monitoring of taxiing aircraft; not asking for confirmation of instructions from ATC; markings obscured by wear; use of two languages; use of two frequencies; poor visibility.

d **Students work in pairs to report the events without looking back at the text.**

e **Go through the example with the class, focusing especially on the use of the past perfect (*had followed*) after *if* to describe an unreal event in the past. Make sure students also understand the meaning of the structure *The accident could have been avoided.* Students then work in pairs to make more sentences, using the factors on the board (from exercise 15c) to guide them. Afterwards, go through the answers with the class.**

Suggested answers:

The accident could have been avoided if:

1 the Cessna pilot had followed Taxiway R5.

2 a single frequency had been used.

3 only English had been used.

4 the crew had confirmed their position and routeing during taxiing.

5 the airport markings had been better maintained.

6 the crew had requested confirmation when they were in doubt.

ICAO FOCUS

Students read the quote to identify examples of good and bad practice [**Answers:** Good practice: Use of full call signs of all traffic; proper conditional clearances. Bad practice: Use of only *Roger* or *Wilco* as acknowledgement]. Students then discuss the four tasks in pairs and feed back to the class.

Suggested answers:

♦ 'Air China 473' is a full call sign; 'China 473', '473' or 'Air China' are abbreviated call signs which could be confused with, e.g. 'China Eastern 473', 'Lufthansa 473' or 'Air China 759'.

♦ If partial call signs are used on the frequency there is a greater risk of similar call signs being confused.

♦ Except in totally unambiguous situations, the response *Roger* or *Wilco* does not enable the person having made a request or given an instruction to be sure that the request or instruction has been correctly understood. Hence the importance of full readbacks or acknowledgements.

♦ Conditional clearances are departure clearances conditional upon another aircraft arriving or departing first. They require the memorisation of more information by the pilot and are used in circumstances where there are quite a lot of simultaneous traffic movements.

16 Go through the example with the class, focusing on how the first cue is changed into a full transmission. Students then work in pairs to exchange information. You may need to check the meaning of *respectively* (see *Background notes*).

If you have an odd number of students you will need to have a group of three, where the third student takes cues 1 to 3 from Student A and cues 8 to 10 from Student B.

Suggested answers:
Student A

1 Thai 1648, behind landing A320 on short final, line up behind.

2 Stripe 328, taxi to holding point Bravo 2 via Alpha and Bravo. Hold short of Runway 08 Left.

3 Southwest 761, caution: (there will be considerable) jet blast from (the) departing A380.

4 Vietnam 466, vacate via Alpha 2. Contact Ground 121 decimal 35.

…

Student B

1 Turn second right onto Taxiway Tango 4. Contact Ground 121 decimal 9.

2 Regional 028, cross Runway 31 Left and taxi to holding point 31 Right. Hold short of Runway 31 Right.

3 Libair 496, caution: taxi slower due (to) dense fog.

4 Turk Air, behind landing A320 on short final, line up behind.

…

Background notes:

♦ A *dew point* is the temperature at which, under normal conditions, condensation begins in a cooling mass of air. The dew point varies with different levels of atmospheric pressure, air humidity, etc.

♦ *Current information K* means ATIS Information Kilo. ATIS information is given in a series of updates (… India, Juliet, Kilo …) pilots are advised of the current information so that they can check easily that they have the most recent meteorological information about the airport.

♦ '*RVR of 350, 325 and 275 at touchdown, midpoint and stop end respectively*' means the RVR (Runway Visual Range) is 350 metres at touchdown, 325 metres at the mid-point and 275 metres at the stop end.

Sterile cockpit

Communicative and operational issues:

A *sterile cockpit* means that the flight crew should not cause or be subjected to any distractions which reduce their ability to focus on operating the aircraft and being fully aware of their environment. The errors pilots have made which are listed in the ICAO focus box could easily have been caused, at least in part, by the crew not maintaining a sterile cockpit.

ICAO FOCUS

Students read the quote to identify which of the four mistakes is most serious and which most common. In fact all four mistakes are potentially deadly. Students then discuss the three questions in pairs and feed back to the class.

17a **○1.47** In exercises 17a and b, students will use their listening skills to analyse a situation and identify the source of the distraction. Tell students to close their books. Discuss with the class what the term *sterile cockpit* means (see *Communicative and operational issues*). Elicit from the class on the board a list of events which may lead to distraction. Students then open their books and compare their list from the board with the list in exercise 17a. Discuss the list briefly with the class, making sure students understand all the events and eliciting examples, but avoid going into too much detail, as this will spoil the discussion in 17b. You may need to check the meaning of *saturation* (= the absolute maximum level). Then play the recording for students to complete the task. After they have checked in pairs, you could play the recording again for students to check before going through the answers with the class.

Answers:
1 e – There is communication saturation which results in the message being interrupted at times and essential information missing.
2 d – There is no standard take-off clearance and new information is given to the crew too late while they are preparing for the take-off roll.
3 b – The crew are obviously in a hurry to make their slot and so are failing to check.
4 a – The before-take-off checklist is not performed in the correct sequence and so the crew are not sure whether they have checked one of the items (the speed bugs, which indicate critical speeds: V1, V2 etc.) on the air speed indicator.
5 f – The use of non-aviation language and jargon ('*buttoned up*' = doors are closed and locked) will create confusion in a non-native English-speaking environment.
6 c – The crew may have missed this transmission as there is a lot of noise on the flight deck; this is not a sterile cockpit.
7 g – Different languages are being used on the frequency depriving the crew of situational awareness. In addition, standard phraseology is not being used.
8 h – This is non-standard ICAO phraseology: the United States, where this was official phraseology, adopted the ICAO '*Line up and wait*' in September 2010.

Background notes:
- *Aviation English* is broader than *ICAO standard phraseology*. Most of the language in this book can be described as aviation English, even where it departs from standard phraseology. Non-aviation English would include vocabulary from completely unrelated fields, idiomatic language, slang, etc.
- *Window heat* refers to the electrical resistances in the windshield and side cockpit window panels which prevent the formation of ice and condensation.
- *Anti-ice* covers all the pneumatic systems which prevent the accumulation of ice on the wing leading edges and engine air intakes.
- *Pitot heat* /ˈpɪtəʊ hiːt/ refers to the electrical heating of the various air data probes: pitot probe, angle of attack sensor, static port etc.
- A *yaw damper* /jɔː ˈdæmpə/ is a flight control system which gives the rudder small deflection orders throughout the flight to prevent the oscillation of the tail which is called 'Dutch roll'.
- *Speed bugs* or *V bugs* are small plastic markers, now often replaced by digital displays, which are set manually or automatically around/along the airspeed indicator scale to give the crew easily visible references to critical airspeeds during take-off and approach: V1 or decision speed, when the pilot must decide to take off or reject take-off; V2, take-off safety speed at which the aircraft can be safely airborne with one engine shut down; various flap retraction/extension speeds; Vref, final approach speed.
- *Buttoned up* is an example of aviation jargon, meaning *doors and panels closed and locked*, which, like most idiomatic language, will often be confusing for many speakers. Even Americans and Britons do not always understand each other's jargon.

b Students choose one of the events, ideally so that each event is chosen at least once. When they have described it to the class and given examples, open up the discussion to allow others to contribute.

Suggested answers:
- Flight crew distractions include: talking together about a non-operational subject (e.g. football, private life etc.); being subjected to undue noise; being interrupted by the cabin crew; making a passenger announcement during a critical phase of taxiing or flight; attempting to multitask; not performing checklists in the correct order; working under stress; receiving changed instructions; use of non-standard phraseology; use of different languages on the frequency etc.

- Controller distractions include: being distracted by their colleagues (e.g. talking about private life; colleagues asking them questions at critical times; colleagues talking too loudly to other colleagues nearby or pilots over RT etc.); events on another sector; visitors or technicians working nearby.
- Pilots are subjected to many more stimuli and have to handle many more unexpected and varied situations in the course of a flight. However, because controllers' work is more routine, they may be liable to the effects of boredom or expectation bias.

18a In these exercises, students can use either standard phraseology or plain English: this is not a radiotelephony course. The purpose of the exercises is to use language precisely to give directions. Go through the example with the class. Students then work in pairs to ask for and give directions. Afterwards, check with the class for any problems.

Extension activity:

You could repeat the activity for an airport your students know well, either using a printed map or getting students to draw one.

b Students use the diagram and the cues to describe the events. Make sure they know to use past simple. Then have each pair present one of their descriptions to the class as feedback. They could mark the events and times on the diagram. Afterwards, they could take turns to use only their maps/notes to retell the whole sequence of events.

If you have an odd number of students you will need to have a group of three, where the third student only listens, asks for clarification and takes notes. That student then has to retell the whole sequence of events, using only the notes.

Putting it together: Situational awareness

Communicative and operational issues:

Situational awareness through the combination of different informational inputs runs through the book. The illustrations at the beginning of this section illustrate both the limitations (restricted visibility from the cockpit, or indeed the control tower) and the new technologies which enable pilots and controllers to monitor ground movements accurately even in poor visibility and at night.

19a, b, c Discuss the first question with the class, making sure they fully understand the meaning of situational awareness. Students then discuss the other two questions in pairs and feed back to the class.

Suggested answers:
a The photos refer to just three ways in which pilots and controllers may have their situational awareness enhanced or impaired on the ground.
  1 Pilots' sight of what is happening on the ground and around them being severely restricted by the nose of the aircraft and their inability to see behind them; closed-circuit cameras are increasingly being mounted on aircraft.
  2 Eyes remain one of the prime examples of how to know what is happening; in this case a controller is using binoculars to see more detail. It should be remembered that visibility from the tower is not always unrestricted and that often parts of the apron are concealed by terminal buildings.
  3 Finally, new technologies are being increasingly used to extend awareness of the environment. Here a HUD (Head-Up Display) enables a pilot to combine more information in one place while still continuing to look outside, i.e. to be 'head up'. Controllers have surface movement radar and other monitoring devices to improve their sources of information.
b On the ground, situational awareness can be obtained by: ground radar; ATC instructions; monitoring exchanges between other aircraft and ATC on the frequency; ATIS; reports on meteorological conditions from other aircraft; display of the aircraft's position on the Navigation Display (ND) or even a Head-Up Display (HUD); simply looking through the windshield or from the top of the control tower; taxiway and runway lights, markings and signs; stop bar lights; information from ground staff during turnaround and pushback etc. However, radiotelephony remains the main source of precise and confirmed situational awareness in all circumstances.
c The main ways of obtaining situational awareness on the ground are: 1 visual, 2 radiotelephony and 3 electronically.
  1 Sight remains our predominant and most immediate way of acquiring information about the situation we are in. However, for pilots sight is limited by the fact that the flight crew can only see forwards and to the side and that the nose of the aircraft hides what is directly in front of them. Tower controllers have the advantage of a high view point from which to monitor movements, and the use of binoculars, but the airport area is vast and complex and parts of it may be masked by airport buildings. Both pilots and controllers are subject to conditions of lighting and visibility – night time, fog, haze, heavy rain or snow severely restrict vision.

2 Radio communication is probably the most universal and constantly reliable way of acquiring situational awareness because it is not dependent on environmental conditions or on distance and allows two-way communication to clarify or confirm information. It uses a VHF technology which is generally reliable and there are back-up frequencies if one fails. However, it is dependent upon the speakers' language proficiency and communication skills.

3 Technologies such as HUD and more sophisticated ground radar are increasingly providing valuable support in conditions of poor visibility and lighting; however, they are far from being generalised worldwide and can only be used in conjunction with conventional visual and audio sources of information and communication.

Preparation

20a ⊙**1.48** Go through the example with the class. Students then work in pairs to make sentences. Note that the sentences all require an infinitive of purpose, but a longer structure (e.g. *in order to*) would also be possible. Play the recording for students to check their answers. Discuss any other possible answers, where your students' answers are different from those in the recording.

Suggested answers:
1 Controllers use surface movement radar to monitor traffic on the ground.
2 Pilots sometimes use 121.9 to contact Ground Control.
3 Controllers use call signs to identify individual aircraft.
4 Pilots use all their senses to create situational awareness.
5 Inertial navigation uses laser gyros to calculate aircraft position.
6 Controllers use electronic flight strips to manage separation and flow of traffic.
7 Controllers use binoculars to follow aircraft movements visually.
8 Pilot and controllers use VHF to communicate with each other.

Background notes:

◆ *Surface movement radar* is a radar system to monitor aircraft movements on the ground.
◆ *Inertial navigation* is a system of laser gyros and accelerometers which sense all aircraft movements on all three axes and so calculate the aircraft's present position to a high degree of accuracy.
◆ *Separation* is the distance between aircraft, a crucial thing for ATCOs to get right.

◆ *Flow* refers to managing the movement of one flight after another.
◆ *VHF* (very high frequency) describes radio waves.

Extension activity:

You could discuss with the class how situational awareness techniques have changed over recent decades, and how they might improve in the future.

Possible answer: Since the development of Human Factors research, largely pioneering in and for aviation, people have become much more aware of the effect of various interpersonal communicative skills and the nature of cognitive processes in an operational environment. As a result, flight crews are now trained more systematically in Crew Resource Management (CRM) to work as a team, verbalise and share information.

See Reason, J.: *Human Error* and *Managing the risk of organisational accidents* and his famous 'Swiss cheese' model.

Especially since the introduction of glass cockpits (A320 in 1986), and more experience with sophisticated man–machine interfaces, ergonomics has been applied more extensively to cockpit design. One consequence of this has been a better understanding of how crews can best integrate different sources of information to maintain their situational awareness: radiotelephony inputs from ATC; listening to communications between ATC and other flights; monitoring their flight instrument displays (Primary Flight Display, Navigation Display etc.); crosschecking captain and First Officer inputs; picking up information from physical sensations ('flying by the seat of your pants'); using visual references in Visual Meteorological Conditions; knowing how to use the Flight Management and Guidance System (FMGS); Traffic Collision Avoidance System (TCAS); Ground Proximity Warning System (GPWS); Head-Up Displays (HUD) and Global Positioning System (GPS) for greater control and anticipation.

During the same period, Air Traffic Control has benefited from more sophisticated radar systems and ground radar has become widespread.

b ⊙**1.48** Play the recording again, pausing after each sentence for students to repeat, either individually or together. Make sure the sentences are pronounced clearly and accurately. Students could also work in pairs to practise the sentences.

c Students discuss the task in pairs to come up with a list of sources of input and to prepare their descriptions of how each source of input is used. Encourage them to think laterally, i.e. not just to focus on obvious sources of input. Then brainstorm all the ideas and write them on the board. Discuss the ideas with the class to focus on the most important.

Suggested answers:
Pilots receive instructions from ATC about how to taxi to the active runway. During pushback, they communicate with the ground handling crew who guide them out of the stand and use hand signals to inform them that the tow-bar is disconnected and the nose-wheel steering lockout safety pin is removed from the nose gear. The ATIS recording provides them with up-to-date weather information. They use airport charts to plan and follow their taxiing progression. Airport ground markings and signs indicate to them where they are. The anti-collision and navigation lights on other aircraft show them where other aircraft are located and in which direction they are moving. Stop-bar lights confirm when they are authorised to enter the active runway.

ATCOs receive acknowledgements and readbacks from flight crews about their position, movements and intentions, as well as any problems which may occur. Many airports are equipped with ground radar which enables ATC to monitor aircraft movements at night or in poor visibility. Controllers use binoculars from the Tower to see any suspect aircraft or vehicle movements.

21a **⊙1.49** Play the first transmission and go through the example with the class. Make sure students know to note consequences, not causes. Then play the rest of the recording. You may need to check the meaning of *swerve* (= turn suddenly to avoid something) and *tight* (= with little time to spare).

Background note:

If a plane *overshoots* the runway, it fails to stop before the *turn-off* (= exit).

b Students compare their notes with a partner before listening again to check. Finally, go through the answers with the class.

Answers:
1 aircraft landing gear fire / TWY N blocked
2 tyre debris / delays on RWY 26L
3 ice patches intersection TWY R and T / taxi with caution
4 RWY 13R turn-off overshot, Fedex backtracking / delays on RWY 13R
5 ATR stopped on TWY F3 / departures delayed
6 stop-bar lights inop RWY 29R / caution
7 737 on TWY G with open bulk cargo door / 737 Return to gate
8 RWY 18R 275 m / CAT IIIA conditions

Background notes:

◆ (1) A brake overheat and possibly gear fire caused by hard braking during landing.
◆ (2) Debris from a burst or de-treaded tyre on the runway: tyre debris can cause considerable damage to other aircraft moving at speed. There have been several cases of wing fuel tanks being perforated.
◆ (3) Aircraft can skid on ice patches. Crews usually report any unusual phenomena.
◆ (4) The landing aircraft has not been able to stop in time to vacate the runway by the last exit. The crew will have to turn around at the end of the runway and taxi back to the first suitable exit.
◆ (5) An ATR turboprop is blocking the taxiway and the other aircraft's access to the runway. If they are delayed they may miss their slot and be further delayed.
◆ (6) The stop bar lights are not working so flights at the holding point are not sure that they can enter the active runway.
◆ (7) A crew is reporting that the bulk cargo door [small rear cargo compartment] seems not to be closed. All doors and handles should be flush.
◆ (8) RVR 275 metres means the visibility is very poor.

Communication

22 Explaining why being unable to comply with an instruction (from a controller) or a request (from a pilot) is a common occurrence which may require the use of plain language. The cues provide fairly detailed input about the lexis to be used and the situations; the students must make correct sentences from these cues inserting appropriate verbs, articles, function words etc. Go through the example with the class. You may need to check the meaning of *comply* (= to obey/agree) and *non-compliance*. Make sure students realise they have eight requests each and eight response cues, and that each dialogue should start with a request cue. Students then work in pairs to make dialogues. Afterwards, ask volunteers to act out their dialogues for the class. Discuss with the class the best ways of phrasing each explanation of non-compliance.

If you have an **odd number of students** you will need to have a group of three, where Student C takes numbers 7 and 8 from Student A (both pilot and ATCO cues) and 1, 2 and 3 from Student B.

Suggested answers:
Pilot requests / ATCO non-compliance

1

Pilot: Jamaica 496, request(ing) nose-in stand due full load, adverse weather and late arrival.

ATCO: Jamaica 496, unable. Sorry. All nose-in stands are currently occupied. Taxi to Mike 24.

Pilot: Taxiing to Mike 24, Jamaica 496.

2

Pilot: Uzbek 560, we are stopped on Taxiway Romeo. Request taxi via November and Tango because Sierra is blocked by a Boeing 787.

ATCO: Uzbek 560, unable. A trench is being dug along Taxiway Tango, so it is closed. Taxi to holding point Alpha 3, Runway 27 Left via Taxiways November, Oscar and Papa.

Pilot: Taxiing to holding point Alpha 3, Runway 27 Left via November, Oscar and Papa, Uzbek 560.

3

Pilot: Varig 845, we are at stand Bravo 19. Request departure information.

ATCO: ATIS unavailable. Wind 210 degrees, six knots. QNH 1017, departure runway 19 Left.

Pilot: 210 degrees, six knots. QNH 1017, departure runway 19 Left, Varig 845.

4

Pilot: Virgin 2336, request backtrack from Bravo 2 Runway 17 for departure.

ATCO: Unable. Air France A340 (is) lining up on 17 Left from Bravo 1. You are Number 3 for departure.

Pilot: Roger. Holding. Number 3 for departure, Virgin 2336.

...

ATCO instructions / Pilot non-compliance

1

ATCO: Singapore 977, taxi to holding position Charlie 2, Runway 27 Left, via Golf and Charlie. Hold short of Runway 27 Left.

Pilot: Unable. Our Number 4 engine N2 is fluctuating. We have requested Engineering and are remaining on the apron, Singapore 977.

ATCO: Singapore 977, advise us of the situation.

2

ATCO: Japan Air 389, taxi to terminal via Taxiways India and Juliet.

Pilot: Unable. There is almost nil visibility with this thick fog. We are uncertain of our position. We seem to be on Taxiway Kilo. Request assistance, Japan Air 389.

ATCO: Roger. Will instruct follow-me car to assist you.

3

ATCO: Regional 553, line up and wait Runway 05 Right.

Pilot: Unable. There is a Learjet still on Runway 05 Right; it missed turn-off Charlie 3, Regional 553.

ATCO: Regional 553, hold position.

4

ATCO: Lan 475, push back to face north.

Pilot: Unable. We have one passenger missing and the ramp handlers are unloading his baggage. We'll be ready in five minutes, Lan 475.

ATCO: Roger. Keep me advised.

...

Background notes:

◆ *Engineering* is the technical department, responsible for aircraft maintenance.

◆ A *radio management panel* is a control panel located on the centre pedestal between the two pilots which allows them to tune to different VHF and HF radio frequencies as well as various navigation aids. There is an ACTIVE and a STANDBY window, which enables a new frequency to be pre-tuned and then selected when needed.

◆ If a vehicle *pulls in*, it moves to the side of the road/taxiway, etc., to allow another vehicle to pass.

◆ A *trench* is a long hole, typically dug in order to lay underground pipes or cables.

◆ A *triple seven* is a Boeing 777 wide-body, twin-engine jet airliner.

Debriefing

23 **Discuss the question with the class. Give and elicit feedback on the strengths and weaknesses of the role-plays, and elicit suggestions as to how to overcome the weaknesses.**

Progress check

Students work alone to complete the progress check and then discuss their answers with a partner. Elicit any remaining weaknesses and plan with the class how to overcome them.

DVD: *When attention is diverted*

Communicative and operational issues

The first Eurocontrol clip in this unit, *When attention is diverted*, pursues the theme of distraction already explored in the core of the unit. A-Jet 123 (fictional call signs are used) is on approach to Runway 31 Right. Meanwhile a second aircraft, B-Jet 456, is holding short of Runway 31 Right. ATC instructs them to line up on the active runway. The crew report that the stop-bar lights are still illuminated red. The controller fails to be alerted by this fact and switches off the lights. B-Jet 456 enters Runway 31 Right forcing A-Jet 123 to go around when they are below 200 feet.

In the second short clip, *Fog and poor procedures*, we see two airport maintenance staff members in the fog. Although they are talking about the weather, one of them is more concerned about driving back to the apron to have his break. The controller confirms his request to drive to the apron via Taxiway Alpha, but fails to warn him of an approaching aircraft. As a result he almost drives onto the active runway. Familiarity can easily breed contempt of basic safety procedures.

In the final clip, *40 seconds*, C-Jet 333 is number one on approach to Runway 15 Left. B-Jet 110 is instructed to hold short of Runway 15 Left on Taxiway Alpha 3. Another aircraft, A-Jet 234, is cleared for take-off on Runway 15 Left. B-Jet 110 is given a conditional clearance to line up once the aircraft on short final has landed. In poor visibility, and holding farther down the runway, they mistake A-Jet 234 taking off for the landing aircraft (C-Jet 333) and enter the active runway. At that moment the landing aircraft C-Jet 333 passes in front of them performing its roll-out and they have to swerve to avoid it.

24a **Play the first clip for students to answer the questions. When you go through the answers with the class, elicit the call signs of the two aircraft and the name of the runway.**

> Answers:
> 1 two aircraft: A-Jet 123 and B-Jet 456
> 2 A-Jet 123 is on approach to Runway 31 Right; B-Jet 456 is about to depart from Runway 31 Right.

b, c **Students first discuss in pairs any errors they noticed, and then watch the clip again to take notes. After they have discussed the errors in pairs, discuss the answers with the class. You may want to play the clip a third time, so students can see all four errors.**

> Answers:
> 1 An incoming message to the controller from A-Jet 123 and a controller transmission to B-Jet 456 occur simultaneously.
> 2 'ASTOR 1 Bravo for B-Jet 456' is not a complete instruction using standard phraseology.
> 3 The controller instructs B-Jet 456 to line up while A-Jet 123 is already on final.
> 4 The crew of B-Jet 456 correctly question the fact that the stop-bar is on, but the controller incorrectly overrides it even though A-Jet 123 is on short final.

25 **Students work in pairs to report the incident, either as pilot or as ATCO. Afterwards, elicit the best answer from the class. See summary of the incident above in *Communicative and operational issues*. Note that the report could also be written as a homework task.**

> Suggested answer:
> A controller at a single runway airport (13L – 31R) was handling two flights: A-Jet 123, cleared for a visual approach to Runway 31 Right and a departing flight, B-Jet 456, taxiing to take off from Runway 31 Right from taxiway Romeo 1. An incoming transmission from A-Jet 123 confirming they were on the downwind leg was probably not heard by the controller as he was giving B-Jet 456 a taxi instruction. The controller was further distracted by the fact that B-Jet 456 requested a change in their departure taxiway (from R1 to R3) during taxiing and he then gave the crew new departure instructions. The controller instructed B-Jet 456 to line up on Runway 31 Right despite the fact that A-Jet 123 was on short final. The controller overrode the stop-bar although it was correctly showing red. B-Jet 456 entered the active runway as instructed and A-Jet 123 was forced to go around at the last minute.

26a **Play the second clip for students to answer the three questions. At the end of the clip, students discuss their answers in pairs before feeding back to the class.**

> Answers:
> 1 The men are working on a taxiway (Alpha), probably installing bollards to indicate that a taxiway is closed.
> 2 The second driver decides to return to the terminal to have something to eat.
> 3 F-Jet 123 landing on the runway almost collides with the vehicle in the fog.

b, c **Students discuss the questions in pairs and then feed back to the class. Play the clip a second time to make sure students notice all the contributing factors.**

> Suggested answers:
> ◆ The contributing factors to this incident are: 1 the very poor visibility in fog; 2 the fact that the driver does not give his exact position when requesting authorisation to return to Apron 1 and the controller does not give him precise routeing instructions; 3 the driver seems to be complacent about an airport he thinks he knows well; 4 the driver does not realise he is approaching the active runway, is unaware of the stop-bar and does not hold short; 5 it is evident from the map animation that he had in fact lost his way.

♦ The incident could have been avoided if: 1 the driver had given his exact position; 2 the controller had given him precise routeing instructions to Apron 1; 3 the driver had taken more care in poor visibility conditions and had slowed down to watch the taxiway markings; 4 the driver had contacted the Tower when he saw he was approaching the active runway.

27a Students watch the clip and then discuss the questions in pairs. Afterwards, discuss the questions with the class.

> **Suggested answer:**
> One aircraft, C-Jet 333, is cleared to land at night on Runway 15 Left. Two other aircraft are departing: A-Jet 234 is cleared for take-off from the end of the same runway (15R) and B-Jet 110 is instructed to hold at intersection A3. B-Jet 110 is given a conditional clearance to take off after the landing C-Jet 333, but on seeing A-Jet 234 pass by on the runway during its take-off run, mistakes it for the landing aircraft and starts to line up on the active runway, only narrowly missing the actual landing aircraft a few seconds later.

Background note:

A *checklist* is a document with a series of items which must be performed or checked at specific phases of flight.

b, c Students work in pairs to put the transmissions in order and then watch the clip again to check.

> **Answers:**
> 1 C-Jet 333, continue approach, Runway 15L, Number 1.
> 2 Continue approach Runway 15L, C-Jet 333.
> 3 B-Jet 110, taxi to and hold at intersection A3 for Runway 15L.
> 4 Holding at intersection A3 for Runway 15L, B-Jet 110.
> 5 Checklist completed.
> 6 OK, thank you. Checklist completed.
> 7 A-Jet 234, Runway 15L, cleared for take-off.
> 8 Cleared for take-off, Runway 15L, A-Jet 234.
> 9 B-Jet 110, behind landing 15L, line up and wait behind.
> 10 Behind landing (traffic) Runway 15L, lining up and wait behind, B-Jet 110.
> 11 OK, that's our landing. Lining up.
> 12 C-Jet 333, wind 170 degrees, 7 knots, Runway 15L, cleared to land.
> 13 Cleared to land, Runway 15L, C-Jet 333.
> 14 What's that? Right! Go right!

d Students work in small groups to make a list of the errors. When you have checked with the class, you could play the clip again to make sure all students notice them.

> **Suggested answers:**
> ♦ The controller, knowing that two aircraft were departing and another was on approach at night, should have given B-Jet 110 direct instructions rather than a conditional clearance in poor visibility conditions.
> ♦ The crew of B-Jet 110 should have checked with the controller before entering the active runway; conditional clearances should always be confirmed before being executed.
> ♦ They should also have been aware of A-Jet 234 taking off, from monitoring the frequency and from following the aircraft's take-off and taxiing lights.
> ♦ There is a breakdown of situational awareness.

28 Brainstorm a list of errors on the board and discuss students' experiences as a class.

> **Suggested answers:**
> **Clip 1:** two simultaneous messages are not clarified; an aircraft is instructed to line up while another aircraft is on short final; the controller is distracted by changes in taxi routeing; the controller overrides the stop bar rather than questioning why it is on
>
> **Clip 2:** complacency by the driver; imprecise location and routeing instructions; lack of proper attention to signage in poor visibility
>
> **Clip 3:** the controller should have been aware of the risk of confusion giving a conditional clearance in poor visibility; the flight crew should have confirmed to ATC that they were entering the runway and have checked that the aircraft they saw was the arriving, not the departing, aircraft

PART A
Review

Review units Teacher's brief

Review units are to be found after each of the three parts of *Flightpath*: Hazards on the ground; En route; and Approach and landing. The Review units focus on the six ICAO language proficiency skills detailed in the rating scale and Doc. 9835: Pronunciation; Structure (grammar and syntax); Vocabulary; Fluency; Comprehension and Interaction (See the ICAO Rating Scale and Holistic Descriptors, Teacher's Book, pages 8–9). Apart from Interactions, most of the activities in the Review units can be done individually by the students out of classroom time, if you prefer.

Pronunciation

1a ⊙**1.50** Play the recording once or twice for students to underline the words they hear. Note that one sentence is given twice, as it contains a word for both question 9 and question 10. When you check the answers, students could say 'first' or 'second' to clarify which word is correct. You could also check answers by asking students to raise their hands ('*Who thinks it was the first word?*') in order to assess where students' main problems lie.

Answers:

1	**light** / right	11	near / **rear**
2	chart / **cart**	12	**wheel** / will
3	**won't** / want	13	tired / **tyre**
4	**low** / load	14	quite / **quiet**
5	again / **against**	15	**steel** / still
6	services / **surfaces**	16	**fly** / flight
7	**hand** / and	17	fuel / **full**
8	**least** / last	18	lose / **loose**
9	**then** / than	19	**feel** / fill
10	way / **away**	20	clear / **clean**

Background notes:

* A *ground cart* is any one of the auxiliary power sources used during the turnaround: Ground Power Unit; Air Start Unit; Low Pressure Air Conditioning Unit; etc.
* A *loadsheet* is the document which contains all the information about the aircraft's payload and the location of the baggage and cargo.

b ⊙**1.51** Play the recording, pausing after each pair of words, for students to repeat, either individually or as a class. Listen carefully to their pronunciation, and keep working on any problematic sounds.

Extension activity:

Students test each other in pairs by reading one of the words from exercise 1a. Their partner has to work out which word they said (i.e. the first or second word). They swap roles after each word, and come back to any problematic words as often as necessary.

c ⊙**1.52** Tell students to read the ten sentences to predict which word(s) should receive the main stress and then to listen once or twice to check. They compare their answers in pairs before feeding back to the class.

Answers:

1 rear		6 dog
2 marshaller		7 odour
3 east		8 stomach
4 will		9 assistance
5 seagulls		10 oil

Background note:

Brake fans are used to cool the wheel brakes after landing, especially on short-haul aircraft which have a short turnaround time.

d Play the recording, pausing after each sentence, for students to repeat, either individually or as a class. Listen carefully to their pronunciation to make sure they are using stress clearly and appropriately.

Structure

2a Students work alone to complete the sentences. They check in pairs before feeding back to the class.

Answers:

1 out of		6 at
2 on		7 back
3 down		8 to
4 in		9 ahead
5 behind		10 onto

Extension activity:

Students test each other in pairs by reading one of the sentences aloud, stopping before the gapped word (e.g. *There is still some smoke coming* ...). Their partners have to complete the sentence with the correct preposition and an appropriate ending.

b Students work alone to complete the sentences. They check in pairs before feeding back to the class.

Answers:
1 heard	5 smell
2 see	6 appears
3 felt	7 don't think
4 looks	8 noticed

Extension activity:

Students test each other in pairs by reading one of the sentences aloud, stopping after the gapped word (e.g. *We heard* …). Their partners have to complete the sentence with an appropriate ending.

c Students work alone to complete the sentences. They check in pairs before feeding back to the class.

Answers:
1 a	4 a	7 b	9 c
2 b	5 c	8 b	10 a
3 c	6 a		

Vocabulary

3a **○1.53** Play the recording for students to complete the task. When they have checked in pairs, you could play the recording a second time before going through the answers with the class.

Answers:
1 tow-bar
2 visual docking guidance system
3 conveyor belt loader
4 stop bar
5 jetway
6 crew minibus
7 chocks
8 follow-me car
9 GPU
10 fire engine

b Students work alone to complete the sentences. They check in pairs before feeding back to the class.

Answers:
1 missing	5 bogged down
2 congested	6 dented
3 leaking	7 overflowing
4 delayed	8 deflated

Background note:

A *hydraulic union* is a connector or fitting which attaches one piece of hydraulic piping to another.

Extension activity:

Students test each other in pairs by reading one of the sentences aloud, substituting the word 'blank' for the gapped word. Their partners have to insert the correct word from memory.

c **○1.54** Play the recording for students to complete the task. When they have checked in pairs, you could play the recording a second time before going through the answers with the class.

Answers:
1 ground handler	5 aircraft engineer
2 passenger service agent	6 tug driver
	7 police
3 paramedic	8 flight attendant
4 dispatcher	

Background note:

If you *sprain your ankle*, you injure it by suddenly stretching or twisting it too much.

Fluency

4a **○1.55** Play the recording, pausing after each transmission for a volunteer to ask an appropriate question. Discuss the best questions with the class before moving on to the next transmission. Afterwards, students can test each other in pairs using audioscript 1.55 on page 179.

Suggested answers:
1 How long are the delays expected to be?
2 What can you see (on the taxiway)? / What is there on the taxiway?
3 Why weren't you able to contact the Tower?
4 What sort of trouble is there?
…

b Make sure students realise that there should be ten dialogues – each cue is the beginning of a separate dialogue. Students work in pairs to make dialogues. Afterwards, ask volunteers to act out their dialogues for the class. Discuss the effectiveness of students' communication with the class.

Possible answers:
Student A
1 What problems are you having with your computer? How will this affect turnaround and departure?
2 Which stand can we use?
3 Say what sort of difficulties we should expect.
4 How long will it take to clear the snow?
…
Student B
1 When will you be ready?
2 What is the matter with your cabin attendant? Have you got a replacement crew member? Confirm when you know whether she will be disembarked.
3 Do you need to return to the gate? Do you require maintenance? Can you resolve your problem?
4 Why are you unable to proceed? Say reason you are unable to proceed.
…

Background notes:

◆ An *electrical caution* is information given to the crew about an abnormal condition in the electrical system, but which is not as serious as a warning.

◆ *Industrial action* is a general name for strikes and similar events organised by workers in order to put pressure on their employers.

If you have an odd number of students you will need to have a group of three students, where the third student takes Pilot cues 1 and 2 and ATCO cues 4 and 5.

Comprehension

Before you begin:

If you have suitable facilities (e.g. a language laboratory or two teaching rooms), you may want to run exercises 5 and 6 as a jigsaw listening task, where some students listen to 1.56 and some listen to 1.57. This means that in exercise 6, they will be passing on new information to their partners.

5a **◐1.56 Go through the table with the class to elicit what type of information could go in each gap. Then play the recording for students to take notes. They compare notes in pairs before listening again and then feeding back to the class.**

> Answers:
> | | |
> |---|---|
> | 1 MD-11 | 6 yes |
> | 2 run-up area east of RWY 19L | 7 2,500 ft from Taxiway Foxtrot |
> | 3 Alpha, Bravo Echo, Foxtrot 1 | 8 in excess of 70 kts |
> | 4 B767 | 9 800 ft |
> | 5 01L | 10 Juliet |

b **◐1.57 Go through the table with the class to elicit what type of information could go in each gap. Then play the recording for students to take notes. They compare notes in pairs before listening again and then feeding back to the class.**

> Answers:
> 1 B747-400 cargo
> 2 Tokyo
> 3 21:25
> 4 14L
> 5 Chicago O'Hare
> 6 taxi Bravo and Mike, hold short Runway 09R/27L
> 7 break in transmission; readback errors, hearback error
> 8 B737
> 9 14R
> 10 1,500 ft

Interaction

6a **Students take turns to report one of the incidents from exercise 5a or 5b to a partner. When they are listening, make sure they know to ask about precursors and causal factors. Afterwards, ask volunteers to present their reports and discuss the effectiveness of the reports with the class.**

> Suggested answers:
> a A tractor was towing an aircraft from the terminal to the run-up area on the east side of Runway 19L. The tractor driver had been authorised to tow via Taxiways Alpha and Bravo, turn right onto Taxiway Echo, and to hold short of the mid-point of Runway 1 Left / 19 Right on Taxiway Foxtrot 1.
> At the same time, a B767 was cleared to line up on Runway 01 Left.
> …
> b A B747-400 cargo aircraft arrived from Tokyo and landed at 21:25 hours on Runway 14 Left at Chicago. During the landing roll, the crew was instructed by ATC to taxi via Bravo and Mike and hold short of Runway 09 Right / 27 Left to reach the south-west cargo area. The crew's readback seemed uncertain.
> …

If you have an odd number of students you will need to have a group of three students, where the third student can choose which incident to report.

b **Go through the instructions with the class. Students then work in pairs to perform the scenario. Afterwards, ask volunteers to act out the scenario for the class. Finally, discuss with the class how well they managed the situation.**

> Possible answers:
> **Pilot:** Tower, Alitalia 3845, request push-back and start-up approval for departure to Rome, Alitalia 3845.
> **ATCO:** Alitalia 3845, unable for the moment. There is approximately a 15-minute delay on all departures due traffic and Runway 18 Right closed.
> **Pilot:** Roger. Standing by your instructions.
> **ATCO:** Alitalia 3845, push-back and start-up approved.
> …

If you have an odd number of students you will need to have a group of three students, where the third student is a co-pilot, who takes half of the pilot's cues.

UNIT 5
Environmental threats

Operational topics	Types of weather phenomena; Pilot reports; METAR, ATIS, TAF; Effects of weather on flight paths; Handling environmental phenomena; Weather radar and safety strategies; Wind shear; Dealing with icing; Volcanic ash
Communication functions	Communicating weather information; Asking about the weather; Communicating orally from coded and numerical data sources; Communication errors: expectation bias; Correcting; Describing a flight path; Reading back and confirming; Clarifying and rephrasing; Saying why unable
Language content	Environmental vocabulary; Stressed syllables; Modal verbs; Interrogative expressions; Synonyms; Pronouncing word pairs and whole transmissions; Giving advice; *result in* and *prevent*; Changing conditions; Parts of speech

Unit 5 Teacher's brief

Meteorological and other environmental phenomena not related to weather (e.g. **volcanic ash**, bird strikes, wake turbulence) have immediate, fast-changing and very significant effects on flight. As a result, they are a prime example of unexpected circumstances which may require communication in plain language, not only to transmit information, but also to manage the sometimes complex effects on air traffic.

Pilots have several sources of weather and environmental information:

◆ **ATIS** (Automatic/Automated Terminal Information Service): A regularly updated, pre-recorded message providing pilots with information about the conditions at a given airport at a given time. The report is identified by a sequence of letters (Kilo, Lima, Mike, etc.). See exercise 7a.

◆ **METAR** (Meteorological Airport Reports): A METAR is a weather report from an airport or weather station often used by pilots as a print-out during the pre-flight briefing. It can be obtained for any location in the world and is usually updated hourly. See exercise 5b.

◆ **TAF** (Terminal Aerodrome Forecasts): TAFs use a similar format and coding to METARs, but provide weather forecast information (rather than current weather reports) for a five-mile radius around a given point. See exercise 5b.

◆ **PIREP** (pilot reports): Weather information from official sources is complemented by live updates from pilots about weather conditions they encounter en-route, or during approach and landing.

◆ **Live ATC inputs**: Controllers may relay weather reports orally to flight crews, especially in cases of fast-changing weather conditions, or reports sent in from other flight crews. See exercise 6a.

◆ **On-board weather radar returns**: Aircraft are fitted with weather radar systems using a radar antenna in the radome, covering a range of up to several hundred miles. Crews use the colour-coded displays provided by this system to detect the presence of weather systems (cumulonimbus clouds, thunderstorms and resulting turbulence) in order to request a change of flight path if necessary. See exercise 8a.

Weather information is transmitted in a pre-established sequence: location; time; wind velocity, i.e. direction and speed; any gusting; horizontal visibility in kilometres or metres (except in the US where miles and feet are used); cloud cover at different altitudes in feet; temperature; dew point; altimeter setting; and sometimes duration of validity. It is usually transmitted orally, but also textually using a set of international symbols, see exercise 5a.

Environmental phenomena may have the following effects on aircraft movements:

◆ the **ability to land and take off** (poor horizontal and vertical visibility), see Unit 4

◆ the **choice of the runway**(s) in use for departures and arrivals (wind velocity)

◆ challenging approaches and **hard touchdowns** (crosswinds, gusting and windshear), see exercises 1, 15, 16

◆ **change of flight path**, deviations, flying to alternates (cumulonimbus, thunderstorms), see exercises 11, 12

◆ **aquaplaning** and increased landing distances (wet, icy or snow-covered runways), see Unit 3

◆ increased aircraft weight, **impaired flight control movements** (freezing conditions), see exercises 19, 20

◆ **damage** to the windshield, radome, leading edges (hailstorms)

- structural damage and effect on electrical components (lightning)
- damage to the engines, **engine failure** (bird ingestion), see Unit 7
- damage to the engines, engine stall (volcanic ash), see exercises 22, 23
- longer flight times (headwinds)
- shorter flight times (tailwinds)

In Unit 5, we will be looking at most of these conditions, their effects on operations and how to communicate in plain language in order to manage the resulting situations.

Unit 5 Sources

- Airbus Flight Operations Briefing Notes: *Adverse Weather Operations* (Exercises 10a–d; 11a–b)
- Airbus: *Getting to grips with Cold Weather Operations* (Exercises 21a–b)
- ALPA/Boeing: *Volcanic ash hazard DVD* (Exercises 29a–34c)
- Aviation Safety Network: *Convair 580-ZK-KEU*, 3 October 2003 (ice build-up) (Exercises 21a–b)
- Boeing: *Aero*, issue 9 (volcanic ash) (Exercises 24a–b)
- http://www.flyingineurope.be/ METAR, TAF (Exercises 5a–c; 7a)
- ICAO Circular 323: *Guidelines for aviation English training programmes, 3.8.3*
- ICAO Doc. 9835: *Manual on the implementation of ICAO Language Proficiency Requirements*, 2nd edition 2010, Appendix A–14
- Lacagnina, M.: *Escape from a microburst, AeroSafety World*, April 2010 (Unit lead-in; Exercise 16)
- Qantas B744 at Sydney on Apr 15th 2007, *Microburst at 100 feet AGL* (Exercises 17a–b)
- UK CAA: *Airworthiness Communication on volcanic ash*, 23 April 2010
- http://www.ukweather.freeserve.co.uk METAR, TAF (Exercises 5a–c; 7a)
- http://weather.noaa.gov/weather/
- Withington, T.: *Clearing the air, AeroSafety World*, November 2010

Lead-in

The lead-in quotation gives a very physical and detailed description of the sensations and effects of a microburst during landing, and the way in which the crew responds. All pilots will have experienced similar situations and should have stories to tell. ATCOs, many of whom are also private pilots, will be very aware of the importance of wind phenomena especially during approach and landing. Reporting actual incidents of all sorts is something which pilots have to do in debriefing sessions, and controllers do when they report to their supervisor. In addition, many aviation language proficiency tests

include an oral reporting task. Therefore, students should be encouraged to make reports on various subjects throughout the course whether it is, like here, informally during a lead-in, or during exercise scenarios.

Quote: **Discuss with the class the meaning of environmental threats and elicit some examples. Note that examples are given in exercise 2a. Students then read the quote and the information about its source to find out what the environmental threat was, what happened, and what the outcome was.**

> Answers:
> - Environmental threats are threats (dangers) to air traffic caused by natural factors, especially the weather, other natural phenomena (e.g. volcanic eruptions) and wildlife (e.g. bird strikes). See exercise 2a for some examples of environmental threats.
> - The threats in this case were the sudden changes in wind velocity (direction and speed), which were the result of windshear and the downdraught, which characterises a microburst.
> - In the end, the plane landed with a hard landing but safely.

Background notes:

- A *microburst* is a very localised, descending wind which hits the ground and spreads out. It is extremely dangerous for landing aircraft as it causes an increase in airspeed as the aircraft enters it, followed immediately by a decrease in airspeed as the aircraft exits the microburst. They are severe cases of downdraught.
- A *downdraught* is a sudden vertical descending movement of a mass of air.

1a **Students discuss the questions in pairs and then feed back to the class.**

> Suggested answers:
> 1 final approach and touchdown
> 2 *Flare* is the final nose-up pitch movement of a landing airplane; *pitch attitude* is the angle between the aircraft's longitudinal axis and the horizontal plane; the *sink rate* is the rate of descent of a body in free fall.
> 3 See *Teacher's brief* for a list of information contained in weather reports.
> 4 See *Teacher's brief* for a list of sources of weather information.

b **Students make lists in pairs and then compare their lists with another pair before feeding back to the class. You may need to check the meaning of *precipitation* (= moisture released from the atmosphere and falling as rain, etc.) and *obscuration* (decreased visibility caused by fog, etc.).**

Suggested answers:
1 rain, snow, hail (= ice pellets), sleet (= snowy rain), drizzle (= light rain)
2 crosswind, tailwind, downdraught, microburst, headwind, gusts, windshear
3 fog, mist, smoke, sandstorm, snow, fumes, rain
4 bird strikes, volcanic ash clouds, wake turbulence, black hole phenomenon (spatial disorientation and erroneous perception of altitude caused by a dark approach area and bright lights beyond the active runway), snow blindness

Extension activity:

1 Discuss with the class the differences between similar terms, e.g. *fog* and *mist*, *sleet* and *hail*, *fumes* and *smoke*, *snow* and *slush* etc.
2 Discuss with the class which threats are minor inconveniences, which are serious causes for caution and which are serious enough to cancel flights.

Suggested answers:
Minor inconveniences: mist, rain, drizzle

Serious causes for caution: ice, wake turbulence, hail, gusting wind, bird activity, windshear

Serious enough to cancel flights: volcanic ash clouds, thunderstorms, sandstorms

Background notes:

◆ *Drizzle* is very light but constant rain.
◆ *Haze* is fine dust or vapour causing a lack of transparency in the air.
◆ *Wake turbulence* is a downdraught caused by the movement of a large aircraft through the air. For this reason, ATC usually provides additional horizontal separation after the passage of particularly large aircraft.

Environmental phenomena

Communicative and operational issues:

In the first section, students perform several communication tasks which they have to be able to perform in working situations:
◆ describing the environmental phenomena they recognise (exercises 2a, 3b)
◆ describing the effects and precautionary or avoidance measures (exercise 2b)
◆ visualising weather phenomena from oral descriptions (exercise 3a)
◆ reporting phenomena and incidents related to environmental phenomena (exercise 4)

2a **Students work alone to match the phenomena with the correct pictures. They then check in pairs before feeding back to the class.**

Answers:

a fog	b bird strike
c lightning strike	d ice build-up
e wake turbulence	f cumulonimbus
g volcanic ash	h crosswind
i rain	j standing water

Extension activity:

Students test each other in pairs by pointing to a picture to elicit the name of the threat from their partner.

b **You may need to provide some useful phrases for speculating about results (X *could/might lead to / result in / cause* Y). Encourage students to think about each flight phase in their discussions (taxiing, take-off, climb, cruise, descent, landing). Students then discuss the question in pairs and then feed back to the class.**

Suggested answers:
Many of the dangers of environmental phenomena are listed in the *Teacher's Brief*. The golden rule for dealing with bad weather is to avoid it.
◆ **Thunderstorms** can often be avoided by flying around them.
◆ **Icing conditions** in clouds may be avoided by requesting a higher flight level and flying above the clouds.
◆ **Volcanic ash** can be avoided by flying outside contaminated airspace.
◆ **Ice and snow on the ground** can be removed from the aircraft by de-icing.
◆ **Ice in flight** can be removed or prevented by the aircraft's de-icing and anti-icing systems.
◆ **Bird strikes** and bird ingestions can be made less likely by airports using audio bird scares and birds of prey to deter birds.
◆ The effects of **runways contaminated by ice and snow** can be reduced by snow removal using snow ploughs, and by pilots planning for longer landing distances.
◆ The effects of **poor visibility** can be attenuated by the use of ILS approaches and ground movement radar.
◆ **Changing or threatening wind conditions** require ATC to provide flight crews with up-to-date wind velocity reports and any pilot reports of windshear.

3a ◉ **2.01 Go through the conditions in the box to elicit what they mean. Then play the recording for students to identify the conditions. They discuss their answers in pairs, including as much as they remember about each transmission, before feeding back to the class.**

Answers:

1 gusts	5 glare
2 low ceiling	6 hail
3 windshear	7 smoke
4 drifting snow	8 drizzle

Background notes:

- *Drifting snow* is snow that has been blown by the wind to form a deep deposit.
- *Glare* is bright reflected or refracted light.
- A *gust* is a sudden rush of wind. If wind *gusts*, it blows in gusts / accelerates momentarily.
- *Hail* is precipitation in the form of compacted ice and snow.
- A *low ceiling* refers to the height of the first layer of cloud cover.
- *Windshear* is a large dangerous local wind gradient and change in wind direction characterised by a sudden downward gust causing the aircraft to lose airspeed and altitude.
- In transmission 2, *two kilometres* refers to the horizontal distance it is possible to see. *400 feet* refers to the height of the cloud cover.
- When it is *overcast (OVC)* there is *0.9+* (i.e. over 90 per cent) cloud cover.
- A *radome* is a conical protective cover over the weather radar antenna and forming the nose of the aircraft.
- A *shift* is a change of wind direction.
- *Fumes* are chemical or industrial gases.

Extension activity:

Write the following numbers and notes on the board:
1 170 / 12 / 18
2 2 / 400
3 incoming / sudden / last mile
4 NE / runway surface / markings
5 snow / sun / visibility
6 737 / damaged / descent
7 shift / approach path / fumes / SW
8 light rain / final descent

Students work in pairs to reconstruct the transmissions, word for word. Elicit the reconstructions from the class and play the recording to check. Pay particular attention to the use of tenses (e.g. present perfect continuous, transmission 3), pronunciation (e.g. downdraught, descent), *have something done* ('*had its windshield damaged*', transmission 6), etc.

Language note:

In Unit 3, the structure *have something done* was presented as a way of describing things that people arrange for others to do (e.g. *I'll have the wheels looked at*). In transmission 6, the same structure is used, in the past simple, to describe a problem that somebody suffered. Another example of this meaning would be '*I had my car stolen*'.

b Students work alone to choose the correct adjectives and then compare their answers with a partner.

Answers:
1 thick smoke	6 bright glare
2 scattered cloud	7 poor visibility
3 heavy rain	8 strong wind
4 severe turbulence	9 scattered showers
5 deep standing water	10 thick fog

Background notes:

- *Scattered (SCT) showers* or *clouds* are distributed irregularly.
- For information about pilot reports (PIREPs), see: www.weather.aero www.maps.avnwx.com
- The seriousness of weather is generally reported using the following terms: *smooth to light*; *light to moderate*; *moderate to severe*; and *extreme*.

c ◉2.02 Play the recording for students to check. Then play the recording again, pausing after each phrase for students to repeat, either individually or as a whole class.

Extension activity:

Students could test each other by reading an adjective to elicit from their partner the best noun(s), or vice versa.

4 Go through the example with the class, focusing especially on the phrase '*reporting ...*' (for pilots) and '*Be advised ...*' (for ATCOs), and on the use of present perfect in the ATCO's transmission. Students then work in pairs to prepare and deliver reports and transmissions. Afterwards, elicit example transmissions for each phenomenon from the class.

Note that the Students' Book recommends that students prepare four transmissions each, but, in fact, they could prepare all ten, or they could swap roles after four or five transmissions.

Possible answers:
Pilot: Lufthansa 3675 reporting strong gusting crosswinds during flare and touchdown on Runway 31 Left.
ATCO: Be advised that incoming flights have experienced strong gusting crosswinds near the threshold of Runway 31 Left.

Pilot: Qantas 209 reporting moderate bird activity 200 metres to the left of the far end of Runway 17 Left. I believe we may have suffered a bird strike on our wing leading edge.
ATCO: Be advised that a departing flight has observed moderate bird activity 200 metres to the left of the far end of Runway 17 Left.

Pilot: Regional 27, reporting severe ice build-up on our leading edges between 1,500 and 7,000 feet after departing from Runway 05 Right.

ATCO: All departures from Runway 05 Right, be advised of severe ice build-up between 1,500 and 7,000 feet.

Pilot: Tower, Singapore 384 reporting moderate standing water towards the mid-point of Runway 28 Left during roll-out. As a result, we missed our Bravo 2 turn-off.

ATCO: Be advised that the previous flight has reported the presence of moderate standing water near the mid-point of Runway 28 Left and that your stopping distance may be increased.

…

If you have an odd number of students you will need to have a group of three, where each student prepares three (or more) transmissions. The third student can choose whether to be a pilot or an ATCO.

Background notes:

♦ A full pilot report (PIREP) may take something like this form:

This is a Routine Upper Air (UA) PIREP. The aircraft observation was 20 nautical miles west of the Buffalo-Niagara (BUF) VOR/DME (270 due west 020 miles) at 23:20 UTC. The aircraft was at 6,000 feet (FL 060) and is a Boeing 737 (TP B737). The clouds were broken at 2,000 feet AMSL with tops at 4,000 feet and an overcast layer at 11,000 feet AMSL. The temperature is –14 Celsius and the winds are from the NE at 45 knots. (030 @45) There is moderate clear air turbulence (MDT CAT) between 6,000 feet and 8,000 feet. There is light rime icing between 2,000 feet and 4,000 feet. (This would indicate that the icing is picked up in the cloud.) The remarks section says that light freezing rain was encountered in the cloud. (RM LGT FZRA)

In coded form this would be transmitted as follows:

UA / OV BUF 270020 / TM 2320 / FL 060 / TP B737 / SK 020BKN040 1100VC / TA –14 / WV 030045 / TB MDT CAT 060-080 / IC LGT RIME 020-040 / RM LGT FZRA INC

♦ *rime icing* is the most common form of icing. Rime ice forms when small supercooled drops of water freeze on contact with a sub-zero surface. The ice deposit is rough and crystalline. Rime ice forms on the leading edges and can affect aerodynamic characteristics of wings and engine air intakes; it also considerably increases the weight of the aircraft.

Communicating weather information: METAR, TAF and ATIS

Communicative and operational issues:

In exercises 5 and 6, students have practice interpreting international weather abbreviations, listening to METAR, TAF and ATIS reports, giving weather reports and asking and answering questions about changes in the weather.

While the weather abbreviations are only used in print-outs, pilots and controllers need to be able to say the corresponding conditions in full in order to communicate them. Most of the abbreviations or contractions are quite easy to understand, but some are derived from French, from a time before World War II when, with Clément Ader, Santos Dumont, Blériot, Guynemer, Mermoz, Saint Exupéry and the Aéropostale, France was the cradle of aviation and French was its predominant language. A fuller list of abbreviations can be found at: http://www.dixwx. com/abbreviations.htm. And a more exhaustive treatment of METARs and TAFs at:
http://en.allmetsat.com
http://skylinkweather.com
http://stoivane.iki.fi/metar/
http://www.nws.noaa.gov
http://www.ukweather.freeserve.co.uk

5a **Elicit the difference between METAR and TAF reports (see *Teacher's brief*). Students work alone to match the abbreviations with the words and then check in pairs. Go through the answers with the class, making sure all students fully understand the 18 terms.**

Answers:			
1 RA	rain	10 VA	volcanic ash
2 DU	dust	11 TS	thunderstorm
3 DZ	drizzle	12 FU	smoke
4 SN	snow	13 SCT	scattered
5 HZ	haze	14 BCFG	fog patches
6 BR	mist	15 DRSN	drifting snow
7 GR	hail	16 FZRA	freezing rain
8 SQ	squall	17 RASH	rain showers
9 IC	ice	18 MIBR	shallow mist

Background notes:

♦ A *squall* is a sudden, violent wind often with rain.
♦ *Shallow mist* is a thin layer of mist near the ground, above which the aircraft climbs quickly.
♦ The order in which some information is given may vary slightly, e.g. in the US they may say '2,500 feet overcast', whereas in the rest of the world 'Overcast 2,500 feet' is more usual.

Extension activity:

Students test each other in pairs by saying a symbol to elicit the correct word, or vice versa.

b ○2.03 Before the students listen, go through the reports with the class to discuss what the symbols mean (see *Background notes* below) and what type of information is missing. With experienced pilots and ATCOs, this will be fairly easy, but inexperienced pilots and ATCOs will struggle and need plenty of support. Then play the recording for students to complete the reports. Students check in pairs and then listen again to check. Finally, go through the answers with the class, and deal with any problems with understanding.

Answers:
1
METAR KBUF (Buffalo Niagara International) 12**1755Z** AUTO **21016G24KT 180**V240 1SM **R11**/P6000ft – **RA** BR BKN**015** OVC025 **06**/04 A**2990**
2
METAR EPKK (Krakow) 06**1800Z** 1206**KT** 1400 **R12**/P**1500**N +SN BKN017 M04/**M07** Q**1020** NOSIG
3
TAF SBRF (**Recife**) 070801Z 210**12**KT 9999 BKN010 – RA BKN**008** TEMPO 0712/0718 **SCT**015=

Background notes:

	Report 1	Report 2	Report 3	Notes
Type of report	METAR	METAR	TAF	
Airport code	KBUF	EPKK	SBRF	
Date	12	06	07	
Time	17:55Z	18:00Z	08:01Z	Z = *zulu, GMT/UTC*
Wind direction	AUTO 210	120	210	AUTO = *information provided automatically*
Wind speed	16G24KT	6KT	12KT	G = *gusting*
				KT = *knots*
Direction of gusts	180V240			V = *varying between … and …*
Visibility	1SM	1400	9999	1 SM = *1 statute mile* (see page 94)
				9999 means *effectively unlimited visibility* (see page 94)
RVR information for specific runways	R11/ P6000ft	R12/ P1500N		RVR = *runway visual range* R = *runway number* P = *in excess of* (see below) ft = *feet* N = *to the north*
Ground-level weather	– RA BR	+ SN		– = *light* + = *heavy*
Level of lowest clouds	BKN015	BKN017	BKN010	BKN = *broken* (see page 94) (numbers in hundreds of feet)
Weather at higher level	OVC025		–RA BKN008	OVC = *overcast*, i.e. complete cloud cover
Time of weather condition			TEMPO 0712/0718	TEMPO = *temporary* 0712 = *12:00 UTC on 7th*
Weather at higher level			SCT015=	SCT = *scattered clouds* The equals sign (=) shows that this is the end of the message.
Temperature and dew point	06/04	M04/M07		M = *minus*
Pressure	A2990	Q1020		A = *altimeter* Q = *QNH*
Change		NOSIG		NOSIG = *no significant change*

Background notes:

Weather reports follow the same sequence, as explained in the *Teacher's brief*. The first METAR comes from Buffalo airport in the north-eastern United States. Visibility is given in statute miles and feet rather than kilometres and metres and the altimeter setting (29.90) is given in inches of mercury rather than hectoPascal (1012 hPa). The second METAR is from Krakow, Poland and the TAF is from Recife, Brazil.

The three reports from exercise 5b are explained, step by step, in the table.

- *broken (BKN)* = cloud cover of between 0.5 and 0.9 (i.e. 50 per cent and 90 per cent) of the sky
- *clear (CLR)* = no cloud cover
- *9999* = horizontal visibility of more than ten kilometres
- *P* = greater than highest reportable sensor
- *scattered (SCT)* = intermittent or irregular cloud cover or precipitation
- *statute mile (SM)* = 1,609.34 metres, land mile as opposed to nautical mile (1,853.18 metres)
- *VV* = vertical visibility, indefinite ceiling
- The IATA and ICAO airport codes are:
  Bordeaux, France: BOD - LFBD
  Karachi, Jinnah International Airport, Pakistan: KHI - OPKC
  Seoul, Incheon International Airport, South Korea: ICN - RKSI
  Fujairah, United Arab Emirates: FJR - OMFJ
  Maastricht, Holland: MST - EHBK
  Dubai, United Arab Emirates: DXB - EGLC
  London City, UK: LCY - EGLC
- Report 6 includes the term *becoming*. This is shown in weather reports as *BECMG*.
- In report 7, '*probability 30 per cent*' is written as *PROB30*.

c **2.04** Tell students to listen first to take notes. If they are not familiar with such reports, it might be useful to use a table format (as above) for students to organise their notes. You could write the seven airport codes (see below) on the board to help them. Make sure they realise that there are eight reports, so they will need to listen and concentrate for a long time. Afterwards, students compare their notes in pairs to identify any discrepancies. They then listen again to check their notes. When they are confident that their notes are accurate, they take turns to make weather reports, using their notes. Finally, ask a volunteer to deliver each report, which you can check using audioscript 2.04 on page 180.

Extension activity:

Elicit from the class a written form of each report from exercise 5c, and write it up on the board. You could do this before students have to make their spoken reports. The objective of this exercise is not technical accuracy; any combination of coded and plain language would be quite acceptable.

Answers:
1 METAR LFBD 070850Z 21012KT 9999 BKN023 20/14 Q1017=
2 METAR OPKC 081225Z 18006KTS 8000 SCT030 SCT100 34/24 Q1002 TEMPO NE 30KTS TSRA FEW025CB=
3 METAR RKSI 071200Z 20011KT 9999 BKN037 17/13 Q1022=
4 METAR OMFJ 081200Z 10009KT 040V130 6000 FEW025 34/25 Q1001 A2955=
5 METAR EHBK 071350Z 21008KT 160V250 9999 BKN008 17/14 Q1019=
6 TAF OMDB 081056Z 0812/0918 34012KT 8000 NSC BECMG 0815/0817 10007KT BECMG 0908/0910 35012KT BECMG 0915/0917 11008KT=
7 TAF EGLC 070800Z EGPA 070805Z 0709/0718 18010KT 9999 FEW030 BECMG 0709/0712 19020G32KT PROB30 TEMPO 0712/0718 8000 SHRA

6a **Students work alone to prepare their weather forecasts. Make sure they realise to use plain English. Note that in plain English, it is usual to use *will*, not *going to*, to make predictions in weather forecasts.**

b **Students read their reports for their partners to make notes and ask for clarification. Again, remind them to use plain English.**

Extension activity:

Students use the notes they made in exercise 6b to give a METAR or TAF-style weather report to their partners.

7a **2.05** Go through the tables with the class, eliciting the type of information missing from each box. Then play the recording for students to complete the tables. They check their notes with a partner and listen again to check, if necessary. Finally, go through the answers with the class.

Answers:
ATIS 1

Airport	NZCH Christchurch	Visibility	5,000 m
Information	G	Cloud	SCT 3,000 ft BKN 11,000 ft

Time	2200Z	Temperature	12°
Departure RWY	20	Dew point	10°
Wind velocity	110° / 20 kts	QNH	1001 hPa

ATIS 2

Airport	Prague	Visibility	10 km or more
Information	L	Precipitation	light rain showers
Time	10:59	Ceiling	Few 500 ft; few CB 1,500 ft; BKN 4,000 ft
ILS RWY	24	Temperature	15°
RWY condition	wet	Dew point	14°
Transition level	50	QNH	1019 hPa
Runways closed	13/31	Special instructions	NOSIG
Wind velocity	340°/ 14 kts		

Background notes:

◆ The first ATIS comes from Christchurch in the South Island of New Zealand. It contains just the basic weather information. The second is from Prague in the Czech Republic; in addition to the weather information, it also provides information about the state of the runways, the transition level and precipitation.

◆ The *transition level* is the flight level at which flight crews reset their altimeters from local atmospheric pressure (QNH or QFE) to standard atmospheric pressure at sea level (1013 hPa). Below this point *altitude* rather than *level* is used by pilots and controllers.

◆ *Few* = 0.25 or less of the sky covered by clouds.

b **Discuss the questions with the class.**

Suggested answers:
◆ The order in which information is given is generally that used in the examples, but regional variations exist. The first example contains the essential mandatory transmission and weather information: location; information identification (India, Juliet, Kilo ...); Zulu time (UTC); runway; wind velocity; visibility; ceilings; temperature; dew point and altimeter setting.

◆ Additional information may be given in case of rapidly changing or hazardous weather conditions, or modifications to the runways etc.

◆ The information in the ATIS is absolutely critical for flight, especially for take-off and landing. It determines the runway(s) in use, any special precautions (de-icing, aircraft anti-icing, runway length required), the conditions of climb-out, IFR (instrument) or VFR (visual) flight and expectations about the way the aircraft will respond.

c **Students work in pairs to give their ATIS reports and to make notes. Point out that there is a table in the Pairwork section for them to take notes in.**

If you have an odd number of students you will need to have one group of three, where Student C listens and takes notes from both reports. Student C then reads back both reports in exercise d below.

d **Students use their notes to repeat the weather reports, while their partners check.**

Language focus: Changing conditions

Tell students to close their books. Ask questions to elicit the information from the *Language focus* box (e.g. *How can we describe positive/negative changes in wind strength/direction?*, etc.). Write the elicited phrases on the board. Then allow students to check in their books to see if they have missed any phrases (or found some that are not in the book). Draw attention to the form of present continuous to describe changes. You may need to check the spelling and pronunciation of *strengthening* /'streŋθənɪŋ/ and *deteriorating* /dɪ'tɪərɪəreɪtɪŋ/.

Extension activity:

Students test each other in pairs by reading the beginning of a sentence from the *Language focus* box (e.g. *The wind is …*) to elicit a suitable ending from their partner, whose book is closed. They could use body language (e.g. pointing upwards or downwards) to encourage their partner to use a positive or negative word to complete the sentence.

8 **This pairwork exercise develops the students' ability to talk about changing weather conditions using the appropriate language seen in the *Language focus* box, and to use the present continuous in a naturally suitable context. It also develops the students' ability to produce language from a combination of oral and symbolic inputs, which is something they have to do frequently in their operational environment where they respond to oral questions while referring to information on their displays. Go through the examples with the class to draw attention to the types of questions and responses. Students then work in**

pairs to ask and answer about changing weather conditions. Afterwards, ask volunteers to act out their dialogues for the class.

If you have an odd number of students you will need to have one group of three, where Student C takes the first two reports from Student A and the last report from Student B.

Communication errors: Expectation bias

Communicative and operational issues:

Expectation bias, which is the subject of this section, is, of course, not restricted to environmental issues, but changes in flight plan or the times at which clearances are given may well be affected by the state of the weather. In commercial aviation, where there is a lot of routine and procedures indeed constitute safety measures, pilots and controllers may sometimes understand not what they hear, but what they expect to hear. When routings, changes of level, runways and taxiways, radials and altitudes are always the same or always given at the same time or in the same conditions, it may happen that a change in information may be overlooked. In such a case, readback is the immediate safety net.

ICAO FOCUS

Elicit from the class what is meant by expectation bias [**Answer:** see *Communicative and operational issues* above]. Students then read the quote to identify the two pieces of information that are confused in the example. Students discuss the two questions in pairs and then feed back to the class.

Possible answers:
- In the example a heading of 280° is confused with Flight Level 280.
- Information which may be confused in transmissions includes: active runways (28R/ 28L); FL 100 / FL 110 (one zero zero / one one zero); a clearance and information to expect (climb to Flight Level 260 / expect Flight Level 260 at 35); navaid identifiers (ALD/ADL); call signs (Fedex 2835 / Fedex 2385); 5 and 9 if not said correctly as *fife* and *niner*; squawk transponder identifiers (3645/3465); *taxi into position and hold / taxi to holding position*; altimeter settings (1003 hPa / 1013 hPa) etc.

9 This exercise is especially designed to improve students' skill in recognising discrepancies between an instruction and its readback and being able to correct the misunderstanding fluently. Go through the example with the class, drawing attention to the mistake that the pilot makes. Point out that each

student has input cues and readback cues. Students then work in pairs to make dialogues. Afterwards, ask volunteers to act out their dialogues for the class.

Suggested answers:
Student A initiating

1
ATCO: White Eagle 268, expect joining clearance at time 55. Time is 45.
Pilot: Expect joining clearance time 45, White Eagle 268.
ATCO: White Eagle 268, negative. Expect joining clearance at time 55.

2
ATCO: Gulf Air 395, recent rain showers, standing water at midpoint Runway 34 Left, braking action medium.
Pilot: Heavy rain, braking action poor (on) Runway 34 Left, Gulfair 395.
ATCO: Gulfair 395, negative. I say again standing water at midpoint of Runway 34 Left. Braking action medium.

3
ATCO: Broken 2,500 feet; overcast 5,000 feet; temperature minus four degrees; dew point minus six degrees, QNH 979 hectoPascal.
Pilot: Broken 2,500 feet; overcast 5,000 feet; temperature minus four degrees; dew point minus six; QNH 997 hectoPascal.
ATCO: Negative. I say again, QNH 979 hectoPascal.

...

Student B initiating

1
ATCO: Lufthansa 3165, caution: there is a thunderstorm 200 miles ahead of you and ten miles to the south-east of your projected flight path, moving north-west.
Pilot: Roger. Confirm thunderstorm 200 miles ahead and ten miles north-west of our flight path.
ATCO: Negative. The thunderstorm is ten miles south-east of your projected flight path and moving north-west.

2
ATCO: Aeroflot 3587, climb and maintain FL 190.
Pilot: Maintaining heading 190, Aeroflot 3587.
ATCO: Aeroflot 3587, negative. I say again, climb and maintain Flight Level 190.

3
ATCO: Kyrmal 591, maintain FL 310, expect descent after Minsk.
Pilot: Maintaining Flight Level 310, expect descent after Minsk, Kyrmal 391.
ATCO: Kyrmal 391, negative. That transmission was not intended for you.

...

If you have an odd number of students you will need to have a group of three students, where Student C takes the first two input and readback cues from Student A and the last two from Student B.

Background notes:

- *Controlled airspace* is airspace of defined dimensions within which ATC service is provided.
- *Delaying action* involves holding or orbiting to slow down the progress of a flight.
- *Joining clearance* is authorisation to join a circuit prior to approach and landing.
- In *IFR* (Instrument Flight Rules), *straight-in* means an instrument approach in which the final approach is begun without a prior procedure turn. In *VFR* (Visual Flight Rules), *straight-in* means the entry of a traffic pattern by interception of extended runway centreline without executing any portion of a traffic pattern.

Extension activity:

Discuss with the class what can be done to minimise the risk of expectation bias.

Suggested answer: The simplest technique is simply to be aware that it exists and that it can be extremely dangerous. Pilots and ATCOs should be constantly alert not only for instances when they themselves fall into this trap, but also for their colleagues and the people they are communicating with. As mentioned above, readback and hearback are the most important safety nets. Applying good crew resource management by discussing decisions, verbalising actions, crosschecking different sources of data, using common sense, breaking out of tunnel vision, are also effective barriers against expectation bias.

The effect of the weather on a flight path

Communicative and operational issues:

This section explores changes to the projected flight path due to encountering a weather system first through using two Airbus weather radar displays and then listening to an authentic example of a flight in the vicinity of a thunderstorm in Florida.

The Airbus example is taken from the Airbus Flight Operations Briefing Notes (FOBN) on Adverse Weather Operations. These FOBNs are an invaluable source of genuine professional expertise in an accessible form.

Quote: **Students read the text to identify what the numbers 40, 160 and 80 refer to. [Answers: The flight crew needs to make decisions while 40 nm away from a storm; the pilot non-flying range is 160 nm and below; the pilot flying range is 80 nm and below]. You may need to check the meaning and pronunciation of *adverse* /ædˈvɜːs/ (= likely to cause problems).**

10 a, b, c, d **Students discuss the four questions in pairs and then feed back to the class.**

Suggested answers:
- Given the speed at which the aircraft moves, it is necessary to take any avoiding action while 40 nautical miles (nm) away from a thunderstorm. This is why the weather radar is especially useful in IMC (Instrument Meteorological Conditions) or at night. The two pilots will have their displays set at different ranges covering a 90° arc, for instance, in this example, 40 and 80 nm ahead of the aircraft. This enables the crew to have advanced warning of a storm and see what change of heading they need to make to avoid it effectively, while having a more detailed view on the shorter range display.
- The airborne weather radar usually displayed on each pilot's Navigation Display uses Doppler technology to give information about cloud formation, not the presence of other aircraft. On most controllers' radar screens, weather returns are suppressed in favour of the identification and position of aircraft under their control.
- En-route or arriving traffic taking avoidance measures will result in a concentration of flights and increase ATC workload by requiring additional communication, unexpected flow management, possible conflict resolution and possible deviations to alternates.
- In cruise, weather avoidance is usually fairly simple and localised: a temporary change of heading and then return on course after circumventing the obstacle; a possible climbing to a higher flight level to avoid icing conditions or turbulence. During approach, more traffic is concentrated in a smaller airspace. Thunderstorms in the vicinity of the airport may make approaches to the glide path more complicated and cause holding traffic to build up, generating further delays. Very bad weather (storms, poor visibility) at the airport itself may make it impossible for some flights to land if conditions are below their minima in terms of decision height, visibility or CAT III capability. This in turn will mean that flights have to be re-routed to alternate airports.

Background notes:

- The *range* is the distance that can be covered by an aircraft without refuelling, or the distance that can be covered by a radar / radio / navigation aid signal or an instrument.

♦ The terms *pilot flying* (*PF*) and *pilot non-flying* (*PNF*) are used to designate the pilot who is actually doing the hands-on flying of the aircraft at a given moment and the pilot who is monitoring the PF, entering data, communicating with ATC etc. Captain and First Officer take these roles in turn.

♦ *Avoidance* is the action of distancing oneself from an obstacle, danger etc.

♦ *Doppler technology* is used in radar and consists in reflecting beams off objects, in this case cloud formations, to sense their density and velocity. Pulse Dopplers are used to detect precipitation particles, e.g. rain, ice, hail.

11a **Students discuss the four questions in pairs and feed back to the class.**

> Answer:
> The two screens show simultaneous views of the same area ahead of the aircraft but with different ranges. On the more detailed, shorter range left-hand display, one has the impression that it is possible to avoid the two storm formations by flying a heading of 343° between them. The longer range right-hand display shows that after flying between the two cloud formations at just under 40 nm, one will encounter a much larger one straight ahead, 60 nm from the aircraft's present position. In other words, a heading of 315° is a better avoidance manoeuvre.

b **Discuss the question with the class.**

> Answer:
> Green indicates weather of moderate intensity; yellow of heavy intensity and red of extreme intensity. Some displays have gradations of colour such as light green, dark green, pale yellow, dark yellow, orange and red and allow the identification of different types of weather.

12a **Students role play the situation in pairs.**

If you have an odd number of students you will need to have one group of three students, where there are two PNFs (pilots non-flying).

b **In the same pairs, students plan what they will say to ATC. Then ask volunteers from several groups to act out their communications. Then discuss and agree on the best course of action as a class.**

> Suggested answers:
> Basically, they need to obtain authorisation to enter a new course and follow a different heading from their next waypoint in just under 20 nm from their present position (small yellow aircraft symbol), by flying a heading of 315° or 294° instead of 343°.

13a ⊙**2.06 In this recording, while flying south off the Florida coast to land at Daytona International Airport, a Comair commuter flight (Comair 580) is unable to pursue its approach by turning west towards the airport because a tornado centred near the airport causes a power cut which makes all the controllers' equipment momentarily unserviceable. The flight crew pursue their flight south before turning north to make a new approach.**

Tell students to read the report to get a general idea of what happened and to start thinking about the order of events. They discuss their ideas in pairs. Then play the recording for them to put the events in order and write the correct times. Allow them to discuss their answers in pairs before listening again to check if necessary. Finally, go through the answers with the class.

> Answers:
> | | | | |
> |---|---|---|---|
> | 1 e | 3 a | 5 c | 7 b |
> | 2 g | 4 h | 6 f | 8 d |

Background notes:

♦ If an aircraft is *nearing* something, it is approaching it.

♦ A *landing sequence* is the series of manoeuvres (outbound track, base turn, inbound track) prior to landing.

b **Volunteers re-tell the story to the class.**

Extension activity:

Use the following questions to generate a class discussion based on the story, eliciting students' own similar experiences where possible. Note that the discussion here is more important than the correct answers.

♦ Why do you think the airport lost power? [**Possible answer:** There was a severe storm, which may have brought down power lines, caused overvoltages or caused short circuits.]

♦ Is this a common problem? [**Possible answer:** It is fairly rare.]

♦ What can be done to avoid such situations? [**Possible answer:** ATC needs to have contingency plans, i.e. use of a back-up generator.]

♦ How long was the plane out of contact with the airport? [**Answer:** Around three minutes.]

♦ What should a pilot do if he loses contact with the airport? [**Possible answer:** Climb to the Minimum Safe Altitude, perform a circuit and attempt to contact ATC on the previous frequency used.]

♦ Do you think the tornado was a complete surprise? [**Possible answer:** In this case, it seems to have been unexpected, as planes were still arriving just before the tornado struck.]

- Is it possible to predict where a tornado will hit? [**Possible answer:** Not precisely, but it is possible to make judgements based on worsening weather conditions. In this case there seems to have been a failure to interpret the weather conditions properly, although it should be remembered that the airport had no power at the critical time.]
- Did anyone make mistakes on the day of the event? [**Possible answer:** Possibly the weather forecasters and planners, who failed to predict the tornado, but the exact location of a tornado is almost impossible to predict.]
- What should have been done to avoid such situations? [**Possible answers:** There should have been a back-up electricity supply to prevent such power cuts. There should have been a more effective weather forecasting system.]

14a ◉ **2.07 Go through the example with the class. Then play the recording, pausing after each transmission for volunteers to confirm or read back. Discuss the most suitable responses with the class. Afterwards, students can test each other in pairs using audioscript 2.07 on page 180.**

> Suggested answers:
> 1 Freezing rain is expected at destination.
> 2 Strong windshear on approach.
> 3 Current ceiling is 3,000 feet.
> 4 Solid cloud from 1,000 to 6,000 feet.
> 5 Moderate to severe icing in clouds.
> 6 Gusty winds reported on (the) approach path.
> 7 Wind 150 degrees, 18 knots, gusting to 23 knots.
> 8 Thunderstorms (in the) vicinity (of) Kuala Lumpur.
> 9 50-mile volcanic cloud moving south west from Iceland.
> 10 Snow flurries at destination.

Background notes:

- The *ceiling* is the bottom of the lowest level of clouds.
- *Snow flurries* are sudden rapid falls of snow.

b ◉ **2.07 Go through the examples with the class. Then play the recording, pausing after each transmission for volunteers to suggest a course of action or give an instruction. Make sure they know to use a modal verb in their responses. Elicit a range of possible responses from the class and then discuss and decide on the most suitable responses. Afterwards, students can test each other in pairs using audioscript 2.07 on page 180.**

Suggested answers:

1
Pilot: We must set the probe heat, window heat and wing and nacelle anti-icing on. We should prepare for a longer landing distance.
ATCO: Up-to-date advisories should be transmitted as required. The longer runway must be used.

2
Pilot: We should be ready to go around. You must call out airspeed during approach. We should ask ATC for the latest update.
ATCO: We must be prepared for flights to go around. You must monitor the incoming flights carefully.

3
Pilot: You should ask ATC if the vertical visibility is increasing or decreasing. We may have to go around if we are below minima / if the ceiling drops below our minima.
ATCO: You must advise incoming flights if the ceiling decreases any more.

4
Pilot: We will need wing ant-icing during climb-out. We must climb out of the cloud as soon as possible. There may be some turbulence during the initial climb / first segment. We will be in IMC.
ATCO: You should advise flight crews of icing conditions. All flights will be in IMC.

5 (See 4, above)

6
Pilot: We may experience some turbulence during our approach. We will decrab just before touch-down.
ATCO: We must update incoming flights on any changes to wind velocity.

...

Background notes:

- In the first example, the phrasal verb *set ... on* means *turn ... on.*
- The *probe heat* is the electrical anti-icing of the air data probes (pitot probe, static ports, angle of attack sensors, outside air temperature probes) which are located on the outside of the forward fuselage. The failure of the probe heat system on the A330 is suspected as being a contributory factor to the loss of Air France Flight 447 over the South Atlantic in June 2009. If the probes become obstructed with ice, the flight crew can lose all altitude, airspeed and angle of attack information and the computers which receive this information will generate erroneous outputs.

◆ *Minima* (answer 3 above) are the lower limits of visibility for a given aircraft depending on its onboard equipment.

◆ If a pilot *decrabs* (answer 6 above), he/she aligns the aircraft with the runway centreline just prior to touchdown in crosswind conditions. *Crabbing* refers to flying with drift due to crosswind.

15 **Go through the example with the class. Students then work in pairs to ask and answer questions. Note that they should swap roles when they have finished. Afterwards, ask volunteers to act out their dialogues for the class, and discuss the best ways of phrasing the responses.**

If you have an odd number of students you will need to have a group of three, where Student C answers questions 1 to 3 from Student A and questions 8 to 10 from Student B.

Suggested answers:
To Student A questions
1 We are still in icing conditions at 8,000 feet. / We left icing conditions at 11,000 feet.
2 We have some moderate weather activity showing 70 miles ahead and ten miles to the right of our flight path.
3 Affirm, but there is a CB formation maybe some 20 miles to the south-west.
4 We experienced some moderate clear air turbulence over Irkutsk.
5 We are at Flight Level 290 with a 45-knot tail wind and occasional mild turbulence.
6 Temperatures were negative from 1,200 feet.
...

To Student B questions
1 At 9,000 feet we are still in IMC with severe ice build-up despite our anti-icing being on High.
2 We experienced moderate wake turbulence at 1,600 feet as we turned right off the extended runway centreline.
3 Our flight conditions are smooth/bumpy.
4 Affirm. Snow has accumulated on our wings.
5 Our weather radar is not displaying any weather activity after HMG 20 miles ahead.
6 It is severe with a very high frequency. It is making the instruments quite difficult to read.
...

Background notes:

◆ *Extend* has two meanings. If a pilot *extends* flaps, slats or landing gear, he deploys them or moves them down. If clouds *extend* over a given area or height, they cover it.

◆ If clouds have *smooth tops*, it means there are no sudden variations, movements or irregularities.

◆ *CB* or *cumulonimbus* is a type of cloud which is high, dense and generates storm activity; it is the type of cloud that represents the greatest threat for aviation and which crews try to avoid.

◆ The *freezing level* is the altitude at which the temperature in the atmosphere drops to 0° Celsius.

◆ A *build-up* is an accumulation.

◆ *Wake turbulence* is a severe disturbance of the air caused by the passage of an aircraft through a mass of air. The wake turbulence caused by a B747 or A380 can upset a smaller aircraft. Consequently, ATC creates about three minutes' separation between aircraft on the same trajectory during climb when aircraft are using full thrust.

◆ *Ride* is jargon for flight.

◆ *Buffeting* refers to the effects of being knocked around by turbulence or the rapid oscillation of flight control surfaces.

◆ A *weather return* is the coloured patterns or outlines which are shown on the weather radar display.

◆ *Overhead* can be used as a preposition (*overhead the field*), meaning *immediately above*.

Windshear

Communicative and operational issues:

Windshear (a large dangerous local wind gradient and change in wind direction characterised by a sudden downward gust causing the aircraft to lose airspeed and altitude) represents a considerable hazard for aircraft during final approach and touchdown as there can be dramatic variations in wind speed which can thrust the aircraft violently downwards. To mitigate this danger, ATC must provide incoming aircraft with up-to-date information about any changes in the reported weather conditions.

Quote: **Elicit from the class what *overshoot windshear* is and what causes it. They then read the quote to check their answers.**

Background notes:

◆ *Overshoot windshear* is characterised by an increase in aircraft airspeed. It contrasts with *undershoot windshear*, characterised by a decrease in aircraft airspeed.

◆ A *head wind* is a wind blowing in a direction opposite to the direction of travel of the aircraft, while a *tail wind* is blowing in the same direction as the direction of travel of the aircraft.

◆ *Indicated airspeed* (*IAS*) is the relative velocity between the aircraft and the surrounding air.

16 Students discuss the questions in pairs and then feed back to the class.

> **Suggested answers:**
> Windshear is particularly dangerous during final approach and touchdown because the effect on the aircraft's airspeed, rate of descent and vertical movement can be so sudden and unexpected at a phase of flight when the aircraft is using reduced engine power, it is close to the ground and its flight control surfaces have less effect. Windshear can result in the aircraft suddenly: losing height and airspeed, and so touching down short of the runway, or making a hard landing; gaining height and airspeed and touching down late on the runway; or being blown away from its flight path on the runway centreline. Given the aircraft's built-in inertia and the response time of the engines and flight controls, the pilot's remedial action may not prevent the aircraft from touching down even if he/she wishes to go around.
>
> The controller's main contribution at this phase of flight is to provide the pilots with the most up-to-date weather information, including reports sent in by pilots who have just landed.

17a **⊙2.08** The story in this exercise highlights the importance of up-to-date weather information in windy and windshear conditions. The crew did not receive the latest ATIS, and so was less prepared for conditions near the ground. Seeing the conditions, the crew disconnected the autopilot to have direct control of the flight controls. The rapid changes in wind velocity during the last couple of minutes before landing demonstrate how unpredictable conditions can be. The aircraft's airspeed increased to 159 knots then decreased to 131 knots, which was 13 knots below the aircraft's reference speed. This caused a rapid descent (sink rate) over the last few feet with 2.34g. In theory, aircraft should touch down at 1g.

Go through the table with the class to check what sort of information is needed for each gap. Then play the recording for students to complete the table individually. They check their answers with a partner and then listen again to check if necessary.

> **Answers:**
>
> | | |
> |---|---|
> | 1 B747-400 | 10 20 kts tailwind |
> | 2 Singapore | 11 continuous wind |
> | 3 Sydney | data call-outs |
> | 4 030°; 17 kts | 12 15 kts headwind |
> | 5 18 nm SW of airport | 13 right crosswind |
> | 6 different frequency | 14 131 kts |
> | 7 3 nm from runway | 15 820 ft/min |
> | 8 16R | 16 go around |
> | 9 180°; 22 kts | |

Background notes:

♦ *CAS* stands for *calibrated airspeed*, i.e. the indicated airspeed corrected for airspeed indicator errors.

♦ The *pilot-in-command* is the pilot flying (PF), i.e. the pilot in control of the aircraft.

♦ An *approach control frequency* is the frequency used by the Approach controllers at a given airport, as distinct from the Tower or Ground frequencies.

♦ A *reference speed* (*Vref*) is the speed at which the aircraft should be flying in a given configuration.

♦ *Surface wind* is measured near ground level.

♦ A *readout* is data which is displayed or played audibly.

♦ *Autopilot* (*AP*) is an airborne electronic system which automatically stabilises the aircraft about its three axes.

♦ *Autothrottle* is an automatic engine power control system.

♦ A *call-out* is spoken data read out by a member of the flight crew.

♦ If you *advance* a thrust/throttle lever, you move it forward to increase engine thrust.

♦ Note that the pilot decided to *go around* after touching down. In other words, the aircraft took off again immediately because it was not properly controlled.

b Students work in pairs or small groups to ask and answer questions about the information they noted down. Note that the aim here is to practise question forms as well as to discuss the events in the story.

> **Suggested answers:**
> 1 What type of aircraft was involved in this incident?
> 2 Where was the aircraft flying from?
> 3 Where was the aircraft flying to?
> 4 What were the wind conditions like at 18:30?
> 5 Where exactly was the thunderstorm?
> …

c Students write their crew briefings or reports as homework.

> **Suggested answer:**
> A Qantas B747-400 was enroute from Singapore to Sydney. Just before descent, the crew requested the latest weather report. The METAR reported fairly strong winds (17 knots) and thunderstorms moving towards the airport. The aircraft was on an approach frequency and did not receive the windshear warnings on the latest ATIS. Three miles from touchdown on Runway 16 Right, the crew learnt of a change in wind velocity. At 1,000 feet, the crew were experiencing a tailwind. The crew disconnected the autopilot and autothrottle. At 500 feet, the wind changed to a crosswind. At 120 feet, the airspeed increased from 146 to 159 knots, then decreased to 131 knots on touchdown; the reference touchdown speed was 144 knots. The aircraft made a very hard landing, but the pilot flying decided to go around in compliance with company standard operating procedures.

Language focus: The same word used differently

Tell students to close their books. Write the following words on the board:

control   go around   call out   clear

Elicit from the class two meanings of each word, with examples. Elicit also, the rules about hyphenation of go-around and call-out. Then tell students to check in their books.

18a ○2.09 Go through the ten pairs of words first to make sure students know which word is a noun (i.e. the first in each pair) and which is a verb (i.e. the second in each pair). Then play the recording for students to mark the correct word. They check in pairs and listen again to check if necessary. Then go through the answers with the class. Elicit what happens to the stress pattern of phrasal verbs when they are turned into verbs and as nouns/adjectives (See *Language note* below).

> **Answers:**
> | 1 b | 3 b | 5 b | 7 b |
> | 2 b | 4 a | 6 a | 8 a |

Language note:

Phrasal verbs are usually stressed on the second word (e.g. *Can you read it OUT?*). When they are transformed into nouns or adjectives, the stress moves to the first word (e.g. *They have requested a READout*).

Background notes:

◆ *Rollout* is an aircraft's ground roll after landing, i.e. its movement along the runway after touchdown while it is decelerating.

◆ *V1* refers to the decision speed, i.e. the speed at which the pilot must decide to continue or abandon take-off.

◆ A *synthetic voice* is an automatic recording triggered in certain configurations, especially during approach and landing, e.g. '*pull up, pull up*'.

◆ *Go-around thrust* is take-off/go-around thrust (TOGA on Airbus); this is the maximum engine power setting.

b ○2.10 Play the recording, pausing after each pair of words for students to repeat the words, either individually or as a class.

Extension activity:

Students can repeat the pronunciation work in exercise 18a in pairs, by reading one word from a pair for their partner to work out which word it is.

19a Go through the tables with the class to elicit what type of information needs to go in each gap. Note that *PF* refers to the pilot flying, so the information should be the Captain or First Officer. The type of circuit could be, e.g. *holding, diversion,* or *vectors for a new approach.* In the box marked *ATC instructions,* students should write abbreviated ATCO instructions.

Students then work alone to fill in the details in their tables, using their imaginations. Both pilots and controllers should be able to find roughly suitable data, but the accuracy of the data is not the purpose of the exercise and indeed any disagreement could generate further discussion between partners. They then work in pairs to ask and answer questions about the information in their partners' tables. See exercise 17b for examples of questions to ask.

If you have an odd number of students you will need to have a group of three, where Student A asks about Student B's flight, Student B asks about Student C's flight and Student C asks about Student A's flight.

b Students take turns to describe their partners' flights using their notes.

Dealing with icing

Communicative and operational issues:

Icing, like wind, is another meteorological condition which can have severe consequences both in flight and on the ground. Ice formation (build-up) on the wings, stabilisers and flight control surfaces increases the weight of the aircraft, changes the centre of gravity, may alter or invalidate airspeed and attitude data by blocking the probes, and reduces the efficiency, or even prevents the movement of the flight controls. It can result in aircraft stall, i.e. the aircraft losing lift and entering an uncontrollable dive, as in the New Zealand example in exercise 20, or in a crash after take-off like Air Florida Flight 90, which ended in the Potomac River in Washington in 1982.

Aircraft are equipped with anti-icing and de-icing systems, which are electrical for the cockpit windows and air data probes; and pneumatic (hot bleed air) for the wing and engine cowl leading edges or using deformable rubber boots on some turboprop aircraft. Usually, turboprop aircraft cannot generate enough spare hot air to de-ice the wing leading edges, so they use another system which consists in inflating and deflating a rubber chamber running along the wing leading edges in order to detach any ice which has built up on it.

On the ground, aircraft are often de-iced by de-icing vehicles or gantries (see Unit 3) in freezing and snowy conditions. When freezing conditions are forecast in dense cloud, flight crews select aircraft anti-icing before take-off. Whenever possible, aircraft fly above freezing conditions, i.e. above cloud.

ATC provide flight crews with up-to-the-minute weather briefings in addition to regular ATIS recordings and have to take into account delays caused by aircraft going through a ground de-icing cycle.

The report in exercise 20 is about the flight of a turboprop aircraft which leaves Christchurch in New Zealand's South Island at night to fly to Palmerston in the North Island. They climb to FL 210 before being cleared by ATC Wellington to descend to FL 130 and then 11,000 feet. As they descended they were cleared to 7,000 feet. The aircraft then disappeared from the controller's radar screen as the aircraft was beginning a left turn. Ice build-up could have obstructed the transponder as it could have made the aircraft air data probes unserviceable.

The accident report said that an ice-induced tail stall likely caused the aircraft to enter a nose-down pitch attitude of about 70 degrees and descend rapidly in a spiral dive. The aircraft was descending through 9,000 feet at about 345 knots when the Cockpit Voice Recorder recorded a terrain awareness and warning system '*Bank angle, bank angle*', indicating that the aircraft was banked more than 50 degrees.

Since 2004, New Zealand's transition altitude is 13,000 feet, where pilots switch from local field to standard pressure settings, and the transition level is FL 150.

See http://www.skybrary.aero/index.php/In-Flight_Icing

Quote: **Tell students to close their books. Elicit from the class what a pilot should do if he/she encounters icing conditions in flight, and write their ideas on the board. Students then compare their ideas with those in the quote.**

Background notes:

◆ The *accretion rate* refers to the speed at which ice is accumulating; it is also referred to as the *accumulation rate* or *build-up rate*.

◆ Types of cloud include: cirrus, cirrocumulus and cirrostratus (above 20,000 ft); altocumulus, altostratus (between 6,500 and 20,000 ft); stratocumulus and altostratus (up to 6,500 ft) and nimbostratus and cumulus (up to 10,000 ft). Cumulonimbus are vertically developing clouds which generate severe thunderstorms and may rise to as high as 40,000 feet. Icing is especially associated with cumuliform clouds, or more locally with stratiform clouds.

◆ A *stratiform cloud* is a stratified or layered cloud, whereas a cumuliform cloud is made of a large aggregate or mass of cloud.

See:

http://eo.ucar.edu

http://www.stuffintheair.com

20 a, b, c, d **Students discuss the questions in pairs and then feed back to the class.**

Answers:

a Flights usually encounter icing at relatively low altitudes (from ground level up to 10,000–13,000 feet), i.e. when flying in cloud in freezing conditions. Once they are above dense cloud formations, there is little humidity in the air although temperatures are often as low as –50°C.

b In flight, pneumatic de-icing is used to remove any ice that has formed on the wing leading edges, which could affect the aircraft's aerodynamic characteristics, and on the engine air intakes, where ice ingested into the engine could damage the engine blades. The cockpit windshield and air data probes are protected electrically from ice formation. On the ground, the aircraft will be sprayed with de-icing fluid from vehicles or a gantry.

d ATC can help flight crews by providing up-to-date weather forecasts for the areas around the departure and destination airports and by providing them with information about the altitudes and the locations where they may expect freezing conditions. In flight, ATC may also help by clearing aircraft to, usually higher, altitudes at which they will not encounter icing.

21a ◉ **2.11 Go through the statements with the class to make sure everyone understands them. Play the recording for students to complete the exercise individually. They then discuss their answers in pairs.**

Background notes:

♦ A *Digital Flight Data Recorder* (*FDR* / *DFDR*) is a device for automatically recording information on aircraft operation (altitude, airspeed, vertical acceleration, heading, elapsed time, attitude, flight control surface position and engine speed). Such recorders are designed to survive crash accelerations, impacts, crushing and fire and often carry underwater transponders or beacons.

♦ A *Cockpit Voice Recorder* (*CVR*) is an automatic recycling recorder storing all crew radio and intercom traffic, including crew speech and background noise.

♦ If the captain was *pilot flying*, it means that it was the captain who was at the controls, while the First Officer monitored the instruments and was in charge of the radio.

♦ *PAR* is the abbreviation for Palmerston North, an airport and Navaid in New Zealand.

♦ An aircraft's *primary radar target* is its blip (symbol) displayed on a controller's radar screen.

♦ A *transponder* is a radio device, which when triggered sends out a pre-coded reply on the same wavelength.

♦ A *transition altitude* is the altitude at which the altimeter setting is changed from local atmospheric pressure to 1013 hPa and vice versa, while a *transition level* is the flight level at which this change is made.

b ●2.11 Play the recording for students to check their answers. Then go through the answers with the class.

Answers:
1 F – 20:32   6 T
2 T   7 T
3 T   8 T
4 F – 1,500 fpm
5 F – only the route instructions

c Go through the example with the class. Make sure students realise that they need to remember the answers to the statements in exercise 21a. If necessary, they could refer to audioscript 2.11 on page 181 to check. Afterwards, go through the questions and answers with the class to make sure the questions were formed correctly.

If you have an odd number of students you will need to have a group of three, where Student C takes questions 1 to 3 from Student A and questions 6 to 8 from Student B.

Suggested answers:
A1 Did the aircraft depart on time? → Yes
B1 Where was it flying from? → Christchurch
A2 Who was at the controls? → the captain
B2 When did the co-pilot request to fly directly to PAR? → At 21:08
A3 To which altitude did ATC instruct the plane to descend? → 11,000 feet
B3 What was the aircraft's rate of descent? → 1,500 feet per minute
…

Extension activity:

Discuss the story with the class: how common are such problems?; what went wrong?; and what could have been done to avoid them?

22 In this exercise, students will deliberately use their cues to make statements in slightly unusual or idiomatic language. Their partner will ask for clarification or explanation using either the phraseology *Say again*, or plain English expressions such as *I'm sorry, I didn't understand*, or *What do you mean exactly?* etc. Elicit some of these phrases for requesting clarification onto the board. Then go through the example with the class. Point out that each cue is the beginning of a new dialogue, making 24 in total. Students then work in pairs to make dialogues. Basically, the responding student says *Say again* or a plain language equivalent (*Can you repeat that?*, *What did you say?* etc.) each time. Afterwards, discuss the dialogues with the class, and agree on the best answers. You may wish to highlight and discuss those words for which it is easy to find satisfactory synonyms and those which do not have any (e.g. snow, flight plan, wings, braking, water, ash cloud, runway lights, turbulence, mountain, climb, hold, ice, radar, squawk).

If you have an odd number of students you will need to have a group of three, where Student C takes cues 2, 6, 10 and 14 from Student A and cues 4, 8 and 12 from Student B.

Suggested answers:
Pilot
1 We are going around.
2 Request a change in our flight plan. / Will you modify our flight plan?
3 Our weather radar return is displaying a weather formation 40 miles in front of us.
4 Snow is accumulating on our wings.
5 We expect to reach / arrive at / overfly Lima at 18 minutes past the hour / at 17:18.
6 Request a longer circuit.
…

ATCO

1 Can you see the runway lights? / Are you visual?
2 There is a possibility of wake turbulence after the A380.
3 There may be turbulence over the Carpathians.
4 Traffic is climbing to Flight Level 290; he is now at Flight Level 210.
5 We will make sure / verify that.
6 You are heading 045 degrees on our radar.

...

Background notes:

* A *missed approach* is a discontinued approach followed by a go-around.
* A *braking coefficient* is a measurement of braking efficiency based on the friction coefficient of the runway, i.e. if the runway surface is wet or icy, it will be slippery, there will be less friction and the braking coefficient will be lower.
* *Mountain wave effects* are the result of a large body of rotating air just after an aircraft has crossed a mountain range.
* *Light chop* refers to mild turbulence
* The *stack* is a superimposed series of holding patterns at assigned flight levels.
* A *radar return* is the reflection of the beam off the 'target' (the aircraft) which causes a 'blip' or display on the controller's screen.

Volcanic ash

Communicative and operational issues:

This short section is devoted to another environmental phenomenon which periodically causes a lot of disruption to aviation: ash clouds from erupting volcanoes. The clouds rise to high altitudes, are carried long distances by prevailing winds and contain abrasive materials and moisture in the form of ice which, when ingested by jet engines, damages the leading edges of the blades and obstructs the airflow resulting in engine malfunction or shutdown. In addition, the dust may enter the air conditioning system distributing toxic gases and reducing visibility inside the cockpit and cabin. Flight crews need to communicate with ATC to avoid or escape from ash clouds by deviating from their flight plan and to manage any aircraft malfunctions caused by the ash.

The content in this section is based on recommendations from Boeing about how flight crews should react to volcanic ash. The full recorded version of the recommendations contains some vocabulary (e.g. *deploy, don, exceed, exit, idle, recovery, shutdown, SOP, surge, thrust*) which can be useful when describing different types of environmental or technical problems.

Quote: **Read the quote aloud. Elicit from the class what happened during the volcanic ash shutdown of Europe, and whether/why the shutdown was necessary.**

Background note:

The volcanic ash shutdown of Europe refers to the events of April 2010, when ash from the erupting Eyjafjallajökull volcano in southern Iceland caused major disruption to flights across Europe. See *Clearing the Air*, in Flight Safety Foundation *AeroSafety* World November 2010.

23 **Students discuss the questions in pairs and feed back to the class.**

Suggested answers:
1 The photos illustrate a volcanic eruption and the effect on passengers of flights cancelled or delayed by the volcanic ash cloud.
2 The shutdown was painful for the many passengers who were stranded or delayed in uncomfortable conditions (e.g. sleeping at airports), and also painful for the airlines and airports who lost a lot of revenue.

24a **O 2.12 Students work alone to match the beginnings of the sentences with the endings, and then compare their answers in pairs. Then play the recording for students to check their answers. Finally, go through the answers with the class.**

Answers:
1 d	3 b	5 c
2 a	4 f	6 e

Background notes:

* An *Auxiliary Power Unit* (*APU*) is an airborne power generation system usually located in the aircraft tail, used to provide electrical and pneumatic power and engine start when the aircraft is on the ground or during an in-flight emergency.
* *Idle* describes the minimum smooth engine operating speed.
* If oxygen masks *deploy*, they extend or drop down from the PSUs (Passenger Service Units) above the passengers' heads.
* If you *don* a mask or life vest, you put it on.
* If a plane *exits* a cloud, it goes outside it.
* *Molten debris* is matter melted or fused with heat.
* *Hot-section components* are the combustion chamber, high and low pressure turbines and exhaust.
* *Bleed air* is hot air taken from the engine compressor for air conditioning and anti-icing etc.

♦ A *surge* is a breakdown of airflow over the engine airfoils (blades and vanes) resulting from compressor stall (i.e. a sudden loss of compressor efficiency) and often accompanied by a muffled bang and an increase in turbine temperature. A *surge margin* is the difference between the current operating rpm and the rpm at which the compressor blades will stall at any altitude in the event of a sudden acceleration.

♦ A *stall* is a sudden breakdown of fluid flow around an aerofoil (wing) or in an engine. An *engine stall margin* is the difference between the gas turbine operating line and the stall line.

♦ *Recovery* is the completion of a flight manoeuvre and return to straight and level flight or return to normal operation, or restarting of the engine.

♦ An *air conditioning pack* is a large unit comprising an air cycle machine and pre-cooler which regulates bleed air from the engine compressor for use in the cabin.

♦ *Shutdown* involves reducing engine power to zero; stopping engine operation.

♦ *Standard operating procedures* (*SOP*) are specific procedures defined by an airline to respond to all contingencies.

b ○2.12 **Make sure students know which points to take notes on and what type of information to record. Then play the recording for students to take notes.**

If you have an odd number of students you will need to have a group of three students, where one student makes notes on points 1 and 4, one on points 2 and 5 and one on points 3 and 6.

c **Students exchange information with their partners and discuss the most important actions. Then open up the discussion to include the whole class.**

d **Discuss the question with the class.**

> Suggested answer:
> Area Control should keep flight crews informed of any developments in the location, extent and direction of movement of volcanic ash clouds and relay any information received from other flights. They must also coordinate any changes to flight plans resulting from avoidance manoeuvres or deviations to alternates caused by serious damage or engine failure.

Extension activity:

Students look back at the sentences in exercise 24a and audioscript 2.12 to underline different ways of describing cause and effect (including prevention).

> Suggested answers:
> ♦ X could/will result in Y (as a result of Z)
> ♦ X prevents/will prevent Y (from happening)
> ♦ By doing X, Y may happen
> ♦ X allows Y to happen
> ♦ X improves the chances of Y happening
> ♦ X can cause Y

Putting it together: Handling environmental problems

Communicative and operational issues:

Putting it together is an opportunity to review many of the environmental threats looked at in Unit 5. It is also an opportunity to develop students' ability to say why they are unable to do something, or comply with instructions or requests (exercise 25), as well as prepare and play out scenarios related to environmental problems (exercise 26).

The quotation in the ICAO focus, from ICAO Circular 323, *Guidelines for aviation English training programmes*, summarizes succinctly the relationship between standard phraseology and plain language and defines the aviation English which is targeted in *Flightpath*. Indeed, difficult weather or environmental conditions are one of the circumstances in which plain language will often be required. The other circumstances are addressed in other units.

Like the second edition of ICAO Doc. 9835 (2010), Circular 323 (2009) should be required reading for all aviation English teachers and their contents and principles fully assimilated. In the *Flightpath* Teacher's Book we have tried to comply with, but not to simply repeat, what is explained in these two ICAO documents. The Teacher's Book aims at expanding and giving practical examples and applications of the principles they contain.

Preparation

25 **Students work alone to match the problems with the consequences. They then check in pairs. Afterwards, go through the answers with the class. You may need to check the meaning of some words, e.g.** *blurred* **(= not in focus).**

> Answers:
>
> | 1 f | 3 a | 5 c | 7 d |
> | 2 h | 4 g | 6 b | 8 e |

Background notes:

- *Clear air turbulence (CAT)* is significant turbulence where no clouds are present, normally at high altitude near a jetstream.
- *Aquaplaning* is when an aircraft's wheels are partially supported by standing water on the runway and not fully in contact with the runway surface so that braking and steering are inefficient.
- A *blade* is an aerofoil designed to rotate about an axis.
- A *flame-out* is a loss of combustion in a gas turbine engine.

Extension activity:

Students could test each other in pairs by reading the first half of a sentence to elicit from their partner the correct ending.

ICAO FOCUS

Students read the quote to find adjectives to describe: standard phraseology [**Answers:** clear, concise, internationally recognised, formulaic]; and non-standard situations [**Answers:** non-routine, abnormal, emergency]. Students then discuss the task and question in pairs and feed back to the class. Note that the issue of when to use standard and non-standard phraseology may generate some strong opinions and a lot of discussion.

Possible answers:
Environmental conditions such as volcanic ash, lightning strikes, ice build-up, bird strikes, thunderstorms, hailstorms, fog and other sorts of obscuration, severe turbulence, windshear, runways contaminated by ice, snow, slush or water etc. will all result in increased communications between the flight crew and ATC. This is due to: 1) the fact that the aircraft may be damaged or its aerodynamic performance modified; 2) there may be a need for an unscheduled and sudden change of flight level or heading; 3) the crew may need to divert to an alternate destination or even declare an emergency; 4) the type of approach may be affected; 5) runway conditions, and so landing and braking, may not be as expected; 6) the crew may require information about a change of routeing or an alternate; 7) the crew may require assistance on arrival. All these factors will generate a lot of communication which cannot be handled by standard phraseology and so which will require plain language.

26 Go through the example with the class. Point out that each student has eight inputs and eight responses. Make sure they realise to swap roles after they are satisfied with their eight dialogues. Students then work in pairs to create dialogues. Finally, ask some pairs to act out their dialogues for the class. Discuss the appropriacy of each dialogue.

Suggested answers:
Pilot responses
1 Negative. Unable. The ILS display seems unreliable; it is fluctuating following a lightning strike.
2 Negative. We are still in thick/dense cloud.
3 Negative. We have not got enough fuel to perform another pattern.
4 Negative. We have only intermittent transmission; we have problems with our receiver. We suspect the antenna was damaged in the hailstorm.
...

ATCO responses
1 Unable due traffic. Expect lower in five minutes.
2 Negative. A Dash 7 has declared an emergency due (to a) bird strike. It is on short final to Runway 07.
3 Unable due traffic restrictions. There are military exercises in the Yaounde area.
4 Unable. Runway 31 Left is closed due (to) flooding near (the) threshold.
...

If you have an odd number of students you will need to have a group of three, where Student C takes inputs and responses 1 to 3 from Student A and inputs and responses 6 to 8 from Student B.

Background notes:

- *CB* stands for cumulonimbus.
- A *tight circuit* has a short radius.
- A *level change* involves climbing or descending. It might be preferable to orbiting because it avoids icing conditions.
- '*Are you visual?*' means '*Have you got the runway in sight?*'
- When the ATCO asks '*Did you read my previous transmission?*' (Student B, Input 4), *read* means hear and understand.
- '*You #3*' means the aircraft has two other aircraft ahead which will land first.
- *Below minimums* means that the vertical and horizontal visibility is less than that for which the airport, aircraft and crew are certificated.

Communication

27a Make sure students realise they are only planning at this stage, and that they will need to invent most of the information for their dialogues. They should make notes, but should not actually script their dialogues.

If you have an odd number of students you will need to have a group of three students, where the third student could be a co-pilot.

Background notes:

◆ a) The *cracked windshield* will cause problems of visibility for the flight crew which are particularly critical during approach and landing. In some cases the crack may also result in a distracting noise. If the crack worsened, it might result in the windshield breaking possibly injuring the pilots, causing a cabin depressurization and a risk of the crew being sucked towards the open window. Therefore, the crew will need to reduce their airspeed and request descent to reduce pressure on the windshield.

◆ b) The effects of *volcanic ash clouds* have been seen in some detail in the previous section through the Boeing recommendations. It will be necessary to manage a diversion.

◆ c) A *bird strike* can either crack or shatter the windshield, with results similar to those in the first scenario, or if there is ingestion of a large bird in the engine(s) result in engine stall or loss. Normally, bird strikes/ingestions are at fairly low altitudes just after take-off, or less often during approach. In any case, a pan-pan urgency call and precautionary landing will be necessary.

◆ d) *Heavy rain during approach and landing* obviously affect visibility through the windshield and cause the approach and runway lights to be blurred. If the rain is very heavy, it may be accompanied by squalls and windshear which make the approach more difficult. It is also likely that the rain water will not be entirely drained from the runway resulting in standing water. This makes aquaplaning possible and in any case reduces the runway friction coefficient and braking efficiency and so increases the distance required to come to a standstill. In these conditions, there is a greater probability of a runway excursion, like that which occurred with the Air France A340-300 at Toronto, Canada, in August 2005. The crew will need to be ready to perform a missed approach, especially if they touch down too far from the runway threshold.

◆ e) *Turbulence*, especially clear air turbulence for which there is no warning, may cause passengers moving in the cabin to be thrown around and injured: concussion, broken ribs and bruising are quite common in this case. If the injuries are serious, the flight crew will have to request a diversion to the nearest suitable alternate so that the injured passengers can be cared for. The crew will need to describe the nature, extent and seriousness of the injuries. Cabin attendants will provide first aid.

◆ f) *Cumulonimbus storm cloud formations* will often cause the crew to change heading momentarily in order to avoid them by 20 or 30 miles, before resuming their route. These dense clouds are often the sign of intense electrical storm activity and violent up and downdraughts which can destabilise the aircraft and damage its electronic equipment.

b, c **Pairs take turns to role play their dialogues for the class. Give and elicit feedback on each dialogue, focusing not only on accurate and effective language but also the success of the communication and ways it could have been improved.**

Extension activity:

As a homework task, students could write out their dialogues as a script and act them out in the next lesson. Alternatively, they could write a short report on the incident and present it to the class in the next lesson.

Debriefing

28 **Students discuss their dialogues and how they could have been improved with the class.**

Progress check

Students work alone to complete the progress check and then discuss their notes with a partner. Then discuss with the class what students still feel uncomfortable with, and how they can overcome these problems.

DVD: *Volcanic ash hazard*

Communicative and operational issues:

The clip in Unit 5 is the simulation of an actual United Airlines Boeing 747 flight (United 869) off the coast of Alaska en route to Japan at night. The crew are unaware of any erupting volcanoes. The first sign of volcanic ash is their detecting a slight smell, which they interpret as an electrical overheat or fire. As a precautionary measure, the Captain instructs the First Officer to don his oxygen mask. The Captain realises that if it is volcanic ash, they might lose their sense of smell and be unaware of it in the flight deck. The crew then notice the presence of dust and call United Airlines Dispatch to know whether there have been any reports of volcanic activity.

The Captain also dons his mask and calls for the 'Smoke, Odour, Fumes' QRC. Then the crew lose engines 4 and 1 (the outboard engines) followed by engines 2 and 3. They shut down the engines, declare an emergency ('Mayday' call) and perform a 180° turn in order to exit the cloud. The Captain then calls for the Indicated Airspeed Disagree / Airspeed Mach Unreliable checklist as the crew have undoubtedly noticed discrepancies in their airspeed indications caused by the Captain and First Officer probes being obstructed to different extents. Airspeed (and attitude) is one of the essential items of situational awareness required to fly the plane.

Two of the four engines relight, presumably once they have flown out of the ash cloud. ATC advise them of reports of volcanic activity near their present position and Dispatch look for a suitable alternate airfield for the crew to divert to (the weather is OK and the runway long enough for a B747 with a heavy load of fuel). ATC also liaise with the airport staff for them to provide the necessary support (engineering, catering, accommodation etc.). Flight 869 lands successfully at Petropavlovsk-Kamchatskiy airport in the far east of Russia.

29a Brainstorm a list of effects on the board.

b Students watch Part 1 to answer the three questions. You could play the clip again to highlight the useful vocabulary from this part: en route /ɒn ˈruːt/ (= on the way to); a whiff (= a slight, almost undetectable odour); to don an oxygen mask; a sense of smell; and desensitised (= no longer sensitive to a sensation).

> Answers:
> 1 at FL 330 over the North Pacific between the United States (Alaska) and Japan
> 2 a whiff, a faint smell which does not last long
> 3 the First Officer dons his oxygen mask

30a Discuss the questions with the class but avoid confirming or rejecting students' suggestions.

> Suggested answers:
> ◆ The captain will probably contact the Area Control Centre for the Flight Information Region in which he is flying and/or his own company's Dispatch.
> ◆ The captain will probably report his position, the phenomena he has encountered, the status of the aircraft, the action he has taken and ask for information about making a diversion.

b Play Part 2 for students to answer the questions. Go through the answers quickly with the class. You could play the clip a second time to focus on the important vocabulary (see Background notes).

> Answers:
> 1 United Airlines Dispatch
> 2 The Captain checks with Dispatch whether they have any reports of volcanic activity and suggests that the First Officer dons his oxygen mask as a precaution.

Background notes:

- ◆ Dispatch is an airline's operations department in radio contact with all the fleet.
- ◆ 'Copy all that' means I understand and will comply with those instructions, requests, etc.
- ◆ A QRC (Quick Reference Checklist) is a concise document listing actions to be performed in abnormal situations.
- ◆ Indicated Airspeed Disagree / Airspeed Mach Unreliable checklist is a checklist performed if the crew suspect that the information provided by their air data probes is incorrect.
- ◆ The obstruction of the air data probes by ice or volcanic ash, for example, is extremely serious since these probes are the only source of airspeed, altitude and attitude information for the pilots' instruments which comprise an essential part of their situational awareness. See Air France flight 447, which disappeared over the South Atlantic in June 2009.

31a Discuss the question with the class.

> Suggested answer:
> The systems which are most immediately affected by a volcanic ash cloud are the engines, air data probes and air conditioning which could all be blocked and damaged.

b Play Part 3 for students to answer the questions. Afterwards, go through the answers quickly with the class.

> Answers:
> 1 First, Engine 4 (the outer right-hand engine) fails and then the indications of Engine 1 approach the operating limits.
> 2 The captain calls for the Engine 4 Failure checklist, then shuts down Engine 1 (outer left-hand engine) and calls for the Engine Surge/Stall Quick Reference Handbook checklist.

32a Discuss the question with the class.

> Suggested answer:
> The captain needs to exit the volcanic ash cloud as soon as possible by performing a 180° turn.

b Play **Part 4** for students to answer the four questions. Students discuss the answers in pairs before feeding back to the class. Elicit from the class which two checklists the pilot called for in this clip [**Answers**: the Indicated Airspeed Disagree / Airspeed Mach Unreliable checklist and the Multiple Engine Flame-out checklist]. You could also check the meaning of some of the useful words: *inadvertently* (= accidentally); *relit* (= past form of *relight*, i.e. started again), and play the clip a second time for students to check how these words were used.

> **Answers:**
> 1 The captain makes a 180° turn, declares an emergency and calls for the Indicated Airspeed Disagree / Airspeed Mach Unreliable checklist.
> 2 The captain contacts both ATC (to declare an emergency) and his company Dispatch.
> 3 All four engines had failed initially; now two engines have been re-started successfully.
> 4 You see the various technicians working in the airline Dispatch department and the air traffic controllers.

33a Discuss the question with the class.

> **Suggested answer:**
> ATC should inform the flight crew of the reported location and altitude of the volcanic ash cloud and its direction of movement. They should provide the flight crew with a new route to avoid the area. They will also alert other aircraft in the area.

b Play **Part 5** of the DVD for students to answer the four questions. They discuss their answers in pairs before feeding back to the class.

> **Answers:**
> 1 ATC receives reports of volcanic eruptions in the area.
> 2 Dispatch looks for the most suitable diversionary airport in the vicinity, collects weather and routeing information and informs the flight crew and the airport authorities.
> 3 The weather is good, the runway is 11,155 feet (3,400 metres) long and the name of the airport is Petropavlovsk-Kamchatskiy (in the Russian Far East).
> 4 The aircraft lands successfully and safely at Petropavlovsk-Kamchatskiy airport.

Background notes:

> ♦ A *sweeping weather check* is a check for weather, which covers a wide area using weather reports from various sources and weather centres.
> ♦ The *arrival weather* is a forecast of weather conditions at the time the aircraft is expected to arrive at a destination.

34 a, b, c Allow about five minutes for students to plan their reports in pairs. Then play all five clips again for students to check their information. They then write up their reports, either in class or as homework.

> **Possible answer:**
> United Airlines flight 869, a Boeing 747, was flying over the North Pacific en route to Japan at night at Flight Level 330 when the crew encountered the first signs of a volcanic ash cloud: a slight smell in the cockpit. The captain instructed the First Officer to don his oxygen mask and contacted United Airlines Dispatch to check whether there had been any reports of volcanic activity in the region. Dust then appeared in the cockpit, the Captain donned his mask and they performed the 'Smoke, Odour, Fumes' checklist.
>
> ...

UNIT 6
Level busts

Operational topics	Level bust situations; Causes of level bust; Communication techniques; Call sign, flight level, frequency and heading confusion; Breakdowns in communication; Memorisation; Recommendations for pilots and controllers for avoiding level busts; Level bust incidents
Communication functions	Reporting incidents; Communication errors: readback/hearback and hearback errors; Distinguishing call signs, frequencies and settings; Identifying causes; Correcting readback/hearback errors; Negotiating and managing separation and level changes
Language content	*Fail to*; Verb forms and active and passive; Movement and location; Pronunciation, enunciation, delivery and stress; Conditionals

Unit 6 Teacher's brief

The second topic in the part of *Flightpath* devoted to the safety aspects of **en-route** situations, focuses on **level busts**. Eurocontrol defines level bust as 'Any unauthorised vertical deviation of more than 300 feet from an ATC flight clearance. Within **RVSM** airspace, this limit is reduced to 200 feet.' RSVM refers to Reduced Vertical Separation Minima, where vertical separation between aircraft is reduced from 2,000 ft to 1,000 ft in order to increase the available airspace for traffic movements.

Eurocontrol further highlights the fact that 'Once every half hour, somewhere in the world, an aircraft is busting its cleared level. Once each day, the loss of separation results in aircraft passing within a mile of each other.' Eurocontrol *Level Bust Tool Kit*. See: http://www.eurocontrol.int/safety/gallery/content/public/level_bust/menuindex.html

Level busts have a variety of causes: pilots mishearing a cleared level; pilots **setting an erroneous level or altitude** on the autopilot FCU (Flight Control Unit) on Airbus aircraft, and MCP (Mode Control Panel) on Boeing aircraft; controllers changing a level clearance (re-clearing) too late so that the aircraft continues through the newly assigned level; **a last-minute change** in type of approach, approach path or runway in use; failure to level off due to **distraction**; failure to change **altimeter setting** resulting in the aircraft being higher or lower than the crew think; **emergency descent** in the event of cabin depressurisation, engine failure etc.; spontaneous avoidance manoeuvre when an aircraft is flying VFR (Visual Flight Rules); loss of altitude due to turbulence, or; pilots correctly following a **TCAS** (Traffic Collision Avoidance System) **RA** (Resolution Advisory), e.g. '*climb, climb*', '*descend, descend*' to avoid conflict with another aircraft; an unjustified response to a TCAS **TA** (Traffic Advisory) where no

change in flight level / altitude is required. See: http://www.skybrary.aero/index.php/Airborne_Collision_Avoidance_System_%28ACAS%29

Level busts are a common occurrence, but most do not have serious consequences: a level bust may occur in airspace where there are currently no other aircraft. However, if separation is lost between two aircraft, an **Airprox** occurs and a report has to be filed. The UK Airprox Board defines an airprox as follows: 'An Airprox is a situation in which, in the opinion of a pilot or a controller, the distance between aircraft as well as their relative positions and speed have been such that the safety of the aircraft involved was or may have been compromised.'

UK Airprox Board: http://www.airproxboard.org.uk/

Skybrary, Flight Safety Foundation and Eurocontrol have excellent websites with documents, videos and Powerpoint presentations which can be used by teachers for informational purposes or to source materials for additional activities.

Unit 6 Sources

- Airbus Flight Operations Briefing Notes: *Effective pilot-controller communications VI.3, VI.15* (Exercises 13c; 15b)
- Airbus Flight Operations Briefing Notes: *Level busts*
- http://www.aviation-safety.net – Ilyushin 76 and B747, 1996 (Exercise 24a)
- Day, B.: *Careful communication,* Flight Safety Foundation
- Eurocontrol: *Level Bust Briefing Notes – General* (Exercise 1a)
- Eurocontrol: *Reducing Level Bust* (Exercises 2a; 9a)
- Eurocontrol: *ATM (Air Traffic Management) 1 – Understanding the causes of level busts 4.1* (Exercises 10–11)

◆ Eurocontrol: *En route to reducing level bust* (Exercise 15a)
◆ Flight Safety Foundation: *ALAR (Approach and Landing Accident Reduction) Briefing Note 2.3 – Pilot/Controller Communication* (Exercise 8a)
◆ National Air Traffic Services (NATS): *Level Best video (DVD)*
◆ Skybrary: http://www.skybrary.aero/ – B737/MD81, en route, Romford UK (Exercise 7a)
◆ Skybrary / Eurocontrol: *Level Bust 2* DVD (Exercises 24a–28b)
◆ UK Flight Safety Committee: *Recommendations for avoiding level busts* (Exercise 21a)

Lead-in

The lead-in quote (taken from another Eurocontrol document) contains a similar definition to the longer one quoted at the beginning of the *Teacher's brief*.

Quote: **Elicit from the class what level busts are, how they occur and why they are dangerous. Students then read the quote to check their answers.**

1 **Students discuss the five questions in small groups and then feed back to the class.**

> **Suggested answers:**
> a Both professional pilots and controllers will have experienced level busts in one capacity or another for any of the reasons listed in the third paragraph of the *Teacher's Brief*. The scenarios used throughout Unit 6 show examples of controllers dealing with different types of level bust situation.
> b The priority is to instruct the aircraft to return immediately to its cleared level or altitude and, if necessary, give avoidance instructions to other aircraft in order to maintain separation.
> c In addition to vertical separation, there is also horizontal separation between aircraft which must be managed by ATC and where relative airspeeds and aircraft types are influential; i.e. a turboprop will probably not be travelling at the same speed as a jet airliner.
> d When *RVSM* (Reduced Vertical Separation Minima) operate, i.e. where vertical separation is reduced to 1,000 feet between aircraft on routes with high-density traffic, the risk is potentially greater because the distance between aircraft and, therefore, the error margin are smaller.
> e The safety nets against level busts are largely related to good communication: making sure that pilots read back instructions and clearances and that the controller monitors these readbacks by effective hearback; making sure that flight crews make call-outs, i.e. verbalise and crosscheck their actions to avoid entering incorrect flight levels and altitudes or failing to change altimeter settings.

Examples of level bust situations

Communicative and operational issues:

The introductory quote refers to a 300-foot level bust during an approach to Munich, Germany, which appears to have been self-corrected by the crew. Last-minute changes in clearance or type of approach during a time of high workload are a common cause of level bust.

Quote: **Read the quote aloud. Discuss with the class exactly what the crew did wrong and how common such mistakes are.**

Background notes:

◆ The quotation shows how a flight crew may be upset and their attention diverted when something unexpected happens at a critical moment with high workload. In this case, having to change the landing runway would have resulted in the crew changing data in the Flight Management and Guidance System, so being heads-down, and carrying out a briefing for the new approach. As a result, they failed to be fully attentive to the new cleared altitude and flew through it.
◆ The *intercept heading* is the heading the crew must follow in order to capture and follow the ILS or visual approach flight path.

2a **○2.13** In addition to being a conventional listening comprehension exercise, this activity also mirrors a very common cognitive process used by operational staff: matching visual and audio inputs.

Discuss the three diagrams with the class to work out whose mistake led to each situation [**Answers**: In diagram a, the pilot has already passed the new level when the ATCO re-clears him to it: the ATCO gives his re-clearance too late. In diagram b, the pilot forgets to reset his altimeter setting to QNH when the ATCO re-clears him to an altitude below the transition altitude after initially clearing him to a level above it. In diagram c, the pilot forgets to adjust his altimeter setting to standard pressure (1013 hPa) when he is re-cleared to a level above the transition level]. Students then listen to match the descriptions to the diagrams.

> **Answers:**
> 1 b   2 c   3 a

Background notes:

◆ If an ATCO *re-clears* a flight, he/she modifies a previous clearance.
◆ *Transition level* is the flight level above which pilots set their altimeter to standard atmospheric pressure (1013 hPa or 29.92 in.Hg) and below which their altimeter is set to local pressure: QNH (relative to sea level) or QFE (relative to the airfield elevation).

◆ *Transition altitude* is the same principle as for transition level, but expressed in feet or metres rather than Flight Level. These levels and altitudes vary from one location to another. In the United States there is a single transition altitude of 18,000 feet.

◆ *Standard pressure setting* is the altimeter setting used universally above the transition level or altitude: it is 1013.25 hPa or 29.92 in.Hg.

b **Students discuss the three scenarios in pairs to make sure they fully understand what happened in each case. You could play the recording again for them to check. Finally, discuss the three scenarios with the class.**

> Answers:
> a ATC issued a late re-clearance: the flight crew had already exceeded FL 190 on their way to FL 250 when ATC re-cleared them to FL 190.
> b The pilot correctly set the standard pressure setting of 1013 hPa in anticipation of FL 80, which is above the transition altitude of 7,000 feet. ATC then re-cleared the flight to 5,000 feet, which is below the transition altitude, but the crew forgot to reset the altimeter to local pressure, which is 1025 hPa. The result of this is that when the crew saw 5,000 feet displayed on their instruments, the aircraft was in fact at about 4,400 feet.
> c The pilot correctly set 990 hPa in anticipation of 3,000 feet to which he had been cleared, which is below the transition altitude. He was then re-cleared to FL 60, above the transition level of FL 50. The aircraft levels out at FL 60, but is in fact at about 5,400 feet.
>
> For more information on altimeter setting procedures, see Eurocontrol, *Level Bust Briefing Notes Ops 2, Altimeter setting procedures.*
>
> http://www.levelbust.com/downloads/bn_ops2. pdf

c **Discuss the question with the class. Note that the Munich incident is described in the quote before exercise 2a.**

> Answer:
> The Munich incident corresponds to scenario *a*, where a new clearance is given too late for the crew to adjust before flying through their cleared level/altitude. The change of approach generates an extra workload and causes a distraction.

d **Discuss the question with the class.**

> Suggested answer:
> Aircraft altitudes/levels are displayed on their radar screens and controllers may also pick up misunderstandings through readback errors. ATC centres may also have Short Term Conflict Alert systems, which detect aircraft on converging courses or with unacceptable vertical separation. See exercise 7a.

3a ○ **2.14 Play the recording, pausing after the first transmission to go through the example with the class. Draw attention to the need to write the call sign beneath each diagram. Then play the rest of the recording for students to complete the exercise. They discuss their answers in pairs and listen again if necessary before feeding back to the class.**

> Answers:
> 1 e – Air France 3762
> 2 c – Emirates 5371
> 3 d – Japan Air (JAL) 1956
> 4 f – Air China 3776
> 5 a – Delta 1982
> 6 b – Air Canada 5718
> The situations are as follows in the six recordings:
> 1 Air France 3762: Air France 3762 is re-cleared to a lower level once they have already flown through it.
> 2 Emirates 5371: Due to an altitude setting error or lack of crosschecking, the crew believe their cleared level is 6,000 feet rather than 5,000 feet.
> 3 Japan Air (JAL) 1956: Japan Air 1956 has descended too far. They believe their cleared level is FL 130 instead of FL 140 due to a misunderstanding or a distraction.
> 4 Air China 3776: Due to radio interference, Air China 3776 took '*expect 3,000 feet*' as a clearance to 3,000 feet. The crew should have asked the controller to say again.
> 5 Delta 1982: ATC interrupts Delta 1982's climb to 9,000 feet due to the presence of aircraft above. However, Delta 1982 has already exceeded 8,000 feet and has to re-descend.
> 6 Air Canada 5718: This is the contrary scenario where Air Canada 5718 has to stop its descent and climb back to 6,000 feet.

Extension activity:

Play the recording again, pausing after each ATC transmission (e.g. the ATCO's instruction) to elicit from volunteers how the dialogue continues (e.g. the pilot's readback). Then play the pilot transmission to compare it with students' suggestions. Continue in this way for each dialogue. As you go, you could draw attention to the following grammar structures:

◆ Present perfect to describe something that has already happened (*we have already passed*) in dialogue 1

◆ The adverb *immediately* in dialogue 2

◆ Past simple to correct a misunderstanding (*you were cleared*) in dialogue 3

◆ Present perfect for news (*have stopped descent*) in dialogue 4

◆ Past perfect for the earlier of two actions (*we had passed* [before we stopped]) in dialogue 5

◆ Present simple after *when* with future meaning (*Let me know when you're climbing*) in dialogue 6

b Students role play the scenarios in pairs. If you have done the extension activity after exercise 3a, you could encourage students to use the same grammar structures, although it is not necessary to insist on a word-for-word reproduction of the original dialogues. Afterwards, ask some pairs to perform the dialogues for the class.

If you have an odd number of students you will need to have one group of three students, where the third student plays a co-pilot in each dialogue. Alternatively, the three students could take turns to sit out while their partners perform the dialogue. Each student in this group will therefore act in four out of six dialogues.

Language focus: Verb forms

Go through the four points with the class, using the following questions to draw attention to the grammar structures:

Impersonal, passive (past)

◆ Looking at the first two examples, how do we form the passive voice in the past simple? [**Answer:** *was/were* + past participle]

◆ Why is the passive used in these two examples? [**Suggested answer:** To make the sentences less personal – to focus on the events rather than the person performing them. In both examples, it should be obvious that: the clearance came from ATC; the autopilot was disconnected automatically or by a crew member.]

Result/objective of an action

◆ What structure is used in the next three examples to show results/objectives? [**Answer:** *to* + infinitive]

◆ In which of these three examples could *to* be replaced with *in order to*? [**Answer:** The third one]

◆ Apart from *clear sb to do* and *instruct sb to do*, what other verbs of instructing are followed by *to* + infinitive? [**Answers:** *tell*, *ask*, *invite*, *encourage*, *urge*, *order*, *command*, *force*, *compel*, etc.]

Personal, active (past)

◆ In which of the next three examples would the passive be possible? [**Answer:** The second one: *The aircraft was cleared* (*by ATC*) *to descend.*]

◆ What is the effect of using the active voice in this example? [**Answer:** It focuses on the person performing the action, making the sentence more personal.]

◆ Why is the passive not possible in the other two examples? [**Answer:** Because the verbs have no object.]

Following *before, after, while, by*

◆ What verb forms follow these words? [**Answer:** *-ing* (the present participle)]

Language notes:

◆ *by* is a preposition. Like all prepositions, it can be followed by a noun phrase (e.g. *by plane*) or a verb in the *-ing* form (e.g. *by flying*).

◆ *while* is a conjunction. Conjunctions are normally followed by a full clause (e.g. *while I was flying*), but some conjunctions allow ellipsis of the subject and the verb *be* (i.e. *while I was flying*). The conjunction *when* works in the same way (e.g. *when flying*). *While* and *when* cannot be used as prepositions (e.g. *while/when the flight*).

◆ *before* and *after* can be used as both prepositions (e.g. *before/after the flight*, *before/after flying*) and as conjunctions (e.g. *before/after I flew*). Other words which work in this way include *since* and *until*.

4a Students work alone to complete the sentences. Point out that sometimes they will need to use the passive. They check in pairs before going through the answers with the class. You could use similar questions to those in the *Language focus* above to draw attention to the correct verb forms in each sentence, especially the use of *-ing* after *when* in question 8 (see *Language notes* above).

Answers:	
1 assigned	6 occurred
2 were assigned	7 following
3 received	8 using
4 rotating	9 was issued
5 taking	10 to contact

b Make sure students realise they may use each word only once. They work alone to complete the sentences and then check in pairs before feeding back to the class.

Answers:

1 through/to	5 away
2 at	6 on
3 from	7 over
4 back	8 right

Background note:

An *outer marker* is an ILS marker beacon usually on the runway centreline approximately 8.3 km from the threshold.

Extension activity:

If you decide your students need extra work on prepositions and similar words, you can make activities such as this one very easily.

1 Choose some sentences that you have already used with your class (e.g. an audioscript from an earlier unit). Underline the prepositions and similar words (e.g. *back*, *away*).
2 Write the underlined words in mixed-up order on the board.
3 Read each sentence aloud, saying 'blank' instead of each underlined word. Students have to choose a word from the board to write down for each blank.
4 When you go through the answers with the class, award a point for each correct answer. The student/team with the highest score is the winner.
5 Repeat with sentences from other texts.

5 **As in all pairwork activities, the emphasis in this exercise is on effective communication, i.e. fluency and interactions, between partners, not the use of correct phraseology. The scenarios reflect the various causes for level bust already covered in this unit, and some of the communication errors (readback error, call sign confusion), which we have seen so far in** *Flightpath*.

Go through the example with the class. Make sure students know they need to take notes and report back from them, and that they should report back on all five incidents at the same time. Students then work in pairs to describe their incidents, take notes and report back from their notes.

Suggested answers:
Student A
1 An Air Force Hercules departing Lagos (Nigeria) was cleared to 8,000 feet, but the pilot entered the wrong altitude and climbed to 9,000 feet. ATC instructed the pilot to descend/ re-descend/return to 8,000 feet.
2 A Saab A340 approaching Bergen (Norway) was cleared to 2,500 feet, but continued its descent to 2,000 feet creating/causing/ resulting in a traffic conflict. ATC contacted the crew to instruct them to take avoidance action/ measures by turning left and climbing (back)

to 2,500 feet / and turn left and climb back to 2,500 feet.
3 An A320 was cleared for a descent / to descend from Flight Level 310 to 250 / to FL 250 from FL 310. Casablanca Control (Morocco) re-cleared the aircraft to stop at Flight Level 280 when passing FL 290. The aircraft levelled off at FL 270 and climbed back to FL 280.
...

Student B
1 A B767 en route from Kuala Lumpur (Malaysia) to Singapore at Flight Level 310 experienced / encountered / was subjected to downdraughts and turbulence. The aircraft dropped 900 feet and then regained FL 310.
2 An A319 departing Riga (Latvia) was cleared to 6,000 feet. The crew requested a higher altitude because of / due to the weather and was cleared to FL 120. As they were levelling off at FL 120 they received a TCAS RA (Resolution Advisory) 'Descend' message. The crew had forgotten to set their altimeter to the standard pressure of 1013 hPa.
3 A B757 descending to Oakland (California) was cleared to FL 110. The Pilot Flying entered FL 100 on the autopilot Mode Control Panel. ATC contacted them and instructed them to climb back to FL 110.
...

If you have an **odd number of students** you will need to have a group of three students, where Student C takes incidents 1 and 2 from Student A and incidents 4 and 5 from Student B. While one student is describing an incident, both the other students should take notes and should report back together at the end.

Background notes:

◆ A *traffic conflict* occurs when two aircraft are at altitudes or on headings which, if maintained, could result in an airprox or a collision.
◆ When an aircraft *levels*, it stops ascending or descending.
◆ *En route* means *on the way*. Although it is French, it is commonly used in English to mean flying between two points, usually in cruise.
◆ A *TCAS RA* (Traffic Collision Avoidance System Resolution Advisory) is an automatically generated warning such as '*descend, descend*'.
◆ *PF* stands for pilot flying.
◆ A *Mode Control Panel* (*MCP*) on a Boeing aircraft fulfils the same function as a *Flight Control Unit* (*FCU*) in an Airbus aircraft, i.e. entering altitude, heading, speed, vertical speed (rate of climb / descent) values into the autopilot and autothrust/autothrottle.

6a Students work alone to match the beginnings of the sentences to the endings. When they have checked in pairs, go through the answers with the class. You may need to check the meaning of *distinguish between* (= tell the difference between).

Answers:
1 d	3 b	5 c	7 f
2 g	4 a	6 e	

Language note:

The technical meaning of *failure* will be familiar to most students, however, the use of *fail* as a verb, often applied to human behaviour, will be less so. *Fail to do* has two related meanings:

◆ to try to do something, but not succeed, e.g. *I fail to understand why you did that*.

◆ to not do something that you are supposed to do, e.g. *She failed to check* (= she didn't check; she forgot to check).

In most of the examples in exercise 6a, the second meaning is used.

Background note:

If you *cross check* something, you check one piece of information from two sources, e.g. the pressure altitude on the Captain's and First Officer's instruments.

Extension activity 1:

Discuss with the class the meaning of '*fail to do*' in each of the seven sentences (see *Language note* above). Note that in some sentences both interpretations are possible. You could also discuss with the class how common each of the seven situations is, in students' own experience.

Answers:
◆ try but not succeed: 1, 6
◆ not do something you should do: 2, 3, 4
◆ both interpretations possible: 5, 7

Extension activity 2:

The completed sentences illustrate operational 'failings' which are of interest in themselves. Use these notes to generate a class discussion: how often they occur and what can be done to minimise their dangers.

1 interrupted or garbled transmissions
2 the importance of flight crew members crosschecking each other's actions and instruments
3 the need to say the complete call sign and not just the last numbers

4 the absence of readback which may conceal a misunderstanding and deprives the interlocutor of situational awareness and a sense of security
5 the need to disconnect the autopilot in some critical manoeuvres such as responding to a TCAS warning or taking avoiding action
6 the number of cases where 11,000 and 10,000 have been confused
7 flying through their cleared level due to distraction, incorrect setting etc.

b Students discuss the question in pairs and then feed back to the class.

7a ◐2.15 Students read through the eight sentences to make sure they understand all the terms, including holding pattern identifier and Short Term Conflict Alert (see *Background notes*). Then play the recording for students to complete the exercise. When they have checked with a partner, play the recording a second time if necessary for them to check. Finally, go through the answers with the class. Discuss with the class who was at fault, the MD-81 crew, the B737 crew or ATC [**Suggested answer:** Based on the facts as presented, the B737 crew were in the wrong, as they descended much too far. ATC were also partly to blame, as they were not paying attention to the situation].

Answers:
1 F – in November (northern hemisphere)
2 F – LAM
3 T
4 T
5 F – the crew read back the instruction, but descended through FL 150 and did not report on reaching
6 T
7 F – 14,052 ft
8 T

Background notes:

◆ This is a shortened version of an authentic report of an incident which occurred near London Heathrow (LHR). A reference to the full report can be found in *Unit 6 Sources* at the beginning of the unit. The action takes place at one of the main holding patterns for LHR, *Lambourne*, identified alphabetically, *LAM*. Note that each airport has its own set of holding patterns, identified by various *holding pattern identifiers*, consisting of three letters. The narration is about how the altitude of the B737 is eroded in the holding pattern until it is only 100 ft above the level of the MD-81 despite a correct initial readback. Once aircraft have been cleared to a given level, controllers are not required to constantly monitor their movements.

♦ *Horizontal separation* is measured in metres here, while *vertical separation* is measured in feet. 1,000 feet separation is normally the minimum safe level.

♦ A *Short Term Conflict Alert* is 'a ground-based safety net intended to assist the controller in preventing collision between aircraft by generating … an alert of a potential or actual infringement of separation minima.' (Eurocontrol) See Eurocontrol: *Standardisation of Short Term Conflict Alerts*

Extension activity:

Students read audioscript 2.15 on page 182 to find the following:

♦ two phrases meaning *on the way to/from* [**Answers:** *en route from*; *bound for*]

♦ a phrase meaning *before* [**Answer:** *prior to*]

♦ a word meaning *later* [**Answer:** *subsequently*]

♦ two verbs describing separation becoming too low [**Answers:** *had reduced to; had closed to*]

♦ three collocations with *attention* [**Answers:** *to devote one's attention to sth*; *to draw sb's attention to sth*; *to require (immediate) attention*]

♦ two adjectives to refer to things happening very soon [**Answers:** *imminent*; *immediate*]

b **Students work in pairs to summarise the incident. Then ask one or two pairs to read their summaries aloud to the class. Discuss the summaries with the class, including any information that is missing or incorrect.**

> **Suggested answer:**
> An MD-81 from Denmark entered the hold near Heathrow at about 16:30. Two minutes later, a B737 from Amsterdam entered the same hold. The MD-81 was cleared to Flight Level 140. The 737 was cleared to Flight Level 150, but a little later the vertical separation between the two aircraft was reduced to 100 feet and the horizontal separation to 750 metres. The 737 descended to 14,050 feet. The controllers received a Short Term Conflict Alert and instructed the 737 to climb back to Flight Level 150. The 737 regained Flight Level 150.

Extension activity:

You could discuss what could be done to avoid such situations, both in the short-term (e.g. *what could/should the B737 pilot have done?*) and in the long-term (e.g. *how can ATCOs avoid becoming distracted? Should the Short Term Conflict Alert be set to activate sooner?*)

> **Suggested answers:**
> ♦ The crew of the B737 should have checked their actual altitude and have been aware of the fact that they were losing height. They may have needed to cross check their altitude readings and double-check their altitude setting.
> ♦ In this particular case, the controllers had no obligation to monitor the aircraft they had cleared, but regular monitoring would have alerted them to the deteriorating situation before the alert sounded. Good practice, working discipline and combating complacency are probably the most effective ways of avoiding distractions.
> ♦ If the Short Term Conflict Alert were set to be triggered earlier in a busy airspace like the one around Heathrow, it would constantly be going off and would become a self-defeating distraction. There is always a balance to be achieved in calibrating warnings in order to achieve maximum efficiency.

Communication errors: Readback/hearback and hearback errors

Communicative and operational issues:

Readback/hearback errors are a major safety concern, which we have already seen. Short definitions are to be found in the ICAO focus box below. To draw attention to a readback error, the contradictory word '*negative*' is used to prefix the correct message; to correct one's own mistake, '*correction*' precedes the correct version of the message.

The types of information that must be read back by the pilot are: Runway in use; ATC Route clearance; ATC Transponder (SSR) Code; Altimeter setting; Clearance and instruction to enter, land and take-off on, hold short of, cross or backtrack on a runway; Heading and speed; and Transition levels.

See: Eurocontrol, *Air-Ground Communication Safety Study – Causes and Recommendations,* 2006

http://www.eurocontrol.int/safety/gallery/content/public/library/AGC%20safety%20study%20causes_recommendations.pdf

Correcting erroneous information is one of the fundamental communication functions identified by ICAO in Appendix B of Doc. 9835. As regards the students, there are different aspects to correcting effectively:

♦ recognising the error (practised in exercise 7a)

♦ possessing the appropriate language to correct the error

♦ having the linguistic self-confidence to correct the error (practised in exercise 7b)

The teacher should monitor all three aspects in the two parts of this exercise.

ICAO FOCUS

Students read the quote to find four problems caused by hearback errors [**Answers:** less-than-required vertical separation; less-than-required horizontal separation; near mid-air collisions / airprox; runway incursions]. Students then discuss the three questions in pairs and feed back to the class. Discuss also the distinction between *hearback errors* and *readback/hearback errors* and elicit a simple example of each.

Answers:
- A *hearback error* is a failure to notice when one's own error is correctly repeated by the interlocutor.
- A *readback error* is a failure to correctly repeat all or part of a message to verify accuracy.
- A *readback/hearback error* is a failure to notice and correct a readback error.

8a ⊙2.16 Tell students to listen to the two communications and to make notes based on the questions. After listening, students discuss their notes with a partner and listen again if necessary to check. Finally, discuss the answers with the class.

Answers:
- Communication 1 is an example of a hearback error: the ATCO notices the pilot's erroneous readback ('*190*' instead of '*150*') and corrects the pilot who reads back correctly.
- Communication 2 is an example of a readback/hearback error: the pilot reads back the clearance incorrectly ('*290*' instead of '*250*'), but the ATCO does not pick up the mistake.

b ⊙2.17 Play the recording, pausing after the first communication to go through the example with the class. Focus on the language used to correct an error (e.g. *negative*; *I say again*; *correction* – see *Communicative and operational issues*). Then play the other communications, pausing after each one for a volunteer to correct the error. Discuss with the class the appropriacy of each response. Afterwards, students can test each other in pairs using audioscript 2.17 on page 182.

Suggested answers:
The errors are:
1 confusion of FL 190 for FL 150
   ATCO: *Cedar Air 385, negative: climb altitude fife thousand feet.*
2 confusion of KLM 4833 for KLM 4388
   ATCO: *KLM 4833, that transmission was <u>not</u> for you.*

3 two errors: first the pilot confuses the frequency 129.400 for 125.900, then the controller corrects incorrectly, by saying 125.400
   ATCO: *Shuttle 771, negative: contact Riga Approach 129.400.*
4 the pilot confuses the time to expect an onward clearance with the duration of the expected hold. The controller makes the correction, but then makes a mistake in flight level
   ATCO: *Shenzhen 3851, negative: expect onward clearance at time 25. Delays at Shanghai 20 minutes ... Correction: hold at Huzhou Flight Level 190.*
5 the pilot makes a readback error for the ATIS frequency which the controller does not correct
   ATCO: *Tarom 458, negative: monitor 128.375 for ATIS.*
6 the pilot confuses heading 290 for 250
   ATCO: *Spanair 3658, negative: turn left heading 290.*
7 the pilot reads back the squawk incorrectly, which goes uncorrected
   ATCO: *Vietnam Airlines 873, negative: squawk 5251; I say again 5251.*
8 the pilot makes a readback error in the altimeter pressure setting, which goes uncorrected
   ATCO: *Air Madagascar 663, negative: QNH 1003, I say again, QNH 1003.*

Background notes:

- *Huzhou Flight Level 190* means that the aircraft should pass over the Huzhou navaid beacon / waypoint at FL 190. Huzhou is 160 kilometres west of Shanghai, China.
- *Onward clearance* is clearance to pursue the flight after a waypoint or holding action.

Causes of level bust

Communicative and operational issues:

The introductory quote from *Reducing Level Bust* draws attention to the fact that those contributing and causal factors which result in level bust are also to be found in other types of incident. As is often the case, it is more interesting to discuss the causes behind phenomena than the phenomena themselves.

Quote: **Elicit from the class causes of level busts (see *Teacher's brief*). Students then read the quote to see if it mentions the same causes. Students could also be asked to provide examples and comment on cases of poor communication, distraction, lack of standard operating practices, high workload and pilot handling (flying skills), and how these might lead to level bust situations or other incidents.**

9a **◐2.18** Go through the six causes (a–f) briefly to elicit a simple example of each from the class. Then play the recording for students to complete the exercise. Students check in pairs before feeding back to the class.

> Answers:
> 1 e   3 f   5 d
> 2 b   4 a   6 c

Background notes:

- ◆ '*ILS 29*' is the ILS approach to Runway 29.
- ◆ *Climb-out* is an aircraft's initial climb from take-off.
- ◆ An *updraught* /ˈʌpdrɑːft/ is an ascending current of air.
- ◆ *Conflicting traffic* refers to other traffic at or near the same flight level heading towards each other.

b, c **◐2.18** Students go through the notes in pairs to see if they can fill in any information from memory and to predict what type of information is missing in each case. Then play the recording for them to complete the notes. When they have checked with a partner, you could play the recording again for them to check. Finally, go through the answers with the class.

> Answers:
> **Incident 1**
> a 3,000 ft b ILS 29 c 2,000 ft d 600 ft
>
> **Incident 2**
> a FL 350 b Flight 578
>
> **Incident 3**
> a descend b stop descent at FL 300 c FL 298
>
> **Incident 4**
> a Brussels b heavy rain c 230 ft
>
> **Incident 5**
> a 6,000 ft b FL 120 c TCAS Descend d QNH
>
> **Incident 6**
> a FL 140 b FL 078 c FL 080

d Discuss the question with the class.

ICAO FOCUS

Read the quote aloud. With the class, check the meaning of *breakdown* (= failure, disintegration, collapse). Students discuss the tasks in pairs and then feed back to the class.

> Suggested answers:
> Communication breakdown can take different forms: radio frequency interference, interruptions or saturation; readback/hearback errors; inadequate language skills, including problems of pronunciation; uncorrected misunderstandings; confusion about whom a message is intended for (call sign confusion); and radio failure. The way in which students grade the frequency of their occurrence will depend on their individual experience and also the conditions in which they operate. Allow students to discuss this if they disagree.

10 **◐2.19** Play the recording, pausing after each sentence for students to repeat, either as a whole class or individually. Students could also work in pairs and take turns to read the sentences aloud using audioscript 2.19 on page 182, paying particular attention to correct pronunciation.

11a Students work in pairs or small groups to prepare their dialogues. The dialogues could be similar in length to those in exercise 8b. Students could use the causal factors listed in exercise 9a as ideas for their dialogues.

b Students take turns to perform their dialogues for the class. Discuss with the class the accuracy and effectiveness of each dialogue.

Communication markers

Communicative and operational issues:

Effective communication does not only depend on the use of correct words (vocabulary), grammar and syntax (structure), and pronunciation. It also depends on the use of stress, intonation and pauses to attract the listener's attention to key information, especially in situations where communication is difficult or corrections must be made. This section of Unit 6 is designed to make students more aware of these techniques and give them an opportunity to practise them.

Another practical language skill is the ability to identify the type of information or transmission one hears, even if some of the detail is missing. Knowing that one is listening to a request, rather than an instruction, creates a mindset which facilitates understanding.

12a, b **◐2.20** Play the recording, pausing after the first transmission to go through the example with the class. Students could either write down the key words in their notebooks or, if you prefer, they could underline them in audioscript 2.20 on page 182. After playing the recording, allow students to compare their answers in pairs. Then play the recording again, pausing after each transmission for students to repeat, focusing especially on the stressed words.

Answers:
1 eight miles ahead
2 heading
3 After
4 under your own responsibility
5 11 o'clock

Background notes:

◆ An *ATR 72* is a twin-engine, short haul regional
turboprop aircraft manufactured by a Franco-
Italian consortium carrying up to 78 passengers.

◆ *11 o'clock* means ahead, above and slightly to
the left. A clock face is used to locate objects in
space from the viewpoint of the pilot.

◆ The *long way round* refers to a change of heading
in which the aircraft turns more than 180°.

◆ In transmission 8, '*Pass your message*' means
'give or transmit your message'.

c ◎2.20 Play the recording again, pausing after each
transmission to discuss with the class.

Answers:
1 where   3 when   5 where
2 what   4 how

Extension activity:

In preparation for exercise 13a, brainstorm onto the
board with the class some examples of ATCO or pilot
phrases used for answering questions beginning with
when, *where* and *how*.

Possible answers (mostly taken from
transmissions in Unit 6):

when	where	how
immediately	*(to/at) Flight level 210*	*direct*
in two minutes		*via*
when you're climbing again	*(to) altitude 5,000 feet*	*under your own responsibility*
on reaching	*at 12 o'clock*	*at your own discretion*
at time 25	*below*	
prior to descent	*at Shanghai*	
after the departing 767	*five miles*	
	crossing left to right	
when you are ready	*the hold*	
	level-off	
	above them	

13a Students work in pairs or small groups to prepare
their transmissions. They decide which key words to
stress and then act out their transmissions for the
class.

b ◎2.21 Make sure students understand the different
types of transmissions, especially the difference
between a clearance and a conditional clearance (i.e.
a clearance given to be executed only after another
aircraft movement has taken place, e.g. after the
departing 767). Then play the recording for students
to identify the purposes. Go through the answers with
the class.

Answers:
1 b – an instruction: '*climb and maintain*'
2 a – a clearance: '*cleared to ...*'
3 g – a confirmation: '*climbing back to ...*'
4 e – a question: '*How many passengers ...?*'
5 c – a conditional clearance: '*after the landing 737*'
6 d – a correction: '*Correction: ...*'
7 f – a request: '*Request ...*'

Background notes:

◆ A *radial* is a magnetic bearing from a navigation
aid e.g. VOR. The VOR transmits signals at a
specific frequency in all directions; the aircraft
identifies this signal by its frequency and also
the direction from which it comes (i.e. the
radial). By comparing the intersection of two VOR
signals the aircraft calculates its position. Like
other bearings (e.g. compass bearings and true
bearings), it is the angular direction of a distant
point measured in degrees clockwise from a
local meridian or other reference.

◆ In transmission 2, '*Alpha Delta November VOR*'
is the identifier (*ADN*) of a *VOR* transmitter which
is 18 miles from the *DME* (Distance Measuring
Equipment) transmitter, which will be located at
the airport and provide distance information for
the aircraft during approach.

Extension activity:

You could work on the skill of identifying purpose
by reading aloud the same seven transmissions at
very fast speed. This will force students to focus
on the purpose, even if they cannot understand the
actual message. You should change the order of the
transmissions, to make it harder for students to do
this from memory.

c ◎2.21 Read the quote aloud and check students
understand the four factors and how they can be
managed. Students then listen again and repeat
each transmission, either individually or as a class,
paying particular attention to the four pronunciation
factors. They can then practise again in pairs, using
audioscript 2.21 on page 182.

Language notes:

- ◆ Intonation here refers mainly to sentence stress: which words are pronounced most emphatically? In the case of a misunderstanding, the misunderstood word or information will be given greater stress in the clarification.
- ◆ Speed of transmission: how fast or slowly are individual words and groups of words pronounced? Speed of transmission should be influenced by the language proficiency of one's interlocutor and any apparent difficulty or misunderstanding he/she may be experiencing.
- ◆ Placement of pauses: between which words does the speaker pause? Pauses are used to separate different items of information or mark a transition or prepare the listener for an important piece of information.
- ◆ Duration of pauses: how long is each pause? There is no absolute rule as to the length of pauses; they are proportional to the rate of speech, i.e. the faster the rate of speech, the shorter the duration of pauses.

Extension activity:

Play the seven transmissions again for students to mark stress and pauses on audioscript 2.21 on page 182. They should mark stress by underlining key words; short pauses with a bar (|) between words; and long pauses with a double bar (||). Afterwards, it should be much easier for students to repeat the transmissions with the same pronunciation patterns.

14 **Go through the example with the class, pointing out that students will need to be creative when they invent their instructions. Make sure students realise they will need to stress the key words to help their partners. Students then work in pairs to complete the activity. When you go through the answers with the class, pay particular attention to the intonation patterns used.**

Answers:
Student A

1 where	6 when	11 what
2 when	7 what	12 when/where
3 how	8 what/where	13 when
4 where	9 where	14 how
5 what/where	10 where	15 when

Student B

1 when	6 what	11 what
2 where	7 where	12 when
3 how	8 what	13 how
4 when	9 where	14 what/where
5 where	10 when	15 where

Possible answers:
Student A
1 Request climb Flight Level <u>390</u>. / Maintaining Flight Level <u>390</u>.
2 We expect to reach Colombo <u>at 14:56</u>.
3 Perform delaying action <u>by orbiting to your right</u>.
4 We are passing <u>over Panama NDB</u>.
5 <u>Climb to</u> and maintain <u>6,000</u> feet.
6 Our expected approach time is <u>08:25</u>.
...

Student B
1 We started our descent <u>ten minutes ago</u>. / We crossed HID <u>ten minutes ago</u>.
2 We are stabilised <u>on the Localizer</u>.
3 Avoid the inbound traffic <u>by expediting your approach</u>.
4 Our ETA is <u>13:26</u>.
5 Request <u>Flight Level 170</u>.
6 <u>Fly heading 210</u> to intercept the ILS.
...

If you have an odd number of students you will need to have a group of three students, where Student C takes cues 1 to 5 from Student A and 11 to 15 from Student B.

Background notes:

- ◆ '*Panama NDB*' refers to the Non-Directional Beacon at Panama City.
- ◆ *Abeam* /əˈbiːm/ means to be level with a given point (at 90° or 270°), i.e. passing next to rather than over a point or the airfield.
- ◆ '*SAN VOR*' refers to the VOR transmitter at San Diego, California.
- ◆ '*QBC VOR*' refers to the VOR transmitter at Bella Coola, British Columbia, Canada.

Memorising headings, call signs and frequencies

Communicative and operational issues:

Both pilots and controllers use their short- and long-term memories intensively in their working environment in order to acquire and maintain situational awareness and draw on their training and know-how. Using one's working memory in a language which is not one's native language may be a challenge. In this section, students explore: how memory functions differently for pilots and controllers; what factors may diminish memory; retain key items of information from recordings; describe level bust incidents as a report or debrief; and perform pilot/controller exchanges managing level bust situations.

15a **Reading is not a language skill covered by the ICAO rating scale. However, all operational professionals read extensively, and the text in this exercise is one of the few reading texts in *Flightpath*, which has been chosen for its intrinsic value and interest.**

Elicit from the class how easy/difficult it is for pilots and ATCOs to memorise headings, call signs and frequencies, and whether such information is equally easy/difficult for pilots and ATCOs. Students then read the text to answer the questions. When they have answered the questions, students discuss their answers in pairs and then feed back to the class. You may need to check the meaning of some words, e.g. *to chunk* (= to break down into small pieces or bits [chunks]).

Answers:			
1 c	3 b	5 b	7 a
2 b	4 a	6 c	

Background notes:

Technically speaking, Eurocontrol used the wrong terms in this text, although the general message is still clear:

- *Sensory memory* is actually about visual, auditory or tactile memory, e.g. where an image is imprinted on somebody's retina for up to half a second, allowing the viewer to retain information after it has disappeared.
- *Short-term memory* corresponds to the phenomenon described as sensory memory in the text. It relies on an acoustic model, either directly hearing the information or imagining listening to the information in one's head, and recalling it for up to a minute. The figure of 7 ± 2 items is now disputed by many psychologists.
- *Long-term memory* is where we store much more information and for longer times, sometimes indefinitely. This is described as working memory in the text.
- *Working memory* is in fact a model to describe how we use short-term memory to manipulate information.

For more information, see: http://www.nwlink.com/~donclark/hrd/learning/memory.html.

Extension activity 1:

Elicit from the class chunks of information that your students have committed to long-term memory (e.g. a radio frequency they often use).

Extension activity 2:

Students read the text and questions to find three words and phrases meaning *pieces of information*.

Answers:
elements, *memory blocks*, *units of information*. The word *chunk* is not used as a noun in the text, but can also refer to a piece of information.

Quote: **Read the quote aloud. Elicit from the class the meanings of *active listening and intensive listening*. [Suggested answers: *Active listening* traditionally involves speaking (repetition, paraphrasing, asking**

for clarification) and body language (nodding, smiling, etc.). In RTF, active listening mainly relies on successful readback and hearback. *Intensive listening* invloves concentrating on every piece of information. It contrasts with *extensive listening* (= listening for a long period of time, to get a general understanding)].

b Students discuss the question in small groups and then feed back to the class. Encourage them to think of examples for each of the ten factors. You may need to check the meaning or pronunciation of some words, e.g. *workload* (= how busy someone is), *familiarity* (= how well the listener knows the other person, the situation, etc.) and *fatigue* /fəˈtiːɡ/ (= tiredness).

16 **○2.22** This listening exercise allows students to practise using their short term memory to distinguish and retain specific items of information in the way they are constantly required to do in operations. Play the recording, pausing after the first communication to answer the first question with the class. Then play the other seven communications. When students have compared their answers with a partner, you could play the recording again for them to check. Then feed back to the class. Afterwards, students could practise the communications in pairs, using audioscript 2.22 on page 183.

Answers:			
1 b	3 a	5 b	7 a
2 c	4 b	6 c	8 b

17a The reports of the level bust scenarios illustrated by the four sketches in this exercise combine descriptions of flight paths and suppositions about the probable causes of the incidents requiring students to use structures such as *probably, perhaps, may have, possibly, I think, it is likely* etc. You could elicit onto the board a list of these structures from the class. Students work in pairs or small groups to describe the incidents. Afterwards, elicit a description of each incident from volunteers.

Suggested answers:
a The Aeroflot A320 was cleared to Flight Level 110, but the flight crew set Flight Level 100 on the autopilot FCU. The flight crew levelled off at FL 100 and was contacted by ATC. The crew climbed back to FL 110.
b The United Saab 340 was cleared to 5,000 feet, but had entered 1003 instead of 1023 as QNH, and so was actually flying at approximately 4,300 feet. Faced with converging traffic at 4,000 feet, the aircraft climbed and levelled off at 5,000 feet.

c The Cathay Pacific B747 was cleared to 9,000 feet, but the pilot understood 5,000 feet. ATC noticed that the aircraft had flown through 9,000 feet and instructed it to climb back to / regain 9,000 feet. The aircraft levelled off at 6,800 feet and climbed back to 9,000 feet.

d The Akira ATR 72 was climbing through a storm from Flight Level 080. On reaching FL 120 the ATR lost 800 feet of altitude and lost separation with a Citation flying in the opposite direction at FL 110. The ATR continued its climb through FL 120.

b Students discuss the question in pairs and then feed back to the class. Encourage students to use a range of structures for speculating about the past, e.g. *probably*, *perhaps*, *may have*, *possibly*, *I think*, *it is likely*, etc.

> Possible answers:
> a There was probably a distraction in the flight deck and the other crew member did not crosscheck the setting or both crew members misheard the instruction.
> b The crew had either misunderstood the altimeter pressure setting or made a mistake when entering the value.
> c The pilot of the B747 had misunderstood '*five*' for '*nine*', or the controller had not pronounced it correctly as '*niner*'.
> d The ATR suffered a loss of altitude due to a downdraught in an electrical storm.

c Students work in pairs or groups of three to make dialogues (where the third student could be the co-pilot). Then ask volunteers to perform their dialogues for the class.

> Possible answers:
> **Incident a**
> A (ATCO): Aeroflot 358, descend to Flight Level 110
> B (pilot): Descend Flight Level 110, Aeroflot 358
> ...
> A: Aeroflot 358, confirm cleared flight level
> B: Flight Level 100, Aeroflot 358
> A: Negative. You were cleared Flight Level 110. Climb to Flight Level 110.
> B: Climbing to Flight Level 110, Aeroflot 358
>
> Answers for incidents b–d would follow a similar format.

Putting it together: Recommendations for pilots and controllers

Communicative and operational issues:

The final section of Unit 6 brings together various receptive and active communication skills:

recognising the nature of the circumstances which are causing a situation (exercise 18); using context to distinguish homophones (exercise 19a); enunciation, intonation and phrasing practice (exercise 19c); recognising the effects of bad communication practice (exercise 20a); discussing recommendations to avoid level busts (exercise 21a); and managing traffic using a chart (exercises 22a, b).

ICAO FOCUS

Elicit from the class what one must pay special attention to when using non-standard phraseology [**Answer**: enunciation; intonation; phrasing; use of simple words; being concise; being unambiguous]. Students then read the quote to compare their ideas. Check students understand all the words in the quote (see *Language notes* below). Note that the quote contains several examples of the type of language that Brian Day warns against: complex words, e.g. *enunciation*, *unambiguously*; and words that can create ambiguity, e.g. *application*, *countless*.

Students then complete the two tasks in pairs and feed back to the class.

Suggested answers:
- Situations in which standard phraseology cannot be applied: aircraft technical failures; ATC navaid or aerodrome ground failures; passenger or crew sickness; crew incapacitation; environmental threats; security issues on board or on the ground; deviations to an alternate; obstacles on the ground or the runway/taxiway; giving reasons for, and describing the consequences of, any unexpected events; describing physical phenomena, appearances, states of health and feelings (fear, concern, expectations etc.); explaining conditional actions (using *if*, *unless* etc.); expressing obligations and constraints; expressing possibility, eventuality, uncertainty; persuading, advising etc.
- Being both unambiguous and concise is extremely difficult. However, being an *effective* communicator should be uppermost in the minds of both students and teachers. Remind your students to concentrate on getting their message across. They should avoid unnecessary words and structures, but be flexible enough to be able to adapt their speech to the level of proficiency of their interlocutor and be able to say things in different and appropriate ways so as to be understood.

Language notes:

♦ *countless* = too many to be counted. Possibility of confusion with similar words in other languages meaning 'not many'.

♦ *applications* = uses. Possibility of confusion with other meanings of *application*, e.g. a job application.

♦ *enunciation* = clear pronunciation of sounds to maximise understanding. A simple way to improve enunciation is to exaggerate normal mouth movements.

♦ *intonation* = (in this context) rhythm and stress

♦ *phrasing* = grouping words, pausing

♦ *unambiguous* /ˌʌnæmˈbɪgjuːəs/ = having only one possible meaning. If a word or sentence is *ambiguous*, it may be interpreted in several ways.

♦ *concise* = short, efficient, not wasteful, like a pocket dictionary. Conciseness is essential in RTF because pilots and ATCOs often have to communicate information fast.

18a ○ 2.23 **Make sure students understand the six causes (a–f), ideally you should elicit examples of each. Then play the recording for students to complete the task. Students check in pairs and then feed back to the class.**

Answers:
1 e   2 c   3 b   4 a   5 d   6 f

Background notes:

♦ A *blocked transmission* is a transmission that fails to get through, typically because of a technical fault or frequency saturation.

♦ A *purser* is the head cabin attendant on a narrow-body aircraft.

♦ *Affirm* is a way of saying '*that is correct*', typically after a request to confirm. It is pronounced with the stress on the first syllable: /ˈəfɜːm/.

b ○ 2.23 **Students listen again and take notes. They then take turns to explain the reasons for the incidents to a partner. Afterwards, go through the answers with the class.**

Suggested answers:
1 Silkair has just descended following a TCAS RA instructing them to avoid traffic.
2 The purser was in the flight deck talking to the crew about a sick passenger; this distraction resulting in their failing to level off at 9,000 feet.
3 On Oman Air 5837 the flight crew entered an incorrect entry on their autopilot panel.
4 A blocked radio transmission prevented the crew from hearing all of the message.

5 Korean Air 3655 takes a message which was intended for another flight (Korean Air 3659).
6 Corsair 3668 makes an altitude readback error which the controller does not detect, making a hearback error.

c **Students discuss the task in pairs or small groups and then feed back to the class. For common causes of level bust, see** *Teacher's brief.*

19a ○ 2.24 **In addition to being an exercise about the use of conditionals and contextual matching, the completed sentences in this exercise describe the consequences of different types of bad communication practice and are intrinsically interesting as a subject of discussion.**

Go through the pairs of words with the class to check students know the meaning and pronunciation of each word. Then play the recording for students to choose the correct word. They discuss their answers and their reasons for choosing their answer with a partner and then feed back to the class.

Answers:	
1 weight	6 crews
2 route	7 too
3 know	8 hear
4 break	9 to
5 due	10 allowed

Language notes:

♦ *Root* and *route* are homophones in British English (/ruːt/) but not always in American English, where *route* is sometimes pronounced /raʊt/.

♦ *Dew* and *due* are both pronounced /djuː/ in British English and both pronounced /duː/ in American English.

Background note:

A *relief crew* is a flight crew on the ground or on board who replaces a crew at the end of their period of duty.

b **Students discuss the tasks in pairs and then feed back to the class. Write up the pairs of homophones on the board. You could turn the feedback into a game, asking each pair in turn to give a set of homophones. Pairs get a point for every set of homophones they contribute to the list (and no points if another pair names it first) and two points if they can argue convincingly that both words in their set are important for aviation English.**

Suggested answers:

acts/axe	aisle/isle	all ready / already	be/bee
blew/blue	bored/board	buy/by	cent/sent
find/fined	flew/flu	for/four	hall/haul
hire/higher	hole/whole	hold/holed	it's/its
missed/mist	new/knew	pair/pear	plain/plane
principle/principal	raise/rays	right/write	see/sea
steal/steel	tail/tale	there/their	waste/waist
weak/week	where/wear	whether/weather	would/wood
you're/your			

In addition to these, there are countless pairs of words which have the same spelling but radically different meanings (e.g. *to fly / a fly*; *to head / a head*; *right* = correct / *right* = not left). In most cases, it should be obvious which word is intended, but students need to be aware of secondary meanings of words they already know in order to minimise the risk of serious confusion.

Extension activity:

Students write pilot or ATCO transmissions containing one of the words from the board. Monitor carefully, to make sure students include enough context for other students to work out the meaning. They read their transmissions aloud for the other students to work out which word from the pair was used.

c ⊙**2.24** Play the recording again, pausing after each transmission for a volunteer to repeat it. Insist on good, clear pronunciation to maximise comprehensibility. Afterwards, students can take turns to read aloud the transmissions in pairs, using audioscript 2.24 on page 183.

Checklist: Students look at the poster quickly to decide if it is aimed at pilots or ATCOs [**Answer:** ATCOs]. Elicit the three points which ATCOs should be sure about as regards their clearances [**Answer:** received by the right crew; received accurately; and read back]. Go through the five points with the class, eliciting whether they or their colleagues always follow the five recommendations.

Background notes:

1 Headings, speeds and flight levels use numerals between 080 and 360.
2 Never be uncertain that your interlocutor has understood.
3 If you are doing something else while a readback is taking place you may be distracted and mishear or miss something.

4 If similar call signs are being used in the same airspace ATCOs should either advise the crews concerned to be especially careful or assign new call signs.
5 If there have been breaks or saturation on the frequency, clearances should be confirmed in case some information was missed.

20a **Students work alone to match the beginnings of the sentences with the endings. When they have discussed their answers with a partner, go through the answers with the class. You could elicit the rules about verb tenses in the eight conditional structures (see *Language note* below).**

Answers:

1 d	3 h	5 f	7 e
2 g	4 a	6 c	8 b

Language note:

The eight sentences are all examples of conditional structures. Each of them could refer to a future possibility (e.g. *When you are flying tomorrow, if you turn your head away from the microphone ...*) or a general statement (e.g. *Whenever you're flying, if you turn your head away from the microphone ...*). Note that *will* is not normally used to refer to the future after *if*, as it is in many other languages. The verb structures in the main clauses (here, the second part of each sentence) include imperatives (*advise*, *ask*) and modal verbs (*may, will, should*). The two halves of each sentence could, of course, be reversed, with some minor changes to pronouns, etc. (e.g. *The pilot may not be able to remember all the instructions if you give too many in the same message*).

Extension activity 1:

Write one or two key words from each sentence on the board (e.g. *head, reception*). Students close their books and have to reconstruct the complete sentences in pairs using only these key words to help them. Go through the sentences with the class, making sure their grammar is correct.

Extension activity 2:

You can also use the eight sentences to generate discussion based on their content, e.g. *Why might a pilot turn his/her head away from the microphone? Have you ever encountered this situation?*, etc.

b **Students work alone to make the beginnings of their sentences and then work in pairs or small groups to come up with endings to their partners' sentences. Collect examples from the class at the end.**

21a **Students discuss the task in pairs and then share their ideas with the class.**

Answers:

1 P	3 C	5 P	7 C	9 C
2 P	4 C	6 C	8 P	10 C

b **Discuss the reasons with the class, including any experiences students have of these recommendations being breached, or of situations where they proved very important.**

Background notes:

♦ Airline *Standard Operating Procedures* (recommendation 1) should identify and describe the standard tasks and duties of the flight crew for each phase of flight and each normal/ abnormal emergency situation.

♦ *SID* (recommendation 2) stands for *Standard Instrument Departure*, i.e. a pre-planned, coded IFR (Flight Instrument Rules) departure routing, pre-printed for the pilot to use in textual graphic form.

♦ A *step climb* (recommendation 2) involves gaining altitude by a series of steps, i.e. periods of level flight, between phases of climbing.

♦ *'Expect'* (recommendation 4) is used by ATC with a time or location reference for a clearance to be given later in the flight. It is important that it is not confused with a current clearance.

♦ Pilots should inform a new controller handling their flight of their current *cleared level/altitude* (recommendation 5).

♦ *Multiple instructions* in the same message increase the likelihood of confusion or failure to memorise (recommendation 6).

♦ For safety and monitoring purposes, it is important that all level busts are reported and recorded even if the aircraft was operating in an empty sky and there was no loss of separation (recommendation 7).

♦ Monitoring the frequency is a valuable source of situational awareness, but also an additional safety net as another pair of ears may pick up information that has been missed. Furthermore, in many cases where language was an issue, the crew on another flight has been able to facilitate or complete exchanges between ATC and another crew in difficulty (recommendation 8).

♦ Controllers must always challenge pilots if they do not provide the required information (recommendation 9).

♦ The airspace under the responsibility of each Air Traffic Control Centre is divided into smaller volumes called *sectors* (recommendation 10), each of which is controlled by one ATCO at a time. The sectors tend to be quite large, as borders between sectors have the most potential for confusion.

On the other hand, they must not be so large that they overwhelm the controller or saturate the radio frequency. If ATC *splits sectors*, they divide controlled airspace vertically (by flight level) or horizontally to accommodate high traffic, preferably using different radio frequencies.

♦ *R/T loading* (recommendation 10) refers to radio frequency overload or saturation.

Communication

22a **This pair work activity requires a certain amount of time and careful calculation to take into account aircraft relative movements and separation. This activity of managing a simplified en-route airspace at high altitude should generate discussion, even disagreement, and negotiation between the partners. The goal of the exercise is less the outcome than the communication between the students. Students work in pairs to complete the task. They then compare and discuss their solutions and reasons with the class.**

Tell students to read the instructions carefully.
Use questions to check they understand:

♦ Why are some planes red and some blue? [**Answer:** Red planes are visible to both partners; blue planes cannot be seen by the other person.]

♦ What can your partner see on his/her chart? [**Answer:** The same red planes plus some different blue planes.]

♦ Who will be the pilot and who will be the ATCO? [**Answer:** Students will take turns. When they make requests based on the cues, they will be pilots and their partners will be ATCOs.]

♦ Why is it relevant that the aircraft are in RVSM conditions? [**Suggested answer:** Because the vertical separation is reduced from 2,000 feet to 1,000 feet.]

♦ What do the numbers 50, 10 and 1,000 refer to? [**Answer:** 50 = horizontal separation, in nautical miles; 10 = approximate horizontal separation, in minutes; 1,000 = rate of ascent or climb, in feet per minute]

♦ Will FL 430 be for inbound or outbound flights? [**Answer:** Outbound, because 43 is an odd number]

♦ Why might you have to delay flights or give step-climbs or step descents? [**Suggested answer:** Because it might be necessary to wait for another plane to pass]

Go through the example carefully with the class. Note that experienced ATCOs should find this task fairly easy, but inexperienced trainees and pilots may well struggle, so you will need to provide plenty of guidance. For this reason, you will need to familiarise yourself with the charts, the suggested answers and the background notes before the lesson, to make sure you know exactly what the charts show. When you are ready, ask students to create their role plays.

Suggested answers:
Request possible:
Pilot: Air Canada 275, we are an Airbus A330, 150 nautical miles inbound from Caribou at Flight Level 300. Request climb Flight Level 360, Air Canada 275.
ATCO: Air Canada 275, climb Flight Level 360. Report reaching.
Request impossible for the moment:
Pilot: Northwest 2693, we are a Boeing 767, 50 nautical miles outbound from Caribou at Flight Level 290. Request climb Flight Level 350, Northwest 2693.
ATCO: Northwest 2693, unable. You have traffic above at Flight Level 310.
Pilot: Northwest 2693, when can we expect higher?
ATCO: Northwest 2693, turn right heading 110. Expect climb to Flight Level 350 in ten miles on heading 090.
Pilot: Turn right heading 110. Expect climb to Flight Level 350 in ten miles on heading 090, Northwest 2693.
…

If you have an odd number of students you will need to have a group of three, where Student C takes pilot cues 3 and 4 from Student A and cue 1 from Student B. Student C also responds as ATCO to Student A's cue 2 and Student B's cue 4.

Situation	Pilot	ATCO
A1	Student A	Student B
B1	Student C	Student A
A2	Student A	Student C
B2	Student B	Student A
A3	Student C	Student B
B3	Student B	Student A
A4	Student C	Student B
B4	Student B	Student C

Background notes:

◆ *RVSM conditions* involve the reduction of vertical separation from 2,000 to 1,000 feet with aircraft flying in opposite directions every 1,000 feet. See http://www.ecacnav.com/RVSM

◆ *Navaid* refers to various radio navigation aids: DME (Distance Measuring Equipment); NDB (Non-Directional Beacon); ADF (Automatic Direction Finder); VOR (VHF Omnidirectional Range); ILS (Instrument Landing System: localizer and glideslope); VORTAC (VOR + Tacan); GPS (Global Positioning System); GNSS (Global Navigation Satellite System); RNAV (Area Navigation). See http://www.allstar.fiu.edu/aero/RNAV.htm; http://www.trevord.com/navaids/; http://www.altairva-fs.com
◆ Caribou is a navaid on the Canadian coast.

b **Make a copy of the chart on the board. Then ask volunteers to explain what happened in each of the eight situations, and to mark the final positions of the aircraft on the board. Discuss any variations in the decisions the ATCOs took.**

Debriefing

23 **Students discuss the questions in pairs and then share their comments with the class. Discuss with the class possible ways of overcoming their weaknesses (e.g. by repeating the same or similar role-plays).**

Progress check

Students work alone to complete the table and then discuss their answers with a partner. Open up the discussion to include the whole class, including suggestions for how to continue to improve any problematic areas.

DVD: *Level Bust*

Communicative and operational issues

The clip in Unit 6 is taken from a NATS (UK National Air Traffic Services) training film entitled *Level Bust 2.* See http://www.scottipc.com/ for the complete film.

The text in exercise 24a defines a level bust and refers to a particularly deadly level bust accident which occurred over India in 1996. This accident in fact was a decisive factor in leading ICAO to take action to set up standards for language proficiency in aviation, which resulted in the creation of the PRICESG (Proficiency Requirements in Common English Study Group) in 2000 and the publication of the amended ICAO SARPS (Standards and Recommended Practices), Rating Scale and Holistic Descriptors in 2003. Poor language skills were a major contributing factor in this accident.

Part 1 (exercise 25a) highlights the importance of pilots declaring their cleared level to ATC at the beginning of each new exchange in avoiding level busts. There follows the re-enactment of an authentic level bust scenario in which an aircraft (Czar 286) descends to FL 100 instead of FL 110 and the

Heathrow controller's failure to notice the incorrect level report, compounded by the use of incorrect UK phraseology ('*FL one zero zero*', which is ICAO standard phraseology, instead of '*FL one hundred*', one of the few cases where the UK has differentiated from ICAO phraseology.)

In **Part 2** (exercise 26a) a controller is operating two sectors simultaneously and is very busy, and the frequency is close to saturation point. Two aircraft lose their vertical and horizontal separation and a TCAS Resolution Advisory is triggered.

Finally, **Part 3** (exercise 27c) refers to the effects of high Radiotelephony use on controllers' workload and how splitting sectors can reduce this. It ends with some advice about practical measures which controllers can take.

The DVD exercises also contain several activities where students work together to write an incident report (exercise 25b) and compare the facts in the video with their own experience (exercise 27a).

24a **Discuss the question with the class. Note that 300 feet is approximately 91.44 metres.**

b **One of the students reads the introductory text aloud while the others have their books closed. Ask factual questions about the date, aircraft involved, location, the altitude at which the accident took place and the type of incident which led to the collision. Students may well be aware of this well-known accident. Ask students about the confusion which was the direct cause of the accident [Answer: The crew of the Ilyushin took the information about another aircraft at Flight Level 140 as an instruction to descend to Flight Level 140], and about how the crew of the Ilyushin reacted [Answer: They initiated a descent from FL 150 to FL 140 believing it to be their newly assigned level. The radio operator, the only crew member to understand the transmission, warned them not to descend]. Ask students what the underlying cause of the accident was [Answer: insufficient language proficiency] and what measures could be taken to prevent such events.**

> Answers:
> This event illustrates the need for the whole crew to have an operational level of language proficiency. Having a radio operator who understood English in this case was insufficient as the pilots reacted without consulting him. Using translation on the flight deck increases response times, is distracting and unreliable. The crew may also have been unfamiliar with Indian accents. If either the flight crew or the controller has any uncertainty, they should request confirmation before acting.

Background notes:

- *Anxious* means being worried, tense or concerned.
- *Mid-air* means in flight, not on the ground.
- *Range* here refers to the distance of one aircraft from the other.
- *Radio operator*: initially, aircraft were flown by a five-man crew: captain, First Officer, flight engineer, radio operator (whose language skills were often better than those of the rest of the crew) and navigator. With the advances of navigational technology and aircraft system automation, these five-man crews have gradually been reduced to the two pilots on modern aircraft.
- This mid-air collision, in which a lack of language proficiency was so clearly the major contributing factor, led to ICAO investigating the use of English in aviation RT communications through the PRICESG and issuing the Language Proficiency Requirements in March 2003.

25a **Discuss the first question with the class to predict what the answer might be. Make sure they understand the meaning of *compounded* (= made worse) in question 3. Then play the clip for students to find the answers to the four questions. Afterwards, students compare their answers in pairs before feeding back to the class. You could play the clip a second time to focus on some of the vocabulary from the *Background notes* below, and to draw attention to the mistakes that were made by the pilot and the ATCO.**

> Answers:
> 1 The crew of Czar 286 confuse FL 110 and 100 and descend through FL 110 to which they were cleared.
> 2 Heathrow Director did not pick up that Czar 286 believed that they had been cleared to FL 100.
> 3 '*FL one zero zero*' instead of UK phraseology '*FL one hundred*'; '*Just stay on that heading for the time being, please*' is also not standard phraseology.

Background notes:

- If a problem is *precipitated* by an event, it is triggered by it.
- The *preventive level bust trial* was a test to measure how many level busts occurred within a given period of time. It was a preventive trial in that it aimed to prevent future level busts by identifying their causes.
- A *safety net* is a system which prevents incidents turning into disasters.

◆ Note that the call signs in this case study are *fictitious* (= invented), but the case study is based on real events.

◆ The *Heathrow Director* refers to the ATC centre in charge of arriving flights. See http://www.vatsim-uk.org

◆ *Shamrock* is the prefix of all Aer Lingus call signs.

◆ *Millibars* and hectoPascal refer to the same unit of barometric pressure measurement.

◆ '*Flight Level one zero zero*' is correct ICAO standard phraseology. However, given the well-documented cases of confusion which have occurred between FL 110 and FL 100, the UK CAA has decided to adopt '*hundred*' (*FL 100: Flight Level one hundred*; *FL 200: Flight Level two hundred* etc.) rather than '*zero zero*'. For this and the other differences between ICAO and UK phraseology notified to ICAO, see CAA CAP 413 Radiotelephony Manual, Appendix 1.

◆ '*just stay on that heading for the time being, please*' is an example of an unjustified use of plain language where standard phraseology is adequate: '*Maintain heading 190 (degrees)*'.

Extension activity:

You could discuss with your students the reasons for the UK Authorities deviating from ICAO phraseology in this instance by preferring *FL one hundred* over *FL one zero zero* and whether they think the decision is justified.

b **Students work in pairs to make their reports, either orally or in writing. You could play the DVD again for them to check any information they missed.**

> Suggested answer:
> Two flights were inbound to London Heathrow: Endol 675 descending to FL 100 in contact with Heathrow Intermediate Director, and Czar 286 cleared to descend to FL 110 by Bovingdon ATC. Czar 286 confused their cleared FL 110 with FL 100 and descended towards the same level as Endol 675. Heathrow Director failed to detect the error by Czar 286. In order to re-establish separation between the two aircraft, ATC instructed Endol 675 to change its heading.

26a, b **Students watch the clip to make notes about the causes of the incident. After they have discussed their answers in pairs, play the clip a second time before going through the answers with the class.**

> Suggested answers:
> ◆ The controller is operating two sectors and the RT frequency is very busy.
> ◆ The controller introduces a call sign error saying '*Victor Yankee Victor*' instead of '*Victor Juliet Victor*' which creates a doubt in the pilot's mind causing confusion over the Flight Level and heading (85 instead of 95), which can be heard in his voice and hesitation. The controller picks up on this, but only requests a readback of the heading.
> ◆ The controller does not take any avoiding action even though the aircraft pass very close to each other: 600 feet vertical separation and 1.1 miles horizontal separation.

Background notes:

◆ *Lambourne* (*LAM*) *departure* refers to the name of one of the VOR/DMEs around Heathrow which is used for departures towards the east and holding.

◆ VSHJV is outbound from *Biggin Hill* (navaid location, business aviation airfield and former RAF base, to the south east of Heathrow) and Lomair 814D is inbound to London Gatwick.

◆ *TMA* means Terminal Control Area or Terminal Manoeuvring Area.

◆ *R/T loading* refers to the amount of traffic on one frequency.

◆ *Handover* refers to the transfer from one controller to another.

◆ ICAO Doc. 4444 specifies '*Descend/Climb to a level*'; '*Descend and maintain*'. ICAO does not require the mention of *degrees* after a heading.

◆ *3325/2325*: there is an uncorrected squawk readback error.

◆ *1,400 metres* is the horizontal separation distance in this incident, which triggers a TCAS Resolution Advisory.

◆ '*Avoiding action*' is an announcement by the controller to alert the crews that they must modify their flight path to avoid coming into conflict with other traffic.

27a **Students discuss the question in pairs and then report back to the class.**

b **Students make their checklists in pairs and then share their answers with the class. Make a list of students' suggestions on the board. Avoid confirming or rejecting their answers at this stage, as they will watch and compare in exercise 27c.**

Suggested answers:
1 Monitor all readbacks.
2 If the frequency gets busy, don't speed up your delivery: it doesn't help.
3 Avoid multiple instructions: ideally, don't include more than two instructions in one transmission.
4 For some operators, consider issuing only one instruction per transmission.
5 Whenever practicable, reduce the number of level change instructions that you issue to each aircraft.
6 Keep frequency changes separate from other instructions.
7 If you detect a level bust which may result in a loss of separation, do not waste time by asking the aircraft involved to confirm the cleared level; pass good and effective avoiding action; use the words '*avoiding action*'; and if it's urgent, then make it sound urgent.

c Play the clip for students to compare it with the list on the board. After students have discussed the answers in pairs, you may need to play the clip again before discussing the advice with the class.

Background notes:

◆ *High R/T occupancy* means there is a lot of traffic on the same frequency. See also *R/T loading*.
◆ *Picking up* is an expression commonly used in an aviation context in different ways. In this case it is being used in the sense of someone detecting something heard on the frequency. In a more technical sense, it refers to sensors, detectors or *pickups*, which monitor various parameters on the aircraft: vibration; end of travel; position etc.
◆ If you *speed up delivery*, you speak faster.
◆ *Pertinent information* is information that is relevant and useful.

28a Students work alone to complete the advice. You may need to play the DVD again before going through the answers with the class.

Answers:
1 waste time
2 avoiding action
3 make it sound urgent

b Discuss the question with the class.

Possible answer:
Urgency is best expressed not by speaking quickly, but by articulating clearly, stressing certain key words, speaking forcefully, using '*I say again*' when necessary and creating micro-pauses to highlight key words or items of information.

Extension activity:

The whole DVD from which these clips are taken is well worth watching. You could ask different students to watch different parts of the video as homework (see http://www.scottipc.com/course/content/view/58/83/) and then in the next lesson share what they learnt with a partner who has watched a different part.

UNIT 7
Decision making

Operational topics	US Airways Flight 1549; ETOPS diversion at night; Decision making and the language barrier; The effects of stress; Tunnel vision; Managing an abnormal situation
Communication functions	Incident reporting and action taken; Question following a condition; Expressing uncertainty; Communication errors: failure to question instructions; Asking and saying why; Dealing with a lack of language proficiency; Feasibility; Describing a flight path; Asking and answering about intention; Negotiating a course of action
Language content	Distinguishing past and present; Pronunciation and intonation in complete sentences; '*Do you want to …?*'; Stressed syllables; '*I am not sure*'; Cause and feasibility; Conditionals; Focused listening; Intention; Stressing key words

Unit 7 Teacher's brief

All the emergency or abnormal in-flight scenarios upon which the various sections of Unit 7 are based have in common the need for the crew to make critical decisions in a short time and under stressful conditions. **Aeronautical decision making** is a skill which is part of most commercial pilots' basic training, as are other 'soft' skills such as **CRM** (Crew Resource Management) and human factors.

The scenarios used in Unit 7 are:
* the **bird strikes**, twin engine failure and successful ditching of United Airways 1549;
* a **seriously ill passenger** requiring a diversion;
* the **diversion** of an ETOPS flight over the North Atlantic due to an engine **oil leak**;
* a **loss of instrumentation** complicated by **language problems**;
* making decisions under **stress**;
* managing a **damaged windshield** and **injured passengers** on a B777 between Japan and Russia.

The complexity of this unit is due to the fact that students' tasks are largely based on a series of decision-making pair work scenarios in which they have increasing scope to improvise. It was felt that it would be useful to give teachers full support here in terms of extensive technical background information and sample dialogues.

Unit 7 Sources

* Eurocontrol: *Network Operations Report*, 2009 (ACCs and charts) (Exercises 9a; 19b; 21b; 24)
* Eurocontrol: *Loss of communication* DVD in *All Clear* toolkit (Exercises 26a–29)
* FAA: *Extended operations of multi-engine airplanes*, November 3, 2003 (Exercises 11a–13b)
* Lacagnina, M.: *Landing on the Hudson*, AeroSafety World, August 2010 (Exercises 3a–d)

* Lacagnina, M.: *Survival on the Hudson*, AeroSafety World, July 2010 (Exercises 3a–d)
* www.metacafe.com; www.flightaware.com; *NTSB News*, May 4, 2010 (Flight 1549) (Exercises 3a–d)
* Rash, C. and Manning, S.: *Thinking things through*, AeroSafety World, July 2009 (Exercise 2)
* Rash, C. and Manning, S.: *Stressed out*, AeroSafety World, August 2009 (lead-in to Exercise 20a)
* www.skybrary.aero; *ETOPS diversion at night* (Exercises 11a–13b)
* UK AAIB: *Incident report EW/C2007/0602* (Exercise 14a–b)
* Werfelman, L.: *Language Barrier*, AeroSafety World, August 2008 (Exercises 14a–b)

Lead-in

The short lead-in quote is the first thing the captain of US Airways 1549 said to ATC after he realised that both the A320's two engines had ingested birds and lost power during the initial climb from LaGuardia Airport, New York on January 15 2009.

NOTE: 'Cactus' is the commonly used call sign for America West Airlines, which merged with US Airways while retaining its own call sign and ICAO code, just as 'Speedbird' is British Airways' call sign and 'Cedar Jet' Middle East Airlines'.

This is one of the most widely reported aircraft accidents in recent aviation history, because of the spectacular way in which the aircraft landed by ditching on the Hudson River, the captain's remarkable flying skills and cool-headedness, and the flight's successful outcome.

Quote: **Read the quote aloud and elicit from the class what the story was. Avoid discussing any details at this stage.**

131

1a, b, c Students work in pairs or small groups to discuss the three questions. After a few minutes, open up the discussion to include the whole class. Write on the board as much information and as many comments as you can elicit.

> **Suggested answers:**
> The twin engine failure was caused by the A320 ingesting Canada geese and the aircraft losing most of its power. As a result, the captain had to ditch in the Hudson River and all the passengers and crew evacuated the aircraft by the emergency exits finding refuge on the wings while they waited to be rescued.
>
> Factors contributing to the success of the operation included: the captain's quick thinking; his ability to eliminate all the solutions to divert to other airfields proposed by ATC; the crew performing the necessary checklists and placing the aircraft in an optimum configuration for landing on water very quickly; the fact that there was no river traffic and it was daytime.

Extension activity:

You could print some maps connected with the story from the internet. For an animation of US Airways Flight 1549, see
http://www.meriweather.com/ and
http://www.flightstats.com/.
For a map of the New York area, showing the flightpath and the locations of LaGuardia and Teterboro airports, see
http://flightaware.com/live/flight/USA1549.
For a recording and transcript of the flight deck – ATC exchanges, see www.aopa.org. Use these maps to elicit from the class exactly what happened and what the pilot's options were at each stage. Note that there will be a chance to discuss the incident in more detail in exercises 3a, b and c.

US Airways Flight 1549

Communicative and operational issues:

Flight 1549 takes off from LaGuardia airport (the smallest of New York's three airports, located in Queens at the end of Long Island) and is instructed to turn left on a heading of 270°. Almost immediately, the captain reports the bird strike and loss of both engines. Notice in the transcript in exercise 3b how he makes a mistake in his own call sign. ATC assumes he wants to return to LaGuardia, gives him a new heading and instructs the Tower to stop all departures. The first controller relays the information to the Tower and makes another, different mistake in the flight's call sign. The Tower is reluctant to believe that the aircraft has lost all power: a very rare occurrence. (NOTE: You may need to explain '*Got it*'.) ATC proposes Runway 13 to the crew. Already

the captain realises that he may not have enough power to perform a circuit and return and may have to ditch. ATC does not fully understand the gravity of the situation and proposes another runway, 31. The captain says he definitely cannot ('*Unable*'). ATC suggests Runway 04. The captain then enquires about Teterboro, another airfield to his right and replies to ATC that he wants to try Teterboro. ATC proposes Runway 01. The captain says he is unable, which ATC interprets as his meaning he prefers another runway at Teterboro. The captain announces his intention to ditch. The controller still does not fully grasp the situation.

Interestingly, under stress, apart from the instructions ('*Turn left heading 270*', '*Turn left heading of 220*') and the captain's '*Unable*', nearly all the communication is in plain language rather than in standard, or even non-standard, phraseology, and both controller and pilot make mistakes about the call sign.

For more information on Flight 1549, see *Survival on the Hudson* in *Aerosafety World*, July 2010, the transcript and recording on www.aopa.org, and the full report on www.ntsb.gov

For another case of a bird strike, which involved considerable communication problems and demonstrates the need for a proficient level in plain language, see the recording and transcript of communications between Flight Swiss 1311 and Pulkovo ATC on January 10 2010. You can find links from www.liveatc.net.

Purpose and relevance of activities:

The ends of the sentences in exercise 4a are the standard responses or consequences of the circumstances in the beginning of the sentences. The responses to abnormal situations in exercise 5 are also quite standard.

The information required for the role-play in exercise 6 will have been explored in exercise 3. The purpose of the exercise lies more in the discussion which it elicits.

Quote: **Tell students to read the quote to find three factors that contributed to the successful outcome.**

> **Answers:**
> training, experience, decision-making skill

2 **Students discuss the question in pairs and then share their best stories with the class. Allow plenty of time for this discussion, as these stories will provide context for discussions throughout the unit.**

3a **○2.25 Go through the instructions with the class. Make sure they cover the script in exercise 3b, as this would spoil the listening activity. Then play the recording for students to complete the task. Afterwards, students discuss their answers in pairs,** focusing on who said each expression and why. Then go through the answers with the class. You may need to check some words, such as *end up* (= finish in an unexpected situation).

> **Answers:**
> a, c, e, f

> **Background notes:**
> ♦ *Ditching* involves alighting (= landing) an aircraft on water in an emergency.
> ♦ *Ingesting* means sucking or pulling into the engine.

b Students read the script to remember or work out what words are missing. They discuss their ideas in pairs. Then play the recording again for them to check before going through the answers with the class.

> **Answers:**
> 1 left   6 both
> 2 birds   7 unable
> 3 towards   8 traffic
> 4 Tower   9 available
> 5 thrust   10 Anything

3c, d Students discuss the questions in small groups and then feed back to the class.

> **Answers:**
> 3c 1 heading 270 / heading 220
>   2 They say three different call signs: 1549; 1539 and 1529
>   3 return to LaGuardia
>   4 LaGuardia Tower
>   5 surprise, disbelief
>   6 RWY 13
>   7 RWY 04
>   8 landing at Teterboro
>   9 RWY 01 at Teterboro
>   10 land in the Hudson River
> 3d The audible signs of stress are: the speed of delivery – a speech rate of some 170 words a minute, which is almost at the limit of what is comprehensible by a native speaker; the confusion of the call sign referred to as 1549, 1539 and 1529; the ATCO's hesitations – '*it's ... he ... ah, bird strike.*'; the ATCO's disbelief when the captain says, '*We're going to be in the Hudson.*'

Language focus: Past and present

Tell students to look back at the script in exercise 3b to find sentences about the present and about the past. Elicit from the class the tenses that are used and why. Elicit also why accuracy with these tenses may be an important safety issue.

Language note:

We use present continuous because the events in the present tend to be incomplete or ongoing. We use past simple because events in the past tend to be complete. The distinction between simple and continuous leads to many mistakes from learners, who overuse the past continuous.

The distinction is not just important for its own sake: it can have safety implications as well. It can be difficult to hear endings such as *-ed*, especially in radiotelephony, so it is easy to mishear *we turn back* as *we turned back* or *we've turned back*. Similarly, unstressed words such as *are* and *were* can be difficult to make out, so *we were turning back* sounds similar to *we are turning back*. There is no such potential for confusion if the correct forms are used: *we are turning back* sounds very different from *we turned back*.

4a ○2.26 Students work alone to match the events with the resulting actions. When they have checked in pairs, go through the answers with the class, focusing on why other possible answers are wrong. You may need to draw attention to the lack of a subject in some of the sentence endings (see *Language note* below).

> **Answers:**
> 1 f   3 h   5 c   7 e
> 2 d   4 a   6 b   8 g

Language note:

The subject may be omitted after *and*, *but* and *or* if it is the same as in the first part of the sentence. For clarity, however, it is fine to keep the subject in both parts.

> **Background notes:**
> ♦ *Area Control* refers to ATCOs responsible for aircraft overflying a large area of airspace at altitude. *Approach* refers to ATCOs responsible for guiding aircraft to capture their glide path and land.
> ♦ *Parameters* are basic definable values or quantities which can be expressed numerically (%, °C, kts, ft, psi etc.).

Extension activity:

Students work in pairs to underline the words they would stress in each sentence and then listen again to check. This will help them in exercise 4b.

b ○2.26 Play the recording, pausing after each sentence for students to repeat, either individually or as a class. Make sure their pronunciation is good. Afterwards, students can repeat the sentences in pairs.

Extension activity:

Students test each other in pairs by reading the beginning of a sentence to elicit from their partner the correct ending. This will be another chance to reinforce the use of present continuous for present actions.

5 Go through the example with the class. Point out that each interaction could start with the same request, '*Report on your status*', and that students should ask for and give clarifications if necessary and read back the information to their partners. Point out also that they should pay particular attention to tenses, and use past simple and present continuous as in the previous exercises.

> Suggested answers:
> **Student A**
> 1 We had a bird strike and lost thrust on Engine Number 1. We are turning back and request ILS approach Runway 21.
> 2 We have lost all our display units and only have our standby instruments. We have performed our checklist and request return to land.
> 3 We are experiencing severe turbulence at FL 370. Eight passengers and two cabin attendants have been injured and are suffering from fractures, concussion and bleeding. The cabin crew are assessing the situation. Request diversion.
> 4 DHL 1274. Some of our cargo pallets have shifted. The flight engineer is trying to secure them. We are concerned about our centre of gravity. Request precautionary landing.
> ...
> **Student B**
> 1 We have encountered volcanic ash and Engine Number 3 has stalled. We can see Saint Elmo's fire on the windshield. We are making a 180 degree turn and request descent.
> 2 We seem to have contradictory captain and First Officer glideslope displays/readings. We have disconnected the autopilot and request a visual approach Runway 31 Left.
> 3 A middle-aged male passenger was showing threatening behaviour. He has been restrained by the cabin crew, but has referred to explosives in the hold. Request immediate diversion.
> 4 A female passenger is suffering from a severe asthmatic attack. She is being given oxygen by the cabin crew at the moment and her condition appears stable. We may request a diversion.
> ...

If you have an odd number of students you will need to have a group of three, where Student C takes cues 1 to 3 from Student B and cues 7 and 8 from Student A.

Background notes:

Student A:

◆ In case of an engine failure after take-off, the aircraft returns to its departure airport.
◆ 2 If the computerised flight instrument displays (*PFD* and *ND*) are lost, there are conventional *standby analogue and mechanical instruments* to provide essential flight data (airspeed, altitude, attitude). *Standby* here refers to an alternate, backup, redundant or precautionary system, instrument or mode of operation. *Analogue* instruments use technology based on continuous variables rather than *digital* technology based on discrete, binary items of information. *Analogue* is spelled *analog* in American English.
◆ If passengers are injured during a flight, the crew will request a diversion to land as soon as possible so that they can receive medical attention.
◆ Containers and *pallets* (= flat platforms transporting goods) may become loose during the flight, especially on cargo flights. This constitutes a very severe threat to the aircraft as it creates an imbalance (a shift in the plane's *centre of gravity*) and may make controlling the aircraft difficult. The crew will request a *precautionary landing* (= a normal landing conducted as soon as possible following a technical failure etc., but not an emergency landing).
◆ A *suspicious parcel* might mean a bomb scare. The procedure is to place the parcel near an aft exit and cover it with layers of material, such as blankets.
◆ Electrical fires are a real danger, especially in the densely packed wiring in the flight deck or the high voltage appliances used in the galley (water heater, boiler, ovens).
◆ If the wing anti/de-icing system fails in cloud, ice will accumulate on the leading edges, change the centre of gravity, increase the weight of the aircraft and possibly prevent some flight control movements.
◆ High-tension *electrical discharges* from lightning can severely damage the electrical and computerised systems.

Student B:

◆ Volcanic ash can cause engine failure due to blade damage and clogging; performing a 180° turn immediately is the correct response. *Saint Elmo's fire* is a visible discharge on blades, windshield etc. caused by build-up of electrostatic potential. While it may be spectacular at night, it is not a direct threat to aircraft safety; however, it may be an indication of the presence of volcanic ash in the atmosphere.

- If two displays are *contradictory*, they show conflicting information, which can't be correct on both displays. Both pilots regularly crosscheck their flight instruments: if there is a discrepancy in their glideslope readings during approach, they will have to fly a manual, visual approach rather than an automated one.
- This is an example of a terrorist/hijacker threatening the flight; the crew has an emergency code to alert the ground.
- Cabin crew monitor any health problems among the passengers and inform the flight crew if they are severe and may require the flight to be diverted.
- A hydraulic failure may directly affect the flight controls, landing gear extension, braking and wheel steering. The principal flight controls are triplexed, i.e. are supplied by three independent hydraulic systems, but roll-out and taxiing may be downgraded.
- The aircraft should make a precautionary landing after an engine failure, but as it has taken place just after take-off, the aircraft may be above its *maximum landing weight*, the weight at which it can land without risking structural damage. In this case, the crew will either have to burn off fuel, or more quickly, dump or jettison fuel to reduce the aircraft weight.
- A drop in engine oil pressure or quantity could cause severe damage to the engine if the engine is not shut down or throttled back to idle. Crews also try to divert to airports (stations) where their aircraft type can receive appropriate maintenance.
- *Electronic racks* are shelves used to house computers in the avionics bay / main equipment centre. A bitter, sharp or *acrid* smell may be a precursor of an electrical fire. The crew will don their oxygen or smoke masks and the First Officer may inspect those areas where a fire is most likely before it increases in intensity or spreads.

Extension activity:

Discuss with the class the captain's use of the phrase '*We may request a diversion*' (Student B's cue 4). Point out that ATC has responded as to full emergencies on several occasions due to the fact that they did not pick up the fact that the flight crew had used the modal verb *may* or *might* in a statement. You may wish to discuss and practise the distinction between '*We may declare an emergency*' and '*We are declaring an emergency*' with your students. The same remark applies to cue 5, when the captain says '*We may require assistance on landing*'.

6a Go through the instructions with the class. You may want to elicit some useful phrases and write them

on the board (e.g. *What happened first / next / after that?*; *No, I think that happened before/after …*; *Didn't that happen earlier/later?*). Students then work in pairs to put the events in order. When you go through the answers with the class, make very brief notes on the board for each event, as this will be useful for exercise 6b.

Answers:				
1 h	3 g	5 f	7 a	9 d
2 e	4 c	6 j	8 b	10 i

If you have an **odd number of students** you will need to have a group of three students, where two students both look at the Student A events.

b Students role play the communication in pairs, using the notes on the board and their own ideas. Point out that they do not need to use the exact words from the script, and they should obviously not make the same call sign errors made by the pilot and ATCO in real life. Afterwards, students swap roles and act out the situation again.

If you have an **odd number of students** you will need to have a group of three, where students take turns to be the pilot or the ATCO, or to listen and compare the dialogue with the script. They should swap roles twice during each role-play (at the points marked '…' in the script).

c Discuss the questions with the class.

> Suggested answers:
> Once he was aware of the bird strike and the twin engine flame-out, the pilot of Flight 1549 had to start or maintain the APU to provide essential electrical and hydraulic power and then assess the situation and decide: whether the engines could be re-started; how much manoeuvrability he had at that altitude without engine power and with reduced flight control response; the safest options for diversion; the best use he could make of the aircraft's momentum; the best angle of attack for ditching etc.

What should we do?

Communicative and operational issues:

This section picks up on two communicative functions to be found in the transcript of US Airways Flight 1549: asking someone if they want to do something in certain conditions; and expressing uncertainty. These are both functions used when pilots and controllers negotiate abnormal situations and work out together the best course of action.

The question '*What should we do?*' is more a question which pilots or controllers might ask each other rather than part of a pilot–controller exchange where roles and responsibilities are clearly defined.

Exercises 7 and 8 prepare the freer and wider use of language in exercise 9, where pairs have to exchange information and discuss various options in an ongoing situation.

7a ❍2.27 Students work alone to match the beginnings with the endings and then check with a partner. Play the recording for them to check. When you go through the answers with the class, elicit why the other answers are incorrect. Note that the answers to questions 4 and 5 could be swapped, but that fire and smoke is always more of an emergency than depressurisation.

Answers:			
1 e	3 a	5 f	7 h
2 g	4 c	6 d	8 b

Background note:

A *low pass* is a flight at low altitude in landing configuration above the aerodrome usually so that the Tower can check whether the landing gear seems correctly extended and locked down.

Extension activity 1:

Elicit from the class whether the sentences refer to the present or the future, and which tenses are used in the *if*-clauses and why. [**Answers:** The sentences are all about future possibilities. The verbs in the first part of each sentence are all in the present simple. *Will* is not normally used after *if*.]

Extension activity 2:

Write one or two key words from each sentence half onto the board (e.g. *relights – continue*; *icing – cloud layer*; *passenger's pain – divert*, etc.). Students then close their books and take turns to make sentences using only the cues to remind themselves.

b ❍2.27 Play the recording, pausing after each sentence for students to repeat, either individually or as a class.

8 ❍2.28 Go through the example with the class. Point out that the three ways of expressing uncertainty are interchangeable. Then play the recording for volunteers to respond. Encourage them to use a range of ways of expressing uncertainty.

Extension activity:

Play the recording again, eliciting continuations for each line.

Possible answers:
1 ... It's completely dead.
2 ... because there's traffic above us.
3 ... Our wings are icing up.
4 ... because we've lost thrust.
5 ... There's a great deal of turbulence.
6 ... because there are large weather systems on both sides of our course.

7 ... We're already at 1,500 feet per minute.
8 ... because there's a strong headwind.
9 ... We have a speed penalty due to the headwinds at this altitude.
10 ... They've jammed at 30 degrees.
11 ... we're running dangerously low on fuel.
12 ... because it's too far away.
13 ... so we're going to make an emergency landing.
14 ... We are short of fuel.
15 ... We're already at our minimum speed.

9a Go through the instructions with the class. Make sure they realise that the pilot will initiate the conversation with the cue marked *7:05*. The ATCO should respond with the cue marked *7:06*, and so on. Point out that students should add their own ideas to those in the cues, and try to use conditional sentences and the language of expressing uncertainty in their conversations. Students then role play the conversation in pairs. They swap roles and repeat the role-play.

> **Suggested answers:**
> **(07:05)**
> **Pilot:** Athens (Area) Control, Royal Jordanian 117. We are an A321 at Flight Level 370 out of Amman bound for Paris. Request Flight Level 390.
> **ATCO:** Royal Jordanian 117, climb Flight Level 390.
>
> **(07:10)**
> **Pilot:** Athens Control, Royal Jordanian 117, Flight Level 390. We have a passenger who is unconscious and has trouble breathing. He is being given oxygen by the cabin crew.
> **ATCO:** Roger. Say intentions / What are your intentions?
> **Pilot:** There is a doctor on board attending the passenger; the situation seems under control for the moment. If the passenger's condition remains stable we will continue to our scheduled destination. If his condition becomes worse, we will contact Area Control for possible alternates, Royal Jordanian 117.
> **ATCO:** Royal Jordanian 117, Athens Control, I will be handing over to Brindisi ACC at time 19. Contact Brindisi ACC 124 decimal 750.
> ...

If you have an odd number of students you will need to have a group of three, where the students take turns to play the roles of pilot, ATCO and a silent observer. They change roles after the three exchanges and again after six exchanges.

Background notes:

♦ In this scenario, a Royal Jordanian Airbus A321 is en route at FL 370 from Amman to Paris via Athens and then up the Adriatic along the east coast of Italy. A passenger on board loses consciousness and is given oxygen by the flight attendants and supervised by a doctor. By the time the flight has begun flying up the coast of Italy the passenger's condition has worsened and the crew requests a diversion to Rome, where Rome ACC gives them the latest information about conditions at the airport.

♦ *ACC* stands for Area Control Centre, a facility where ATCOs work. Each ACC covers an extended area for aircraft en route and passes traffic to and from terminal control centres. In the role-play, the ATCO role actually switches between four different ACCs: the first (unnamed); Athens ACC in Greece; Brindisi ACC in south-east Italy; and finally Rome ACC.

b **Discuss the role-plays and the range of decisions with the class.**

Communication errors: Failure to question instructions

Communicative and operational issues:

There have been several high-profile accidents where communication and language proficiency have been contributing factors. Often, it became apparent after the accident that those involved were unsure of the situation, but probably did not possess the language skills and resulting self-confidence to question an instruction or a piece of information.

Teachers should be mindful that psychological factors are inseparable from the effective use of language and that acquiring greater self-confidence through linguistic proficiency is at the heart of the objectives embedded in *Flightpath.*

The quote from the Flight Safety Foundation *ALAR Briefing Notes* gives just two examples of instructions or information which might need to be questioned by either the pilot or the controller, or between two members of the same flight crew or ATC team. Linguistic self-confidence is one of the things which may make it easier to question a superior's decision, especially in cultures where there is a large hierarchical difference.

In this issue, we have an example of how language is closely connected to both safety and cultural habits.

All of the factors mentioned in the ICAO focus box can affect the likelihood of someone questioning an instruction, but especially those which are largely psychological: respect; language proficiency; trust; expectation bias; and habit. It will be interesting to see how students grade these factors.

ICAO FOCUS

Students read the quote to identify two problems that may result from a failure to question instructions [**Answers:** accepting altitude clearances below minimum safe altitude; accepting headings that place the aircraft near obstacles]. Students then work in small groups to discuss the two questions. Allow plenty of time for the discussion, as each factor is worth discussing properly. Afterwards, open up the discussion to include the whole class, and try to elicit examples and anecdotes relating to each of the factors. Note that *respect* and *trust* are normally seen as positive attributes, but in the context of aviation English, they can be extremely dangerous.

Suggested answers:
In some cases the answers to this question may have a strong social and cultural bias: in cultures where there is a large hierarchical distance, or on the part of young pilots, respect, trust and lack of language proficiency may act as inhibitors. More generally, however, expectation bias as the result of force of habit and distractions and high work-load may make pilots less attentive and less critical about the instructions they receive.

10 ○2.29 **Go through the instructions and the example with the class. With inexperienced students, you may want to draw the two headings (050 and 160) on a diagram on the board, to show that a right turn is needed. Then play the recording, pausing after each transmission for a volunteer to respond as pilot and another volunteer to correct the instruction. Encourage them to stress both the problematic word/phrase in the pilot's question and its replacement in the ATCO's correction. Afterwards, students can work together in pairs or groups of three to practise, using audioscript 2.29 on page 184.**

Suggested answers:
1
Pilot: Heading 160. Our present heading is 050. Confirm turn left, Midland 1263.
ATCO: Midland 1263, correction: turn <u>right</u> heading 160.
2
Pilot: Our present level is 370. Confirm climb Flight Level 350, Shanghai Air 1637.
ATCO: Shanghai Air 1637, correction: maintain Flight Level <u>370</u> / <u>descend</u> Flight Level 350.

3

Pilot: Our present altitude is 4,000 feet; there is terrain at 1,600 metres to the North West. Confirm turn right heading 340, TAM Express 3971.

ATCO: TAM Express 3971, correction: orbit left / turn right heading 240.

4

Pilot: Confirm your instruction, Iberia 4473.

ATCO: Iberia 4473, correction: maintain present Flight Level. Iberia 4373, descend and maintain Flight Level 210.

5

Pilot: Unable. We are too heavy for Level 390, Swiss 1648.

ATCO: Swiss 1648, correction: maintain present level.

...

Background notes:

The situations illustrated in the ten recordings to which students should react are:

1 Midland 1263 is flying a heading of 050° (approximately East North East) and is instructed to turn left heading 160°, i.e. approximately South East by South, which would involve them turning through 250° instead of 110° if they turn right.

2 Shanghai Air 1637 has been instructed to climb to FL 350, but they are already above this level at FL 370.

3 TAM express 3974 is flying at 4,000 ft (1,219 m) and is instructed to turn onto a heading of 340 (North East by North) where there is terrain rising to 1,600 m.

4 ATC gives an instruction to Iberia 4473, but the instruction is actually received by Iberia 4373 (call sign confusion).

5 Swiss 1648 is instructed to climb to FL 390, but the aircraft is too heavy because it is at the beginning of its flight and has not burnt off enough fuel.

6 Malaysian 377 is instructed to make an approach to Runway 12L, but the crew is surprised because they usually land on 12R. A *vectoring ILS approach* involves the controller using radar to instruct the pilot about the headings and altitudes to fly to capture the ILS glidepath.

7 Air Canada 2695 is told to orbit right, but points out that there is *terrain* (i.e. mountains, hills) up to 3,900 m (12,795 ft) in that direction.

8 Air Algérie is instructed to descend to 3,000 ft, but points out that the Minimum Safe Altitude is 4,000 ft to the South West.

9 ATC asks Speedbird 3774 to reduce speed (probably during approach) to 180 kts, which is probably below their minimum speed in their present configuration.

10 Olympic 3345 is instructed to turn right, but can see traffic in that direction.

ETOPS Diversion at night

Communicative and operational issues:

The topic of this section is the eastbound, transatlantic ETOPS flight of a B777 which encounters an oil leak on one engine, and how the crew deals with the decision to divert or not. ETOPS means *Extended Twin Operations*, i.e the use of *long-haul*, twin-engine aircraft over the sea, desert or arctic regions where there is no suitable airport within 60 minutes of flight which can be used in case of a diversion being necessary following the loss of an engine. A more facetious interpretation of the acronym 'ETOPS' is 'Engines Turning Or Passengers Swimming'!

Originally, three- or four-engine aircraft were required to operate in these conditions so that the flight could be continued in the event of an engine failure. With aircraft engines having greater reliability, regulatory bodies have decided that specially-equipped twin-engine aircraft, such as the Boeing B767, B777 and B787 and the Airbus A330 and A350, can fly safely up to 90 or even 120 minutes from the nearest airport on one engine. These aircraft are designated ETOPS and must respect more stringent operating conditions, follow specific routes and have their on-board equipment reinforced.

See www.dutchops.com and Flight Safety Foundation *AeroSafety World*, March 2007 for more information on ETOPS rules.

From an economic point of view, operating twin- rather than multiple-engine aircraft represents a considerable saving for the airlines, hence the popularity of the aircraft types mentioned above.

Flight crew decision making in the case of ETOPS flights is obviously particularly critical and may lead to much exchange of information with ATC and discussions between the flight crew members.

11a **Discuss the questions with the class.**

> Suggested answers:
> See *Communicative and operational issues* above

b **Students work alone to match the sentence halves and then check in pairs. Then go through the answers with the class.**

> Answers:
>
> | | | | | | | | |
> |---|---|---|---|---|---|---|---|
> | 1 c | | 3 f | | 5 a | | 7 b | |
> | 2 h | | 4 g | | 6 d | | 8 e | |

Background notes:

♦ An *eastbound* route is towards the east. A *northerly* route is in or from the north. Similar words exist for other compass points (e.g. *northbound*, *easterly*).

♦ The *first alternate* is the first suitable airport in the vicinity of the flight path to which the aircraft can divert in the event of an emergency or urgent situation.

♦ A *logbook* (*techlog*) is a record of all technical incidents and maintenance action carried out on a given aircraft, signed by the crew and technicians and kept on the flight deck.

♦ *Upper-level winds* are the winds blowing at altitudes typically between 23,000 and 39,000 feet for the polar jet streams and at higher levels for the subtropical jet streams. They blow from west to east and, as a result, make eastbound flying times across the North Atlantic approximately one hour shorter than the westbound ones. See http://cimss.ssec.wisc.edu and http://aviationweather.gov

Extension activity:

Elicit as much as possible about the ETOPS flight, but avoid providing any information yourself or confirming/rejecting students' suggestions:
1 Where was it flying from/to?
2 What problem was observed?
3 What did the crew think was the likely cause?
4 What happened next?
5 What do you think the crew did?
6 Is this problem common?

c ◉2.30 Students work in pairs to underline the syllable that they think is stressed. Then play the recording for students to check. When they have compared their answers in pairs, go through the answers with the class.

Answers:
1 eastbound
2 established
3 alternate
4 diagnosis
5 assume
6 alternatives
7 indication
8 consult

Language notes:

♦ *Alternate* has two pronunciations:
1 as a verb, it is pronounced /ˈɒltəneɪt/ e.g. *The pilot alternated between English and Spanish*.
2 as an adjective, it is pronounced /ɒlˈtɜːnət/ e.g. *She works on alternate weekends*.
3 as a noun, it is also pronounced /ɒlˈtɜːnət/ e.g. *The first alternate was 100 km away*.
♦ In sentence 7, *likely* is used as an adjective, meaning *probably*: *It is likely an indication problem*.

Background notes:

♦ If an aircraft is *established in cruise* it means that it is in level flight at its maximum or cruise altitude, which is typically between 35,000 and 41,000 feet.

♦ An *indication problem* means that an erroneous indication is being given and that there is not necessarily anything wrong with the system itself.

Extension activity:

Make sure students cover the sentences in exercise 11b. Elicit from the class onto the board the whole sentences containing the words in question, using only the words from exercise 11c to help them remember. You may play the recording again (without pausing) to refresh their memories. This will be a chance not only to test their memories, but also to focus on the grammar and vocabulary of the sentences, and the pronunciation of the key words.

d ◉2.30 Play the recording again for students to repeat the sentences, either individually or as a class. Make sure the key words are pronounced correctly.

12a ◉2.31 Students work in pairs to complete as much of the information as they can, based on what they remember from the sentences in exercises 11b and c. Then play the recording for them to check their answers and to complete any missing information. You could pause the recording in the middle (after '*What is your diagnosis of the situation?*') and again at the end to discuss the answer to the question with the class. Afterwards, allow them to check their notes in pairs before going through the answers with the class.

Answers:
1 night
2 350
3 90 degrees West
4 drop in oil quantity on Engine 2
5 dispatch
6 150 minutes
7 120 minutes
8 poor weather

Background note:

Runway length, or *Landing Distance Available* (*LDA*), is a key consideration for pilots when considering which alternate airport to choose for a diversion. This is especially true towards the beginning of a flight when the aircraft is heavy with fuel and, in this case, with one engine only operating at idle resulting in the thrust reversers being unavailable or only partly available. All these factors will increase the landing distance required with the necessary safety margin and may be compounded by a wet or icy runway surface which will reduce the braking coefficient and increase the stopping distance.

For more information on landing distances, see http://www.skybrary.aero/index.php/Landing_Distances

b Students discuss the situation in pairs and then feed back to the class.

Extension activity 1:

Elicit from the class the four options mentioned at the end of the recording, and write them up on the board. You might need to play the last part of recording 2.31 again for students to check. Discuss with the class the advantages and disadvantages of each option, which option looks best/worst, and what other information they would need in order to make the best decision [**Suggested answer**: weather information for each alternate].

Suggested answers:

Option	Advantages	Disadvantages
Fly back 150 minutes	Known airport	Further than other alternates
Divert to another airport 120 minutes away	Not as far as first option; Good facilities	7,500-foot runway; Not as near as third option
Divert to a closer airport	Possible to reach in a short time	Bad weather
Continue the flight	No disruption to schedule	Risk of loss of engine

Extension activity 2:

Before you do exercise 12c, tell students to listen to recording 2.32 to check if the pilot made the same decision as they would. Pause the recording after each question (*What is your next move in view of the developing situation?*; *What task sharing are you implementing at this stage?*) to discuss the questions with the class. For *Background notes*, see exercise 12c.

Suggested answer:
Given that the drop in oil level has not yet affected engine oil pressure, engine operation is not immediately threatened. None of the alternates available at the present time are ideal. The crew is probably right in deciding to pursue the flight while monitoring the engine, but some students may be more cautious and not wish to take any risks. It is a good subject for discussion. See Suggested answer to 12c below for more detailed information.

c ⊙ 2.32 Students read through the eight sentences to make sure they understand all the words. Then play the recording for them to complete the task. When they have discussed their answers in pairs, go through the answers with the class.

Answers:
1 F – decides to continue and informs Dispatch
2 T
3 F – 15 minutes
4 T
5 F – he throttles back Engine 2
6 T
7 T
8 T

Background notes:

♦ A *pan call* involves saying '*Pan pan, Pan pan, Pan pan*'; this radio call is used as an alert, but not at the level of urgency of a Mayday distress call. *Pan* comes from the French *panne* for *failure* and *Mayday* from the French *m'aider*, meaning '*help me*'.

♦ *HF* (high frequency) refers to the high radio frequencies (3 MHz to 30 MHz). HF radio bands are less used than VHF (30 MHz to 300 MHz) in aeronautical radio communication, but are not limited by the line-of-sight characteristic of VHF, so may sometimes be convenient at low altitudes.

♦ *Task sharing* involves dividing the workload between crew or team members in a systematic and integrated way.

♦ A *drift down* involves losing height gradually.

♦ If a pilot *throttles back*, he/she pulls back the throttle/thrust lever(s) on the centre pedestal to reduce the engine speed and the resulting thrust.

♦ An *intercept* involves an aircraft joining a path, trajectory or navigation beam.

♦ A *rupture* is a break or failure.

♦ A *supply line* is hydraulic, fuel or pneumatic piping or electrical wiring which gives a source of energy.

d Ask students to discuss the questions in small groups and then open up the discussion to include the whole class.

Suggested answers:
The flight crew is faced with a series of decisions:
1 Is the drop in oil quantity real or not? They assume it is, although there is no history of oil leaks on that engine in the logbook: it is always better to err on the side of caution. For a second opinion they call the airline's operations Dispatch who consider it more likely that it is a faulty indication, a relatively common occurrence.

2 The drop in oil level continues and so they correctly start to consider various alternates in case they decide to divert. None of the alternates is ideal: flying back 150 minutes to their point of departure is clearly a commercially unattractive solution; the runway at the second alternate is short for a large heavily loaded plane; the weather is bad at the third alternate. As the oil level is still within tolerance, i.e. the oil pressure is still correct, they decide to pursue the flight for the moment, but to collect data about suitable alternates, inform Dispatch and divert if the situation deteriorates. They are following standard operating procedures for such a situation.

3 15 minutes later, the oil pressure starts to drop. They rightly decide to divert. A drop in oil pressure can lead to severe engine damage and engine failure. They correctly make a Pan call and get clearance for a precautionary landing at an airport in Iceland 313 miles away.

4 What precautions do they take? They advise the cabin crew of the situation and make a passenger address announcement. They start a gradual descent and reduce engine speed on the No. 2 engine; this is preferable to an engine shut-down as the engine still produces some thrust and also continues to power accessories such as the electrical generator, hydraulic pumps and bleed air supply.

5 ATC sensibly enables the crew to intercept the ILS early so that they have plenty of time to stabilise their approach to an airport they are unfamiliar with in less than optimum conditions. The landing is uneventful and a subsequent inspection of the engine shows no damage; this validates the crew's decision to keep the engine running.

Overall, the crew made all the right decisions for the right reasons.

13a **Tell students to read their information carefully to make sure they understand what they have to do. Then go through the example with the class. Point out that the ATCO should avoid providing too much information at once – the pilot will need to ask for it. However, they should work together to manage the situation as effectively as possible. They should invent any information that isn't provided, and should respond creatively to the developing situation. Afterwards, they could swap roles and conduct their role-plays again, where the new pilot may of course make a different decision.**

If you have an odd number of students you will need to have a group of three, where the third student plays the role of a co-pilot.

Background notes:

♦ If an engine is *idling*, it is operating at its minimum smooth rotating speed.
♦ *Line maintenance* is aircraft maintenance, servicing and repair which is performed during turnaround rather than scheduled maintenance in a hangar.
♦ A *repair station* is a technical facility where certain types of aircraft, engines and equipment can be repaired and maintained.
♦ *Navaids*: *ILS CAT II, CAT III, CAT IIIC* refer to the various degrees of automation which aircraft and airports are equipped with, and flight crew are qualified to use. These categories involve different landing minima, i.e. vertical and horizontal visibility. In CAT IIIC, using the Autoland autopilot mode, it is possible with zero vertical and zero horizontal visibility. For more information, see http://www.bcavirtual.com/
♦ *Maximum landing weight* is the maximum weight at which an aircraft can land without causing structural damage to the airframe. For this reason, many long-haul aircraft may have to dump or jettison fuel if they have to land prematurely.
♦ A *bearing* is a surface that supports and reduces friction between moving parts. Types of bearing include ball, roller and needle bearings. Note that bearing has a second meaning in aviation English: an angular measurement of direction between a known point and the aircraft in flight.
♦ *STEAM, REDBY, KESIX, SOVED, NETKI* etc. shown on the chart on page 81 are 'landfall points' at the end of a transatlantic flight and 'Oceanic Entry points' at the beginning of a transatlantic flight. They are among the waypoints used to define a flight plan. You can look at the flight data for another transatlantic flight (a Delta Airlines A330-300) between Chicago and Amsterdam (see www.livedispatch.org).

Possible answer:

Pilot: *We are a Boeing Triple Seven dash 300 Extended Range heading 095 at Flight Level 390. We have just experienced an engine failure. Can you give us various alternatives for a diversion?*

ATCO: You are within 320 nautical miles of three airports. ABC is at 160 nautical miles on a bearing of 290 degrees. The runway in use (12L) is 3,120 metres long and is equipped for CAT III (for an ILS approach). There is only Boeing line maintenance. The current visibility (RVR) is 600 metres. Wind is 130 degrees at four knots with rain. The ground temperature is six degrees Celsius.

[When the flight crew have been informed and taken notes about all three alternates, the students will have to discuss the relative advantages and disadvantages of the various options as the flight crew would do in such a situation. This is pilot-to-pilot communication.]

Pilot: ABC is the nearest option at 160 nautical miles and has quite a long runway, which is an advantage as we are currently above our maximum landing weight and so would need to dump less fuel. It is CAT III, no significant weather and the visibility is currently above our minima, so that's OK. But, at 290 degrees, this means flying back [they are flying eastbound, so on a heading around 090] and there is only line maintenance, so no possibility of getting specialised engineering or an engine change on the spot after we land.

...

b Ask each pair to report back to the class. Then discuss with the class the various solutions.

Decision making and the language barrier

Communicative and operational issues:

After the ETOPS flight over the North Atlantic, we look at something which is at the core of the ICAO Language Proficiency Requirements: the effect on safety, human behaviour and operational efficiency of a lack of language proficiency. The case study is based on a real-life incident which occurred near London Heathrow in June 2007. In addition to the August 2008 *AeroSafety World* article quoted in the ICAO focus, there is an account of the incident in 12th June 2007 issue of *Flight International*.

Language proficiency is a two-way process. It also means being able to deal with interlocutors whose language proficiency is either much higher or, in the case of the conversations in exercise 15, much lower than one's own.

In exercise 16, starting from an initial rather bare statement by their partner, students are expected to ask a series of questions to obtain more information about an unusual situation.

14a **2.33** Tell students to read the eight sentences in pairs to predict the order they will be mentioned. They should also try to predict what went wrong, what its causes were and what its consequences were. Then play the recording for students to check their predictions and to mark the correct order. Note that the wording in the recording is different, so students should not listen for the exact sentences written in their books.

Answers:
1 e   3 c   5 d   7 a
2 g   4 h   6 f   8 b

Background notes:

♦ *Instrument meteorological conditions* (*IMC*) are weather conditions, notably a lack of visibility, requiring pilots to fly using their instruments.
♦ The *commander* is the captain of an aircraft.
♦ If two planes *come into conflict*, they are at or near the same flight level heading towards each other.

Extension activity:

Students read audioscript 2.33 on page 184 and listen again to underline the phrases which correspond to the sentences in exercise 14a. They check in pairs before feeding back to the class.

Answers:
a ... the commander ... was not able to understand some of the instructions.
b The ATC controller became concerned that ... the flight crew might be planning to land on Runway 09 Right ...
c ... which involved a 27-minute return flight ...
d ... the aeroplane was flown north instead of north-northeast as directed ...
e ... their electronic flight displays went blank ...
f ... another aircraft, whose crew was issued revised instructions ...
g ... the airplane was not damaged ...
h ... the co-pilot flew the aircraft ...

ICAO FOCUS

Elicit from the class three *burdens* (= complications, difficulties) that the pilots in this incident had to deal with [**Answers:** flying in IMC; using only standby instruments; communicating in English]. Students then read the quote to compare with their ideas. Then discuss the four questions with the class.

Suggested answers:
♦ Other ways of saying you have your hands full: they were busy; they were fully occupied; they had a heavy workload; their attention was taken up; they were preoccupied
♦ IMC, Instrument Meteorological Conditions, means that the aircraft is in thick cloud, fog or generally poor visibility and that the crew must use the aircraft instruments to fly. VMC, Visual Meteorological Conditions, means that the crew has good visibility and can fly according to VFR, Visual Flight Rules.

* Standby analogue instruments, which rely on direct, not computerised, inputs, are used when digital displays are lost for one reason or another. They consist of a separate altimeter, airspeed indicator, artificial horizon and compass and use inputs from standby pitot and static probes rather than Air Data Computer (ADC) and Air Data and Inertial Reference Unit (ADIRU) sources.

* Communicating in a language other than one's own without a sufficient degree of proficiency demands increased concentration and effort, and generates additional stress, at a time when stress and a high operational workload have already probably diminished one's effective language capability. Many Cockpit Voice Recorder (CVR) recordings bear witness to the fact that effective language proficiency decreases significantly under stress and that people often tend to revert to their native language. This is a strong argument for requiring pilots and controllers to achieve at least a very robust ICAO Level 4 when they are assessed in order to ensure a safety margin which takes into account the considerable loss of proficiency which occurs under stress and over time when the language is not used extensively.

b **Students work in pairs to describe the flight path and then feed back to the class. You could ask students not just to describe the flight path, but to use it to reconstruct the whole incident: what happened first; why; what were the ATCO's options at this stage, etc.**

> Suggested answer:
> The Boeing 737-500 took off from London Heathrow towards the east and turned left on a northerly heading. As they were flying on a heading of approximately 010°, they reported a navigation problem just before they were handed over from London Control to Heathrow Director. They then turned left heading approximately 310°.

Extension activity:

Write these questions on the board:

1 What is the language barrier?

2 What causes it?

3 Is it mainly caused by non-native speakers?

4 What can be done to overcome it, in aviation English and in other spheres?

Students discuss the four questions in small groups and then feed back to the class.

> Suggested answers:
> 1 An inability to communicate because the speakers do not share the same language background.

2 Lack of vocabulary and misunderstanding caused by poor grammar (for both the speaker and the listener); poor listening skills; poor coping strategies (e.g. asking for clarification); poor pronunciation; speaking too fast; use of unusual vocabulary, etc.

3 No. In fact many non-native speakers of English find it easier to communicate with each other in English than with native speakers, who may speak too quickly, use idiomatic or unusual vocabulary, and incorrectly assume the listener understands. The non-native may be intimidated by the native speaker's fluency and confidence, and may therefore be reluctant to ask for clarification.

4 In aviation English, it is important to work on language skills, especially vocabulary, listening and pronunciation. Speakers should stick to standard phraseology as much as possible. They should use readback/hearback to check understanding. In both aviation English and other spheres, it is vital to have the confidence to ask for clarification and to admit to a lack of understanding. The most dangerous (but psychologically tempting) strategy is to pretend to understand.

Language focus:

Ask students to read the phrases to identify three pairs of phrases with similar meanings. [**Answers:** *What is the nature of your problem? – Describe / Tell me the situation*; *What do you require/want? – Say what you want*; *I'm listening – I'm here*]. Elicit from the class the connection between the first nine phrases [**Suggested answer:** They can all be used to establish the precise nature of a problem. If the speaker is struggling to communicate, these questions allow the listener to focus on the important parts of the message]. Elicit from the class which phrase(s) they could use if:

a the other person is speaking too fast;

b the other person doesn't seem to understand;

c the other person is taking a long time to make a point.

> Suggested answers:
> a *Say again slowly. / Say all words twice.*
> b *I say again (slowly). / Confirm you received my last transmission.*
> c *I'm listening. / I'm still here.* (Note: The usual phrase for this function in conversation, *OK*, should be avoided, as it may be taken as an agreement. *Go ahead* should also be avoided, as it may be taken as an instruction to move forward.)

15 **●2.34** Go through the example with the class. Make sure students realise that the listening extracts cover only the beginning of each conversation, after which students will need to use their imaginations. In each case, one student should play the role of a pilot with very limited English. The ATCOs should use the phrases from the *Language focus* box where possible. Play the recording, pausing after each conversation for volunteers to respond as ATCOs and pilots. Ask the pilots to make an effort to be awkward, i.e. to restrict their language to a minimum, so that the controllers have to exercise all their communication skills. Allow each conversation to continue for several turns. Afterwards, students can repeat the exercise in pairs, swapping roles after each conversation, using audioscript 2.34 on page 184.

> **Suggested answers:**
> 1 Do you mean a passenger is injured? Is this a medical emergency? Is a passenger dangerous?
> 2 Did you say smoke? Confirm smoke.
> 3 I say again. How ... many ... passengers do you have on board?
> 4 What is the nature of your problem? Confirm (you have an) engine failure.
> 5 Say your conditions. Do you require a change of level or heading?
> 6 Do you wish to declare an emergency? Confirm Mayday.

If you have an odd number of students you will need to have a group of three students, where the third student plays the co-pilot. They swap roles after each conversation.

16 **Go through the example with the class. Point out that the pilot will have to invent most of the details. The pilot may have to use some of the phrases from the *Language focus* box to get more information. Encourage students to continue the dialogues beyond the cues, to include, for example, decision-making about how to resolve the problem.**

If you have an odd number of students you will need to have a group of three, where Student C takes cues 1 and 2 from Student A and cues 4 and 5 from Student B.

Background notes:

The repercussions of the five ATCO situations are:
1 The closure of part of the airspace occurs when, for instance, there are military exercises or VIP flights or navigation aids are being recalibrated in that zone. It will result in traffic being re-routed and so possibly in a certain amount of congestion.
2 Most large international airports have at least two parallel runways: typically, one is used for take-offs and one for landings. If runway maintenance is taking place, one of these runways will be closed resulting in both departing and arriving traffic using the same runway. The necessary separation between aircraft and the delays caused by aircraft vacating and lining up will slow down traffic considerably.
3 ATC computer failure or maintenance and power cuts will create huge constraints for controllers, reduce the information at their disposal and delay traffic movements.
4 Military aircraft usually operate in their own designated airspace, but may at times share civil airspace. Given their different airspeeds, manoeuvres and patterns this requires other traffic to be particularly cautious.
5 Technical problems, maintenance or unscheduled traffic may cause flow management restrictions which could result in holding. *Flow management* involves making the best use of airspace capacity to meet the demands of the traffic at any given time. It may result in aircraft being delayed, holding or being re-routed by ATC.

The repercussions of the five pilot situations are:
1 Windshields can be broken by the impact of a large bird or a heavy hailstorm, although the breakage is usually limited by the fact that the windshield consists of up to five layers of glass and resin. However, a cracked windshield can impair the pilot's vision or even cause cabin depressurisation.
2 Smoking is strictly forbidden anywhere on the aircraft as fire and smoke are among the most threatening of all aviation emergencies. The toilets and under-floor cargo compartments are all fitted with smoke detectors. The crew can use portable fire extinguishers.
3 There is a regulatory minimum ratio of one cabin attendant for every forty nine passengers, so an incapacitated cabin attendant on a full flight can contravene safety regulations.
4 As seen in Unit 6, a TCAS RA (Resolution Advisory) obliges the crew to take evasive action by climbing or descending immediately.
5 Terrorist bomb threats are taken very seriously and both flight and cabin crew have procedures to contain unruly passengers and place suspicious objects in a part of the aircraft where their explosion would cause the least damage. The flight crew would enter an emergency code (*7500 hijack, 7600 loss of communication, 7700 emergency*) and divert immediately to the nearest suitable airport.

Reasons and feasibility

Both pilots and controllers must be able to ask for and explain the reason for, or the cause of a situation, incident or action (exercise 18). Another function which pilots and controllers must be able to ask and reply about is whether something is possible or not (exercise 19).

17a Students work alone to complete the task and then check in pairs. When you go through the answers with the class, check what each abbreviation stands for. Afterwards, students can test each other in pairs by reading an abbreviation to elicit its meaning or vice versa.

Answers:
1 HDG	4 IMC	7 VMC	10 VSI
2 UTC	5 IAS	8 ETOPS	11 ADF
3 RTF	6 VHF	9 DME	12 VOR

Background notes:

The significance of the abbreviations in this exercise can be found in the abbreviation glossary, but they are glossed below contextually in a little more detail. ETOPS and IMC have been glossed in the previous section.

♦ ADF (*Automatic Direction Finder*): airborne radio navaid tuned to non-directional beacon
♦ DME (*Distance Measuring Equipment*): a transponder-based radio navigation device that measures distance by timing the delay of VHF or UHF radio signals
♦ HDG (*Heading*): angle between the horizontal reference datum (north) and the longitudinal axis of the aircraft expressed in degrees from 000° to 360°.
♦ IAS (*Indicated Airspeed*): relative velocity between the aircraft and the surrounding air, corrected for instrument error
♦ RTF (*Radiotelephony*): transmission of speech by radio
♦ UTC (*Universal Time Coordinated*): the standard of time by which all clocks and computers are regulated, formerly known as Greenwich Mean Time
♦ VHF (*Very High Frequency*): the radio frequency band within which 'airband' is located; 'airband', between 108 and 137 MegaHertz, is the bandwidth used in commercial aviation and general aviation for radio navigation and ATC voice radiotelephony
♦ VMC (*Visual Meteorological Conditions*): conditions in which pilots have enough visibility to fly the aircraft and maintain separation from terrain and other aircraft visually, as opposed to IMC
♦ VOR (*VHF Omnidirectional Range*): a VHF ground station which emits a Morse identifying signal. The signal enables the aircraft's receiver to determine a magnetic bearing or radial from the station to the aircraft. The intersection of two radials from different VOR stations provides the approximate position of the aircraft.
♦ VSI (*Vertical Speed Indicator*): instrument which displays the vertical speed, or rate of climb or descent, of the aircraft in feet per minute. It is particularly vital during approach.

b Students discuss the question in pairs and then feed back to the class.

Answers:
♦ ADF is a conventional radio navaid which allows the pilot to find the aircraft's bearing with respect to an NDB (non-directional beacon) or other beacon. It is now mainly used to crosscheck computerised navigational data, especially during approach.
♦ DME is used either en-route or during approach to determine the aircraft's distance from a specific ground transmitter. It is used in conjunction with the ILS.
♦ HDG, the direction in which the aircraft is flying, is, with altitude or flight level, one of the key flight parameters which is always monitored.
♦ IMC means that the pilots are using their instruments, rather than external visual references (VFR) to fly the aircraft.
♦ IAS, indicated airspeed, is highly critical during take-off and approach; the correct airspeed depends on the flaps, slats and landing gear and angle of attack configuration of the aircraft. If the IAS exceeds its envelope, stall will occur.
♦ RTF, radiotelephony, is the fact of air-ground communications throughout the flight and is one of the prime source of situational awareness.
♦ ETOPS we saw in some depth in exercises 11 to 13.
♦ UTC (Universal Time Coordinated) is the single time reference used by aviation throughout the world.
♦ VHF is the main frequency band used for air-ground radio communication and navigation aids.
♦ VMC occur when pilots can use external visual references to fly the aircraft.
♦ VOR, VHF Omnidirectional Range, is one of the main sources of information about the aircraft's position and is more accurate than an NDB. The VOR information is supplied to the aircraft's navigation equipment.
♦ VSI, vertical speed indicator, gives the rate of climb and descent, and must be closely monitored just after lift-off and during approach.

Language focus: Cause and effect

With the class, discuss why it can be important to ask why, when there is a problem. [**Suggested answer:** Because knowing the cause of a problem can often be a first step in identifying a solution; it may lead to the discovery of other problems; it provides ATC with a better understanding of the situation on the aircraft.]

For each of the example sentences, elicit which part refers to the cause and which to the effect. Elicit onto the board the six structures and how they work:

♦ Sth (CAUSE) *caused* sth to happen (EFFECT)
♦ Sth happened (EFFECT) *because* sth else happened (CAUSE)
♦ Sth (CAUSE) *resulted in* sth else happening (EFFECT)
♦ Sth happened (EFFECT) *due to* sth else (CAUSE)
♦ Sth (CAUSE) *has forced* sb to do sth (EFFECT)
♦ Sth happened (EFFECT) *because of* sth else (CAUSE)

18 Go through the example with the class. Make sure students realise to invent their own reasons for each decision. Point out that the event may be in the past or present (e.g. *Why did you make / are you making an emergency descent?*). Encourage them to use the structures from the board in their explanations. Students then work in pairs to ask and answer about causes. Afterwards, elicit from the class a range of answers (using a range of structures) for each cue.

> Possible answers:
> **Pilot responses**
> 1 We made an emergency descent because of a cabin depressurisation.
> 2 We changed heading to avoid a CB cloud formation.
> 3 We reduced our speed because we were instructed to do so due slower traffic ahead.
> 4 We requested a higher level because we are experiencing a lot of turbulence at our present level.
> ...
>
> **ATCO responses**
> 1 I instructed you to increase airspeed so that you could be Number 1 in approach.
> 2 The ILS is/was inoperative because there is maintenance work underway on the glideslope transmitter.
> 3 Runway 32 Right is/was closed because of a runway excursion by a previous flight.
> 4 There is so much holding because Newark Airport is closed and traffic is being diverted to JFK and LaGuardia.
> ...

If you have an odd number of students you will have to have a group of three students, where the third student takes cues 1 to 3 from Student A and cues 8 to 10 from Student B.

Language focus: Feasibility

Tell students to close their books. Elicit from the class the meaning of *feasibility* (= possible), and some examples of ways of asking about feasibility. Elicit also a positive and negative answer to a question about feasibility. Write students' suggestions onto the board. Then tell students to check in their books to see if the same phrases are mentioned.

Language note:

♦ *Can* is not always the best way of asking about feasibility, as it is also often used for requests. The example in the book, *Can you increase your rate of climb?*, could be interpreted in both ways.

♦ Note that *able* is normally followed by *to* + infinitive, but in abbreviated aviation English, the following verb is sometimes omitted (e.g. *Are you able ~~to climb to~~ FL 410?*)

19a ○2.35 Go through the example with the class. Then play the recording, pausing after each cue for a volunteer to make a question. Encourage them to use a range of structures. Ask another volunteer to respond to each question. Afterwards, students can test each other using audioscript 2.35 on page 184.

> Possible answers:
> 1 Are you able / Advise able to maintain present flight level?
> 2 Can you / Is it possible for you to make a straight-in approach?
> 3 Will you be able to stabilise your approach?
> 4 Are you able to give radar vectors to the nearest landing place?
> 5 Can you provide assistance?
> ...

Background notes:

♦ A *straight-in approach* means an approach which does not involve any changes of heading.
♦ *Radar vectors* are heading, altitude and airspeed instructions given by ATC using secondary surveillance radar (an ATC radar system which detects and measures the position of an aircraft as well obtaining its identity and altitude by means of a transponder onboard the aircraft).
♦ If a crew *isolates* a failed system or component, they shut off the electrical, hydraulic, fuel or pneumatic supply to it.
♦ A *foam carpet* is a layer of foam put down on the runway by fire tenders to cushion the impact of an aircraft making a wheels-up landing.

b Go through the examples with the class, pointing out how the cues have been used to create the dialogue. Students then work in pairs to make dialogues. They could swap roles and repeat the task without using their script. Afterwards, ask volunteers to act out their dialogues for the class. Then, discuss the dialogues with the class focusing on reasons for the pilot's decisions.

Possible answers:

Pilot: Shamrock 137, we are an Airbus 330 at Flight Level 380 heading for Boston. The cabin crew have reported an unruly male passenger.

ATCO: Shamrock 137, in what way is he unruly? What has he done? Advise intentions.

Pilot: The man attacked another passenger and then got up, moved around the cabin insulting the cabin crew.

ATCO: Have you been able to restrain him? Is the situation under control?

Pilot: Affirm. The cabin crew have restrained him now.

ATCO: Do you intend to continue to Boston?

Pilot: Affirm. We will continue the flight to Boston if he remains restrained … The cabin crew have just informed me that the man is claiming that there is a bomb in the cargo hold.

ATCO: What is your assessment of the situation? Are you able to continue or do you wish to divert?

Pilot: We need to divert as soon as possible. Can you provide us with suitable airports for an immediate diversion?

ATCO: There are three suitable options: Charlottetown, Prince Edward Island 60 nautical miles from your present position; Halifax, Nova Scotia at 180 nautical miles; and Saint John, New Brunswick, 220 nautical miles away.

Pilot: Are you able to give me the runway specs and the current weather conditions at Charlottetown?

…

If you have an odd number of students you will need to have a group of three students, who play the role of pilot or ATCO, or wait and listen. They rotate roles after cues 3 and 6.

Background notes:

◆ *Shamrock* is the call sign prefix for Aer Lingus (Irish airlines) flights.
◆ *FIR* stands for Flight Information Region.
◆ *46° 17' 21"* is pronounced *forty-six degrees, 17 minutes and 21 seconds*.
◆ *CAVOK* means ceiling and visibility OK.
◆ *Specs* are specifications.

Making decisions under stress

Communicative and operational issues:

The effects of stress were seen with the B737-500 flight crew who lost their digital flight displays; their communication skills were impaired. The lead-in quote will provide a chance for students to talk about stressful situations they have experienced and the effect they noticed it had on their behaviour and cognitive functions.

The pair work scenario in exercise 21b is about the flight of a four-engine aircraft flying east at FL 275 bound for Baku in Azerbaijan, when one of the engines fails. The pilot monitors the condition of the other engines and discusses possible alternates and different routes with ATC. Later in the flight, a flight attendant suffers a head injury.

Quote: **Elicit from the class how stress may affect decision making [Possible answers: tendency to act without reflection and sufficient team work; risk of focusing on one factor only and of forgetting essential piloting tasks; failure to follow procedures and check information]. Then tell students to read the quote to identify the most dangerous types of stress and its consequences [Suggested answers: Prolonged stress (i.e. stress over a long period of time); oversimplification and ignoring important information].**

20a Students work alone to make lists and then discuss their lists with a partner. After a few minutes, ask a few volunteers to present their lists to the class. Make sure the volunteers explain how the factors helped them to avoid oversimplifying the decision-making process. Afterwards, for each volunteer's story, discuss with the class if there are any other factors that could/should have been taken into consideration.

b, c, d Check students fully understand the meaning of the words (e.g. fatigue). Then students discuss the three questions in pairs or small groups before feeding back to the class. For each of the sources of stress in exercise 20c, elicit techniques for dealing with / overcoming it.

Suggested answers:
◆ Sleep deprivation: Get sleep where possible; have energy drinks available if necessary.
◆ Mental fatigue: Share decision-making with colleagues.
◆ Family problems: Don't think about them when on duty.
◆ Hunger: Bring chocolate for emergencies.
◆ Insufficient language proficiency: Ask people to repeat/clarify; make sure that at least one team member has good language skills; respond to any misunderstandings; request additional language training from management.

- ◆ Altitude effects: Be aware that they can occur and that one is not always aware of their onset; and that hypoxia reduces response times.
- ◆ High workload: Delegate work where possible.
- ◆ Information overload: Write things down.
- ◆ Decreased vision: Use other sources of information to reconstruct situational awareness; and be especially vigilant.

Language focus: Intention

Tell students to close their books. Elicit from the class two ways of asking about intentions [**Answers**: *Advise intentions*; *Do you intend to ...*] and a suitable responses to each request. They then compare their ideas with those in the book.

21a Go through the example with the class. Elicit which words should be stressed [**Suggested answers**: *turn back*; *continue*]. Students then work in pairs to make dialogues. Afterwards, ask volunteers to act out their dialogues for the class, and make sure their sentence stress is clear and logical.

If you have an odd number of students you will need to have a group of three students, where Student C takes cues 1 to 3 from Student A and cues 7 and 8 from Student B.

Background note:

A plane *overflies* a waypoint which corresponds to a navigation beacon some of which are located in the vicinity of an airport, in this case Karatau.

b Elicit from the class which part of the world is shown in the map [**Answer**: The Caucasus mountains, with the Black Sea to the west and the Caspian Sea to the east]. Go through the example with the class, focusing on the use of language to ask about and describe intentions. You may need to check the meaning and pronunciation of *deterioration* /dɪtɪərɪəˈreɪʃən/ (= worsening). Elicit onto the board alternative ways of phrasing requests and intentions: *Do you intend?*; *Will you?*; *Are you going to?*; *Advise intentions*. Students then role play the situation in pairs. Afterwards, ask volunteers to act out their role-play for the class.

Suggested answers:
Student A to Student B
1
| **ATCO:** | Do you intend to turn back? / Advise intentions. |
| **Pilot:** | Negative. We intend to continue. |

2
| **ATCO:** | Do you intend / Will you shut down Engine Number 2? |
| **Pilot:** | Negative. We will let it / set it at idle. |

3
| **ATCO:** | Are you going to descend to Flight Level 250? |
| **Pilot:** | Negative. We will maintain Flight Level 310. |

4
| **ATCO:** | Do you intend to make a PAN call? |
| **Pilot:** | Negative. We will continue to our destination. |

...

Student B to Student A
1
| **ATCO:** | Do you intend to fly direct (to) Almaty? |
| **Pilot:** | Negative. We are going to overfly Karatau. |

2
| **ATCO:** | Will you declare an emergency? |
| **Pilot:** | Negative. We will make a PAN call and perform a precautionary landing. |

3
| **ATCO:** | Are you going to switch to the standby frequency? |
| **Pilot:** | Negative. We'll remain on the present frequency. |

4
| **ATCO:** | Do you intend to maintain your present heading? |
| **Pilot:** | Negative. We will request a left turn in five minutes. |

...

If you have an odd number of students you will need to have a group of three students, where Student C plays the co-pilot and takes half of Student B's responses.

Putting it together: Managing an unexpected turn of events

Communicative and operational issues:

In this section, students are given opportunities to discuss concrete cases of stress, describe various potentially dangerous in-flight situations and manage an in-flight scenario using minimal cues.

The final role-play scenario in this unit is about a Japan Airlines Boeing B777 which has just left Tokyo at night bound for London Heathrow. The students are free to make the final decision as to how to handle the situation and where to land.

ICAO FOCUS

Tell students to read the quote and discuss the three questions in pairs. After a few minutes, open up the discussion to include the whole class.

Suggested answers:

- Plain aviation language, the main focus of *Flightpath*, is required especially in unexpected or unusual situations when standard phraseology is insufficient to handle these situations.
- It is much more difficult to communicate in another language in stressful situations because you don't have time to think of the correct words or phrasing. It is also much harder to understand other speakers when you are stressed, because there are likely to be plenty of distractions, and because people tend to speak more quickly. Operating in another language is always mentally taxing, so it may be especially difficult to do this while at the same time monitoring a complex situation and making important decisions. Note: the students have already discussed the effects of stress in a previous section of Unit 7, and in exercise 22 are going to say how they would respond in a series of common stressful situations.
- The answer to the final question, how they should learn English for operational purposes, has already been alluded to, when safety margins were discussed in relation to how one's language skills deteriorate in stressful situations with a high workload. This is an opportunity to further raise their awareness about what is involved in reaching and maintaining language proficiency. Other aspects of operational English which you could explore are: mastering the operational functions listed in Appendix B of Doc. 9835; focusing on lexis and grammar which will have a direct application to operational situations; acquiring effective reflexes in English rather than theoretical knowledge; learning to perform communication tasks in English; developing their ability to paraphrase; developing their ability to pass from phraseology to plain language and back again when appropriate; and developing their ability to deal with interlocutors who have higher and lower levels of proficiency than they have.

Preparation

22a, b **Students discuss the situations in pairs and then feed back to the class.**

Suggested answers:
1 The First Officer will require more time to prepare the approach; will request a straight-in approach; will plan a go-around procedure and make notes; will require possibly greater separation, and ongoing ATC support in terms of data input; and have emergency services standing by as a precautionary measure.

2 This will considerably increase the controllers' workload. ATC will need to manage traffic flow more carefully, prepare for more and longer holding and be ready to prioritise arrivals in case of urgent or precautionary landings.
3 It will be important to try and change your mindset, i.e. put yourself back mentally in a work context and bring yourself up to date about any new conditions or procedures with your colleagues. You will need to apply discipline and try and leave your private life outside, otherwise it will distract from your concentration.
4 You must try and manage this situation by communicating about it with the other crew members and possibly Flight Ops management. You need to be objective enough to decide whether you are able to ensure your flight safely.
5 You will have emergency procedures to follow in such a case. Work may be slower to perform and certain functions or types of approach, for instance, will not be possible. Flight crews must be informed of the effects of such downgrading.
6 You must use your Quick Reference Handbook and Engine Stall checklist, prioritise one pilot to fly the aircraft; monitor engine indications (N1, N2, EPR, EGT, vibrations); reduce thrust on the stalled engine; advance the related thrust/throttle lever gradually to see whether the stall condition persists; decide whether to shut down and/or relight the engine.
7 You will contact the Tower or Approach Control to obtain the latest weather data from them.
8 You will probably have to redistribute roles and sectors and exercise particular care as your workload will be increased.

Background notes:

- If *incapacitated*, he/she is incapable of functioning properly.
- A *non-precision approach* is an instrument approach which uses horizontal guidance (Localizer, DME, VOR, NDB etc.), but not vertical guidance (glideslope).
- If *ATC computerisation is downgraded* it means that some ATC support functions such as current and forecast weather, traffic forecasts, decision support tools etc. and precision data may not be available.

23a **Students brainstorm vocabulary in groups. You could provide some guidance by suggesting they think about nouns, adjectives, verbs and phrases for each situation. Afterwards, collect the words and write them on the board.**

Possible answers:

situation	nouns	adjective	verbs	phrases
a	a mask; oxygen; resuscitation; unconsciousness; breathing; a bottle	unconscious; lying; kneeling	to don (a mask); to breathe; to inhale; to exhale; to faint; to collapse	to provide first aid; to care for; to put on a mask; to put a mask on sb

b Elicit from the class the grammatical structures needed for each of the three parts of the description [**Suggested answers**: 1) present perfect or past simple – the distinction is unlikely to make any difference to communication in these situations; 2) present continuous; 3) *We intend to ...*]. Students then take turns to describe the situations to their partners, using vocabulary from the board.

c Discuss the question with the class, paying particular attention to the language difficulties the students experienced.

Communication

24 Go through the example with the class, showing how the cues have been transformed into the lines of dialogue. Make sure they realise they will need to check the times to see who speaks next. Students then work in pairs to make dialogues. Afterwards, they could swap roles and repeat the role-play, this time without looking at the cues. Finally, ask volunteers to act out their dialogue for the class. Discuss the effectiveness of the dialogues with the class (e.g. were they clear and concise enough) as well as the suitability of the language (vocabulary, tenses, etc.)

Suggested answers:
12:46
Pilot: Khabarovsk Area Control, Japan Air 410, we are a Boeing 777 at Flight Level 310, heading 340 degrees. There is a large CB (cumulonimbus) showing on our weather radar 30 miles ahead. Request turn right 20 degrees, Japan Air 401.
ATC: Japan Air 401, turn right heading 360.
Pilot: Turn right 360 degrees, Japan Air 401.

12:53
Pilot: Japan Air 401, we have just encountered a hailstorm and severe turbulence. There is a small crack on the right-hand outer windshield. Some passengers and cabin crew have been injured, Japan Air 401.
ATC: Japan Air 401, confirm seriousness of windshield damage. How many passengers and crew have been injured? Advise intentions.
Pilot: The windshield damage does not seem serious, but we are monitoring its

condition. There are seven passengers with head injuries, concussion and suspected broken ribs. One cabin attendant is unconscious. We wish to make a precautionary landing. Request suitable alternates, Japan Air 401.
ATC: Japan Air 401, Khabarovsk International Airport KHV / UHHH is located at 358 nautical miles from your present position on a magnetic track of 269 degrees. Runway 05 Right / 23 Left is 4,000 metres long with ILS CAT III. Engineering keeps Boeing spares. There is a university hospital and connecting flights to Moscow and Tokyo. The coordinates are: 48 degrees 31 minutes 41 seconds North, 135 degrees, 11 minutes, 18 seconds East.
Pilot: Request present weather.
...

If you have an **odd number of students** you will need to have a group of three students, where the third student is the co-pilot, who takes half of the pilot cues.

Background notes:

- *KHV / UHHH* are the IATA and ICAO identifiers for Khabarovsk-Novy International Airport in the Russian Far East 5,296 miles from Moscow and 30 miles from the Chinese boarder.
- *Magnetic track* refers to following a track/ course using the Earth's magnetic field. Given the fluctuations in magnetic field in the polar regions, magnetic navigation cannot be used there.
- No *western a/c technical support* refers to the fact that if an aircraft diverts to an airport where there is no technical maintenance support and spare parts for a particular make of aircraft (Airbus, Boeing, Embraer, ATR, Bombardier etc.) it may be difficult to service and repair the aircraft for it to fly out.
- Overcast 600 metres reflects the fact that in Russia, China and the CIS (Commonwealth of Independent States, i.e. former Soviet republics) metres, not feet, are used to measure altitude and cloud ceilings.

25 Discuss the questions with the class.

Students work alone to complete the table and then discuss their answers with a partner. Elicit from the class any remaining weaknesses and discuss ways of overcoming them.

DVD: *Loss of communication*

Communicative and operational issues:

The DVD *Loss of communication* from the Eurocontrol *All clear?* toolkit illustrates how different forms of distraction can cause both pilots and controllers to overlook important information and cause traffic conflict. In the event of a prolonged loss of communication, military fighter aircraft can be called to intercept.

26a **Go through the questions with the class. Then play the DVD for students to answer the questions. You can stop the DVD at times and ask students to describe the information displayed on the ATC radar screens. Similarly, you could ask students to describe how a frequency is changed by a pilot on the Radio Management Panel. At the end of the clip, students discuss their answers in pairs before feeding back to the class. You could play the clip a second time to deal with any questions that students still have about exactly what happened and why.**

> Suggested answers:
> 1 The initial problem is the flight crew being distracted by the arrival of a cabin attendant which results in them making a mistake about the next frequency to contact. At one point, neither pilot is attending to the radio or controls.
> 2 Even before the cabin attendant enters, the flight crew do not appear very focused: they are discussing the impact of the weather on their projected game of golf.
> 3 The flight crew are distracted by the presence and conversation of the cabin attendant; by the sick passenger; by the drinks they are being served; and by asking for sandwiches at a phase of flight, just prior to descent, when there should be a 'sterile cockpit'.

Background notes:

- ♦ In this context, *opposite* means moving in the contrary direction.
- ♦ In this context, to *read* something means to hear it clearly.

26b **Discuss the questions with the class.**

> Possible answers:
> The flight crew enters an incorrectly read back frequency into the STANDBY window. When they activate this frequency they discover that they cannot contact anyone. They consult their chart and enter the frequency they find there, which is still incorrect, but which puts them in touch with a controller on another sector who should not be handling their flight.

27a **Students discuss the errors in pairs and then feed back to the class.**

> Suggested answers:
> 1 The captain makes a readback error and the controller makes a hearback error since she does not notice his mistake.
> 2 The captain is unable to contact ATC on the incorrect frequency. The First Officer had not been listening, so cannot help him.
> 3 A controller on another sector, who should not be handling the flight, clears A-jet 2745 to descend to FL 260. This causes a conflict with other traffic (Z-jet 979) and Controller B is forced to instruct them to make an unexpected descent.

27b, c **Discuss the questions with the class.**

> Possible answers:
> b When the pilot found out that he could not contact ATC, he should have contacted the previous sector again on the original frequency and requested confirmation of the next frequency.
> c Controller A seems distracted: looking away from the screen while she is speaking on several occasions. She fails to pick up the pilot's readback error, probably due to expectation bias. Controller C should have been aware that he had been contacted by an aircraft which was not normally on his sector; he does not inform Controller B until she notices a conflict caused by A-jet's descent.

28 **Students work in small groups to tell their experiences or anecdotes they have heard about similar situations, and then share their stories with the class.**

PART B
Review

Pronunciation

1a **○2.36** Play the recording for students to select the correct verb ending. When you check with the class, elicit what students remember about each sentence.

> **Answers:**
> | | |
> |---|---|
> | 1 asked | 6 climbing |
> | 2 had | 7 cleared |
> | 3 reporting | 8 passed |
> | 4 suffered | 9 passes |
> | 5 remaining | 10 climbed |

> **Background note:**
>
> *Overshoot windshear* is windshear characterised by an increase in an aircraft's airspeed.

b **○2.36** Play the recording again, pausing after each sentence for students to repeat, either individually or as a class. Make sure they pronounce the verb endings clearly and correctly. Afterwards, students work in pairs to practise saying the sentences using audioscript 2.36 on page 184.

c **○2.37** Play the recording, pausing after each transmission for students to repeat, either individually or as a class. Make sure they pronounce the words clearly and correctly and with good sentence stress and intonation. Afterwards, students work in pairs to practise saying the sentences using audioscript 2.37 on pages 184–185.

d **○2.38** Go through the word pairs quickly with the class to make sure everyone knows the meanings of each word (and which meaning goes with which spelling). Then play the recording for students to underline the correct words. When you check with the class, elicit what students remember about each sentence. Afterwards, students work in pairs to practise saying the sentences using audioscript 2.38 on page 185.

> **Answers:**
> | | | |
> |---|---|---|
> | 1 here | 5 whether | 9 ate |
> | 2 missed | 6 mail | 10 to |
> | 3 whole | 7 Sea | |
> | 4 Its | 8 where | |

Structure

2a Students work alone to match the beginnings and endings. They check in pairs before feeding back to the class. You may need to check everyone understands sentence 6, which is another way of saying *If the wind changes ....*

> **Answers:**
> | | | | |
> |---|---|---|---|
> | 1 g | 3 h | 5 b | 7 e |
> | 2 d | 4 f | 6 c | 8 a |

Extension activity:

Students test each other in pairs by reading one of the beginnings (1–8) to elicit a suitable ending from their partner, whose book is closed. Make sure they pay attention to the correct tenses.

b Students work alone to match the beginnings and endings. They check in pairs before feeding back to the class.

> **Answers:**
> | | |
> |---|---|
> | 1 because of | 5 so |
> | 2 because | 6 has made |
> | 3 force | 7 due |
> | 4 resulted in | 8 caused |

> **Background note:**
>
> *Unable to accept FL 390*; in question 7 we refer to the fact that when long-haul aircraft take off they are carrying a very large amount of fuel whose weight prevents them from climbing to very high altitudes before they have burnt some of it off.

Extension activity:

Students test each other in pairs by reading a sentence, inserting the word 'blank' to indicate where the space is. Their partners, whose books are closed, have to try to remember or work out which words to insert.

c Students work alone to choose the correct option and then check in pairs. When you go through the answers with the class, elicit why the incorrect answers are wrong.

> **Answers**
> | | | | |
> |---|---|---|---|
> | 1 b | 3 b | 5 c | 7 c |
> | 2 a | 4 c | 6 a | 8 a |

Vocabulary

3a **Students work alone to complete the sentences. They check in pairs before feeding back to the class.**

> **Answers:**
> | | |
> |---|---|
> | 1 thicker | 5 heavier |
> | 2 veering | 6 lift |
> | 3 increasing | 7 weakening |
> | 4 gusting | 8 scattered |

Extension activity:

Students test each other in pairs by reading a sentence aloud, but stopping before the gapped word. Their partners, whose books are closed, have to continue the sentence in a logical way.

b **Students work alone to complete the sentences. They check in pairs before feeding back to the class.**

> **Answers:**
> | | |
> |---|---|
> | 1 orbiting | 5 climbing |
> | 2 turning back | 6 donning |
> | 3 turning | 7 making |
> | 4 contacting | 8 monitoring |

Extension activity:

Students test each other in pairs by reading a sentence aloud, but stopping before the gapped word. Their partners, whose books are closed, have to continue the sentence in a logical way.

Fluency

4a ⊙ **2.39 Go through the examples with the class. Then play the recording, pausing after each transmission for volunteers to respond. Discuss the best responses with the class. Afterwards, students repeat the activity in pairs using audioscript 2.39 on page 185.**

> **Suggested answers:**
> 1 Say your position. Do you wish to make a precautionary landing?
> 2 Advise intentions. Is the safety of the flight threatened? Do you wish to divert? Will you require police assistance on arrival?
> 3 Your nearest available alternate at the present time is La Paz at 65 nautical miles to the north west.
> 4 Tune to 118.925.
> 5 Confirm that you are able to contain this individual. Do you wish to declare an emergency?
> 6 Are you able to continue your flight? Are any of your primary systems affected? Advise us if the situation changes.

> 7 Recent volcanic activity has been reported from the Mayon volcano on Luzon in the Philippines with ash clouds moving south east.
> 8 The cloud tops in your area are reported to be at 12,000 feet. Are you able to climb Flight Level 150?

Background notes:

◆ '*I am reading you two out of five*' means that radio reception is poor: the quality of reception is measured on a scale of 1 to 5.
◆ The *green hydraulic system* is one of the three hydraulic systems on Airbus aircraft.

b ⊙ **2.40 Go through the examples with the class. Then play the recording, pausing after each transmission for volunteers to respond. Discuss the best responses with the class. Afterwards, students repeat the activity in pairs using audioscript 2.40 on page 185.**

> **Suggested answers:**
> 1 Where exactly was the turbulence located, how severe was it and how long did it last?
> 2 Request the perimeter of the restrictions and re-routeing.
> 3 Why are you unable to hand us over to Gander?
> 4 A Citation crossed our path flying from right to left at what I would estimate at 500 feet below us 30 seconds ago.
> 5 Request instructions for diversion to nearest available alternate. Have you got any more information about the location of the bomb?
> 6 Advise me when we are showing on your screen again.
> 7 We will divert to San Antonio.
> 8 It had a t-tail and rear mounted engines, but it wasn't a McDonald Douglas. The livery was red and green on white.

Background note:

A *blind spot* is a point on a radar screen where information is not displayed or an area outside the aircraft hidden from the pilot by the airframe.

Comprehension

5a ⊙ **2.41 Go through the table with the class to elicit what sort of information is missing from each gap. Then play the recording for students to take notes. Point out that the information is presented very quickly, so inexperienced pilots and ATCOs may find this task very difficult. They compare their notes in pairs and listen again if necessary before feeding back to the class.**

Answers:

Airport	Stockholm, Arlanda	Visibility	5 km	Dew point	08°
Information	E	Cloud	500 few 1,200 SCT	QNH	1009
Time	13:55Z	Ceiling	3,000	ILS RWY	19L
Wind velocity	210°, 8 kts	Temperature	15°	Departures RWY	19R

Background notes:

♦ *Information Echo* identifies the ATIS information in a chronological series: Charlie; Delta; Echo; Foxtrot etc.

♦ '*Advise controller on initial contact that you have Bravo*' refers to the fact that the pilot must inform ATC of the status of the weather information he/she possesses.

b ⊙**2.42** Go through the eight statements with the class to check students understand all the words. Then play the recording for students to complete the task. They check in pairs and listen again if necessary before feeding back to the class.

Answers:
1 F – they are already level at FL 190
2 T
3 F – due to TCAS TA
4 F – he suffers from expectation bias and interprets the communication as a request
5 F – Shannon
6 T
7 T

Extension activity:

At the end of the recording, the speaker asks '*What were the factors in the error chain which caused a serious incident?*' Discuss this question with the class.

Suggested answers:
The various factors in the error chain are:
1 The controller's failure to recognise that Flystar 259 is descending due to a TCAS TA (Traffic Advisory) and not requesting clearance to descend as he had expected.
2 The pilot acting on a TCAS TA when in fact he had no obligation to take immediate evasive action before an RA (Resolution Advisory); he should have liaised with ATC.
3 The controller's failure to realise that Shamrock 148 is flying 1,000 feet below Flystar 259 at FL 180.
4 The controller's failure to respond to any of these situations; finally, the two aircraft resolved the situation themselves by Flystar climbing back to FL 190.

Interactions

6a ⊙**2.43** Go through the example with the class. Make sure students know to keep the conversations going over several turns in order to find a solution. Note that in several of the recordings, the pilots have problems with their English. Students playing the pilots could pretend to have poor English in order to make the situations more challenging for the ATCOs. Play the recording, pausing after the first exchange for students to work in pairs and continue the conversations. After a few minutes, stop to discuss the solutions with the class. Continue to use the same technique for the other seven conversations.

Possible answers:
ATCO: Descend Flight Level 130.
Pilot: We have trouble with descent.
ATCO: Say what exactly the problem is, please.
Pilot: Pitch control … elevator respond bad.
ATCO: Have you any warning lights?
Pilot: Affirm. Actuator failure.
ATCO: Say your heading and altitude.
Pilot: Heading 240 degrees … passing Flight Level 170 … descending to Flight Level 130.
ATCO: What are your intentions?
Pilot: Say again.
ATCO: Say your intentions.
Pilot: We need time to see the situation.
…

UNIT 8
Approach and landing incidents

Operational topics	Expectation; Runway friction coefficients; Runway excursions; Stabilised approach; Loss of situational awareness; Approach hazards; Landmarks, terrain and obstacles; Jeppesen approach chart; On short final; Go-around
Communication functions	Correcting erroneous expectations; Asking about availability; Saying unable; Communication errors: uncorrected erroneous readback; Expressing concern; Describing precautions; Expressing urgency; Relaying information
Language content	*Should*; Giving advice; *Will*: future, intention and undertaking; Relaying information using reported speech; Describing position; Distance

Unit 8 Teacher's brief

After working around communication situations related to hazards on the ground in Units 2 to 4 and en-route scenarios in Units 5 to 7, we now explore situations which occur during approach and landing in the third part of *Flightpath*.

Approach and landing are the most potentially critical phases of flight; final approach and landing represent four per cent of a 90-minute flight, yet over 40 per cent of all accidents occur during final approach and landing. Many of these accidents are cases of what is called **Controlled Flight Into Terrain** (CFIT), which means that an airworthy aircraft is unintentionally flown into the ground by its crew for a whole range of reasons. This is why safety and regulatory organisations such as the Flight Safety Foundation, ICAO, NASA, FAA etc. have devoted a lot of energy to trying to reduce **approach and landing accidents**. One of the main messages to flight crews is that if they are uncertain, they should **go around**, i.e. pull up and perform a **missed approach**.

Some of the reasons which make approach and landing more hazardous are:
- landing is technically more difficult than take-off or cruise
- the aircraft is approaching the terrain rather than moving away from it as after take-off
- weather conditions at destination can change significantly during the flight
- the pilot does not have the advantage of the added control over the aircraft provided by high engine thrust
- the aircraft is more affected by crosswind or windshear during landing

Approach and landing are phases of flight where the workload and the need for concentration are at their highest and response times are the shortest. Therefore, in Unit 8, in terms of communication

tasks, we will be looking at correcting erroneous expectations and misunderstanding, expressing concern and urgency, describing precautions and relaying information in order to maintain situational awareness.

Unit 8 Sources

- Airbus Flight Operations Briefing Notes: *Approach Hazard Awareness*
- Airbus Flight Operations Briefing Notes: *Standard Operating Procedures – Standard calls* and *Normal checklists*
- Boeing: Aero 19 – *ALAR tool kit*
- Flight Safety Foundation: *ALAR tool kit*
- Flight Safety Foundation: *Runway Safety Initiative – Reducing the risk of Runway Excursions*, 2009 (lead-in to Exercises 15a–c)
- Flight Safety Foundation: *It could happen to you*, DVD (Exercises 27a–29b)
- Lacagnina, M.: *Wayward Approach, AeroSafety World*, June 2009 (Exercises 12b–c)
- Lacagnina, M.: *Slippery Surprise, AeroSafety World*, April 2010 (Exercises 2b–e; 3a–c)
- Lacagnina, M.: *Misgauged recovery, AeroSafety World*, July 2010
- Mckinley, R. and Mohn, E.: *Dangerous Approaches, AeroSafety World*, February 2011
- NASA: *Aviation Safety Reporting System* http://ntl.bts.gov/data/letter (Unit lead-in)
- NATS: *Avoiding communication error – top ten tips for controllers* (ICAO focus with Exercise 22a)
- Transport Canada: *Crew Resource Management* (lead-in to Exercise 11a–b)
- UK CAA: *Safety Sense Leaflet 23*
- UK CAA: *CAP 745 Aircraft Emergencies*

Lead-in

The lead-in quote describes a small incident in which an American crew misunderstands an arrival chart because they expect to see something else. Although this is a case of misreading information, the same principles apply to oral information.

Quote: **Elicit from the class what a GLAND SIX Arrival chart is. Students read the quote to find out what went wrong and what happened as a consequence. [Answers: The pilot and co-pilot misread the chart; as a consequence the aircraft approached at too high a speed].**

Background notes:

- ◆ A *GLAND SIX Arrival chart* is a chart for a navigation fix in Texas.
- ◆ If you *expect* an event, you anticipate or think that it will occur in the future.
- ◆ If an action is *mandatory*, it is something you must do.

1a, b, c **Discuss the questions with the class.**

Suggested answers:
a The chart said that there was a 250-knot speed restriction about crossing the GLAND waypoint and that the crew should expect clearance to cross it when they were at 10,000 feet. The crew thought that the chart said that they should expect to be cleared to cross GLAND at 10,000 feet and 250 knots. As a result, they crossed the waypoint 40 knots too fast.
b The anecdote raises the distinction between mandatory restrictions, which are obligatory, and expectation messages which are purely indicative.

Extension activity:

Elicit from the class all the phrases from the quote referring to mistakes. Check the pronunciation of *misread* (infinitive: /mɪsˈriːd/; past: /mɪsˈred/). Students then use these phrases to make sentences about their stories in exercise 1c.

Suggested answers:
misread sth as sth; actually, it said ...; it should have been ...; that was (a mandatory), not (an expect).

Expectation

Communicative and operational issues:

In communication terms, what is important here is the awareness that the same data (e.g. *10,000 ft*; *250 kts*; *at time 25*; *170°* etc.) can be framed in different contexts (e.g. mandatory actions; indicative information; immediate actions; conditional

clearances; expectations; discretionary actions etc.) and so mean something quite different. Students should be reminded of the importance of clearly identifying the context in which the information they hear is transmitted, especially, as in the case quoted in the *Lead-in*, where two pieces of information (i.e. altitude and airspeed) are given together, but not in the same context: the altitude was indicative and the airspeed mandatory. You could ask the students to produce examples of their own.

2a **Students discuss the questions in pairs and then feed back to the class.**

Suggested answers:
- ◆ A *runway incursion* (see Unit 4) is when an aircraft, vehicle, person or animal enters an active runway from a taxiway or another runway. A *runway excursion* occurs when an aircraft fails to stop, usually during landing roll-out, and runs off the end or the side of the paved runway.
- ◆ Runway excursions tend to happen when one or more of the following conditions occur: the aircraft lands too far down the runway; lands too fast; lands on a 'contaminated' runway, i.e. when the runway is very wet or icy; the aircraft braking system or thrust reversers are faulty; when the available landing distance is too short.

b ⊙3.01 **Elicit from the class the type of information required for each gap in the table (e.g. a distance in feet or metres). Students then listen to the recording to complete the table. They compare their answers with a partner and listen again if necessary. Finally, go through the answers with the class.**

Answers:
1 A321	6 800 feet
2 Spain	7 1,200 m
3 Norway	8 RWY 18
4 216	9 2,569 m
5 7	10 45 m

Background notes:

- ◆ *Landing distance available* (*LDA*) refers to the length of the runway which can actually be used for landing and roll-out as declared by the airport authority. It is referred to as the 'available landing distance' in the recording.
- ◆ The length (2,569 m) and width (45 m) of the runway are fairly conventional and certainly adequate for narrow-body aircraft like the A321.

c, d **Students discuss the questions in pairs and then feed back to the class.**

Answers:
c The flight crew expected good visibility and the snow to have been cleared from the runway.
d It started to snow 40 minutes before their arrival and the airport authorities decided to remove the snow from the runway only after the flight's arrival.

Extension activity:

Elicit from the class onto the board a range of ways of talking about expectations which were not met. Ask volunteers to make sentences connected with the incident in exercise 2b for each structure. Students then work in pairs to use the structures to describe unfulfilled expectations from their own experience. Afterwards, ask some volunteers to report back on their partners' stories to the class.

Possible answers:
They *expected / were expecting* ... *to* ... , *but in fact* ...
They *thought* there *would* be .... *However, it turned out that* ...
They *assumed* they *would* ..., *but* they *ended up having to* ...
It should have been.... *But* it was *actually* ...

Language note:

Expect can be followed by a *to*-infinitive (with or without a subject before *to*), a *that*-clause or a noun phrase. Past simple and continuous are both possible, with no change of meaning.

They expected (the aircraft) to land easily.
They expected that they would be able to land easily.
They expected an easy landing.

Other verbs describing expectations (*think*; *assume*) are less flexible. They are usually in the past simple, and are followed by a *that*-clause.

They thought/assumed that they would be able to land easily.

NOT *They thought/assumed ~~to land easily / an easy landing~~.*

e Students describe runways in pairs and then feed back to the class. They could extend the discussion by commenting on whether the runways are well designed, using phrases such as *too short/narrow*; *long/wide enough*.

Extension activity 1:

Elicit from the class onto the board a range of nouns and adjectives to describe dimensions, plus the opposites of the adjectives. Make sure they are all happy with the spellings and pronunciations, especially endings such as *-ght* and *-gth*. You could

also check the difference between *high* (e.g. clouds, a bridge) and *tall* (e.g. a tower). Note that *wide* and *broad* are effectively interchangeable when describing dimensions, but wide is preferred because it is more widely understood.

Suggested answers:

long	length	short
wide/broad	width/breadth	narrow
deep	depth	shallow
high	height	low
tall	height	short

Extension activity 2:

Print some charts of runways in your country, or at least find data about their dimensions. Read the dimensions to the class, who have to guess which airport/runway you are describing.

3a ⊙3.02 Go through the table with the class (see pages 136 and 144), eliciting the type of information missing from each gap. You could also predict what some of the information might be, based on the information provided in the first part of the recording. Make sure students realise they should only fill in half the information. Then play the recording for students to complete their tables. Afterwards, they work in pairs or small groups to exchange information by asking questions (e.g. *What did the ATIS report say about the surface of runway 18? At what time did the crew contact the tower?*) and making notes in their tables. With weaker classes, it may be necessary to elicit these questions from the class onto the board first. You could play the recording again for students to check their information is all correct. Finally, go through the answers with the class. You could also go through the questions they used to elicit each piece of information.

Answers:
Crew actions
1 three minutes before touchdown
2 one dot high
3 780 m from threshold (350 m beyond touchdown zone)
4 140 kts
5 apply maximum reverse thrust
6 half way down the runway
7 engaged parking brake
8 increased deceleration
9 end of hard runway surface
10 minor damage to lower skin and nose-wheel rim and tyre

Environmental conditions
1 dry
2 good
3 2,500 m
4 500 feet
5 060
6 6 kts
7 contaminated with 8 mm of wet snow
8 medium
9 12 mm
10 poor

If you have an odd number of students you will need to have a group of three students, where Student C alternates in each row between completing the left and right-hand columns. This means that for about half the missing pieces of information, two students in that group should have noted the answers.

Background notes:

For ATIS (Automatic Terminal Information Service), see Unit 1 exercise 7 and Unit 5 *Teacher's brief*.

- *Braking action* is measured in MU (pronounced 'mew') on a scale from 0 to 100. If braking action is described as *good*, it is 40 or above; if *medium* or fair, it is between 30 and 40; if *poor*, between 20 and 30. See AOPA *Safety Brief* No. 3
- If a runway is *contaminated* by snow, standing water, ice, slush, oil etc., it is covered with or has patches of these substances, which could affect braking efficiency.
- A *post-incident analysis* is an analysis conducted after the event.
- A *radio altitude* is an altitude above the ground displayed by the radio altimeter during the last 2,500 feet of the approach.
- If a plane is *one dot high*, it is 50 feet above its expected position on the glidescope, although on the glideslope scale the pointer will indicate one dot below the centre. See www.pilotfriend.com (ILS) and www.united-virtual.com (The ILS Approach).
- *Reverse thrust* involves changing the direction of flow of part of the engine exhaust gases during landing roll-in order to assist the braking action.
- *Autobrake* is a computer-assisted system which controls and monitors landing gear brake applications in order to achieve maximum braking efficiency.
- The *parking brake* is used on the ground at the stand until the chocks are in place or for emergency braking as a last resort.
- The *skin* is the fuselage, wing and empennage panels which make up the outer airframe of the aircraft.
- A *wheel rim* is the outer lip of a wheel, which holds the tyre in place.

- A *non-emergency evacuation* involves leaving the aircraft as a precautionary measure while the aircraft is not at its parking stand.

b, c **Students work in pairs or small groups to retell the story. You may want to elicit some phrases first for structuring a report such as this (e.g. *First of all, ...; After that, ...; Next, ...; That was because ...;* etc.). Afterwards, elicit the whole story from the class. This would be a good time to discuss the questions in exercise 3c for each stage of the incident, rather than all together at the end.**

Suggested answer:
c As always, this incident was caused by a combination of factors related to the way in which all those involved reacted to the worsening weather conditions. The captain should have decided to go around when he saw that they were one dot (50 feet) too high on the glideslope scale, and were going to touch down beyond the touchdown zone on a contaminated runway. The Tower did not have accurate or up-to-date information about the state of the runway at their disposal and so they reported to the crew that the depth of snow was less, and the braking action better than they in fact were. The airport authorities had not updated the ATIS recording, had decided not to clear the runway, and had not measured the depth of snow or the runway friction coefficient correctly or recently. All these omissions had a knock-on effect on the Tower and the crew's behaviour.

4a **Students work alone to match the sentence halves and then discuss their answers in pairs. After you have checked with the class, students could test each other in pairs by reading one of the beginnings to elicit a suitable ending (which may not necessarily be the same as the one in the exercise).**

Answers:
1 f	3 a	5 b	7 c
2 h	4 g	6 d	8 e

Background notes:

- *Information K* identifies the order in which information is issued by the ATIS.
- *To be visual* means the crew has the runway in sight.
- *Igaba, Oradi, Krabu* are locations in West Africa.
- If a plane *tracks* a radial, it flies along it to join a navaid or ILS fix.

Extension activity:

You could continue to explore the language of expectations (see *Extension activity* and *Language note* after exercise 2d). Ask students to find examples in exercise 4a of the following:

♦ *to expect/think/assume + that*-clause [**Answer:** *The crew thought they would be visual.*]

♦ *to expect* + noun phrase [**Answers:** *... the crew expected a 210° radial; ... not to expect any holding; The controllers had expected a quiet shift, ...*]

♦ *to expect* + subject + *to*-infinitive [**Answer:** *The crew expected snow to be cleared ...*]

♦ *to expect* + *to*-infinitive [**Answer:** *The pilot expected to be landing ...*]

b **Students discuss in pairs and feed back to the class.**

> **Suggested answers:**
> 1 The crew expected better braking action than they actually experienced.
> 2 A last-minute change of runway has a very destabilising effect on the flight crew at a critical phase in the flight because it requires them to make a new briefing, prepare for a new approach and enter new data at low altitude, with other traffic in the vicinity, and at a moment of high work load and stress.
> 3 The destabilising effect of flying a different radial is similar to that of a change in runway.
> 4 An unexpected change in visibility, although probably not below minima, means that the crew might have to switch from a visual to an instruments approach and anticipate a greater likelihood of a go-around.
> 5 Unexpected holding will obviously affect their fuel consumption and possibly their schedule if this is only a leg in a longer flight.
> 6 A sudden increase in workload due to diverted traffic arriving, increases stress levels and may mean the shift is understaffed.
> 7 Not being visual at 500 feet when they expected to have the runway in sight at 1,500 feet, creates a feeling of uncertainty, makes the crew possibly doubt the rest of the terminal information provided, be forced to review the type of approach and have to suddenly consider the possibility of a go-around.
> 8 A change of vectors to intercept the ILS means that the crew has to enter new navigation data at the last moment, and tends to undermine their sense of security.

5 ○3.03 **Go through the example with the class. Then play the recording for volunteers to respond. In the suggested answers, both plain language and phraseology options have been given. Afterwards, students can test each other in pairs using audioscript 3.03 on page 186.**

> **Suggested answers:**
> 1 Is the full length of the runway available? / Advise take-off distance available
> 2 Is the fire service available? / Advise fire service available

3 Is CAT III C available? / Advise CAT III C available
4 Are the localizer and glideslope available? / Advise ILS available
5 Is Runway 31 Left available? / Advise Runway 31 Left available
6 Are radar vectors to final approach available? / Advise radar vectors to final approach available
...

Background notes:

♦ *CAT III C* (*Category three C*) means that the crew, aircraft and aerodrome are qualified and equipped to land in conditions with theoretically zero feet *vertical Decision Height*, and zero feet *longitudinal visibility*.

♦ *GNSS* (*Global Navigation Satellite System*) refers here to the underlying technology behind the *GLS* (*GNSS Landing System*), which combines satellite and local data to provide very accurate navigational positioning for landing. For more information, see Boeing: *Global Navigation Satellite System Landing System* in Aero 21

♦ *VOR-DME approach* is an approach using a combination of two types of navaid: VHF Omnidirectional Range and Distance Measuring Equipment.

♦ *Lower level* here refers to a lower flight level which the crew wishes to descend to for operational, technical or meteorological reasons.

ICAO FOCUS

Tell students to read the quote carefully to find out exactly what a proficient speaker should be able to do [**Answer:** to be able to easily and successfully deal with linguistic challenges presented by complicated and/or unexpected situations]. Students then discuss the two questions in small groups and feed back to the class.

Background note:

This is a key quotation from ICAO Doc. 9835 as it refers explicitly to the need to use plain language in a complicated and unexpected turn of events, and the linguistic challenges this involves. As we have seen, this linguistic challenge is usually accompanied by a higher workload and a degree of stress, meaning that the students' linguistic mastery should be robust enough to handle unexpected turns of events at times when their cognitive, emotional and psychological processes are under pressure.

Language note:

The use of *shall* in the quote may cause some confusion. In this context, it is close in meaning to *must*: a statement of obligation rather than a prediction. *Shall* is commonly used in legal and regulatory documents.

6 **Go through the example with the class. Elicit which words should be stressed [Answer: 19 Left]. Note that the purpose of this exercise is not to reproduce standard phraseology, but students may feel that this is a more appropriate and easier solution and this is perfectly correct. Students then work in pairs to make dialogues. Students then swap roles and repeat the role-plays. Afterwards, ask volunteers to perform their role-plays and discuss the best answers with the class.**

Suggested answers:
Student A to Student B:
1
A: Request ILS approach to Runway 26 Right.
B: Unable. Wind 180 degrees at ten knots. Runway in use <u>19 Left</u>.
2
A: Request (Can we have a) lower level in 12 miles?
B: Negative. (There is) Heavy traffic. Expect lower in <u>20 miles</u>.
3
A: Request straight-in approach to Runway 29 Left.
B: Due terrain, make a step-down approach to Runway <u>29 Right</u>.
...

Student B to Student A:
1
B: Our current rate of descent is / We have set a rate of descent of 1,000 feet per minute.
A: Expedite your descent at <u>1,500</u> feet per minute.
2
B: We have a forecast of visibility 2,000 metres overcast.
A: Negative. Current weather is visibility <u>600</u> metres in <u>rain</u>.
3
B: Request ILS approach to Runway 07 Left.
A: Unable. Runway 07 Left (is) <u>closed</u>. Runway 07 <u>Right</u> is in use.
...

If you have an odd number of students you will need to have a group of three students, where Student C takes cues 1 and 4 (both expectations and changes/corrections) from Student A and cues 3 and 6 from Student B.

Background note:

PADDY is the identifier of a navaid in New Jersey, US.

Communication errors: An uncorrected erroneous readback

Communicative and operational issues:

We have already looked at the critical phenomenon of uncorrected readback error (hearback error) in an en-route environment in Unit 6. Given the numerous constraints associated with approach and landing, the safety margin for correcting hearback errors is narrower in this phase of flight.

Quote: **Elicit from the class what is meant by an uncorrected erroneous readback, and what problems it might lead to [Answers: an uncorrected erroneous readback is a hearback error; they can lead to deviations from assigned altitudes, or non-compliance with an altitude restriction or radar vector]. They then read the quote to compare it with their ideas. You may need to check the pronunciation of some words, such as *erroneous* /ɪˈrəʊnɪəs/, *deviation* /ˈdiːvɪˈeɪʃən/, *assigned* /əˈsaɪnd/ and *compliance* /kəmˈplaɪəns/.**

7a, b **Students discuss the two tasks in pairs and feed back to the class**

Suggested answers:
a **ATCO:** ILS Asiana 482, expect ILS approach Runway 19 Right, QNH 1023.
 Pilot: ILS approach Runway 19 Right, QNH 1013, Asiana 482.
b Readback errors are most likely to occur during periods of high workload, e.g. during a technical incident, in dense traffic conditions, when the crew are distracted etc.

Background notes:

 ◆ An *altitude restriction* is an obligation for the crew to not fly above or below a certain altitude at a given point or in a given area.
 ◆ A *radar vector* is a heading issued as part of radar navigation guidance.

8 **⊙3.04 Go through the example with the class, focusing on the mistake the pilot makes and its possible cause [Suggested answer: He says 245 instead of 255, presumably because his call sign is 245]. Then play the recording, pausing after each communication for two volunteers to continue the dialogue. They may repeat either all of the original message, or simply the part which was read back incorrectly. Make sure they stress the corrected information. Afterwards, students repeat the exercise in pairs or small groups, using audioscript 3.04 on page 186.**

Suggested answers
(with stressed words underlined):

1 **ATCO:** CSA lines 245, negative. Turn right heading 2<u>55</u>, I say again turn right heading 2<u>55</u> degrees to intercept Localizer Runway 24. Read back.

2 **ATCO:** Speedbird 1872, negative. Expect Trujillo direct in <u>two</u> <u>zero</u> miles. Confirm.

3 **ATCO:** Oscar Kilo Alpha 14<u>78</u>. Confirm.

4 **ATCO:** Silkair 496, negative. Traffic <u>ten</u> o'clock, <u>one one</u> miles westbound. Confirm.

5 **ATCO:** Foxtrot Alpha Bravo 159, negative. I say again turn right heading 0<u>80</u> degrees. and contact Radar 1<u>18</u> decimal 825. Confirm.

6 **ATCO:** Negative. Orient Eagle <u>359</u>, I say again <u>359</u>, cleared ILS approach Runway 26 Left. Confirm.

7 **ATCO:** Enkor 153, negative. Intercept Localizer <u>one niner</u> miles from touchdown. Confirm.

8 **ATCO:** Cyprus 766, negative. I say again, QNH 10<u>31</u>.

Expressing concern and making suggestions

Communicative and operational issues:

The crash of Avianca Flight 52 near New York JFK airport in January 1990 (see Aviation Safety Network: www.aviation-safety.net) is often referred to as an example of the flight crew being unable to communicate the gravity of the situation on board. In fact, the aircraft crashed due to fuel exhaustion, which the crew were aware of, but did not manage to communicate to ATC.

It is important, therefore, even in much less dramatic circumstances, to have the language and the self-confidence to be able to express concern and make suggestions about action to be taken. Part of this ability is being able to paraphrase if one's interlocutor does not understand one's original message. Doing this effectively involves not only the lexis and structures used, but also word stress and tone of voice.

Language focus: Expressing concern

Tell students to close their books. Elicit from the class a range of ways of expressing concern. Students then compare their ideas with those in the book.

Extension activity:

Read the beginning of one of the examples (e.g. *I am puzzled ...*) to elicit a suitable ending. Note that this will draw attention to dependent prepositions (*about*, *by*) and other structures that follow these phrases. Students could then test each other in pairs.

9a ○**3.05** Go through the instructions with the class. For each of the eight reasons, elicit why it might be a cause for concern. Play the recording for students to complete the exercise. When they have checked in pairs, play the recording again for them to check, if necessary. Then go through the answers with the class. Note that the recordings contain remarks made from pilot to pilot or from controller to controller.

Answers:			
1 g	3 h	5 e	7 d
2 b	4 a	6 c	8 f

Background notes:

◆ If one aircraft is *gaining on* the aircraft ahead, it is reducing the distance between them.

◆ If you *key in* data, you enter it into a computer system using a keyboard.

Extension activity:

Students look at audioscript 3.05 on page 186. They work in pairs to decide which words and syllables in each communication they would stress and then listen to check.

Suggested answers:
1 I am very con<u>cern</u>ed about our rate of <u>descent</u>.
2 I'm getting <u>worr</u>ied about whether we'll be able to <u>hold</u> much longer.
3 I'm a<u>fraid</u> that we've lost <u>radio</u> con<u>tact</u> with Air India 45<u>81</u>.
4 I thought that he read back 2<u>90</u> not 2<u>50</u>.
5 The Boeing 737 is <u>gaining</u> on the <u>turbo</u>prop ahead.
6 I am <u>puzzled</u> by our <u>altimeter</u> reading. I thought we were <u>higher</u> than 4<u>,000</u> feet.
7 I am con<u>cern</u>ed about the flights being di<u>vert</u>ed from Oslo.
8 Don't you think it's <u>strange</u> that they've instructed us to turn <u>left</u>? I thought there was ter<u>rain</u> at more than 3<u>,000</u> metres to the north<u>west</u>.

b ○**3.05** Play the recording again, pausing after each communication for students to repeat, either individually or as a class. They could practise again in pairs, using audioscript 3.05 on page 186.

Language focus: *should*

Tell students to close their books. Elicit some examples onto the board of sentences with *should*. Ideally at least one sentence for each of the three functions listed in the *Language focus* box, plus at least one example of *should have* (for criticising a past mistake or talking about a past probability). Make sure students know which structures follow *should* and *should have* (i.e. *should* + infinitive; *should have* + past participle). For each sentence, elicit the function of *should*. Students then compare their ideas with those in the book. You could discuss with the class any potential problems with the fact that *should* has several meanings, and ways to avoid these problems (see *Language note* below).

Language note:

◆ The first use of *should*, for strong recommendations and advice, is the most common and the most useful for students to learn. The following verb is usually an action verb.

◆ The second use of *should*, for probability, is unlikely to be confused with the first meaning, as it tends to go with state verbs denoting present or future ability (e.g. *You should [be able to] see the runway now.*), or with future actions (e.g. *They should come into sight in about a minute*). However, to avoid confusion, it may be safer to use questions about ability (e.g. *Can you see the runway?*), or words like *probably* (e.g. *They will probably come into sight.*), or *expect* (e.g. *Expect them to come into sight*).

◆ The same risk of confusion exists with *should have*. *They should have landed by now* could be interpreted as a prediction (= I expect they have landed) or as an expression of concern (= I'm worried because they haven't landed as expected). This confusion can be avoided by using *should have* only for regrets and criticism (e.g. *You shouldn't have pressed that button*).

◆ The fourth use of *should*, in conditional sentences, is especially likely to cause confusion when speaking with less proficient speakers of English, and should therefore be avoided, although it is a use which is fairly common in the pilots' Flight Manuals, e.g. *Should the runway not be in sight at Decision Height, perform a go-around.* However, *if* should be recommended for the students' own speech production instead.

c Students work in pairs to discuss the meaning of *should* in each sentence and its context. They then feed back to the class.

Answers:

1 if	5 must
2 must	6 if
3 must	7 must
4 probably	8 probably

Background notes:

◆ The *Decision Height* (*DH*) is the height above the ground shown on the radio altimeter in final approach at which the pilot must decide to land or go around.

◆ If a pilot calls '*Go around*', he/she decides to pull up and perform a missed approach.

Extension activity:

Students work in pairs to rewrite the sentences without using the word *should* and then feed back to the class.

Suggested answers:
1 *If* the runway isn't in sight at Decision Height, I'll call '*go-around*'.
2 *I recommend that* you always read back clearances and instructions.
3 *Would you advise us to* change frequency now?
4 *We expect to* be crossing the ZUVMU waypoint in five minutes.
5 *It would be a good idea for me to* ask for confirmation of our routing.
6 *If* you notice anything unusual, inform me.
7 *I want you to* inform me if you notice anything unusual.
8 The forecast is good. You *probably won't* encounter any weather.

d ◐ **3.05** Go through the example with the class. Then play the recording, pausing after each communication for volunteers to respond appropriately, ideally using *should*. There are several possible responses and reactions to each situation. Some typical suggested answers are given in the key, but the teacher should expect to hear others and, if in doubt, throw the answers open to the group for discussion. Discuss the best responses with the class. Students then repeat the exercise in pairs using audioscript 3.05 on page 186.

Suggested answers:
1 We should crosscheck with the altimeter reading. / We should use the airbrakes. / You should ease back on the stick.
2 You should contact Approach. / We should divert. / We should declare an emergency.
3 You should try and contact them on the previous frequency. / You should check whether any aircraft in the sector have heard them.
4 You should ask him to confirm / read back again.
5 You should instruct the B737 to reduce his airspeed/orbit.

6 We should cross check the two instruments. /
We should contact the Tower.

7 You should ask for our shift to be reinforced. /
You should warn ground handling that they will
need more staff.

8 You should question that instruction. / We
should maintain our present heading until we
have confirmation.

10 In this exercise too, pilots and controllers are
speaking amongst themselves about subjects of
concern and giving each other advice. Students
can imagine that a less experienced controller or
pilot is seeking advice from an instructor or more
experienced colleague. Go through the examples with
the class. Make sure students realise they will be
playing different roles when they initiate a discussion
and when they respond to an expression of concern.
Students then work in pairs to make dialogues.

Suggested answers:
ATCOs
1
A: I am not sure it was Aeromexico 562 which
responded.
B: You should ask for confirmation. / You should
request a full readback. / You should ask him
to read back his full call sign.
2
A: I am worried that Air France 585 and 985
have similar call signs.
B: You should assign a new call sign to one of
them.
3
A: I thought he said Runway 26 Right and not
Runway 26 Left.
B: You should ask for confirmation. / You should
ask him to make another readback.
4
A: It's strange he didn't read back.
B: You should remind him to read back. / You
should call him back.
...
Pilots
1
A: I'm worried about the shifting wind direction
on Runway 07.
B: You should request an updated weather
report. / You should ask for the latest wind
velocity. / You should check with the Tower.
2
A: I thought the controller said an ILS approach
to Runway 31 left.
B: You should ask her to repeat the clearance.
3
A: It's strange that ATC instructed us to approach
from the South.
B: You should ask for confirmation. / You should
question the instruction.

4
A: I'm concerned about our radio-altimeter
readings.
B: We should go around. / We should crosscheck
our instruments.
...

If you have an **odd number of students** you will need
to have a group of three students, where the third
student takes cues 1 to 3 from Student A and cues 8
to 10 from Student B.

Background note:
Converging flight paths are heading towards each
other.

Loss of situational awareness

Communicative and operational issues:

Acquiring and maintaining situational awareness
is one of the primary aims of oral communication.
As the lead-in quote from Transport Canada makes
clear, this is a process which is constantly going
on between the pilots in the air, controllers on the
ground, and between pilots and controllers at critical
points in the flight (e.g. clearances, level changes,
changes of heading, approach, holding, unexpected
events etc). In addition, situational awareness is
consolidated by the crew monitoring communications
between other aircraft and the ground. So, losing
situational awareness could become the equivalent
of 'flying blind'.

Quote: **Students read the quote to identify what
situational awareness is, what it promotes and
what it requires. Elicit from the class what each of
the key words means in this context. [Suggested
answers:** *to accurately perceive* = to be aware of and
correctly understand a situation; *on-going* = constant,
repeated, non-stop; *questioning* = asking questions,
not accepting the obvious or expected answer without
checking; *crosschecking* = exchanging information
between pilots and confirming that all instruments
are displaying the same data; *refinement of one's
perception* = updating and improving the way one
understands a situation; *constant and conscious
monitoring* = monitoring in an active way all the time,
not simply waiting for warnings, etc.]

11a, b **Students discuss the two questions in pairs and
then feed back to the class.**

Suggested answers:
a Situational awareness is a mental picture
which can be built up from: pilot-controller
communications (explicit oral information);
instrument displays (airspeed, altitude,
attitude, rate of climb, engine parametres,
compass, inertial navigation, radio-altimeter
etc.); glideslope and localizer displays; weather

radar returns (pilots); ATC radar screens; monitoring communications between ATC and other flights; ATIS; TAF; pilot reports; feeling the way the aircraft responds ('flying by the seat of your pants'); feedback from other crew or team members; direct vision through the windshield (other traffic, weather conditions, terrain, approach and runway lighting), or from the control tower etc.

b Situational awareness can be lost partially, or completely, by phenomena such as: aircraft instrument failure or incorrect instrument data (especially anything related to the radio-altimeter and ILS); VHF radio blackout; incomplete transmissions; incorrect phraseology; poor language proficiency; erroneous readbacks; ATIS recordings which are not up to date; poor crew resource management depriving other crew members of feedback; technical failures (radar, lighting, ILS) of the ground equipment; visual effects such as snow blindness or black hole effect (impaired assessment of height caused by a dark stretch of ground prior to very bright city lights); poor visibility etc.

12a Students work alone to complete the sentences. When they have checked with a partner, go through the answers with the class. Discuss with the class what facts about the incident they can work out and what they can guess. Elicit what the cause of the problem was [**Answer**: The crew mistook hotel lights for runway lights]. Elicit how common this problem is [**Suggested answer**: It is a well-documented visual phenomenon in certain conditions, especially at the end of a long flight with the effects of fatigue]. And elicit how it can be avoided [**Suggested answer**: The crew must crosscheck all the data sources which provide them with situational awareness: instruments; visual references; ATC communications. If in doubt, they must question ATC and always be ready to go around].

Answers:
1 schedule	6 edge
2 descent	7 distracted
3 course (path)	8 noticed
4 deviate	9 initiated
5 due to	10 vectors

Background notes:

◆ *Minimum descent altitude* (*MDA*) is the altitude in the terminal area (around the airport) below which no aircraft must descend unless it is on its approach path. In some airports, the MDA will be different in different directions depending on the terrain.

◆ If a pilot *initiates* a manoeuvre or procedure, he/she starts it.

b ○3.06 Students read through the statements to predict the answers. Then play the recording for them to complete the task. They compare their answers in pairs and listen again if necessary. Then go through the answers with the class.

Answers:
1 F – Runway 28
2 T
3 F – at 5 nm
4 F – confused the lights of a hotel with runway approach lighting
5 T
6 F – distracted by communications with airport maintenance personnel
7 F – at an altitude of 580 feet
8 T

Background note:

An *MD-83* is a McDonnell Douglas narrow-body jet aircraft of an older generation (1990s) with twin engines mounted on the rear fuselage.

c Students discuss the questions in groups and then feed back to the class.

Suggested answers:
◆ Environment: planned runway closed; easily confusable lights in the vicinity of the airport
◆ Flight crew: crew had to plan for a different approach at the last moment; flight crew mistook the lights of a hotel for the runway approach lights
◆ ATC: the controller was distracted by communications with airport maintenance and did not monitor the approach; a third runway (RWY 16) was finally selected

Language focus: *will*

Tell students to close their books. Read the six examples from the *Language focus* box aloud. Elicit in each case what the function of *will* is. Elicit also the difference between saying *I'll call you back* and *I will call you back* (with *will* stressed) [**Suggested answer**: The second version stresses the promise, which is intended to reassure the other person who may be worried that the speaker might not call back]. Students then read the information in the box to compare it with their ideas.

Language note:

It is important that students realise that *will* is not always about the future. In the sentence *Our nose landing gear won't extend*, the pilot is simply saying that he has tried, perhaps several times, but the gear 'refuses' to extend. This is an example of *will* for attitude/willingness.

13 Go through the example with the class. Students then work in pairs to ask questions and give responses. Afterwards, students swap roles and repeat the exercise without looking at the response cues.

Suggested answers:
ATCO responses to pilot input:
1
Pilot: We have to make an emergency landing on 08.
ATCO: I'll position you for a ten-mile final ILS Runway 08.
2
Pilot: Our nose landing gear doesn't seem to have extended.
ATCO: If you make a low pass, we'll have a look.
3
Pilot: We need to expedite our approach.
ATCO: I'll make you Number 1.
4
Pilot: We need to alert our maintenance base.
ATCO: I'll relay your message to your base.
...

Pilot responses to ATCO questions:
1
ATCO: What will you do if the thunderstorm is still overhead the field on arrival?
Pilot: We'll divert to Tashkent.
2
ATCO: The ILS is inoperative, I'm afraid. Say your intentions.
Pilot: We'll make a VFR approach.
3
ATCO: If your oil leak gets worse, what will you do?
Pilot: We'll shut down the engine and divert to Merida.
4
ATCO: What will you do if the warning does not come on again?
Pilot: We'll continue the flight.
...

If you have an odd number of students you will need to have a group of three, where the third student takes the first two responses from Student A and the last two responses from Student B.

Background notes:

◆ The *field* here is used as a common shortened form of airfield meaning aerodrome.
◆ *#1* here simply means number one, i.e. the first in the queue.

14 Elicit/Remind students of the different elements of situational awareness and how they can be lost (see answers to exercises 10a and b) and make notes on the board. Students then make their own dialogues based on the situation as described. There are no cues for these dialogues: students should use their imaginations and the notes on the board for guidance. Allow about five minutes for students to plan their role-plays and then ask each pair to perform their role-play for the class. Discuss with the class which role-plays were most successful at resolving the situations.

Possible answer:
A Korean Air Boeing 737-800 from Seoul is on approach at 11.15 to Aomori (Japan) with 106 passengers and six crew members on board. During the approach, the crew loses various elements of situational awareness.

ATCO: Korean Air 767, turn left heading 014, vectoring for ILS Approach 24.
Pilot: Turn left heading 014, Korean Air 767
Pilot: Aomori Approach, Korean Air 767, unable receive Information Delta.
ATCO: Korean Air 767, Information Delta: 10:59Z, Wind 260 degrees, seven knots; Visibility three kilometres; Overcast 600 feet; Temperature 11 degrees, dew point 10 degrees, QNH 998 hPa.
...

If you have an odd number of students you will need to have a group of three students, where the third student could play the co-pilot or any other role they choose.

Reducing the risk of runway excursions

Communicative and operational issues:

As the Flight Safety schematics introducing this section show, runway excursions remain a common type of aircraft incident and accident, and the majority of runway excursions occur during landing.

Further resources on runway excursions are:

www.tsb.gc.ca: Air France flight 358 at Toronto, Canada
www.skybrary.aero: Skybrary: *Beyond the runway end safety area*

Quote: **Tell students to read the quote to decide which of the two graphs it relates to [Answer: the left-hand graph].**

15a, b, c Students discuss the questions in groups. After a few minutes, open up the discussion to include the whole class.

> **Suggested answers:**
> b A *runway incursion* occurs when an aircraft, vehicle, pedestrian or animal inadvertently enters an active runway. A *runway confusion* is the fact of a pilot entering or landing on the wrong runway.
> c Runway excursions occur more often during landing because of the higher speed and greater momentum of a landing aircraft. Runway excursions do occur during take-off especially when a take-off is rejected after V1 or if the runway surface is slippery due to ice, snow or standing water, or the aircraft suffers a brake failure.

16a Students work in pairs to discuss who is responsible for each of the factors. They should also discuss any experience they have of these factors. Afterwards, open up the discussion to include the whole class. Allow plenty of time for this discussion to develop, including any anecdotes students have connected with these factors.

> **Suggested answers:**
>
> | | | | |
> |---|---|---|---|
> | 1 P | 5 C | 9 P | 13 A |
> | 2 C | 6 P | 10 P | 14 P |
> | 3 P | 7 A | 11 C | 15 C |
> | 4 A | 8 C | 12 C | 16 P |

Background notes:

- *Crew resource management* (*CRM*) is a branch of human factors which analyses the ways in which team work and good communication can reduce the effects of human error. CRM training has become part of mainstream pilot training. See James Reason's seminal works in this field: *Human Error* (1990) and *Managing the risks of organisational accidents* (1997).
- *Standard Operating Procedures* are specific procedures defined by an airline to respond to all contingencies.
- *Approach high* refers to the fact that the aircraft is above the glideslope beam during approach; as a result, the aircraft will probably touch down beyond the touchdown target zone.
- *Touchdown long* refers to the aircraft touching down beyond the touchdown target zone.
- *Approach fast* refers to the fact that the aircraft is flying faster than its reference speed for that particular configuration and at that particular phase of the approach. This may result in a hard landing and more of the runway length being required to stop. A fast approach may be the result of a flaps-up landing.

b Students work in pairs or small groups to list some of the consequences of each factor before feeding back to the class. Students then work in pairs to make sentences for each of the sixteen factors. They can do this orally, if you are sure they will use *will* properly. If you think they will make lots of mistakes, ask them to write their sentences down. Afterwards, collect the best sentences from the class and write some onto the board.

> **Possible answers:**
> 1 If the pilot has inadequate directional control, the aircraft will veer off the runway.
> 2 If the controller fails to allow the aircraft to fly appropriate speeds, the aircraft will not respect Vref.
> 3 If the pilot does not conduct a go-around, the aircraft may land too fast or too far down the runway and not be able to stop in time.
> 4 If the airport authorities do not construct and maintain the runways to maximise effective friction and drainage, the pilots will find that the braking action is not as efficient as they expect.
> 5 If controllers fail to select the appropriate runway based on the wind, the aircraft may encounter cross-winds which make landing more hazardous, or tailwinds which make the ground speed on touchdown higher and so the roll-out distance required longer.
> 6 If there is poor crew resource management, crew coordination, crosschecking and reactivity will be affected.
> …

Background notes:

- If a plane *veers* off course, it changes direction or moves diagonally away from the centreline or correct path.
- *Vref* is an aircraft's *reference velocity*, i.e. the speed the aircraft should be flying at, especially during approach.

Extension activity:

Students test each other in pairs using their own conditional sentences, or those from the board. They read one of the *if*-clauses to their partner, who should complete it in an appropriate way, without looking at the original sentence.

c Students discuss the question in groups and then feed back to the class.

> Suggested answer:
> Common solutions include: deciding to go around if in doubt; providing up-to-date runway and weather information; stabilising the approach early; not changing the type of approach at the last moment; good crew and team coordination; effective and reactive airport management and maintenance; compliance with Standard Operating Procedures.

Language focus: Relaying information

Give the following instruction: *'We've finished that part. Now close your books. We're going to study the language of relaying information.'* Then elicit from the class how they could relay your instruction and explanation to a third person. Write examples on the board. Then tell students to compare the structures they used with the ones in the book. You could draw attention to the different tenses that are possible in several of the examples, and elicit why they are both possible and which version might be preferred in aviation English (see *Language note* below).

> Possible answers:
> ◆ *The teacher reported that we had finished the previous part.*
> ◆ *He/She told us to close our books.*
> ◆ *He/She told/advised us that we are going to study ...*
> ◆ *Be advised that we are going to study ...*

Language note:

The issue of relaying information is closely connected with *reported speech*, i.e. rules for 'backshifting' tenses, so that present continuous becomes past continuous, *will* becomes *would*, and so on. In the context of aviation English, and in particular in life-or-death decision-making, such rules may be considered superfluous or even dangerous. As a general rule:

◆ If the information is still true and relevant, it is normal not to use backshifting. The tense can remain the same as it was in the original statement.

◆ Backshifting is possible where a reported statement may or may not be true (e.g. *They said that the runway was contaminated*). However, this may lead the listener to assume that the runway was contaminated in the past and has since been cleared, so for clarity, a statement without backshifting (e.g. *They said that the runway is contaminated*) is less ambiguous and therefore preferred.

◆ Backshifting is most appropriate in situations where the speaker disagrees with a statement, or the statement is no longer true (e.g. *We thought we ~~will~~ would land on runway 16L, but in fact we landed on 16R*).

17a **◉3.07 Go through the example with the class. Then play the recording, pausing after each communication for a volunteer to relay the information. Encourage students to use a range of structures from the *Language focus* box. Afterwards, students can test each other using audioscript 3.07 on page 186.**

> Suggested answers:
> 1 Be advised that Runway 29 Left is closed for scheduled maintenance. Runway 29 Right is the runway in use.
> 2 Regional 385, report rate of descent. You appear to be above the glide path.
> 3 Be advised that Airport Maintenance has reported ten millimetres of standing water on the far end of Runway 15 Left.
> 4 Jetblue 582, reduce speed or go around. Traffic ahead.
> 5 Be advised that the wind direction is now 140 degrees.
> ...

Background notes:

◆ A *Saab 340* is a small twin turboprop regional transport, still in operation, but no longer in production.

◆ *'Offset 500 metres'* here describes the location of the chimneys. They are 500 metres to the side of the localizer beam and extended runway centreline, i.e. from the flight path of a landing aircraft.

b **Go through the instructions and examples carefully with the class. Check that they understand that Student C is always a colleague of the student listening to the information. Use the two examples to reinforce this. Make sure students realise that they do not need to use backshifting in any of these sentences (see *Language note*). The aim here is rather to practise the skills of listening carefully, taking notes, checking and reporting. Afterwards, go through the conversations with the class.**

If you don't have a multiple of three students you will need to have at least one group of four, where the third and fourth students take turns to ask for clarification.

Suggested answers:
ATCO input, pilot response:

1
A: Runway 15 Left is closed.
B: They said that Runway 15 Left is closed
C: Did you say Runway 15 Left is closed / was closed? / Confirm Runway 15 Left (is) closed.

2
A: You are cleared for an ILS approach Runway 21 Left.
B: They said that we are cleared for an ILS approach Runway 21 Left.
C: Did you say that we have cleared for an ILS approach Runway 21 Left?

3
A: The wind has veered to 240 degrees.
B: They reported that the wind has veered to 240 degrees.
C: Did you say the wind has veered to 240 degrees.

...

Pilot input, ATCO response:

1
A: We have 246 passengers on board.
B: They said they had/have 246 passengers on board.
C: Did they say they had/have 246 passengers on board? / Confirm 246 passengers on board.

2
A: We are passing through 6,000 feet.
B: They reported they are passing through 6,000 feet.
C: Confirm they are passing 6,000 feet.

3
A: We are flying the 9 DME arc from the initial approach fix.
B: They said they are/were flying the 9 DME arc from the initial approach fix.
C: Did you say they were/are flying the 9 DME arc from the initial approach fix?

...

Background notes:

◆ A *9 DME arc* is a segment of a circle which is flown as a transition from en-route flight to begin an instrument (ILS) approach. For more information, see www.pilotoutlook.com: DME arc.
◆ An *initial approach fix* (*IAF*) is one of the points from which the initial segment of an ILS approach begins.
◆ The *black hole effect* describes spatial disorientation and erroneous perception of altitude caused by a dark approach area and bright lights beyond the active runway.

Saying your position

Communicative and operational issues:

Being able to report your position accurately or the position of another aircraft, environmental phenomenon, topographical feature, navigational aid etc. is a vital communication skill which is practised in this section.

In aviation, distances are measured in the following units:
◆ distance in the air (including distance to touch-down) in nautical miles;
◆ horizontal distance on the ground in kilometres and metres, and in the United States in statute miles and feet;
◆ altitude in feet for most of the world, but in Russia, China, Kazakhstan and in other CIS (Commonwealth of Independent States, i.e. many of the former Soviet republics) in metres.

www.flightsafety.org: Flight Safety Foundation *CFIT Checklist*
www.skybrary.aero: Skybrary *Ground Proximity Warning System*

Language focus: Distance

Go through the examples with the class, eliciting in each case what is being measured (i.e. from where to where).

Suggested answers:	
from the Final Approach Fix	to the threshold
from Biggin Hill	to London Gatwick
from MID	to the extended centreline of Runway 26
from OCK	to your present position
from LaGuardia	to JFK
from the glide scope	to our present altitude
from one end of the runway	to the other

Background note:

See *Background notes* for exercise 19 for *MID*, *OCK*, etc.

18 Students work in small groups to make sentences about their chosen airports, using as many of the phrases and structures from the *Language focus* box as possible. Afterwards, elicit some examples from the class.

Background notes:

The actual location of these items will obviously vary from one aerodrome to another and so it is each student's description which should be listened to for clarity and accuracy. However, a few general tendencies may be useful.

♦ The *final approach fix* is on the extended centreline of the runway in use, typically some four nautical miles from touchdown, from which the final part of an ILS approach is made.

♦ The *control tower* may be located either among the terminal buildings or, increasingly, in a remote location for better visibility.

♦ The *Area Control Centre* (*ACC*) is usually located in the vicinity of a large airport, but often in the countryside some distance away.

♦ The *ILS transmitters* consist of the localizer and glideslope transmitters. The localizer transmitter is aligned with the runway centreline within the airport perimeter some distance from the runway threshold. The glideslope transmitter is located perhaps some 100 metres to the left or right of a runway, near the touchdown zone.

♦ The *runways* have different designated orientations (QFU) such as 05L / 23R 180° apart and are generally some distance from the terminal buildings. The runways may be parallel, offset or intersecting.

♦ *Obstacles* may be found anywhere, but more significantly in the proximity of the flight path and are typically such things as factory chimneys, electrical pylons, hills, tall buildings.

♦ Aerodromes tend to be built on the flattest ground: *terrain* is any rising ground, north, south, east or west. Its height and direction are important. Terrain determines the value of the *Minimum Safe Altitude* (*MSA*) or *Minimum Descent Altitude* (*MDA*) in the aerodrome area.

♦ The rotating *radar antenna* is often located in an open space in proximity to the control tower.

Extension activity:

If you think your students will all be familiar with several airports in your country/region, you could read some sentences about distances at one of those airports for students to guess which airport you are describing. This could also be student led: they could prepare some descriptions as homework, and read them aloud in a follow-up lesson for others to guess which airport they are describing.

19 Students work alone to complete the sentences and then check in pairs. Finally, go through the answers with the class.

Answers:	
1 to the southwest	5 long
2 to the south	6 outbound
3 from	7 between
4 above	8 to the north

Background notes:

♦ The *NATS chart* for the Gatwick area upon which this exercise is based contains some information which requires an explanation. *VOR/DME* and *NDB* navigation beacons are identified by specific symbols and three-letter identifiers: *MID* for Midhurst, *EPM* for Epsom and *OCK* for Ockham. Obstacles and high ground are indicated by a vertical dotted chevron with the altitude value next to it. The minimum initial altitude within this area, i.e. the altitude before starting an approach procedure, is 2,000 feet. See NATS Aeronautical Information Circular 7/2008 – ATC Surveillance Minimum Altitude charts.

♦ *Terrain* refers to the contours and relief of the land as a potential obstacle for aircraft; '*Terrain, terrain*' is the audio warning triggered by the *Ground Proximity Warning System* (*GPWS*).

♦ A *Surveillance Minimum Altitude area* is a designated area in the vicinity of an aerodrome, in which the minimum safe levels allocated by a controller vectoring IFR flights with radar equipment have been predetermined.

♦ *Mean sea level* describes the average height of the sea surface.

Extension activity:

Tell students to cover the sentences and work in pairs to try to remember as many as possible, using only the chart to help them.

20 **Go through the examples with the class. In this exercise, flight crews communicate with ATC about various complications they are encountering during descent and approach. The controllers respond by providing information which may assist the pilots in resolving a problem or being better informed about landing conditions. 'Pilots' can then read back or acknowledge information received. Students then work in pairs to make dialogues. Afterwards, ask volunteers to act out their dialogues for the class.**

Suggested answers:

1

Pilot: We are landing heavy. Request conditions for Runway 13.

ATCO: Runway 13 available: width 34 metres covered with ice patches; braking action poor; snow along the edges.

2

Pilot: Request ILS approach Runway 12.

ATCO: Cleared ILS approach Runway 12, obstacle clearance altitude 700 metres. Maintain 2,000 feet. Check minima.

Pilot: Cleared ILS approach Runway 12, maintain 2,000 feet.

3

Pilot: We are indicated on the glideslope, but have just received a GPWS warning.

ATCO: Adjust your rate of descent. Your altitude should be 900 feet.

...

Background notes:

- *GPWS* (*Ground Proximity Warning System*) is a system designed to warn the flight crew that they are closing on terrain or obstacles.
- *LHR* is the airport code for London Heathrow.

21a **Students work alone or in groups to prepare their information. You could set the preparation as a homework task. When the information is ready, students ask and answer questions about their airports, using the questions in the example as a model.**

Possible answers (based on Seattle, Washington State, USA):

- What's the name of your airport? → It's Seattle, Washington State.
- What are the ICAO and IATA identifiers? → The ICAO code is *Kilo Sierra Echo Alpha* and the IATA identifier code is *Sierra Echo Alpha*.
- What are the ATIS and Tower frequencies? → The ATIS and Tower frequencies are 118.0 and 119.9.
- What is the ILS Decision Altitude? → The Decision Altitude is 630 feet.

...

Background notes:

- *Jeppesen charts* are used by pilots worldwide and represent a very high quality of cartography. The chart used as a model in this exercise is an arrival chart for an ILS or LOC approach to Runway 16C at Seattle International Airport (Boeing Field), Washington State. Different charts exist for each arrival and type of arrival. Other Jeppesen charts include Standard Instrument Departures (SID), airport charts, approach charts, route plotting charts, VFR charts and high level en-route charts for larger regions. Many charts have a validity of only two weeks and must be constantly updated. See the sample answers to exercises 21a and 21b for details of the information contained on this approach chart.
- Useful websites:
  Jeppesen: www.jeppesen.com
  SkyVector: http://skyvector.com/
- *Decision altitude* (*DA*) is the altitude (above sea level) at which the pilot must decide to land or go around.
- *Decision height* (*DH*) is the height (above the ground) at which the pilot must decide to land or go around.
- *Missed approach point* (*MAP*) is the point at which the pilot must land or go around, i.e. perform a missed approach.

b **Students complete the tasks in small groups and then feed back to the class.**

Possible answer (based on Seattle):
Fly inbound from an altitude of 6,000 feet at radar fix *Whisky Echo Mike Alpha Tango* 18.2 DME *India Sierra Zulu India* on a heading of 163 degrees and perform a step-down approach to Runway 16 Centre. Intercept the three-degree glideslope at altitude 1,900 feet, or as instructed by ATC. The missed approach point (MAP) is at 2.5 DME. In the event of a missed approach, climb to 2,000 feet on a heading of 161 degrees via *Sierra Echo Alpha* VOR Radial 161, then continue to climb to 5,000 feet outbound and hold at 5,000 feet.

Putting it together: On short final

Communicative and operational issues:

The pair work activity in this section is based on the authentic scenario of a badly managed approach in suddenly worsening meteorological conditions. It illustrates the need for good communication discipline, especially in challenging circumstances.

You could construct many valuable and interesting additional student activities suitable for this section and the Unit 8 DVD using the documents in the *ALAR Toolkit*:
Flight Safety Foundation: *ALAR Toolkit* (http://flightsafety.org/current-safety-initiatives/);
6.2 Manual go-around;
7.1 Stabilised Approach;
8.1 Runway excursion and runway overruns;
8.5 Wet or contaminated runways.

ICAO FOCUS

The quote from NATS (UK National Air Traffic Services) draws attention to the importance of the non-lexical and non-grammatical aspects of language: speed of delivery; clarity; concision; and tone of voice. Teachers should always have these characteristics in mind when monitoring students. The three related questions draw directly on the students' personal experience.

Students read the quote to find two types of delivery and reasons for choosing each one [**Suggested answers:** measured, clear and concise – especially when the frequency is congested; sound urgent – when urgent]. Students then discuss the questions in pairs and feed back to the class.

Suggested answers:
♦ *Measured* = calm, controlled; *Clear* = easy to understand, both in terms of vocabulary and pronunciation; *concise* = not containing unnecessary information.
♦ *Frequency congestion* can result in important information (clearances, flight levels, headings, times etc.) being lost or only partially heard; conditional clearances and advice to expect, being taken as clearances; pilots not being able to pass urgent information; information intended for one flight being adopted by another; and a general loss of communication quality with the ensuing stress.

22a ◐**3.08** Tell students to read through the 15 statements to check they understand all the words. Then play the recording for students to complete the task. They compare their answers in pairs and listen again if necessary before feeding back to the class.

Answers:
1 T
2 F – Lufthansa 338 is on short final; another aircraft has not vacated
3 T
4 T
5 T
6 F – 2,710 metres
7 T
8 T
9 T
10 F – an excessive sink rate

Background note:

CFIT (*Controlled Flight into Terrain*) happens when an aircraft, which is airworthy and under the control of the flight crew, is flown unintentionally into terrain, obstacles or water, usually without the crew being aware. For more information, see: www.casa.gov.au: CFIT; Flight Safety Foundation: *CFIT Checklist*

b ◐**3.08** Play the recording again, pausing after each communication for a volunteer to give advice or a warning. Make sure they convey a sense of urgency in their voices. Afterwards, students can repeat the activity in small groups, using audioscript 3.08 on page 186.

Suggested answers:
1 Regional 259, pull up and go around. Traffic on active runway.
2 Lufthansa 338, go around. I say again, go around. Traffic on 07 Right.
3 Be advised that braking action is poor on the mid section of Runway 28 Left due (to) standing water.
4 Caution. The last incoming flight reported severe windshear and a 20-knot decrease in airspeed half a mile from the threshold of Runway 15 Right.
5 Ryanair 3548, caution. You are cleared to Runway 26 Right, I say again 26 Right.
...

23a Students discuss in pairs and then feed back to the class.

Suggested answers:

f Caution. Visibility is now down to 400 metres.

d Be advised of a factory chimney rising 148 feet one mile to the north west of the approach flight path and two miles from the threshold.

e Caution. The runway lights can be confused with the motorway and city lights.

g Braking action is poor due (to) the contaminated state of the runway.

a Be advised of the presence of a high tension power line rising to 180 feet across the approach path three miles from the threshold.

c Caution. Look out for a Beechcraft without radio contact in the terminal area.

b There is a line of hills up to 2,300 feet, five miles to the south east of the approach path to Runway 09.

h Strong, variable and gusting winds have been reported over the last three miles of the approach.

Background note:

Flight crew and controllers should be able to report and describe many different types of obstacle or problem they encounter and react by giving appropriate advice or instructions. Accurate descriptive language and the integration of suitably phrased advice into their cognitive decision-making processes are essential links in the chain which ensures operational safety.

b ◉3.09 Play the recording for students to complete the task and then go through the answers with the class. Discuss with the class which of the obstacles or hazards would be most worrying [**Suggested answer**: All are potentially dangerous depending on circumstances: the hills and the cloudburst are probably the worst as there are more documented cases of incidents and accidents where terrain (CFIT) and windshear during final approach are major contributing factors than with the other hazards].

Answers:

1 f	3 e	5 a	7 b
2 d	4 g	6 c	8 h

Background note:

If an aircraft *strays* into the terminal area, it enters by accident.

Extension activity:

Students work in pairs or groups of three to write a short ATCO-pilot dialogue based on one of the situations from audioscript 3.09 on page 187. They then act out their dialogues for the class. They could also do a similar activity without a script, by improvising some of the situations. Afterwards, discuss the dialogues with the class in terms of how well the students reported problems and offered advice.

24 **Students work alone to complete the sentences and then check in pairs. When you go through the answers with the class, make sure students fully understand all the words from the sentences.**

Answers:

1 slippery	5 rate of descent
2 missed	6 past
3 busy	7 collided
4 threshhold	8 passed

Communication

25a **Go through the instructions with the class. This pairwork scenario uses a fictionalised version of an actual runway excursion. Alphajet Flight 473 is approaching Runway 23 Left after a nine-hour flight. The First Officer is the pilot flying (PF) and is landing at this runway for the first time. The runway is said to be '*slippery when wet*'. You may need to check the meaning of *slippery*, using examples of slippery surfaces such as ice and oil. Point out that only the pilot has information in italics. Point out also that the timings of the cues indicate the order they should be communicated. The pilot will still need to read the italicised information aloud, so that the ATCO knows what is happening. Students work in pairs to act out the dialogue. Afterwards, they swap roles and repeat the role-play without looking at the cues.**

Suggested answers:

21:14

Pilot: Approach, Alphajet 473.

21:15

ATCO: Alphajet 473, Information for Runway 23 Left: wind 250 degrees at ten knots; visibility eight kilometres; rain and thunderstorm in the vicinity; runway length available 3,220 metres.

21:16

Pilot: Runway 23 Left, wind 250 degrees, ten knots; visibility eight kilometres, Alphajet 473.

21:17

ATCO: Be advised of fumes from a factory four miles from threshold and one mile from approach path that are being carried by wind.

21:17

Pilot: Factory fumes, roger, Alphajet 473.

21:18

ATCO: Alphajet 473, the high intensity lights on Runway 23 Right are unserviceable due (to) maintenance work.

...

If you have an odd number of students you will need to have a group of three, where the third student is the co-pilot, and takes half of the pilot cues.

b Students discuss the questions in pairs and then feed back to the class.

> **Suggested answers:**
> There was a series of mistakes made by both flight crew and controllers in these suddenly worsening weather conditions. At 21:20 the flight crew did not acknowledge the ATCO's warning of the heavy rain and reduced visibility and the ATCO did not request an acknowledgement. At 21:26 the flight crew did not acknowledge the ATCO's warning of poor braking having been reported by a previous flight and again the ATCO did not challenge this absence of response. At 21:27 the flight crew did not take into account that the B767 ahead of them had decided to go around. At 21:28 the flight crew decided to continue their approach despite the ATCO's apprehension. At 21:30 the aircraft crossed the threshold too high and too fast; this should already have caused the captain to go around. The captain then decided to go around, too late to prevent a hard touch-down, but not too late to lift off again and go around. Then he changed his opinion, again too late, and applied reverse thrust. The aircraft was by then so far down the wet runway that it was impossible to decelerate sufficiently to stop in time.
>
> The decision to go around should have been made well before the threshold when the crew realised that the approach was not stabilised (correct altitude, speed and rate of descent).

Debriefing

24 Give and elicit feedback on the effectiveness of the communication in the role-plays, and identify any remaining concerns/weaknesses.

Progress check

Students work alone to complete the table and then discuss their notes with a partner. Elicit from the class any remaining weaknesses and strategies for overcoming them.

DVD: *Call sign confusion*

Communicative and operational issues:

The Eurocontrol video used in this unit is not particularly complex or challenging from either a technical or linguistic point of view. It does, however, give some effective illustrations of the importance of attitude in an operational environment, and most of the questions relate to attitude and the effects personal attitude can have on operational outcomes. The controller, who is just back from holiday and takes over the shift, is visibly very complacent. The Captain of B-Jet 3158 is very dismissive of his First Officer and does nothing to create a good working relationship; he disregards the First Officer's suggestion to reduce their airspeed and as a result there is a level bust.

27a Tell students to watch the clip carefully to identify the kind of incident. Point out that the title of the clip is *Call sign confusion*, so students should expect some problems with call signs, which they should note down as they watch. Point out also that A-Jet and B-Jet are fictional airline call signs. After playing the clip, students discuss as much as they remember about the incident and then report back to the class.

> **Answers:**
> ◆ Level bust and airprox
> ◆ The call signs were: Lufthansa 3EM (three echo mike), SAS 1142, B-Jet 3158 and B-Jet 3518. The private aircraft was a PA28/180, but this is not its call sign.

Background notes:

> ◆ A *PA28/180* is a Piper Cherokee; a popular single-engine light aircraft.
> ◆ *3EM* (three echo mike) is part of the call sign.
> ◆ The *published speed* is the reference speed which is published in the flight manual for this phase of operations.

b Check students understand all the words, especially *complacency* (= being too relaxed, not worrying enough about potential problems). Students discuss the factors in pairs, with examples of each type of problem. Point out that there will be a chance to watch the clip again later, so students should not worry if they miss something. Afterwards, discuss the answers with the class, but avoid going into too much detail or providing too much information from the answer key, as you can come back to these questions after the second viewing.

> **Suggested answers:**
> ◆ Complacency: Controller 1 returning from holiday, not being proactive; B-Jet Captain not questioning his airspeed or taking into account his First Officer's concerns
> ◆ Expectation bias: Controller 1 not monitoring airspeed of B-Jet; B-Jet Captain misinterpreting first TCAS message
> ◆ Similar call signs: B-Jet 3158; B-Jet 3518
> ◆ Poor team work: B-Jet Captain disregarding his First Officer

28a, b Tell students to watch Part 1 again and to pay close attention to the ATCO's attitude. They discuss his attitude and its possible effects in pairs and then feed back to the class.

> **Suggested answers:**
> a The controller who is starting his shift takes very little trouble about being briefed by the controller he is relieving.
> b Especially after a holiday, the second controller will not immediately have the correct mindset and should take more time and care when starting his shift. His very relaxed attitude may well result in him not anticipating sufficiently and being overtaken by events.

29a, b Tell students to watch Part 2 again and to pay close attention to the interaction between the Captain and the First Officer, and to the traffic that the ATCO is handling. Students discuss the two questions in pairs and then share their ideas with the class.

> **Suggested answers:**
> a The Captain is very dismissive and rude about his First Officer from the start, which can only make the First Officer ill at ease. The Captain pays very little attention to what he says.
> b The controller is controlling Lufthansa 3EM, SAS 1142, B-Jet 3158, B-Jet 3518 and A-Jet 1582: five aircraft in all.

c Discuss this with the class. Make sure they fully understand the meaning of *conflict* (see *Background note*).

> **Suggested answer:**
> The controller has a rather irresponsible, 'laid-back' attitude to his work: normally, a controller should anticipate and take appropriate and immediate action to avoid a conflict between aircraft developing.

> **Background note:**
> A *conflict* is the risk of two aircraft losing their horizontal or vertical separation. The controller's job is to anticipate and take steps to avoid this from the outset.

30a, b, c Students watch Part 3 again and then discuss the three questions in pairs, trying to remember as much as they can from the clip. Allow them to discuss their answers again in pairs before feeding back to the class.

> **Suggested answers:**
> a The situation has not developed on the flight deck of B-Jet 3158; the aircraft is still travelling too fast and the First Officer is right to be concerned; they are well above their published speed and will have difficulty reacting in time at lower altitudes in a more crowded airspace.
> b The PA 28 (Cherokee) is blocking traffic by flying in the flight path of departing aircraft, and increasing the controllers' workload. The private pilot should have filed a flight plan and should not be occupying this airspace.
> c The controller instructs B-Jet 3158 to stop its descent because there is traffic (A-Jet 1582) below at 5,000 feet. B-Jet 3158 fails to stop at 6,000 feet because the crew miss the transmission which is picked up by another flight with a similar call sign (B-Jet 3518), and because they are travelling too fast. This causes a level bust and the TCAS to trigger a warning ('Adjust vertical speed').

31a Make sure students know to focus only on the human factors. Students work in pairs to make their lists and then feed back to the class.

> **Answers:**
> ◆ complacency, a lack of commitment, and expectation bias by the controller
> ◆ a condescending, dismissive attitude by the Captain, who disregards his First Officer's valid concerns

b Students work in pairs to report the incident, either orally or in the form of a written report. Afterwards, ask some volunteers to present their reports to the class.

> **Suggested answer:**
> Controller X returned to work after his holidays. His colleague handed over the east sector to him and showed him the five aircraft he was controlling, but controller X was very complacent and arrogant and did not seem to pay much attention.
> One of the inbound flights he was controlling was B-Jet 3158, which was travelling at 240 knots: 30 knots above their published speed. The First Officer was concerned about their speed, but his opinion was disregarded by the Captain. Controller X was aware that a conflict could develop, but chose to ignore it.
> …

c Students discuss the questions in small groups. Afterwards, go through the factors with the class, eliciting any examples of students' experience of them and how they are managed.

UNIT 9
Handling a technical malfunction

Operational topics	ATC technical failures; Aircraft system failures; Consequences of a technical failure; Flight crew discussions; Electrical failure during approach; Monitoring a situation; ILS malfunction
Communication functions	Summarising; Suggesting action; Communication errors: Failure to request clarification; Announcing a change; Self-correcting; Asking and answering about consequences and reasons
Language content	Technical conditions; Language of consequences; Conjunctions and function words; Phrasal verbs 1; Using context to distinguish between similar words

Unit 9 Teacher's brief

A technical malfunction on the aircraft: on the ground, or while the aircraft is in flight is one of the most common 'unexpected events' which can cause much additional communication in plain language between the flight crew and controllers, first describing the malfunction, then discussing its consequences and agreeing on a solution.

Most technical failures are unexpected and so cause a certain amount of stress and require time for the flight crew to assess them and then respond to them. In all cases, the crew needs to prioritise flying the aircraft. They may need different types of assistance from ATC: changes in flight path, level, destination; modifications to their planned type of approach; technical support on the ground; and emergency services.

Like environmental factors, which we saw in Unit 5, technical failures will require both pilots and controllers to be familiar not only with the names of the aircraft systems and main parts, but also with the possible symptoms and consequences of a failure, so that they understand what action and precautions need to be taken and what the flight crew may not be able to do.

Unit 9 Sources

- Airbus Flight Operations Briefing Notes: *Human Performance – CRM aspects in incidents/accidents*
- Air New Zealand: *NZ60 – a free lesson* DVD (Exercises 27–28d)
- ATSB: *Report on Boeing 747 electrical system event on 7 January 2008* (Exercises 13–15b)
- ATSB: *Report on Qantas Airbus A380 VH-OQA. Flight 32, 04.11.2010*
- Civil Aviation Authority of New Zealand: *Occurrence report 00-2158 – NZ 60 'Erroneous' Glideslope Capture, Autocoupled Approach, and Go-around* http://www.caa.govt.nz (Exercises 23a–24b)

- Commercial Aviation Safety Team: *Aviation Occurrence Categories*
- Eurocontrol: *Guidelines for Controller training in the handling of unusual / emergency situations* (Exercises 9a–c)
- ICAO: *Threat and error management in Air Traffic Control*
- Lacagnina, M.: *Check flight goes bad*, AeroSafety World, April 2010
- Lacagnina, M.: *False localizer signal*, AeroSafety World, September 2010
- Lacagnina, M.: *Rapid Depressurization*, AeroSafety World, December 2010–January 2011
- Roelen, A. and Wever, R.: *An analysis of flight crew response to system failures*
- Safety posters: http://www.levelbust.com/downloads.htm
- Skybrary: *Loss of communication*
- Skybrary: *Engine failures – guidance for controllers*
- Smart Cockpit: *Failure reports*, www.smartcockpit.com

Lead-in

The lead-in quote from the *Aviation Herald* reports briefly on one case of what is not an uncommon occurrence: various types of technical failures on the ground, which affect ATC and navigational equipment and services. The most common causes are computer or power failures, although most centres have standby power supplies and equipment. Unlike aircraft system failures, these unexpected failures on the ground affect the handling of many aircraft simultaneously, require modified procedures, result in delays, holding or diversions, cause a sudden increase in controller workload and generate a large amount of additional ATC–flight crew communication requiring the use of plain language. There tends to be a 'knock-on' effect whereby the original failure will set off a chain of events affecting not only the airport or ATC centre in question, but flights scheduled to arrive at or depart the airport, or enter, leave or pass through the area.

Quote: **Students read the quote to identify what went wrong, what the crew did and what the final result was [Answers: ATC radar and radio equipment failed; after holding for two hours, the aircraft had to declare an emergency and attempt to land without a landing clearance (most likely because it had limited fuel endurance) the aircraft landed safely]. You could also ask students what they would have done if they had been (a) the crew or (b) ATC in this situation.**

1a, b, c **Students discuss the three questions in small groups and then share their ideas with the class.**

> Suggested answers:
> a A dual radar and radio failure was probably caused by a power cut, which may have affected ATC computerisation.
> c Failures on the ground which affect ATC management and flow control, and therefore have a direct effect on flights, include: general and specific system power cuts; ATC computer failures; interrupted VHF/UHF radio communications; stuck microphone selectors; secondary surveillance radar (SSR) ground movement radar not being available; Mode S transponder positioning incorrect; VOR/DME beacons unserviceable or undergoing maintenance or recalibration; NDB beacons being unreliable or unserviceable; glideslope and localizer transmitters errors or maintenance; visual approach slope lighting (PAPI) having a power failure; decision bar not available; runway centreline and edge lighting being maintained.

d **Students make lists in pairs and then compare their lists with other groups. Then elicit a definitive list from the class.**

> Suggested answers:
> Note that you can find background information for many of the technical issues described below at the Skybrary website (http://www.skybrary.aero/index.php/Main_Page).
>
> The number of technical failures and malfunctions which can occur on board an aircraft is almost limitless, even if most systems are designed to be failsafe, i.e. have built-in redundancy by which a secondary, standby or alternate system can ensure the same function. Failures in the main systems include:
> ◆ **Engines:** stall/surge; bird ingestion; low oil pressure; high oil temperature; oil leak; bearing failure; high EGT (Exhaust Gas Temperature); vibrations; fuel starvation; blade rupture; engine fire etc.

> ◆ **Electrical power:** IDG (Integrated Drive Generator) disconnect; AC, DC and Essential busbar faults; GCU (Generator Control Unit) failure; short circuits etc.
> ◆ **Flight Controls:** servocontrol failure; hydraulic system failure; yaw damper loss; flap/slat asymmetry or jam; flight control computer faults etc.
> ◆ **Fuel:** fuel pump fault; fuel filter clog; fuel tank leak; crossfeed valve fault; fuel trim transfer fault etc.
> ◆ **Navigation:** pitot probe, static port and angle of attack sensor anti-icing failure; discrepant air data; FMGC (Flight Management and Guidance Computer) malfunction; IRS (Inertial Reference System) malfunction; gyro fault; ADIRU (Air Data Inertial Reference Unit) fault; glideslope and localizer indication faults; antenna faults etc.
> ◆ **Pressurisation and air conditioning:** pack fault; duct overheat; crossbleed valve fault; discharge valve not fully open or closed; avionics bay ventilation fault; bleed valve fault; cabin depressurisation; trim valve fault etc.
> ◆ For overviews of civil aircraft systems and system failures, see:
> www.b737.org.uk
> The Transair *System Guides* for various aircraft
> Thomas W. Wild, *Transport Category Aircraft Systems,* Jeppesen
> Philip Shawcross, *English for Aircraft*, Volume 2, Editions Belin

Extension activity:

You could conduct the feedback for exercise 1d as a game, where you collect an idea onto the board from each group in turn. Of course, you should only accept sensible suggestions from the groups, so make sure all other students agree with a suggestion before writing it up. Keep going until some pairs run out of ideas. The pair with the last idea is the winner.

Reporting system failures

2a **Go through the six examples of aircraft failures and elicit from the class what exactly they involve (see *Background notes*). Students then work alone to match the other 13 failures to the systems they relate to. They discuss their answers in pairs before feeding back to the class. Make sure students fully understand what each failure involves.**

> Answers:
>
> | | |
> |---|---|
> | 1 b | 4 d, j, m |
> | 2 c, k | 5 h, i, l |
> | 3 a, f | 6 e, g |
> | (See also suggested answers for 1d) | |

Background notes:

- The *IDG* (*Integrated Drive Generator*) is installed on each modern commercial aircraft engine; it is a combination of a constant speed drive and an electrical generator driven by the engine through the accessory gearbox. It is the main source of A.C. electrical power on the aircraft.
- The *Aileron Power Control Unit* is a hydraulically powered servo-control which moves the ailerons on the outer wings.
- An *INS warning* is a warning about a malfunction in the Inertial Navigation System, i.e. the main system using gyros and geographical coordinates to calculate the aircraft's precise position.
- If a warning is *spurious* /ˈspjɜriːəs/, it is not based on true facts, and may in fact be the result of a problem with the warning system.
- An *outflow valve* is a valve which regulates cabin pressure by controlling the amount of air which is allowed to flow out of the cabin. They are large door-type valves which are quite visible on the outside of the fuselage.
- *Stabiliser trim runaway* means that the Trimmable Horizontal Stabiliser (THS), or tailplane, on the aircraft tail fails to stop at the selected position and continues to deflect up or down.
- *GEN 1* is the electrical generator on Engine 1.
- A *crossfeed valve* is a valve which allows fuel to be transferred from one wing to another.
- A *flow control valve* is a valve which regulates fuel supply to the engines and APU.
- *Flap asymmetry* occurs when the flaps are not extended the same amount on both wings.
- A *pack controller* is an electronic device which regulates airflow and temperature within the air conditioning pack / air cycle machine, which in turn adjusts the temperature of hot engine compressor bleed air for use in the aircraft.
- An *air data computer* is a digital computer serving as a central source of information on the surrounding atmosphere and the aircraft flight through it. It provides the pressure altitude, outside air temperature, airspeed, Mach number and angle of attack data to the automatic flight control system, the flight instruments and other systems.
- A *filter clog* occurs when a fuel or hydraulic filter is blocked or obstructed with particles.
- An *AC bus* is an electrical power distribution point for alternating current to which several circuits are connected.
- *DME 1* is one of the two Distance Measuring Equipment systems which measure the time signals transmitted from the aircraft take to reach a ground station and return to the aircraft. This is converted into distances in nautical miles and is one means of calculating the aircraft's position.

Extension activities:

Students can test each other in pairs in various ways. In each case, Student B has his/her book closed:
1 Student A reads the name of a failure for Student B to explain what it means.
2 Student A describes a failure for Student B to name it.
3 Student A names a system for Student B to name all the failures connected with that system.
4 Student A reads the name of a failure for Student B to name the system it relates to.

b, c **Students discuss the questions in pairs and then feed back to the class.**

Language focus: Technical conditions

Go through the list of technical conditions carefully with the class, eliciting the opposite to each condition. Note that not all the conditions have opposites, but the purpose is not to find exact opposites but rather to generate some discussion and focus on the meaning of the sentences in the book.

Suggested answers:
The cable has been fixed/replaced.
The filter is clean.
The windshield is intact.
The situation is safe.
The autopilot is connected.
The oil pressure is rising.
The tanks are almost full.
The transmission was clear.
The oil temperature is too low.
The indication is constant.
The slats are moving freely.
The hydraulic reservoir is tight/sealed.
The lever is moving freely.
The oil level is high.
The wing tip is present/intact.
The Localizer is serviceable.

Background notes:

- If the indication is *intermittent*, it appears and disappears.
- The difference between *locked* and *jammed* is that *locked* or *seized* is more often used about a simple mechanical part and *jam* tends to be used about the flight controls.

Extension activity:

Students can test each other in pairs by reading the beginning of a sentence from the *Language focus* box to elicit its ending.

3a Tell students to cover the *Language focus* box. Students then work alone to complete the sentences and compare their answers with a partner. When you go through the answers with the class, elicit a wide range of possible answers for each sentence.

> Possible answers:
> 1 jammed, locked
> 2 disconnected
> 3 cracked, missing
> 4 empty
> 5 garbled
> 6 high, dangerous
> 7 broken, unserviceable
> 8 leaking

Background notes:

♦ A *static discharger* or wick is an electrical conductor on the outer trailing edges of the wings and stabiliser designed to discharge static electricity which accumulates in the aircraft during the flight or as the result of a lightning strike.

♦ *Autothrust* is an automated system connected to the autopilot which controls the power delivered by the engines.

♦ Most of the aircraft fuel is stored in the wings in separate tanks: the smaller *outer tanks*, which are emptied first, the inner tanks, and often a centre tank between the two wings.

♦ *Line* refers to any fuel, hydraulic or water pipe or electrical wiring.

Language note:

Students may be unfamiliar with the structure *to report sth* + adjective (e.g. *They reported the lever missing*). You could elicit a few more examples of this structure onto the board (e.g. *They reported the Localizer unserviceable*).

Extension activity:

For each of the eight sentences, elicit from the class a possible cause and some possible consequences of the failure. This is intended to generate discussion, so encourage plenty of creative thinking.

> Suggested answers:
> 1 The flaps may be jammed if there is a seal failure on one of the transmission gearboxes which results in the flap linkage seizing up. A flap failure results in the crew not being able to extend (or retract) the flaps fully. Partial extension will mean that the crew will have a higher airspeed on landing or a lower airspeed during climb.

> 2 The autothrust may be disconnected due to a discrepancy in the FMGS system inputs or an electrical failure. It means that the crew will have to adjust engine thrust manually. Static dischargers are often lost when the aircraft encounters an electrical storm or suffers a lightning strike. The result is that static electricity will build up more in the aircraft airframe and may affect some electronic units.

> 4 The outer tanks being empty is a normal occurrence during the early part of the flight as they are emptied first; the aircraft wings are usually cambered and the fuel flows towards the centre of the aircraft by gravity. Once they are empty, the wings tend to become more flexible.

> 5 Garbled messages are usually caused by static interference or frequency saturation when several messages are being transmitted simultaneously. This is potentially serious as an essential piece of information may be lost or misunderstood. Pilots and ATCOs should therefore always ask their interlocutor to '*say again*'.

> 6 If the cabin becomes depressurised, the cabin altitude rises and passengers and crew are threatened by hypoxia (lack of oxygen). In this case the oxygen masks will drop automatically in the cabin, and the crew will don their masks and make an emergency descent.

> 7 The APU provides electrical power, air conditioning and high pressure air to start the engines on the ground. However, it can also be used in flight in case of engine failure to provide a back-up source of electrical generation.

> 8 Hydraulic leaks are relatively frequent, especially on the landing gear, which undergoes considerable stress on landing. Leakages are measured by mechanics in drops per minute and there are tolerances which enable the aircraft to be dispatched without a repair being carried out. The most common source of a hydraulic leak is a faulty seal. Serious hydraulic leaks can lead to slow landing gear or flight control operation, or degraded braking.

b Students discuss the task in pairs. When you go through the answers with the class, discuss the meaning of difficult words and the context in which they would be used.

Answers:
1 cracked; the other defects are fluid system, not structural, faults
2 missing; all the other faults are related to fire or overheat
3 loose; *loose* is a mechanical problem not an electrical fault
4 loss; all the other defects are mechanical malfunctions
5 contaminated; contaminated is usually related to fluids, whereas the other defects are related to radio communications
6 stall; stall is an engine or aerodynamic phenomenon while the aothers are structural failures

Background notes:

♦ If a circuit is *de-energised*, it is without electrical power; not electrically supplied.
♦ If a component is *grounded*, it is connected to the aircraft's electrical ground.
♦ *Humming* is a low buzzing noise.
♦ *Noise* refers to unwanted signals within an electronic system.
♦ If a mechanism is *seized* is has been blocked by friction.
♦ A *short circuit* is an inadvertent electrical connection which causes an electrical failure or electrical fire.
♦ If something is *stuck*, it is blocked in one position, unable to move.
♦ A *surge* is a sudden irregular flow of fluid or electrical current, especially in the engine, electrical or hydraulic system which causes a malfunction: in the case of an engine, this results in an engine stall.
♦ *Tight* has two meanings in aviation English. In the case of a tank, a pipe or a union, it could mean secure/leakproof or, in the case of a nut or a fastener, it means difficult to turn.
♦ If a surface is *worn*, material has been removed by use and rubbing.

Extension activity:

Students work in groups to sort the words into grammatical categories: nouns, verbs and adjectives. Note that some words belong in several categories. Note also that many of the adjectives (e.g. *leaking*, *worn*) are derived from verbs, but are classified as adjectives because they can pre-modify a noun (e.g. *a leaking pipe, a worn tyre*). When you go through the answers with the class, elicit also some related words (e.g. *to leak, a crack, to seep*). You may need to check the pronunciation of *overheat* as a noun (/ˈəʊvəhiːt/) and as a verb (/əʊvəˈhiːt/), as well as the difference between *loose* /luːs/ and *lose* /luːz/.

Answers:

Nouns	Verbs	Adjectives
seepage, an overflow, a surge, smoke, fire, overheat, a transient, a short circuit, a loss, noise, humming, a stall	to overflow, to surge, to smoke, to overheat, to short-circuit, to stall	leaking, clogged, cracked, over-temperature, missing, burnt, transient, loose, de-energised, overvoltage, grounded, locked, seized, stuck, jammed, tight, saturated, congested, garbled, contaminated, humming, worn, ruptured, broken, scratched
Related words		
a leak, a crack, transience, a jam, saturation, congestion, contamination, a rupture, a breakage, a scratch	to leak, to clog (up), to crack, to seep (out), to burn, to loosen, to ground, to stick, to jam, to tighten, to lose, to hum, to wear (out), to rupture	overflowing, surging, smoking/ smoky, overheated, noisy

4a ◉ 3.10 Go through the example with the class. Then play the recording, pausing after each transmission for volunteers to respond. Discuss the best responses with the class. Note that the suggested answers below use several different openings (So, Therefore, You may, Do you mean?, Does this mean?, Confirm) which can be used as alternative ways of asking for confirmation if you wish them to extend their language. Strictly speaking, the most direct response (Confirm) would probably be most commonly used in any stressful operational situation. Afterwards, students can test each other in pairs using audioscript 3.10 on page 187.

Suggested answers:
1 So, you have a problem with the flight controls and the flaps are probably jammed.
2 Therefore you are now using the standby instruments.
3 You may have to throttle back on Engine Number 3 and this may affect your ability to climb.
4 Do you mean it's likely that you will need to divert to make a precautionary landing?

5 So, you are flying manually and have to rely on your standby instruments. We will have to speak slowly and clearly.

6 Does this mean that you have shed some electrical load and have donned your oxygen masks?

7 Confirm the present status of your instrumentation. Have you been able to engage the autothrust again?

8 Confirm whether you will make a visual approach or go around.

Background notes:

◆ Transmission 3 refers to both a caution message and a warning. A *warning* is a crew alert symbolised by the colour red and requiring immediate crew action. A *caution* is a crew alert symbolised by the colour amber and is less urgent than a red warning. An *advisory* is information displayed to the crew which does not require immediate action

◆ *Degraded mode* means operating at a reduced capacity, or in a mode with fewer capabilities.

◆ The *overhead panel* is an instrument panel above the pilots' heads in the cockpit which contains most of the system control panels on aircraft with a two-man crew.

◆ A *power transient* is a temporary electrical surge or impulse, causing a sudden peak of variables, especially at power up.

◆ *Indication oscillations* are variations in the display which may be caused by instrument malfunctions rather than actual changes in the parameters.

◆ *System 1*, in this case DME 1, refers to the fact that nearly all systems are 'duplexed', i.e. there are two systems operating in parallel. In the case of instrumentation, System 1 usually provides the Captain with information and System 2 the First Officer.

b Go through the examples with the class. Make sure they realise that the cues offer only minimal guidance, and that they will need to use their imaginations and experience to develop the dialogues. Students then work in pairs to make dialogues. Afterwards, ask volunteers to act out their dialogues for the class. Finally, discuss with the class which dialogues reported the technical conditions and their consequences most clearly and effectively.

> Suggested answers:
> **Technical problems on the ground**
> 1
> **ATCO:** The glideslope is unserviceable. ILS approach not available.
> **Pilot:** How long will the glideslope be unserviceable? What type of approach will we be able to make?

2
ATCO: The runway lighting level is low. You may not be visual until your Decision Height.
Pilot: Confirm present ceiling and RVR. / What is the current visibility?

3
ATCO: The PAPI is inoperative. Make an ILS approach.
Pilot: Request clearance for an ILS approach to Runway 31 Left.

...

Technical problems in the air
1
Pilot: We have a cabin pressurisation fault. Unable to accept a higher level.
ATCO: What level is acceptable to you?
2
Pilot: We have shut down Engine Number 2. We will be making a precautionary landing.
ATCO: Do you require emergency services on arrival?
3
Pilot: We have lost a hydraulic system, but the flight controls are operating normally.
ATCO: Will your braking and steering be affected on roll-out?

...

If you have an odd number of students you will need to have a group of three students, where the third student responds to pilot cues 1 and 2 and to ATCO cues 4 and 5.

Background notes:

◆ *Captain probe heat* is a system of electrical resistances inside the angle of attack probe, pitot probe, static port etc. which supply the captain's instruments with attitude, airspeed and altitude data. The heating prevents the probes from being obstructed or seized up by ice.

◆ *U/S* stands for unserviceable.

◆ A *PAPI* (*Precision Approach Path Indicator*) is a series of lights leading to the runway threshold which enable pilots to control their rate of descent visually.

Consequences of system failures

Communicative and operational issues:

As we saw in Unit 6 with the engine oil quantity dropping in the ETOPS diversion scenario, technical failures, or other operational situations, often develop over time. Good CRM dictates that crew members discuss in advance what they will do in such a contingency. Equally, they will need to inform ATC of these possibilities in order to allow controllers to anticipate and take precautions, if necessary.

Language focus: Consequences

Elicit from the class the meaning of *consequence* (= result or effect), and use the examples in the box to elicit how it relates to similar concepts such as *cause* and *effect* [**Suggested answer:** *Causes* and *effects* tend to be about events in the past: *X happened because Y happened.* *Consequences* are more about the future: *if X happens, Y will/ might happen*]. Use these questions to focus on the differences between the structures:

♦ What is the difference between *if* and *in the event of*? [**Answer:** *If* is followed by a clause (*if X happens*); *in the event of* is followed by a noun phrase (*in the event of X*)].

♦ Which other word could replace *as* and *since* in these examples? [**Answer:** *because*]

♦ What is the difference between *so*, *as a result* and *therefore*? [**Answer:** *So* can be used to link two clauses in a single sentence. *As a result* and *therefore* tend to link separate sentences. *As a result* tends to be followed by a comma (or a pause in speech), while *therefore* may be used without the comma/pause].

5a ○**3.11** Students work alone to match the sentence halves and then discuss their answers in pairs. Then play the recording for them to check. When you go through the answers with the class, discuss the meaning of the technical terms in each sentence.

Answers:
1 g	3 a	5 b	7 c
2 d	4 f	6 e	8 h

Background notes:

Briefly, the consequences referred to in exercise 5a are as follows:
1 The loss of certain hydraulic systems can affect braking capability and automatic braking.
2 The *yaw damper* is a flight control system which sends inputs to the rudder in order to counter the effects of turbulence and avoid the aircraft oscillating from side to side, which is called *Dutch roll*. If the yaw damper fails the aircraft may suffer from Dutch roll.
3 In the event of cabin depressurisation, the cabin altitude increases and at 14,000 feet cabin altitude the passenger oxygen masks will be deployed in the cabin.
4 Especially on a twin-engine aircraft, if one engine is shut down, fuel will only be taken from the other wing, which will result in a weight imbalance between left and right. As a result, the fuel crossfeed valve is opened to allow fuel to flow from one wing tank to the other.

5 If the crew does not have the autopilot and autothrust, they fly manually without automation.
6 If one main generation is lost, for instance in case of an engine shutdown, the APU will be started (at or below 25.000 feet) in order to provide a second source of electrical generation.
7 If one of the pilots loses his/her air data input from the *Captain* or *First Officer probes*, then he/ she will switch over to the *standby probes*. There are three sets of probes: one usually connected to the captain's instruments; one to the first officer's; and a standby set which can be used if either of the others fails, or for crosschecking. The importance of the air data supplied by the probes cannot be overestimated as can be seen from the suspected cause of the disappearance of Air France Flight 447 in 2009.
8 If the crew is not sure that the landing gear is extended and locked down, they will make a low pass in front of the Tower so that the controllers can check.

Extension activity:

Elicit from the class some more possible consequences of these system failures. See *Background notes* above.

b ○**3.11** Discuss with the class where would be a good place to pause in each sentence, and then play the recording to compare it with students' ideas. Then play the recording again, pausing after each sentence, for students to repeat the sentences, either individually or as a class. Afterwards, students can repeat the exercise in pairs.

6 ○**3.12** Verbalising situations, actions and options is an important CRM habit to enhance safety by clarifying the rationale behind all the decisions which are made. In multinational crews, this may well be done in a common language: English. Remember that the technical environment in which the flight crew work is very largely in English through inscriptions in the cockpit, flight manuals and checklists, and the data displayed on their screens.

Go through the example with the class. Discuss whether there are any more consequences of this failure. Then play the recording, pausing after each sentence for volunteers to suggest consequences. Encourage them to use a range of structures from the *Language focus* box. Afterwards, students can repeat the exercise in pairs, using audioscript 3.12 on page 187.

Suggested answers:

1 As the flaps are jammed, we'll have to make a flaps-up landing. So, the touch-down speed will be higher and the stopping distance longer. We'll need the longest runway and we must also request emergency services to be on standby.

2 We have just lost our PFDs and NDs, so we must use our standby instruments. As a result, we will no longer be able to make an ILS approach because there will be no glideslope and localizer display. We are going to request a visual approach.

3 The oil level on Engine Number 3 is low, but we have reduced to flight idle and there is no low pressure oil warning. Therefore we'll be able to continue the flight and the engine running at idle will continue to provide electrical generation.

4 Because Engine Number 2 was shut down, we have started the APU to ensure electrical generation. All our systems seem to be fully operational and we will be making a normal approach.

5 Due to the electrical malfunctions, we should perform the electrical failure checklist, set Essential power, shed the galleys and expedite our descent.

6 To reduce the electrical load, we have selected load shed and selected Essential power. We should deploy the RAT (Ram Air Turbine) and request a precautionary landing.

7 There were obviously unwanted signals going to the flight controls, so we disconnected the autopilot and are flying manually. We should check the fault messages on the EICAS / ECAM and try to isolate the faulty computer.

8 As a result of the lightning strike, we had a lot of discrepant indications and seem to have lost FMGC 2. The data transfer seems to have taken place normally. We have crosschecked Captain and First Officer displays and have seen no anomalies. However, we should request an ILS approach to Runway 13 Left and turn back to make a precautionary landing in order to have our systems checked by Engineering.

9 We are making a missed approach as a result of unreliable glideslope indications. We will climb to 3,000 feet on the extended runway centreline and request a visual approach.

10 The stick-shaker warning was triggered and the autopilot disconnected. Once we have reached a safe altitude, we will perform the autopilot disconnect checklist.

Background notes:

◆ The *main equipment centre* is a term used by Boeing for the under-floor avionics bay where computers and other electronic equipment are located.

◆ A *stick shaker* is an aircraft stall warning system which when triggered by the angle of attack sensor causes the stick or control column to vibrate so that the pilot gives a nose-down order.

◆ *Galley Shed* means cutting off the electrical power supply to the galleys, which consume a lot of electrical power (ovens, boilers), in order to supply essential systems.

Extension activity:

Before you do the listening task in exercise 7a, ask students to discuss in pairs what airport ground equipment the eight pictures show, and what could go wrong with each one.

Suggested answers:

a glideslope transmitter
b PAPI (Precision Approach Path Indicator)
c radar antenna
d TAF report as part of an ATIS
e runway edge light, which is on a stalk so that it is visible even in snow
f Localizer transmitter
g VHF frequencies of various ATC services
h runway centreline light, which is flush with the runway surface

7a ○3.13 **Play the recording for students to complete the matching exercise. Afterwards, students discuss their answers with a partner and listen again to check if necessary. When you go through the answers with the class, discuss what exactly is wrong with each item.**

Answers:			
1 c	3 a	5 g	7 f
2 h	4 d	6 e	8 b

Background note:

Roll-out is when a plane rolls along the ground after landing.

b **Students discuss the task in pairs and then feed back to the class.**

Communication errors: Failure to request clarification

ICAO FOCUS

Tell students to read the quote to find two things that pilots might do wrong [**Answers:** accept an inappropriate or incorrect instruction; use guesswork and anticipation bias to decide on the most probable interpretation for themselves]. You may want to check the meaning of some of the words from the quote, perhaps by reading definitions (see *Language notes*) in a mixed-up order to elicit the correct words from the quote. Students then discuss the four questions in pairs and then feed back to the class.

Suggested answers:
- Flight crews may not wish to ask for clarification for fear of appearing foolish, because they believe, or want to believe, that they did understand, through expectation bias or because they do not have enough confidence in their language skills.
- An inadequate instruction might omit the aircraft's call sign, might use non-standard phraseology, might be delivered too quickly or unclearly.
- One's own interpretation may be based on an expectation, or knowledge of the situation; which could be erroneous.
- If you think incorrectly that you have been cleared, you will be entering airspace which ATC does not wish or expect you to enter and may well be in conflict with other traffic.

Language notes:

The following words may cause problems.
- *reluctance* (to do something) = a lack of willingness, often because of fear of embarrassment or simply to save time and effort
- *inadequate* = not good enough, incomplete
- *over-reliance* = depending on somebody or something too much, which creates dangers when that person or thing is unavailable or wrong
- to *determine* /dɪˈtɜːmɪn/ = to work out, to calculate
- *interpretation* = a way of understanding something
- *erroneously* /əˈrəʊnɪəslɪ/ = by mistake

8a **○3.14 Go through the example with the class. Note that for the purpose of this exercise and the pedagogical objectives of *Flightpath* in general, either plain language or standard phraseology may be used.**

Play the recording, pausing after each transmission for volunteers to request clarification. Discuss the best responses with the class. Afterwards, students repeat the exercise is pairs using audioscript 3.14 on page 187.

Suggested answers:
1 Which runway is in use? / Advise runway in use.
2 On which side of the approach path is the rising terrain located? / Say precise position of rising terrain.
3 What effect has the downgraded ILS had on the system? / Say status of ILS.
4 What is the current visibility (RVR)? / Say RVR.
5 On which part of (Where exactly on) the runway is the debris located? / Say location of debris.
...

Background note:

A *surveillance radar approach* is an approach guided by primary radar determining position, track and (with secondary surveillance radar) identity of an aircraft.

b **The cues at the back of the book are similar to those which students have just heard and responded to with the recording. Each statement is incomplete and requires additional information or clarification. The students will produce their own answers in the pair work exercise; most of the answers will be numerical data, but should be grammatically expressed.**

If you have an odd number of students you will need to have a group of three students, where Student C takes the first three cues from Student A and the last three from Student B.

Controller response to aircraft system failures

Communicative and operational issues:

This section is designed from the controller's perspective: what should a controller know and expect in the event of various technical failures aboard the aircraft? In the case of mixed pilot/controller classes, it is also an opportunity to develop mutual understanding. Controllers are familiarised with the fundamentals of aircraft systems as part of their basic training and should be able to recognise the specific consequences of the different failures in exercise 9d; pilots will be able to develop these subjects further.

Several of the principles (Separate, Silence, Support and Time) are about providing the flight crew which is experiencing an emergency situation with a 'sterile' environment without distractions in which to resolve their problems.

FAA: *Trends in accidents and fatalities in large transport aircraft*, 2010
UK CAA: *CAP 745 – Aircraft emergencies* (concise analysis of the impacts of various emergencies)

9a With inexperienced classes, you may want to elicit the parts of ASSIST onto the board with the whole class, but avoid discussing/explaining too much at this stage, as this would spoil the pairwork discussion. Students then discuss the questions in pairs. After a few minutes, open up the discussion to include the whole class.

> **Suggested answers:**
> **Acknowledge:** It is important that the controller listens carefully to pilot input on the nature of the emergency, requests clarification if in doubt, and gives the crew reassurance that their problem is understood. Requesting and providing clarification, paraphrasing, confirming and acknowledging all play a key role in such exchanges.
> **Separate:** An aircraft in difficulty will need more airspace; manoeuvring may be slower and more difficult; the crew need to be able to concentrate on handling the failure and not on possible conflicts with other aircraft.
> **Silence:** Silence is twofold: first, it means instructing other aircraft and controllers on the frequency to maintain radio silence, if necessary, ('*Stop transmitting*') so that the frequency is fully available for the aircraft in distress; second, it is keeping the controller's transmissions to a minimum so as not to disturb the flight crew.
> **Inform:** All ATC staff concerned should be aware of the emergency or distress situation.
> **Support:** In an unexpected situation caused by a technical failure, the crew will need additional information about alternate airports, weather conditions, runway surface conditions, priority landing, emergency services on the ground, airport facilities etc.
> **Time:** The crew must be given time to respond to the failure, perform the relevant checklists, make decisions, carry out a briefing etc. in a 'sterile cockpit' (see Unit 4). This may involve holding for a while so that they can focus on the technical situation on board and take all necessary precautions before paying attention to the navigation required to perform an approach.

Extension activity:

If you have a group of controllers, you could still use the pilot questions to generate discussion, and vice versa. You may need to change the wording of some questions slightly (e.g. *Why do **pilots** expect these things of a controller?*)

b ⊙3.15 Tell students to listen to the conversation to find out what is happening. You could use these questions, either for the listening task or as a follow-up activity, to check understanding:

1 What was the first sign that something was wrong? [**Answer:** There was a loud crashing noise.]

2 What was the cause of the incident? [**Answer:** A cargo pallet had shifted.]

3 What does the pilot request? Why? [**Answer:** A straight-in approach; to avoid sudden manoeuvres]

4 What course of action do the pilot and the ATCO agree? [**Answer:** A visual approach behind an Airbus 330]

Background notes:

♦ A *pitch-down moment* involves a nose-down movement of the aircraft attitude.
♦ A *long straight-in approach* means that the approach does not involve a turn and that the crew has time to stabilise.
♦ *Maintain own separation* means that the crew uses its vision of other aircraft to keep the necessary distance from other traffic.

Extension activity:

Elicit from the class what tenses were used in the first part of the recording, when the pilot was describing the problem. Then play the recording again to check, and elicit the reasons for the tenses the pilot used.

> **Answers:**
> ♦ He used past simple to describe the incident (*was, had, went, found*).
> ♦ He used past perfect to describe the reason for the incident (*had come, had slid*).
> ♦ He used present perfect to describe present result of a past action (*has secured*).
> ♦ He used present continuous to describe the present situation (*are trying*).

c Students work in pairs to rank the situations and then compare their answers with those of other pairs. You may want to check the language of comparisons first, especially ways of grading comparisons (e.g. *much / far / a lot / even / slightly more serious*). You could also check the language of possible consequences (*could lead to / might end up*, etc.). Note that this exercise is intended to generate plenty of discussion, which is more important than the 'correct' answers. You could extend the discussion by disagreeing with students' rankings in order to get them to justify them.

Suggested answers:
1 smoke or fire in the cockpit
2 a bomb warning; unlawful interference
3 birdstrike; depressurisation
4 hydraulic, fuel and gear problems
Note that there are no correct answers: this is more of a discussion opportunity, but the emergency situations have been graded basically according to the urgency with which they must be dealt with. Each situation can be potentially very dangerous, but usually crews will have more time to deal with hydraulic, fuel and gear problems and all these systems are failsafe, i.e. have built-in redundancy with back-up systems.

Background notes:

The eight emergencies discussed in exercise 9c will probably have the following consequences:

♦ **Unlawful interference:** There is a specific code (7500) to alert the ground of any attempted hijacking as the flight crew may not be able or wish to communicate orally. There may be unexplained and unscheduled changes to the aircraft's course if the crew is threatened and is complying with the hijacker(s). Threatened in this way, the crew may not reply, or may not reply normally, to ATC and may not follow ATC instructions.

♦ **Gear problem:** If the crew is not sure that all the landing gear is properly extended, they will probably decide not to land, request a low pass so that the Tower can check the status of their gear and go around to give themselves time to try and perform a manual gear extension. Many aircraft have an emergency gravity extension system which is activated manually by a crank handle in the cockpit.

♦ **Bomb warning:** Even bomb scares which do not seem credible have to be taken seriously and the aircraft must divert and land as soon as possible.

♦ **Fuel emergency:** Fuel emergencies do not usually occur suddenly, but are the result either of incorrect automatic or manual fuel management or prolonged holding. Avianca Flight 052 remains the classic case of a fuel emergency where inadequate communication, non-standard phraseology and poor language skills by the crew led to fuel exhaustion on all four engines. Different degrees of urgency (distress – pan calls; and emergency – Mayday) are at the crew's disposal once they have communicated their fuel endurance to ATC.

♦ **Smoke or fire:** Both smoke and fire remain number one hazards on board the aircraft. Response time is critical. The crew's priority is to land as soon as possible while deploying fire extinguishing, fire containment and smoke protection. The flight crew will be working under a lot of stress. Communication will be less clear as they crew will be wearing masks. It will be necessary to make an emergency evacuation using the escape slides as soon as the aircraft is on the ground.

♦ **Birdstrike:** Birds can hit the aircraft at different points. Effects will depend on the location of the impact and the size and number of the birds (see Units 5 and 6). The ingestion of large birds may cause engine stall or failure. Although windshields are tested for birdstikes, large birds can crack or break windshields impairing vision and affecting cabin pressurisation. The crew will need to make a precautionary landing.

♦ **Hydraulic problems:** Several aircraft systems depend on hydraulic power: flight controls, landing gear, brakes, thrust reversers. However, most commercial aircraft have triplexed hydraulic systems, i.e. three separate hydraulic systems, at least two of which supply each hydraulically driven component. However, the complete loss of a system can cause the secondary flight controls (flaps, slats) to be downgraded and affect aircraft braking. If the flaps are not fully extended, the aircraft will land faster and so will require a longer stopping distance. If there is not full braking capability, braking will be less effective and again the stopping distance will be increased.

♦ **Depressurisation:** Cabin depressurisation is a perfectly manageable failure, but will result in the passenger oxygen masks dropping, an unscheduled descent, poor communication as the crew will be wearing their oxygen masks and possibly injuries (concussion, broken ribs, bruises, cuts) among the passengers and cabin crew who did not have their seat belts attached.

d **Students work alone to complete the matching exercise and then check in pairs. When you go through the answers with the class, elicit how likely each consequence would be (e.g.** *a birdstrike* **might** *lead to ...;* **it** *could possibly result in ...;* **it** *would definitely mean ...).*

Answers:			
1 g	3 b	5 h	7 d
2 f	4 e	6 a	8 c

Background notes:

See *Background notes* to exercise 9c for full information.

Extension activity:

Students cover the table of consequences. They then test each other in pairs by reading aloud one of the situations from exercise 9c to elicit from their partner all the consequences from exercise 9d. As above, you could encourage them to use full sentences to describe the situations and their consequences (e.g. *a birdstrike might lead to ...*).

10a Students discuss the question in pairs and then feed back to the class.

b ◯3.16 Go through the instructions with the class. Then play the recording for students to complete the task. They check their answers in pairs and listen again if necessary. When you go through the answers with the class, elicit exactly what is happening in each transmission, and what the pilot intends to do.

> **Answers:**
> 1 fuel problems 　　　 5 unlawful interference
> 2 gear problems 　　　 6 hydraulic problems
> 3 bird strike 　　　　 7 smoke or fire in the cockpit
> 4 depressurisation 　　 8 bomb warning

Background notes:

◆ If you *recycle*, you perform a complete flight control, landing gear or door operation (extend-retract-extend, close-open-close etc.)
◆ An *explosive device* is a bomb.

Extension activity:

You could play the recording again, pausing after each transmission for volunteers to continue the dialogues over several turns, with one student playing the role of ATCO, responding to the emergency situation, and another playing the pilot responding to the ATCO. They could also work in pairs to make dialogues using audioscript 3.16 on page 187.

11 Go through the example with the class. Point out that cues are only provided for the first line of each dialogue: the rest will have to come from students' imaginations and experience. Students then work in pairs to make dialogues. Afterwards, ask some pairs to act out their dialogues for the class. Finally, discuss the effectiveness of the dialogues with the class.

> **Suggested answers:**
> **Student A**
> 1 For the moment, the situation is under control and we can continue in the hold normally.
> 2 There is a small leak from the door which may affect our pressurisation and it is causing considerable inconvenience to the passengers. We are reducing our airspeed and request a lower level.
> 3 One of our outflow valves will not close and so the cabin altitude is rising. Request lower level and information for a precautionary landing.
> ...

> **Student B**
> 1 We will be unable to reach Porto Alegre. Request heading for diversion to São Paulo.
> 2 Our Number 1 engine seems to be under control, but we are monitoring the parameters. However, our speed penalty means that we will not be able to pass NEB at 45.
> 3 Request landing distance available and runway surface condition for Runway 27 Left.
> ...

If you have an odd number of students you will need to have a group of three students, Student C takes cues 1 and 3 from Student A and cues 3 and 6 from Student B.

Background notes:

◆ An *outflow valve* is a valve on the lower fuselage which by opening and closing regulates the pressure inside the cabin.
◆ *Cabin altitude* describes the air pressure in the cabin. Air pressure is artificially maintained at approximately 6,000-8,000 feet inside the cabin. Flying for prolonged periods above 10,000 feet may cause hypoxia, altitude sickness, decompression sickness and acute earache and intestinal pain. Oxygen masks are deployed automatically if cabin altitude reaches 14,000 feet.
◆ If an extinguisher has been *discharged*, it has been activated and emptied of its extinguishing agent (e.g. freon).
◆ Some long-range aircraft have fuel tanks in the horizontal stabiliser; the weight of this fuel is used to regulate the aircraft's centre of gravity (CG). The *trim fuel valve* allows fuel to flow from the *trim tank* to the main fuel tanks in the wings and wing centre box (between the wings).
◆ *EGT* means engine exhaust gas temperature.
◆ A *penalty* is a reduction in aircraft or system performance caused by a failure.
◆ *IDG 2* is the integrated drive generator on Engine 2.
◆ A *horizontal stabilser*, also called a tailplane or THS, is the horizontal part of the rear empennage which can be trimmed, i.e. deflected to a position in which it produces the least aerodynamic resistance.
◆ *NEB* is a VOR navaid station identifier.

Electrical problems approaching Bangkok

Communicative and operational issues:

This section is mainly devoted to the case study of a particular failure when a water leak in the forward galley of a B747 resulted in the loss of several computers in the main equipment centre / avionics bay, and in a large part of the aircraft's electrical power supply.

12 Students work alone to complete the sentences. When they have checked their answers with a partner, go through the answers with the class

Answers:

1 print out	5 lifted off	9 pull up
2 look after	6 put out	10 running away
3 running out of	7 read back	11 pass on
4 looking for	8 make up	12 ran up

Background notes:

♦ The *centre pedestal* is a large standing panel between the two pilots which contains the thrust/throttle levers, radio and navigation control panels.

♦ *Akita* is a town in north-eastern Japan.

♦ If an *EGT reading* is *running away*, the engine exhaust gas temperature is increasing in an uncontrolled manner.

♦ If you *retard the thrust lever*, you move it back to reduce engine power.

♦ If you *run up* an engine you test it at full power in an isolated location on the airport in order to test it after an engine change or a repair.

♦ A *Quick Engine Change* is the replacement of an aircraft engine in the field.

Extension activity:

Use questions to check students fully understand all the verbs. Students could also test each other in pairs using the same questions, or by asking '*What does ... mean?*'

♦ Which phrasal verb means *to deliver a message to a third person*? [**Answer**: pass on]

♦ Which phrasal verb means *to recover lost ground*? [**Answer**: make up]

♦ Which phrasal verb means *to discontinue an approach*? [**Answer**: pull up]

♦ Which phrasal verb means *to extinguish*? [**Answer**: put out]

♦ Which phrasal verb means *to have less and less of something*? [**Answer**: run out of]

♦ Which phrasal verb means *to lose contact with the runway and go into the air*? [**Answer**: lift off]

♦ Which phrasal verb means *to move or increase out of control*? [**Answer**: run away]

♦ Which phrasal verb means *to test engine operation on the ground*? [**Answer**: run up]

13 ⦿3.17 Go through the instructions with the class. Students should read through the information in the table (Student A on page 137; Student B on page 145) to make sure they fully understand what information is missing in each case. Then play the recording for them to take notes in their column. Afterwards, students work in pairs to exchange information and complete the second column. They should ask and answer questions (e.g. *What route was the aircraft on? What happened at 08:40? How many passengers and crew were on board? Which AC buses were not powered?* etc.), rather than simply providing the answers. You could play the recording a second time for them to check their notes. Finally, go through the answers with the class, including the questions they asked to obtain the information.

Answers:

Circumstances of the flight			Consequences		
1	Route	London to Bangkok	1	Event at 08:40	bus-control-unit-status message
2	Passengers: Crew:	346 19	2	AC buses not powered:	1, 2 and 3
3	Altitude at 08:37 UTC	21,000 ft	3	System disconnected:	autothrottle
4	Flight phase:	descent	4	System disengaged:	autopilot
5	Incident in forward galley:	water leak	5	Displays lost:	right-hand displays
6	Incident reported by:	customer service manager	6	Status of AC bus 4:	normal
7	Nature of the water:	smelly	7	State of circuit breakers:	all closed
8	Cabin crew action:	soak up water with blankets	8	Strength of radio transmissions:	less than normal
9	State of cabin lights:	extinguished	9	EPR indication available:	only on Engine #4
10	Time, RWY and type of landing	09:07, RWY 01R, VMC	10	State of cabin lights:	extinguished

If you have an odd number of students you will need to have a group of three students, where Student C completes as much information as he/she can from both columns. This student will probably find it impossible to note everything, but they should aim to complete around half the information.

Background notes:

◆ The difference between *disconnected* and *disengaged* is that in disconnection the system is off, while in disengagement the system drops out of the mode it was in (e.g. level change, altitude hold, altitude acquire, vertical navigation, vertical speed etc.), but is still armed, i.e. ready to be engaged.

◆ A *circuit breaker* is a protective device which opens a circuit in the event of excess current flow. Most circuit breakers are located on the flight deck overhead and rear bulkhead panels, and can be opened or reset by the crew.

◆ *EPR indication* refers to the display of the Engine Pressure Ratio, the ratio between engine turbine discharge pressure and compressor inlet pressure, which is used on certain engines.

◆ The *customer service manager* is the chief cabin attendant on board a large aircraft.

◆ A *bus control unit* is a computer controlling the connection of the electrical busbars.

◆ If a display *blanks*, all information disappears from the screen.

Extension activity 1:

Discuss the following questions with the class:

◆ What might have caused the leak? [**Suggested answer:** The water may have come from a leaking potable water connection in the galley.]

◆ What was the relationship between the leak and the subsequent problems? [**Suggested answer:** Water must have seeped through the floor onto some wires, causing a short circuit.]

◆ What was the danger? [**Suggested answer:** The aircraft could have lost all electrical power.]

◆ Did the crew do the right thing? [**Suggested answer:** Yes. They checked the systems and landed as quickly as possible.]

◆ What would you have done?

Extension activity 2:

Elicit which phrasal verbs from exercise 12 could be used to describe this incident? [**Suggested answers:** The crew looked for the source of the leak; They passed on the information to ATC; There was a danger of running out of battery power]

14 ○3.18 Go through the example with the class. Elicit why a different tense has been used to report the actual words [**Answer:** When the reporting verb (e.g. *notified*) is in the past, the verbs in the reported

speech also move into the past]. You may also want to check why the example answer uses the present perfect (*has occurred*) and not past simple [**Suggested answer:** Because the result of the event is more important than when it occurred]. Then play the recording for volunteers to say what the speaker actually said. Note that several of the sentences do not actually refer to people speaking, so students should imagine what those people are saying. This is not an exercise on reported speech, but on recovering likely direct speech from information which might be in a written report or debriefing. Write the changes in verb form onto the board (e.g. *had occurred → has occurred*).

Suggested answers:
1 A substantial water leak has occurred in the galley.
2 The water is smelly.
3 Four or five blankets are saturated.
4 The bus control unit status message has disappeared.
5 AC busses 1, 2 and 4 are not powered.
6 The autothrottle has disconnected automatically.
7 The status of AC bus 4 appears normal.
8 We have checked the cockpit circuit breakers.
9 The strength of the transmissions is less than normal.
10 The cabin lights have extinguished.

15a Students work in pairs or small groups to write their scenarios. Encourage them to be creative and to invent any details they need.

Suggested answer:
Pilot: Bangkok Approach, Qantas 438. We have experienced electrical failures on three of our four electrical buses. Request expedite descent and approach, Qantas 438.

ATCO: Qantas 438, descend to altitude 8,000 feet. Report the effect of the failures on your flight.

Pilot: Descend altitude 8,000 feet. We are reading you only three out of five. The autopilot has disengaged and the autothrust has disconnected. We have lost some of our displays. The batteries are supplying some systems, Qantas 438.

...

b Students role play their scenarios for the class. Give and elicit feedback not only on the correct use of grammar and vocabulary, but also on their pronunciation/delivery.

Monitoring a situation and announcing a change

Communicative and operational issues:

In the event of a technical problem, it is good practice to monitor the situation regularly and report any change in order to maintain situational awareness in the air and on the ground.

ICAO FOCUS

Go through the quote together, pointing out that these are all proficiency requirements, i.e. skills that the students should be able to use effectively. For each requirement, elicit one or two useful phrases or grammatical constructions. Students then work in pairs to think of example sentences for each requirement. Afterwards, elicit some examples from the class.

16a Students work alone to complete the matching exercise and then check with a partner. Then go through the answers with the class.

Answers:
1 e	3 a	5 c	7 b
2 h	4 f	6 d	8 g

Background notes:

- The *dots* mentioned in sentence 4 are the dots on the ILS glideslope and localizer displays. When the aircraft is on the glideslope or localizer beam, the index is centred; any deviation (too high, too low, too far left, too far right) is measured and referred to in 'dots'. There are four dots on each scale. If the needle indicates two dots low, the pilot needs to lose altitude.
- *N1* is the engine fan or low compressor rotation speed measured as a percentage, but ranging as far as 107 per cent.
- *N2* is the engine high compressor rotation speed measured as a percentage, but ranging as far as 107 per cent.
- The *tolerance* for cabin altitude (see *Background notes* for exercise 11) is between 6,000 and 8,000 feet.
- *Yaw control* refers to control of the aircraft about the vertical axis managed mainly by the rudder.
- *Rudder deflection* refers to the movement of the rudder from side to side.

Extension activity:

Students could test each other in pairs by reading a sentence (1–8) to elicit from their partner a suitable sentence (a–h). This will raise their awareness of the grammar constructions used in the announcements of change, especially present perfect (in announcements a, d, e, g and h).

b **Discuss the question with the class. Allow this to generate some discussion as students speculate about what may be happening.**

Suggested answers:
1 The crew is watching the engine performance because low and high pressure compressor speeds and exhaust gas temperature have decreased.
2 The crew are looking at the vertical speed indicator because their rate of descent has increased to 1,600 feet per minute, which may be a subject of concern during approach.
3 The Captain has lost all his displays (PFD and ND) which are supplied by one source, but the First Officer has got his back; they are supplied by a different source. Usually, in such a case, the Captain can switch to the First Officer source and recover his screens.
4 The crew were two dots above the glideslope – a large deviation. When they next report, they have adjusted their rate of descent and come back to the glideslope in a stabilised approach.
5 The Pilot Not Flying (PNF) is monitoring the frequency, i.e. he/she is listening to transmissions on the same frequency between ATC and other aircraft. The controller has just spoken in Russian to another aircraft. Although the transmission was not intended for this crew, because it was in Russian they were unable to gain any additional situational awareness from it.
6 There may be a pressurisation problem, but cabin altitude is still within a correct operating range. A little later, the cabin altitude has obviously reached 14,000 feet as the oxygen masks have dropped.
7 The crew are concerned about rudder operation, but rudder travel seems to be normal. Now, there is no response from the rudder; they will have to use differential engine thrust and aileron control to turn the aircraft, but it will be less responsive.
8 The landing gear did not extend correctly the first time, so the crew retracted it and then proceeded with a new extension. This time the gear extended and locked down correctly.

c Students work in pairs to describe their incidents. Encourage them to ask plenty of questions while their partners are describing incidents. With weaker classes, you may want to elicit some of these questions onto the board first. When they have finished describing their incidents, elicit the best stories from the class.

Language focus: Linking words

Ask students to read the information in the box and then discuss these questions:

◆ In the first example, what is the reason and what is the consequence? [**Answer:** Reason: *We are not sure of gear extension.* Consequence: *We will make a low pass.*]

◆ In the second example, what question is answered with *by ...*? [**Answer:** *How* (*will you do it*)*?*]

◆ In the third example, what is the function of (*in order*) *to*? [**Answer:** to express purpose, i.e. why someone plans to do something]

◆ In the fourth example, why is the first verb in the present tense? [**Answer:** because we don't normally use *will* after *if*]

◆ In the fifth example, is the order of events important? [**Answer:** yes; *and* often has the function of showing the order of events]

◆ How could you change the sixth example so it contained the word *if*? [**Suggested answer:** *We won't have to divert if the visibility improves.* / *We'll have to divert if the visibility doesn't improve.*]

◆ How could you change the seventh example so it contained the word *when*? [**Suggested answer:** *We'll stop holding when we get clearance.*]

◆ In the eighth example, could you replace *then* with *and*? [**Suggested answer:** Yes, but *then* is better because it makes the sequence of events much clearer. Note that there should be a comma before *then*, but not normally before *and*.]

◆ In the ninth example, what grammatical constructions can come after *for*? [**Answer:** nouns, typically those referring to events]

17 Students work alone to complete the sentences and then check in pairs. Then go through the answers with the class. Afterwards, students can test each other in pairs by reading the beginning of a sentence (up to the linking word, e.g. *The Flight Officer's display units are blank, but ...*) for their partner to think of a logical ending.

Answers:	
1 but	6 to
2 until	7 so
3 then	8 and
4 if	9 unless
5 by	10 for

Background note:

BONA refers to the alphabetical identification of a waypoint radio beacon.

18 Go through the example with the class, paying particular attention to the language of asking for confirmation (*Confirm ... / Did you say ...?*) and the way the corrected sentence should be stressed. Students then work in pairs to make dialogues. Afterwards, ask some pairs to perform their dialogues for the class, and make sure they stress the corrected words.

Suggested answers:	
1	
Pilot:	Our autopilot has disconnected.
ATCO:	Confirm your autopilot has disconnected.
Pilot:	Correction. Our autothrust has disconnected.
2	
ATCO:	Maintain heading 120.
Pilot:	Did you say maintain heading 120?
ATCO:	Correction: maintain heading 220.
...	

Background notes:

◆ *Green system / blue system* refers to two of the hydraulic systems on Airbus aircraft; the third one is yellow. Boeing identify their hydraulic systems numerically.

◆ A *damper* is a hydraulic shock absorber.

◆ A *lift dumper* is a function of the ground spoilers on the upper surface of the wing during landing to reduce the lift of the wing and improve wheel brake traction.

◆ *Outboard / inboard spoilers* refers to the spoilers on the upper surface of the wing; there are several surfaces and they are commonly identified as inboard or inner and outboard or outer spoilers.

◆ *Crossfeed valve / crossbleed valve*: the crossfeed valve is part of the fuel system and allows fuel to be transferred from the tanks in one wing to those in the other during refuelling on the ground, or in case of an engine failure in flight. The crossbleed valve is part of the pneumatic system and allows hot 'bleed' air, taken from each engine compressor for air conditioning purposes etc., to be transferred from one side of the aircraft to the other.

If you have an odd number of students you will need to have a group of three, where Student C takes the first three cues from Student A and the last three cues from Student B.

19a ○**3.19** Go through the pairs of words with the class to elicit (a) what they mean and (b) how they are pronounced differently. Then play the recording for students to choose the correct answers. When you check the answers with the class, play any problematic words again for students to practise saying them.

Answers:

1 full	4 lose	7 loss	9 warm
2 lift	5 far	8 way	10 clean
3 dumper	6 last		

Language notes:

♦ The distinction between *damper* and *dumper* is especially problematic, as many languages do not distinguish between /æ/ and /ʌ/. Fortunately, it should be possible to tell them apart from context.

♦ Many students confuse the adjective *loose* /luːs/ with the verb *lose* /luːz/.

♦ *Worn* and *warm* may also be difficult to tell apart in rapid speech, as they share the same vowel sound /ɔː/.

b Students work in pairs to practise saying the words. You could turn this into a game: one student says one of the words from a pair and their partner has to decide if it is the first or the second word in that pair.

20a Go through the example with the class. Students then work in pairs to make dialogues and, in the case of ATCOs, take notes. They should swap roles after the first situation. Afterwards, ask volunteers to act out their dialogues for the class. Finally, discuss the effectiveness of the dialogues with the class.

Suggested answers:
__Situation 1__

Pilot (15:27): Bahrain Centre, Gulfair 571. We are an A320 descending to Flight Level 290 en route to Dubai. We have just had an AC Bus failure and are requesting a lower level to be able to start our APU, Gulfair 571.

ATCO: Gulfair 571, descend and maintain Flight Level 190. Report reaching.

Pilot: Descend and maintain Flight Level 190. Thank you, Gulfair 571.

Pilot (15:38): Bahrain ACC, Flight Level 190, our APU is running and electrical power is normal, Gulfair 571.

ATCO: Gulfair 571, roger.

Pilot (15:41): Gulfair 571, Flight Level 190, we have an AC Essential Feed fault. There has been a load shed and we are in an emergency power configuration. Request diversion for precautionary landing Bahrain. We have 116 passengers on board, Gulfair 571.

...

__Situation 2__

Pilot (19:21): Hanoi Tower, China Eastern 794. We are a Boeing 737-700 passing through altitude 3,000 feet climbing out from Runway 29 Right. We experienced a bird strike at 1,600 feet with Engine 2 surge. We have reduced Number 2 to idle. Request return for precautionary landing, China Eastern 794.

ATCO: China Eastern 794, cleared ILS approach Runway 29 Right. You are Number 3.

Pilot: Cleared ILS approach 794.

Pilot (19:22): China Eastern 794, we have had to shut down Engine Number 2; we suspected engine damage. Our standby hydraulic system is operating. Request vectors for ILS approach Runway 29 Right, China Eastern 794.

ATCO: Turn left heading 120 degrees closing localizer from the right, descend on glidepath QNH 998 hecto Pascal.

Pilot: Turn left heading 120 degrees, localizer from the right, QNH 998.

Pilot (19:24): China Eastern 794, our PTU has failed and we have lost our outboard spoilers and trailing edge flaps.

...

If you have an odd number of students: You will need to have a group of three students, where the third student is a co-pilot, who takes half of the pilot's cues.

Background notes:

- *AC Essential Feed* is the main alternating current power supply.
- *Load shed* refers to the fact of disconnecting non-essential electrical power users (notably the galley) if there are electrical generation failures in order to give priority to the essential systems.
- *RAT extended* or deployed means that the Ram Air Turbine, a small electrical generator driven by a propeller, is lowered into the airstream below the wing to provide essential electrical (and hydraulic) power in the event of multiple engine driven generator failures.
- *Vref +15* means that the plane is flying at a speed 15 knots faster than its Vref, i.e. the speed it should normally be flying.

b **Students could either give their report orally in pairs or write it as a homework task. Afterwards, ask some volunteers to report back to the class.**

Suggested answers (beginnings only):
Situation 1
We were Gulfair Flight 571, an A320 descending to Flight Level 290 bound for / en route to Dubai. We had an AC Bus failure and requested a lower level to be able to start our APU. ATC instructed us to descend to FL 190. Our APU started and our electrical power was normal. Then we had an AC Essential Feed fault.
...

Situation 2
We are China Eastern Flight 794, a Boeing 737-700. As we passed through 3,000 feet climbing out from Runway 29 Right, we experienced a bird strike on Engine 2 which caused an engine surge. We reduced Number 2 to idle and requested to return, in order to carry out / execute a precautionary landing.
...

Putting it together: ILS System Failure

Communicative and operational issues:

The scenario which forms the core of *Putting it together* is about a very unusual ILS malfunction which a New Zealand B767 crew encountered during an approach to Faleolo International Airport in Western Samoa. It demonstrates not only how a failure can be handled, but also the whole decision-making process and crew member interaction using effective Crew Resource Management, which we saw in Unit 7.

21a, b **Discuss the questions with the class.**

Suggested answers:
The localizer antenna is aligned on the runway centreline beyond the runway threshold. It is a succession of 1.50–2.50 metre posts perpendicular to the length of the runway on which antennas are mounted, aligned with the runway centreline. The glideslope antenna is located near the touchdown zone, but at some 300 metres from the edge of the runway. It consists of one or two tall pylon-type structures with horizontal antennas.
The localizer (LLZ, LOC) ground antenna at the end of the runway transmits beams in the form of two overlapping lobes. The two lobes overlap to provide a five-degree path either side of the extended centreline. The localizer gives the aircraft horizontal guidance.
The glideslope ground antenna transmits a signal, typically at three degrees of slope, to enable the aircraft to follow a regular glidepath and touch down on the touchdown zone.
Air Pilots Manual volume 5: *Radio Navigation and Instrument Flying*, Air pilot Publishing, pp. 289–313
Nav Canada: www.navcanada.ca: *ILS*
Skybrary: www.skybrary.com: *ILS*

Background notes:

- *LLZ, LOC*: the localizer part of the ILS, which provides tracking guidance along the extended centreline of the runway. Both abbreviations are in common usage.
- *LOC*: locator, non-directional beacon providing the pilot with accurate fixes along the flight path. The abbreviation LOC is also often used for Localizer.
- *G/S*: the glideslope part of the ILS, which provides vertical guidance towards the runway touchdown point usually at a slope of approximately three degrees.

Preparation

Language focus: Requesting and giving reasons

Tell students to close their books. Elicit from the class at least two ways of asking for reasons and two ways of giving reasons. Students then read the *Language focus* box to compare it with their ideas.

Background note:

If a transmitter is in *bypass mode*, e.g. for testing, the circuit is shunted and is not transmitting an operational signal to approaching aircraft.

22 ⏺ **3.20** Go through the example with the class. Play the recording, pausing after each transmission for two students to respond. Encourage students to use a range of structures in their responses, and to pay attention to tenses. Afterwards, students can repeat the exercise in pairs, using audioscript 3.20 on page 188.

> **Suggested answers:**
> Note: The controller's question always begins, *Why did / have you …?'*
>
> 1 We shut the engine down because of a fuel leak.
> 2 We made a go-around because there was traffic crossing the runway.
> 3 We have lost the pilot's PFD and ND displays due to a computer failure.
> 4 We have donned our oxygen masks because we smelt smoke in the cockpit.
> 5 We have initiated an emergency descent because of a cabin depressurisation.
> …

23a ⏺ **3.21** Students quickly read through the statements to check they understand everything. Then play the recording for them to complete the exercise. When they have discussed their answers in pairs, play the recording again for them to check and then go through the answers with the class.

> **Answers:**
> 1 T
> 2 F – 165
> 3 T
> 4 T
> 5 F – first the localizer, then the glidepath
> 6 T
> 7 T
> 8 F – at an altitude of 400 feet

Background notes:

- ◆ *FALE* (Foxtrot Alpha Lima Echo) is a VOR DME navigation beacon near Faleolo International Airport in Western Samoa in the Pacific.
- ◆ An *arc* is the ground track of an aircraft flying a constant DME distance from a navaid to intercept the ILS localizer inbound course.
- ◆ When an aircraft *captures* a glide path, the ILS system on board detects the localizer and glide slope ground transmitter signals and the aircraft's descent to the runway is automatically controlled under the crew's supervision.
- ◆ *Visual references* or *visual cues* are topographical features which contribute to situational awareness.
- ◆ A *low-drag approach profile* is a high-speed approach using a flaps-up (clean) aircraft configuration in the early stages.

- ◆ If *APPROACH is armed*, the Approach mode of the autopilot is made ready for use, but is not yet engaged.
- ◆ An *auto-flight system* refers to the combination of autopilot, autothrottle/autothrust, flight director, autoland systems etc. used to control the flight.
- ◆ If a plane is *abeam the runway*, the runway is at a bearing approximately 90° or 270° relative to the aircraft, i.e. to the right or the left.

b Students discuss in small groups and then feed back to the class. Allow plenty of time for students to speculate about possible reasons, ideally using language from the *Language focus* box. Avoid confirming or rejecting students' ideas.

> **Suggested answers:**
> Flight NZ60, an Air New Zealand Boeing 767 with 165 passengers and 11 crew members on board, was cleared to Faleolo via the FALE VOR DME navigation beacon on a 15-mile arc to intercept the ILS approach to Runway 08. The aircraft captured the ILS course 14 nautical miles from touchdown. One second after selecting the APPROACH mode, the autopilot captured the glideslope and almost immediately the rate of descent increased. The cockpit instruments showed the aircraft to be on the glideslope and the Localizer, but the PNF was surprised by the location of visual references. Six miles from touchdown, the crew performed a missed approach (go-around) when the aircraft was at only 400 feet (extremely low for an aircraft six miles outbound). The instruments continued to show that the aircraft was on the glideslope until the aircraft was level with the airport, which was manifestly incorrect.
>
> This erroneous glideslope indication, which concealed the fact that the aircraft was much lower than indicated, could have been caused, either by an on-board equipment malfunction, or by a malfunction or incorrect setting of the glideslope transmitter on the ground.

24a ⏺ **3.22** Students read through the statements to predict the answers. Then play the recording for students to choose the correct answers. When they have discussed their answers in pairs, play the recording again for them to check. Then go through the answers with the class.

> **Answers:**
>
> | | | | |
> |---|---|---|---|
> | 1 b | 3 a | 5 a | 7 c |
> | 2 c | 4 c | 6 c | 8 a |

Background notes:

- The *localizer beam front course* is the course indicated by the localizer transmitter antenna along the approach path of the aircraft.
- The difference between *no deviation* signal and *zero deviation* signal is that in the first case no information is displayed, and in the second, the display shows that the aircraft is correctly on the glidepath.
- If something is *out of phase* it is not following, in harmony, or aligned with something else.

b **Students discuss the three questions in pairs and then feed back to the class.**

> Suggested answers:
> 1 The incident was caused by the glideslope transmitter on the ground having been unintentionally set in bypass mode with an unserviceable transmitter selected. Due to the bypass mode, the transmitter monitor was unable to select the serviceable transmitter.
> 2 The transmission of a 3.5° glideslope meant that the aircraft autopilot ordered the aircraft to follow a steeper rate of descent which would have brought the aircraft to touch down 5.5 miles from the runway and crash.
> 3 The crew was alerted by two factors: what felt an extremely fast rate of descent; and by visual cues (topographical features) seeming closer than they should have been.

Communication

25a **Make sure students realise that Student A is to describe the <u>actual</u> flight path and Student B is to describe the <u>planned</u> flight path. Make sure they know to mark the differences on their own charts. Go through the example with the class, drawing attention to the language used: past simple for Student A's debriefing and *should have* + past participle for Student B's analysis. Students then work in pairs to describe and discuss the flight path. Afterwards, they may swap roles to repeat the activity. Finally, discuss with the class what should have happened and what the crew should have done differently.**

> Suggested answers:
> **Student A:** They captured the Localizer at 3,000 feet (second 26) and extended the flaps to position one, eight seconds later. They captured the glideslope almost immediately (second 33) at 2,800 feet.
> **Student B:** They should have levelled off at 2,500 feet and captured the glideslope over a minute and a half later (second 136) at 2,500 feet.
> ...

If you have an odd number of students you will need to have a group of three students, where Student C takes half of Student A's descriptions.

Background note:

IAP (Instrument Approach Procedure) is the procedure for an ILS approach.

b **Students complete the task in pairs.**

Debriefing

26 **Discuss the question with the class. Use these questions to guide the discussion:**

- How successful were they in describing the actual and planned flight paths?
- How well did they describe what the aircraft should have done?
- How could they improve?

Progress check

Students work alone to complete the table and then discuss their answers with a partner. Discuss with the class any remaining weaknesses and elicit ways to work on them.

DVD: *NZ60 – a free lesson* (Part 1)

Communicative and operational issues

The Air New Zealand DVD illustrates the facts already presented in exercises 23 and 24 in more detail and with the advantage of a simulator reconstitution.

27 **Remind the class of the events as described in exercises 23, 24 and 25. Make sure students realise that *Apia* is pronounced /ˈɑːpɪə/ in the clips. Go through the questions with the class. Then play the first part of the DVD for students to answer the questions. They discuss their answers in pairs before feeding back to the class.**

> Answers:
> 1 the glideslope capture
> 2 that the aircraft was correctly on the localizer and glideslope
> 3 with trying to decrease the speed and manage the high-energy situation
> 4 the crew extended the flaps, the speedbrakes and the landing gear to try and reduce speed

Background notes:

- *Vertical Speed mode* is the basic pitch autopilot mode.
- If you *reconcile* two or more pieces of information, you try to see how they fit together to identify any mistakes.
- A *flag* is a red strip on a display which indicates that the instrument input is incorrect.
- If you are *preoccupied* with an activity, you are too busy with it to notice other things.
- *Speedbrakes* refer to upper wing flight control surfaces, or spoiler function, which decrease airspeed in flight.
- *Flap 15 ... / Flap 25 ... /* refer to the various flap settings. As the aircraft descends, begins its approach and loses speed, the flaps are extended gradually from the retracted position to positions such as 5 degrees, 15 degrees, 25 degrees, 40 degrees and Full, depending on the aircraft type.

b Students discuss with a partner what they remember about the three questions and then watch the clip again to take notes. Afterwards, they discuss their answers again in pairs and then feed back to the class.

Answers:
1 a tailwind and a heavy aircraft
2 excessive pitch-down attitude, high engine speed, incorrect vertical speed mode data
3 the crew might disengage the autopilot and fly manually; they might go around; they might lose control of the aircraft

Extension activity:

Write the following words on the board:

moonless Vertical Speed Mode accelerate arc rushed reconcile flag focus preoccupied

Elicit from the class what was said about each word or phrase. You could play the clip again to check students' answers.

Suggested answers:
- It was a dark, *moonless* night.
- The plane was in *Vertical Speed Mode* to control the descent.
- The aircraft seemed to *accelerate* as it pitched down.
- The second First Officer said everything was fine as they came round the *arc*.
- Everything became *rushed* at glideslope intercept.
- The Captain *reconciled* the conflicting information (the ILS readings and the feeling that everything was rushed) by assuming it was connected with a tailwind or the heavy weight of the aircraft.
- There were no *flags* to indicate that there was anything other than an ILS capture.
- The First Officer does not remember contacting the Apia tower because he was *focused* on assisting the Captain.
- The Captain was *preoccupied* with managing the aircraft, slowing down and configuring.

28a, b Play Part 2 of the DVD for students to check if their predictions in exercise 27b were correct. They discuss the answers in pairs and then feed back to the class.

Suggested answer:
All the crew members were uncomfortable about the rate of descent and about the difficulty they had controlling the speed of the aircraft. However, the glideslope and localizer indications showed the aircraft to be on its correct flightpath. The Captain and the the third pilot (on the jump seat) performed a DME crosscheck, i.e. tried to make sure that their current altitude corresponded to their distance from touchdown. But it was the fact that they did not see the airport lights as they were nearing 500 feet and the nearness of the lights to the side of the aircraft, which really caused them simultaneously to realise they had to go around.

Background notes:

- *Unease* is a feeling that something is wrong.
- If a crew member is *heads-down* he/she is focused on the flight instruments rather than looking outside.
- The name *windscreen* is used for the front window in British English (as well as New Zealand English, as in the clip), while *windshield* is used in American English.
- A *mishmash* is a mixture, nothing seems distinct/clear.
- A *dim* light has low intensity
- *Adjacent* means next to.
- If you check one thing *against* another, you compare them to see how they relate to each other.
- If you *assess* something, you evaluate it in order to make a decision.

c Play the clip a second time for students to check their ideas. You could pause the DVD regularly during this second viewing to discuss key vocabulary (see *Background notes*) and to evaluate the crew's decisions. Afterwards, discuss with the class what they think happened next.

d Tell students to read the account to compare it with their own ideas.

e Students discuss the question in pairs and then share their ideas with the class. The decision-making process and the human factors involved will be explored in the DVD clip in Unit 10.

> Suggested answer:
> Even though the glidepath transmitter malfunction was not a failure they would normally expect, the flight crew members worked well as a team in the following ways: the Captain, who was PF, was heads-down monitoring the instruments closely and trying to control the speed using all the usual means (flaps, gear, speedbrakes); the First Officer was heads-up looking for visual references (lights, topography) which would confirm the instrument readings; their senses made them aware of the unusually fast glideslope capture and rate of descent; once the decision to go around was made, they climbed to a safe altitude to give themselves time to reflect before making a manual approach.

UNIT 10
Reducing approach and landing risks

Operational topics	Avoiding action; TCAS; Visual References; Landing hazards; Do-lists and checklists; VOR DME procedures; Crew and Team Resource Management; ATC functions; Threat and error management; ALAR; Problem solving
Communication functions	Saying unable; Announcing a compulsory action; Announcing a (nearly) completed action having an effect on the present; Announcing an avoided problem; Communication errors: Expectation bias 2; Reporting a previous communication
Language content	Phrasal verbs 2; Saying why unable; Present perfect tense; *still* and *yet*; Summarising; Expressing preferences; Reported speech; Phrasing, stress and intonation.

Unit 10 Teacher's brief

Our final unit focuses on various measures and precautions which can be taken to reduce **approach and landing risks**. The Flight Safety Foundation has pioneered work in this area through its ALAR Tool Kit which was updated in 2010; we have drawn extensively on this toolkit throughout *Flightpath* and most specifically in this last unit.

Approach and landing are the most critical phases of flight and Unit 10 addresses some of the safety issues and safety aids which pilots and controllers must manage. Both pilot-ATC and **pilot-to-pilot communication** play a key role in this process where various sophisticated technologies, good **crew resource management** and pilot skills are combined.

The communicative activities will be referring to TCAS, **expectation bias**, controlled flight into terrain (**CFIT**), approach briefings and handling anomalies during approach.

Unit 10 Sources

+ Airbus Flight Operations Safety Notes: *Approach and Landing* (Exercise 12c)
+ *www.theairlinepilots.com* : *The TCAS Display*, December 2006
+ www.alpa.org: *Hold short for runway safety*
+ Eurocontrol: *ACAS Bulletin 8, 9, 10, 11* (Unit lead-in; Exercises 2a–c; 3a–c; 8a–b)
+ Eurocontrol: *TCAS version 7.1*
+ Flight Safety Foundation: *ALAR Tool Kit Briefing Note 7.3* (Exercises 11a–c; 12a–b)
+ Flight Safety Foundation: *ALAR Tool Kit Briefing Note 2.2* (Exercises 19a–c)
+ Flight Safety Foundation: *Approach Briefing DVD* (Exercises 30a–34b)
+ Flight Safety Foundation: *CFIT Checklist*
+ ICAO Circular 314: *Threat and Error Management in Air Traffic Control* (ICAO focus with Exercise 22a–b)
+ Lacagnina, M.: *Blown away, AeroSafety World,* October 2010

+ Lacagnina, M.: *False localizer signal, AeroSafety World,* September 2010
+ Landry, D.: *Automation Addiction*, IFALPA Human Performance Committee Meeting, May 2007
+ Rosenkrans, W.: *Flight Path Management, AeroSafety World*, November 2010
+ Skybrary: *Night visual approaches*
+ Transportation Safety Board of Canada: *Runway overrun and fire aviation investigation report on Air France Flight 358*
+ Werfelman, L: *New approach, AeroSafety World*, February 2011

Lead-in

The lead-in quote refers to a situation in which two aircraft are on conflicting flight paths. In this situation the larger aircraft (the Fokker 100) is equipped with TCAS, which will warn the crew of the conflict, while the other aircraft, flying on Visual Flight Rules, will not be alerted. The situation is made more complex by the fact that the two aircraft are being managed by different controllers who have not briefed each other.

Quote: **Tell students to read the quote to find out what problem it describes [Answer: Two aircraft on a collision course, due to lack of coordination between controllers].**

Background notes:

+ A *track* is the path of the aircraft over the Earth's surface; the angle between a reference datum and the actual flight path of the aircraft over the Earth's surface, measured clockwise from 000° to 360°.
+ A *VFR traffic* refers to a flight following Visual Flight Rules, i.e. in this case, making an approach using visual references rather than flying on the instruments (IFR) making an ILS approach. For more information, see Unit 9.

1a, b, c Students discuss in pairs and then feed back to the class.

> **Suggested answers:**
> a Most commercial aircraft are now fitted with versions of *TCAS*, but light aircraft, and older generation aircraft, are often not. In the case of two aircraft on converging headings, the crew of the aircraft with TCAS will receive first a *Traffic Advisory* (TA) informing them of the presence of traffic in their vicinity. A TA does not require crew action. This allows them time to seek the traffic visually and question ATC. If the two aircraft continue to close on each other, a **Resolution** *Advisory* (RA) will be delivered by the TCAS instructing the crew to climb or descend. An RA requires the crew to take immediate action. If there is a conflict between an ATC instruction and a TCAS Resolution Advisory, ICAO requirements state that the crew must obey the Resolution Advisory. If the TCAS instructs the crew of one aircraft to descend, and ATC also instructs the non-TCAS equipped aircraft to descend, the TCAS will give the crew a contrary instruction after a few seconds in order to avoid collision.
> b TCAS is a communication between aircraft equipped with an appropriate transponder. Each TCAS-equipped aircraft 'interrogates' all other aircraft in a determined range about their position, and aircraft reply to other interrogations. This interrogation-and-response cycle may occur several times per second. Through this constant back-and-forth communication, the TCAS system builds a three-dimensional map of aircraft in the airspace, incorporating their bearing, altitude and range. Then, by extrapolating current range and altitude differences to anticipated future values, it determines if a potential collision threat exists.

Avoiding action

Language note:

The phrase *avoiding action* is a good illustration of the importance of word stress in English. If the second word is stressed (avoiding <u>ac</u>tion), the phrase means *not taking action*. With the stress on the first word (a<u>void</u>ing action), however, it becomes a compound noun referring to *an action taken in order to avoid something*, in this case to avoid a collision.

2a ◉3.23 Discuss with the class what the photograph and diagram show. [**Answer:** The photograph shows an IVSI, a vertical speed indicator used by the flight crew as part of TCAS. Increasingly, TCAS displays are integrated into the Navigation Display. The diagram shows the avoiding action taken by the two planes]. Go through the table with the class, eliciting the sort of information needed in each gap. You may need to check the last gap (8) carefully, as this refers to *what would have happened* (i.e. the unreal past). Then play the recording for students to complete the task. When they have checked in pairs, play the recording a second time if necessary. Then go through the answers with the class.

> **Answers:**
> 1 climb immediately to 5,000 feet
> 2 Descend RA
> 3 after
> 4 disregarded ATC and descended
> 5 climbed, made 90° turn
> 6 increased horizontal separation
> 7 0.9 nautical miles, 560 feet
> 8 less than 300 feet

Background notes:

- If an event *triggers* a second event, it causes or starts it automatically.
- If you *disregard* an instruction, you ignore it or decide not to follow it.
- The separation distances mentioned in the recording are 0.9 nm horizontally and 560 feet vertically.

b Discuss the question with the class. You could also discuss whether the ICAO regulation is sensible in this regard and how the pilot of the VFR knew to do the opposite.

> **Suggested answers:**
> - A TCAS RA takes priority over a controller's instruction.
> - The ICAO regulation is sensible because both aircraft receive an opposite TCAS RA simultaneously. ATCOs can only speak to one pilot at a time, the available response time is very short and this type of high-stress situation can easily lead to mistakes and confusion on the part of the ATCO or pilots.
> - The pilot of the VFR automatically received a TCAS RA at the same time.

c Students work in pairs to take turns to report the events. Afterwards, ask volunteers to report the events to the class.

> **Suggested answer:**
> See audioscript 3.23 on page 188.

3a, b **Students work alone to complete the matching exercise and then discuss their ideas in small groups. Finally, go through the answers with the class.**

> **Answers:**
> 1 e   2 f   3 c   4 d   5 a   6 b

> **Background note:**
> A *miss* is a near collision.

c **Discuss the question with the class.**

> **Suggested answers:**
> 1 The vertical miss distance above 20,000 feet is 600 feet. This value takes into account the vertical separation of 1,000 feet under RVSM conditions (see Unit 6).
> 2 The vertical speed required by the Climb and Descend RAs is 1,500 feet per minute. This is a regular vertical speed.
> 3 The factor of collision risk reduction thanks to TCAS II in the operational world is five. That means that TCAS II has made aircraft collision five times less likely.
> 4 The vertical miss distance at low altitudes is 300 feet. This lower value takes into account the greater traffic density and lower airspeeds at low altitude, but also the fact that the vertical separation is also often 1,000 feet.
> 5 The current (2011) TCAS version is version 7.1. It was trialled between 2008 and 2010 and approved by EASA in September 2010.
> 6 The average number of flight hours between RAs on short and medium haul aircraft is 1,000. On long-haul flights, occurrences are three times less frequent given the longer cruise durations. Most TCAS incidents occur in the more crowded lower airspace.

4 **Students work alone to complete the task and then compare their answers with a partner. Then go through the answers with the class.**

> **Answers:**
>
> | | |
> |---|---|
> | 1 touch down | 7 shut off |
> | 2 turn back | 8 switch over |
> | 3 take over | 9 start up |
> | 4 turn up | 10 turn off |
> | 5 shut down | 11 speak up |
> | 6 take off | 12 switch off |

> **Background notes:**
> ◆ *Ambient lighting* is the general lighting of the cockpit provided by the dome light.
> ◆ A *dome light* is a cockpit ceiling light.

Extension activity 1:

Use these questions to check students fully understand the 12 verbs.
◆ Which verb refers to the moment of landing a plane? [**Answer:** touch down]
◆ Which verb means *leave a runway or taxiway*? [**Answer:** turn off]
◆ Which verb involves removing the power from something, typically by turning a switch? [**Answer:** switch off]
◆ Which verb would you use if someone is speaking too quietly? [**Answer:** speak up]
◆ Which verb means *stop a fluid supply*? [**Answer:** shut off]
◆ Which verb refers to increasing the volume or intensity of something? [**Answer:** turn up]
◆ Which verb means *stop an engine or APU*? [**Answer:** shut down]
◆ Which verb means *transfer from one system, frequency, etc. to another*? [**Answer:** switch over]
◆ Which verb means *head back towards the place you came from*? [**Answer:** turn back]
◆ Which verb means *turn on the engines*? [**Answer:** start up]
◆ Which verb means *replace someone in the function they are performing*? [**Answer:** take over]

Extension activity 2:

Elicit from the class the four patterns for phrasal verbs, with examples from exercise 4. Note that some verbs have more than one pattern with a similar meaning:
◆ phrasal verbs with no object (= intransitive phrasal verbs) [**Suggested answers:** touch down; turn back; take over; shut down; take off; switch over; start up; speak up; switch off]
◆ verbs where the object always comes last (= prepositional verbs) [**Suggested answer:** turn off sth (e.g. turn off the runway/taxiway)]
◆ phrasal verbs where the object may come before or after the particle (= separable phrasal verbs) [**Suggested answers:** take sth over; turn sth up; shut sth down; shut sth off; start sth up; switch sth off]
◆ three-part phrasal verbs (= phrasal prepositional verbs) [**Suggested answers:** touch down on sth; turn back to sth; take over from sb; switch over to sth]

Note that some of these phrasal verbs have different patterns with different meanings, e.g. *turn off the runway* (not ~~turn the runway off~~); *turn off the light / turn the light off* (but not ~~turn off it~~).

5a ◯ **3.24 Go through the instructions with the class. You could elicit some examples of reasons for non-compliance before you listen – see *Suggested answers* from some examples. Make sure students have their notebooks open, ready to take notes. Then** play the recording. Afterwards, students compare their notes in pairs and listen again if necessary. Finally, go through the answers with the class.

> **Suggested answers:**
> The reasons why pilots are unable to follow ATC instructions in these cases are:
> 1 Pilots must obey TCAS RAs rather than controller instructions.
> 2 The aircraft's minimum airspeed in approach in this configuration is 140 knots, so they cannot decrease speed to 130.
> 3 The crew's localizer appears not to be working and so they cannot stabilise on the localizer beam.
> 4 If there is a hydraulic failure, the responsiveness of the flight controls may be affected and all manoeuvres will be slower and more difficult.
> 5 In single-engine operation there may be a loss of speed: an airspeed penalty (see Unit 8).
> 6 If the Captain (left-hand seat) is the pilot flying, then it is easier to turn or orbit left as his visibility to the right will be unobstructed during the turn.
> 7 ATC asks the crew to hold until 35 minutes past the hour, but the crew say that they will have already started using their reserve fuel by then.
> 8 Runway 28 Right must be a shorter runway. If the crew make a flaps-up landing, their landing speed will be higher and so deceleration will require more distance.

Background note:

Sequencing refers to ATC's role in placing aircraft in order with a safe separation during approach.

b ⊙3.24 Play the recording, pausing after each exchange for volunteers to repeat. Make sure their pronunciation is good, that they stress the correct words, etc. Afterwards, they can repeat the activity using audioscript 3.24 on pages 188–189.

c Go through the examples with the class. Students then work in pairs to make dialogues. Afterwards, they could swap roles and repeat the exercise, this time without looking at the response cues. Finally, ask some pairs to act out their dialogues for the class. Discuss with the class how clearly they gave and refused the instructions.

> **Suggested answers:**
> **Pilot responses**
> 1 Unable, we have a hydraulic failure. Request ten minutes to hold over Minimum Safe Altitude to carry out checklists.
> 2 Unable, we are experiencing strong headwinds; we estimate (reaching/passing) ALBA at 25.

> 3 Unable, the cabin crew have reported a passenger with / suffering from very severe chest pains. Request expedite approach.
> 4 Unable, the Minimum Safe Altitude is 4,000 feet in our present position.
> 5 Unable, our frequency selector has a faulty connection. We must remain (on) this frequency.
> ...
>
> **ATCO responses**
> 1 Unable, Runway 26 Right is being used for departures. Cleared ILS approach Runway 26 Left.
> 2 Unable, (there is) traffic above. Expect higher at time 45.
> 3 Unable, there has been a runway excursion; the landing runway is closed for 30 minutes.
> 4 Negative/Unable, there is traffic in the hold. Turn left heading 080 degrees.
> 5 Unable, the radar is unserviceable.
> ...

If you have an odd number of students you will need to have a group of three students, where the third student takes both instruction and response cues 1 to 3 from Student A and instruction and response cues 8 to 10 from Student B.

Background notes:

◆ A *radar surveillance approach* is a type of radar instrument approach provided by ATC. Only an operational radio transmitter and receiver are required. The radar controller vectors the aircraft to align it with the runway centreline.

◆ *Downwind* refers to the direction away from the source of the wind.

◆ A *touch and go* landing, also referred to as 'circuits and bumps', is a training exercise by which pilots practise approaches, touch down on the runway, but do not roll out and stop.

◆ *MSA* stands for Minimum Safe Altitude.

◆ *ALBA* is the identifier of a radio beacon.

◆ *Cumulonimbus* is a type of cloud characterised by its density, large size and height, its tendency to create stormy conditions and the hazard it represents for aircraft. It often has a characteristic 'anvil' shape.

◆ *Controlled airspace* is airspace managed by ATC.

◆ *Antonov precautionary landing* means that an Antonov aircraft is making a priority landing because they have a technical problem or a situation on board which requires attention, while not being an emergency.

◆ A *full stop landing* is a normal landing which ends with the aircraft stopping and exiting the runway.

Announcing completed actions and avoided problems

Language focus: Announcing what has happened

Go through the examples in the *Language focus* box with the class, eliciting which tense is used and why. For each example, elicit what the present result is, using the words *now* or *no longer*.

> **Suggested answers:**
> The verbs are in the present perfect. In each case, the present result is more important than the time it happened, e.g.:
> ◆ The emergency services are here *now*.
> ◆ The fire is out *now*.
> ◆ Most of the passengers are safely out of the plane *now*.
> ◆ We are *no longer* flying towards / We are now flying away from the thunderstorm.
> ◆ The unruly passenger is *no longer* a threat to others.
> ◆ The fire is under control *now*.
> ◆ The engine is working properly *now*.

6 ◉3.25 Go through the example with the class. Point out that the first version uses an abbreviated form of the present perfect, where the words *have* + *been* may be omitted. Students can use the abbreviated phraseology-type response or a more extended grammatical response. Alternatively, you could ask them to respond first in one way, then in the other. The suggested answers give examples of both types of response. Play the recording, pausing after each transmission for volunteers to respond. Discuss the best responses with the class. You could also elicit a series of negative responses, saying that it will be done soon or is being done at the moment, e.g. '*Negative, we have not deployed the foam carpet yet, but we will deploy it immediately*' or '*We are currently deploying the foam carpet*'. Afterwards, students repeat the activity in pairs, using audioscript 3.25 on page 189.

> **Suggested answers:**
> 1 Affirm. Foam carpet deployed. / Yes, we have deployed the foam carpet.
> 2 Yes, the fire fighters have arrived.
> 3 Affirm, MD-90 (has) vacated runway.
> 4 Yes, we have re-established the high-intensity runway lighting.
> 5 Yes, we have measured the braking action. / Yes, the braking action has been measured. / Yes, we have had the braking action measured.
> …

Language note:

This abbreviated form of the present perfect is only possible with a passive meaning (e.g. (*the*) *runway* (*has been*) *vacated*).

7a ◉3.26 Go through the example with the class, drawing attention to the grammar forms in the two versions: abbreviated present perfect and present simple. Then play the recording, pausing after each transmission for volunteers to respond. Discuss the best responses with the class. Afterwards, students repeat the activity in pairs, using audioscript 3.26 on page 189.

> **Suggested answers:**
> 1 Negative, passenger restrained. / Negative, the passenger is under control / Negative, the passenger has been restrained.
> 2 Negative, we have stopped the fuel leak by closing the isolation valve.
> 3 Affirm, we have turned right heading 230 degrees.
> 4 Negative, we have climbed to Flight Level 370 and are not experiencing any turbulence at this level.
> …

Background notes:

◆ The *fuel manifold* is a fuel distribution line to which nozzles are attached.
◆ A *generator overload message* appears when an excessive amount of electricity is drawn from a generator.

b ◉3.26 Go through the example with the class, making sure students can hear the rising intonation. Then play the recording, pausing after each question for students to repeat, either individually or as a class.

8a ◉3.27 Copy the diagram onto the board and elicit the type of information that might be added to various parts of it [**Answers:** Flight Level; heading; climbing or descending]. Then play the recording for students to complete the information. You will probably have to play the recording several times, as there is a lot of information to process. With weaker classes, you might ask them to only listen the first time, to get an idea of what happened, and only to complete the flight paths when they listen again. Allow plenty of opportunity for students to compare their answers in pairs before eliciting the answers onto the board.

> **Suggested answer:**
> See Students' Book answer key, page 173.

Background notes:

- ◆ If two aircraft are *converging*, they are moving towards each other.
- ◆ If an action *induces* an RA, it triggers it.

b Students complete as much as they can from memory and then listen again to check their answers. Go through the answers with the class. Note that the last question may generate some discussion, but the answer, according to ICAO procedure, is clear.

Answers:
1 ATR 72	4 climb
2 IMC (Instrument	5 descend
Meteorological	6 increase descent
Conditions)	7 SW3
3 60	8 TCAS

c, d Elicit the best tenses to use for reporting an incident of this nature [**Suggested answer:** past simple for most of the events; past continuous and past perfect for some background details]. You could ask students to do either task **c** or task **d**, depending on their real-life job, but consider also getting students to perform both tasks, as it is always useful to see things from the other person's perspective. Students work in pairs and take turns to describe the incident in full. Afterwards, elicit a full description from the class.

Suggested answers:

c

B737: We were flying at Flight Level 70 heading 345 degrees when we received an ATC instruction to descend to Flight Level 60. As we were initiating our descent, we received a TCAS RA to climb, but I disregarded this and pursued our descent. ATC then repeated the order to descend to Flight Level 60 to avoid traffic and in fact we passed through Flight Level 60.

ATR 72: We were flying at Flight Level 70 heading 185 degrees when there was a TCAS 'descend' RA. We initiated our descent and then during the descent received a second TCAS message: 'increase descent'. So, we passed through Flight Level 60 towards Flight Level 50.

d

ATCO: I saw on my screen that an ATR 72 and a B737 were on opposite headings at Flight Level 70. I instructed the B737 to descend to Flight Level 60. I then saw that the ATR was also descending. The B737 passed through Flight Level 60 and the ATR 72 continued its descent and entered into conflict with a third aircraft at Flight Level 50.

9 Go through the example with the class. You may need to check they understand the meaning of *belligerent* (= aggressive, rude). Make sure students know to use the time codes to plan their dialogues. Students then work in pairs to make dialogues. Afterwards, they could swap roles and repeat the dialogues, this time without using the cues. Finally, ask one pair to act out their dialogue for the class. Afterwards, discuss the effectiveness and accuracy of the language used, including the use of the present perfect.

Suggested answer:
ATCO: Springbok 3571, report level.
Pilot: Nairobi Approach, Springbok 3571 maintaining altitude 4,000 feet. Request precautionary landing due (to) unruly passengers who are threatening the cabin crew. We have some belligerent football fans on board, Springbok 3571.
ATCO: Springbok 3571, turn left heading 110 degrees to intercept localizer. Cleared ILS approach Runway 06, QNH 1017.
Pilot: Turn left heading 110 degrees. Cleared ILS approach Runway 06, QNH 1017. Springbok 3571.
ATCO: Springbok 3571, has the cabin crew got the unruly passengers under control yet?
Pilot: Negative. One passenger has been injured. The crew has contained the belligerent passengers in the rear cabin. Request police presence on arrival, Springbok 3571.
...

Background notes:

- ◆ A *PA* is a passenger address system, i.e a means for the flight and cabin crew to talk to all the passengers.
- ◆ *HDG* stands for heading.

If you have an odd number of students you will need to have a group of three students, where the third student is a co-pilot, who shares the pilot cues.

Communication errors: Expectation bias (2)

Communicative and operational issues:

We have already looked at expectation bias in Unit 5. We are looking at it a second time because it is a common occurrence which affects all human beings in their everyday behaviour: we tend to see and hear what we expect to see and hear. Good communication is the most effective net to catch expectation bias errors. Developing focused and critical listening skills and not hesitating to question a transmission if in doubt are uses of language which are fundamental to enhancing safety in aviation operations.

ICAO FOCUS

Elicit from the class some examples of expectation bias [**Answers:** see *Background note* below]. Then tell students to read the quote to compare the two examples mentioned with their own ideas. Students then discuss the question in small groups and feed back to the class.

Background note:

Other cases of expectation bias involve not noticing that: a routeing, a radial or a level is not the one the crew usually flies; the approach is different; the left-hand runway is being used, instead of the usual right-hand one.

10 ●**3.28** Go through the example with the class, focusing especially on the pilot's mistake. Elicit good pronunciation, to stress the key information (i.e. *Negative, I am calling Malaysian 485*). Then play the recording, pausing after each communication for volunteers to respond appropriately. Afterwards, students test each other in pairs using audioscript 3.28 on page 189.

Suggested answers:
1 Negative, I am calling Malaysian 485. I say again, Malaysian 485 cleared to Sierra Bravo November, squawk 3164 and IDENT.
2 Negative, expect 9,000 feet in one-five miles.
3 Negative, cleared to Jiddah via Zalim and Al Birkah, I say again Zalim and Al Birkah.
4 Negative, contact Radar 118.6.
...

Background note:

VOR calibration refers to the need for all navaids to be checked and adjusted by technicians on the ground periodically.

Visual references

Communicative and operational issues:

We saw the importance of visual references for Flight NZ60 in Unit 9. Even in IMC conditions, visual references allow pilots to make sure of the accuracy and consistency of their instruments.

11a, b, c **Read the quote aloud and discuss the questions with the class.**

Suggested answers:
a The most common visual references used by the flight crew during approach are: the topographical characteristics of the surrounding terrain such as hills and rivers; features such as towns, factory chimneys, electrical pylons etc., which they also find on their approach charts; Precision Approach Path Indicator (PAPI) and Visual Approach Slope Indicator (VASI) lights; runway centreline, touchdown target and edge lights.
b The horizontal flight path is defined by the aircraft's heading, left and right turns, flying over fixes etc. The vertical flight path is defined by the aircraft's altitude, rate of descent (and climb) and glidepath angle.
c ATCOs' answers will vary widely depending on individual airports and personal experience, but some approaches and runways are much more challenging than others, especially due to high terrain or water surrounding the airport, step-down and complex circling approaches etc.

Background notes:

◆ *Step-down approach* refers to approaches in which phases of descent are followed by phases of level flight usually to fly over obstacles.
◆ A *complex circling approach* is an approach in which the aircraft follows one or more arcs before making its final straight-in approach.

12a **The relative width and length of the runway may affect the pilot's perception of his/her height above the ground, glidepath angle or point in the approach at a given moment and appear to contradict the information displayed on the instruments. In other words, if the runway is long and narrow, the pilot may have the impression that the glidepath angle is less, and the aircraft higher and farther from the threshold than it actually is.**

Students work in pairs to complete the task. Afterwards, discuss with the class the problems presented by such runways, and any examples students have come across in their experience.

Answers:
1 C   2 B   3 A

Language note:

Shallow and *steep* here describe angles of flight paths rather than depths. A shallow glide slope would be 2°, for instance, while a steep angle would be 3.5° or 4°.

Background note:

The relative width and length of the runway may affect the pilot's perception of his/her height above the ground, glidepath angle, or point in the approach at a given moment, and appear to contradict the information displayed on the instruments. In other words, if the runway is long and narrow, the pilot may have the impression that the glidepath angle is less, and the aircraft higher and farther from the threshold than it actually is.

b **Students work in small groups to discuss the pictures and then feed back to the class. Avoid confirming or rejecting students' ideas at this stage, as this would spoil the next exercise.**

> Suggested answers:
> a Rain on the windshield which creates refraction and the impression that one is too high: this could cause the pilot to overcompensate and increase the rate of descent or altitude unnecessarily.
> b Haze which makes one think that the runway is farther away than it is: this could cause a certain complacency and lack of situational awareness and then surprise when the pilot realises the actual position.
> c A snow-covered field under cloud which creates a phenomenon of whiteout: this eliminates the pilot's perception of height above the terrain and may result in spatial disorientation and failing to see significant detail.
> d A crosswind which will make all the lights and markings appear angled, and so make it more difficult for the pilot to align the aircraft on the centreline.
> e A wet runway which does not reflect light as much and gives the impression of being farther away with similar effects to (b), above.
> f Breaking out of low cloud which may mask the farther VASI/PAPI lights and may deprive the pilot of visual clues and make it more difficult to estimate present position, angle of descent and altitude.

c ◉3.29 **Students listen to the descriptions to match them with the pictures. They then discuss the pictures again in pairs. You may want to play the recording again for students to get all the information. Afterwards, go through the descriptions with the class. Elicit any anecdotes students have about these situations.**

> Answers:
> 1 b　2 d　3 a　4 e　5 c　6 f

Background notes:

- *Haze* refers to an unclear, clouded atmosphere.
- If a plane *lands long*, it lands after the target/ touchdown zone.
- A *drift correction* means that the pilot corrects the horizontal flight path by bringing the aircraft back onto the extended runway centreline or localizer beam.
- *Refraction* is the deflection of a light ray from a straight path. Refraction through the windshield can cause external references and their relative positions to be distorted.
- A *nose-down correction* means that the aircraft altitude is too high, and so the pilot pitches down.
- A *pitch-down input* refers to the pilot pushing on the control column or stick.
- If a plane *lands short*, it lands before the target/ touchdown zone.
- A *late flare* occurs when the aircraft passes the runway touchdown target area before it is rotated.
- *Whiteout* is the phenomenon of spatial disorientation caused by the intense glare of a snowy landscape.
- *Slant visibility* means seeing something at an angle rather than head on.

13 **Go through the example with the class, eliciting onto the board some useful language for describing airfields and terrain (e.g. *There is a ...*; *I can see ...*; *... appears to be ...*). Students then work in pairs to describe their photos to a partner. While their partners are describing, students should make notes and afterwards read them back to make sure they have noted all the information correctly.**

> Suggested answers:
> **Student A**
> The airport is located on an island or a peninsular and surrounded by water on three sides. On the near side of the photo / in the foreground, there is a built-up area, a marina and a raised highway. It looks like a tropical country. There are two intersecting runways. The longer of the two runways has water at each end. The airport buildings, hangars and apron are located on the edge of the water on this side. It seems like quite a small regional airport.
> **Student B**
> The photograph is taken in winter and the land is covered in snow although the runways have been cleared. The airport is surrounded by a built-up area / a town on three sides and a wooded area on the fourth side. There is one runway running parallel to the wooded area and a complex network of taxiways. The terminal buildings are located between the runway and the wood.

If you have an odd number of students you will need to have a group of three students. Find and print another aerial view of an airport (e.g. search Google Images for 'airport') for the third student to describe.

Extension activity:

You could repeat the activity for airports your students are likely to know well, or you could find more aerial photos of airports on the internet. If you have enough photos (i.e. at least six), you could turn this into a game, where students take turns to describe an airport for their partners to guess which picture they are describing.

Procedures

Communicative and operational issues:

Aviation operations are based on procedures. These procedures are often materialised by checklists which are read out in what is called a 'challenge-response' manner between two pilots, where one pilot says an action and the second pilot confirms when the action has been performed, e.g.

Pilot 1:   *Engine Fire pushbutton ...*
Pilot 2:   *Pushed*

This verbalisation of actions is part of good crew resource management (CRM) and ensures that each action is double-checked: crew members describe and comment on their actions as they perform them. As both pilots spend most of the flight looking forward, and do not often exchange eye contact, this is an effective way of working together and being aware of each other. Checklists and do-lists are often displayed on the EICAS / ECAM screens and the lines of text are deleted as the actions are effectively performed.

Language focus: Describing procedures

Tell students to close their books. Elicit from the class what happens when a pilot pushes the *ENG FIRE pb* (= pushbutton) [**Answer:** cancels the audio warning; arms the fire extinguisher squib; closes the fuel valve; and de-activates the IDG]. Students then read the information in the *Language focus* box to check their ideas. Elicit also the structure of the verbs in the checklist items [**Answer:** past participles with a passive meaning] and the tenses used to describe the current events [**Answers:** present continuous; present perfect and present simple].

Background notes:

- An *audio warning* is a standardised, repetitive sound which draws the crew's attention to an anomaly.
- A *fire extinguisher squib* is an explosive cartridge which discharges a fire extinguisher and releases the fire extinguishing agent.
- *LP* stands for low pressure.
- An *IDG* or Integrated Drive Generator is a unit installed on the engine (and APU) and driven by the accessory gearbox; it comprises a constant-speed drive and an AC electrical generator.

14 Discuss the questions with the class.

Suggested answers:
A *do-list* is a series of actions to be performed in the form of a procedure: it may be performed by one crew member, technician or controller. It is often used for routine actions. A *checklist* is performed by two people: one reads out the action to be performed, the other performs the action and confirms aloud that it has been performed. Checklists are typically performed at specific phases in the flight (e.g. 'Before descent' checklist), or in abnormal or emergency situations (e.g. 'Engine fire' checklist). They are contained in the Quick Reference Handbook. A *process* describes a series of actions or events.

Extension activity:

Students work in pairs to give instructions to their partner based on the do-list (e.g. *Push the ENG FIRE pb*) to elicit from their partner a statement that the action is completed (e.g. *ENG FIRE pb pushed*).

15a Students work in pairs to write their lists, ideally an example of all three lists (do-list, checklist and process) based on the examples in the *Language focus* box. Afterwards, they discuss their lists with the class to decide if they have missed any stages. If you think students will struggle to come up with these lists, or if you want to make the exercise a little less serious, you could ask them to make do-lists, etc. for everyday processes (e.g. making a sandwich, using a pedestrian crossing, sending an email, etc.)

 b ◑3.30 Go through the example with the class, drawing attention to the tenses used in the question and answer. Then play the recording, pausing after each transmission for volunteers to respond appropriately. Students repeat the activity in pairs using audioscript 3.30 on page 189.

Suggested answers:
1 We are repairing it now.
2 We are completing/performing the Descent checklist now.
3 We are extinguishing / in the process of extinguishing the fire now.
...

Extension activity:

Students could repeat the activity using their checklists from exercise 15a to ask and answer questions.

c Elicit from the class what the pictures show [**Answers:** an ATC console and a Multipurpose Control and Display Unit]. Note that the illustrations are only examples: one for pilots and one for controllers. Elicit onto the board, a range of systems, stations, screens and control panels that students could describe. You may need to elicit from the class some useful phrases for describing layout (e.g. *at the top/bottom*; *in the middle; to the left/right of the ...*; *above/below/ between the ...*; etc.). You may also need to elicit the names of parts of a control panel, e.g.:

◆ pushbutton
◆ key
◆ line key
◆ rotary selector
◆ switch
◆ light
◆ dial
◆ knob
◆ LCD (Liquid Crystal Display)

Students then take turns to describe their chosen item. You could make this into a game by telling the other student to guess which item from the board is being described. Alternatively, while their partners are describing, students could attempt to draw the item being described. The drawer should simply draw what is being described, avoiding using his/her own knowledge to improve the drawing.

16a Go through the example with the class. Draw attention to the use of the present simple to describe regular, repeated processes. Students then work in pairs to describe their processes and take notes of their partners' processes.

Suggested answers:
Student A
1 The aircraft flies a step-down approach (downwind) on a course of 090 degrees. It then turns right onto a heading of 135 degrees, performs a left-hand turn onto a heading of 315 degrees until it turns left onto the extended runway centreline.

2 The aircraft is level at 2,600 feet heading 062 degrees. At FLAKE, 7 DME inbound, it initiates a descent and levels off at 2,000 feet before continuing its descent at 1.5 DME passing over the VOR and levelling off at 980 feet. At DME 1.3 outbound, it descends further and passes over the marker at 2.5 DME outbound where if initiates a climb.

Student B
1 The aircraft flies a step-down approach on a heading of 063 degrees at 3,000 feet. At OBALE, 14.1 nautical miles DME, the aircraft descends towards 2,000 feet and levels off again. At ADEDE, 7.1 DME, the aircraft captures the glideslope and descends towards 1,440 feet, passing below the glideslope, but is on it again at BOLFY at 5.1 DME. It passes over the Middle Marker high and at 1.8 DME the crew decides to perform a missed approach and climbs out on a heading of 050 degrees.
2 The aircraft flies an inbound track heading 231 degrees and turns right onto an outbound/ downwind track of 051 degrees before joining the inbound track of 231 degrees. The aircraft discontinues the approach and climbs out on the extended runway centreline before making a left-hand turn.

Background notes:

◆ In Student A's first diagram, the crossed lines on the left are airport runways. *Back course* refers to the fact that a reverse ILS localizer signal can be used for an approach.
◆ In Student A's second diagram, *FLAKE* is the identifier of a beacon.
◆ *UNZ VOR R-242* refers to a VOR radial to follow in case of a missed approach.
◆ In Student B's first diagram, *OBALE*, *ADEDE* and *BOLFY* are beacon identifiers and MM stands for Middle Marker.
◆ The arrowhead shape is the glidepath cone.
◆ In the same diagram, the flight path which the student should describe is the dotted line; the continuous line shows the theoretical glideslope.

If you have an odd number of students you will need to have a group of three students, where Student C takes one process from Student B. Alternatively, Student C could draw his/her own processes (using his/her imagination) and describe these to his/her partners.

b Students use their notes to report back. Make sure they know to use past simple in their descriptions. They should correct any mistakes in their partner's description. Finally, elicit descriptions from the class.

Suggested answers:

Student A

1 The aircraft flew a step-down approach (downwind) on a course of 090 degrees. It then turned right onto a heading of 135 degrees, performed a left-hand turn onto a heading of 315 degrees until it turned left onto the extended runway centreline.

2 The aircraft was level at 2,600 feet heading 062 degrees. At FLAKE, 7 DME inbound, it initiated a descent and levelled off at 2,000 feet before continuing its descent at 1.5 DME passing over the VOR and levelling off at 980 feet. At DME 1.3 outbound, it descended further and passed over the marker at 2.5 DME outbound, where if initiated a climb.

Student B

1 The aircraft flew a step-down approach on a heading of 063 degrees at 3,000 feet. At OBALE, 14.1 nautical miles DME, the aircraft descended towards 2,000 feet and levelled off again. At ADEDE, 7.1 DME, the aircraft captured the glideslope and descended towards 1,440 feet, passing below the glideslope, but was on it again at BOLFY at 5.1 DME. It passed over the Middle Marker high and at 1.8 DME the crew decided to perform a missed approach and climbed out on a heading of 050 degrees.

2 The aircraft flew an inbound track heading 231 degrees and turned right onto an outbound/ downwind track of 051 degrees before joining the inbound track of 231 degrees. The aircraft discontinued the approach and climbed out on the extended runway centreline before making a left-hand turn.

17a, b ○3.31 Go through the notes with the class to elicit what sort of information might be required for each gap. Then play the recording for students to complete the notes. When they have checked in pairs, you may need to play the recording a second time for them to check. Finally, go through the answers with the class.

Answers:
1 098°
2 109°
3 3,800 ft
4 8 DME
5 265°
6 MDA (Minimum Descent Altitude)
7 4.5 DME
8 3,900 ft

Background notes:

- The *outbound track* is the flight away from the fix.
- A *base turn* is a turn executed by an aircraft during the initial approach between the end of the outbound track and the beginning of the final approach track.
- The *final approach track* is the heading flown by the crew during the final approach.
- *FAF* refers to the Final Approach Fix.
- A *step-down fix* is an identified point permitting descent in a segment of an ILS approach once an obstacle has been overflown.
- *Track 098* here refers to the heading to be followed.

18a Make sure students understand what they have to do. Students then work in pairs to give their instructions to their partners, who may either take notes or sketch a diagram of the approach path. They ask questions to make sure they have fully understood. Afterwards, elicit from the class diagrams of the two approaches onto the board.

If you have an odd number of students you will need to have a group of three students, where Student C describes an approach path they know from their operational experience.

Suggested answers:

Student A

After passing Initial Approach Fix 14 miles DME on radial 009, turn left to fly DME arc radius 12 miles DME descending to 4,600 feet. Crossing lead radial 075°, turn right to establish final approach track 265° descending to 3,800 feet. At Final Approach Fix, 6.1 miles DME, descend to Minimum Descent Altitude to cross step-down fix 4.5 DME at 3,290 feet.

Student B

Leave VOR (Sierra Kilo Alpha) to establish Radial 186° (Delta Papa November), maintain Flight Level 65. After passing Initial Approach Fix 15 miles DME, turn left to fly DME arc of 13 miles DME, passing Radial 213°, descend to 2,600 feet. Crossing lead radial (270°) turn right to establish final approach track 107° (Radial 287°). At Final Approach Fix, 6.3 DME, descend to Minimum Descent Altitude.

b Students complete the activity in pairs, again making sketches based on their partners' instructions. Afterwards, elicit some examples from the class.

Crew and team resource management

Communicative and operational issues:

Crew and team resource management are never more critical than during approach when the number of threats and hazards is greatest and the time frame for decision making is tightest.

ICAO FOCUS

Tell students to close their books. Elicit onto the board a list of CRM (crew resource management) factors that may contribute to approach-and-landing accidents and incidents. Students then compare their ideas with those in the book. You may need to check students understand the meaning of *complacency* (= a false sense that there is nothing to worry about). Students then discuss the three questions in small groups.

Suggested answers:
- Pilots and controllers can be proactive by using their instruments and screens to anticipate any developments and identify any discrepancies in flight path as soon as possible. They must both stay 'ahead of the aircraft'. The latest generation of aircraft have screens which display the projected trajectory and airspeed of the aircraft.
- Changing situations can best be prepared for by thinking about their possibility, having briefings and establishing contingency plans in advance; pilots and controllers should never be complacent or unquestioning.

Background note:

If a crew is *ahead of the aircraft* they can anticipate what the aircraft will do and what they should plan for in advance.

19a Students work alone to complete the exercise and then discuss their answers with a partner. Encourage students to discuss and decide on a final set of answers as a class before eliciting / going through the correct answers.

Answers:
1 d	3 d	5 b	7 b
2 c	4 c	6 a	8 d

b, c Students discuss the questions in pairs and then feed back to the class.

Suggested answers:
c Actions which the crew can take to reduce the impact of factors which contribute to approach and landing accidents include: good pre-flight briefings; careful approach briefings at a moment when the workload is low; verbalisation of all actions performed; good communication between the crew members: the first officer should feel free to express his opinion, concerns etc.; obtaining up-to-date data about weather and runway conditions; using the resources of the Flight Management

and Guidance System; having a pilot head up and another head down; clarifying any information or instruction which does not seem clear; maintaining a sterile cockpit to avoid any distractions; airing any personal problems (stress, impatience, fatigue, frustration etc.) so that they do not impact personal performance and decisions; having well-defined contingency plans; being ready to go around in case of any uncertainty.

20a **Tell students to cover the photo and diagram. They discuss the question in pairs and then compare their lists with the ideas in the diagram. When you go through the answers with the class, elicit as much information as you can about these seven communication partners.**

Suggested answers:
In addition to flight crews, a controller communicates with: other sectors in the same area (east, west, higher lower, A, B); other ATC units (Area Control Centres [*ACC*], Tower [*TWR*], Approach [*APP*], Departures, Ground); Flow management (in charge of maintaining a reasonable overall flow of traffic in and out of a given area); the supervisor (a more experienced controller in charge of a given team or shift); Air Traffic Management [*ATM*] Support staff (providing logistical and IT support); Flight Data Assistance (providing controllers with additional information about weather, traffic and equipment); and other controllers on their own shift or sector.

b Students complete the exercise alone and check in pairs before feeding back to the class. As a follow-up, they could test each other in pairs by reading an item (1–7) to elicit a definition from their partners.

Answers:
1 g	3 e	5 f	7 c
2 a	4 d	6 b	

Extension activity:

Elicit from the class any anecdotes of misunderstandings, disagreements or breakdowns in communication between ATCOs and the other groups of people listed in the diagram.

21a Students take turns to describe one of the aspects of CRM/TRM. They may, of course, describe more than one aspect. Afterwards, elicit as much information as possible about each aspect of CRM.

b Explain to students that there are five short exchanges on the page which are all examples of poor crew or team resource management (CRM/ TRM). Students work in pairs to complete the sentences with the most appropriate words and then report back.

Answers:
1 announcing, say
2 sounded, worry
3 expect
4 seem, published
5 look

Extension activity:

Ask pairs to read each exchange aloud as written. Then ask them to re-enact the exchange as they think it should have been.

Suggested answers:
1
First Officer: ATC are announcing heavy rain on arrival.
Captain: Yes. Request the latest weather data.
2
ATCO 1: Selair 396, sounded concerned about the approach.
ATCO 2: Ask them if they require any support or additional information.
3
ATCO: Mexicana 1285, expect Flight Level 350 in 20 miles.
Pilot: Expect Flight Level 350 in 20 minutes, Mexicana 1258.
4
First Officer: I can't seem to contact Haneda Approach on 119.9.
Captain: Contact Tokyo Centre and ask them to confirm the frequency of Haneda Approach.
5
First Officer: Should I request a weather update? The weather radar doesn't look good.
Captain: Yes, certainly. Request the latest weather and forecast.

Background note:

Haneda Approach is the Approach Control for one of the two main airports serving Tokyo; the other one is Narita.

c Ask students to describe what is happening in each of the five situations and what is wrong with the way the situation is handled.

Suggested answers:
1 The Captain is not paying attention either to the frequency or to what his First Officer is saying. It suggests that he is either preoccupied by something else, or dismissive of the First Officer's input. It is a demonstration of inattention and poor team work as the information flow between the two crew members is poor and time is wasted repeating information.

2 Controllers should pick up verbal and non-verbal clues about a flight crew's state of mind (as well as purely factual information) and act on it. The second controller, probably a superior, shows complacency and is taking risks by not following up on the first controller's impression.
3 The controller fails to detect and correct the pilot's readback error and probably suffers from expectation bias.
4 This is a case of poor radio practice. If a crew cannot contact a new frequency, they should re-contact the previous frequency for confirmation of the new frequency and not try and improvise themselves.
5 The Captain does not take the First Officer's suggestion into account and is complacent about the most recent weather returns on the aircraft's weather radar.

Managing threats

ICAO FOCUS

Tell students to close their books. Elicit from the class examples of contextual complexities that ATCOs have to take into account in order to manage traffic [**Answers:** dealing with adverse meteorological conditions; airports surrounded by high mountains; congested airspace; aircraft malfunctions; errors committed by other people outside the air traffic control room (e.g. flight crews or ground staff etc)]. You may need to check the meaning of *contextual* (= related to the circumstances or context of a situation). Students then read the quote to compare it with their ideas. They then discuss the two tasks in pairs and feed back to the class.

Suggested answers:
A *threat* is an external factor (weather conditions, technical failure, someone else's error) which may endanger the flight. An *error* is a mistake or an omission committed by a person.

22a ○3.32 Go through the diagram with the class, eliciting explanations/examples of each threat. Then play the recording for students to complete the task. They compare their answers in pairs, remembering as much as they can about each transmission, and then listen again to check. Then go through the answers with the class.

Answers:
1 h	3 b	5 a	7 g
2 f	4 e	6 c	8 d

Background notes:

- A *sticking mike/mic* (microphone) is a microphone which is blocked in the open position.
- A *shift handover* is when one group of controllers is replaced by another.
- *Coast guards* are members of a state service in charge of protecting territorial waters.
- *System malfunctions* include such things as IT failures and electrical power cuts.
- *Airspace restrictions* may be caused by military or VIP traffic operating in certain areas, or navaids being inoperative.
- *Distractions* may come from a sudden unexpected traffic movement, an emergency which could have a knock-on effect, from people visiting the control room, technicians doing maintenance work, or staff talking among themselves.
- *Similar call signs* may be call signs such as Air India 2863 and Air India 2386.

b Students discuss their anecdotes in pairs. After a few minutes, open up the discussion to include the whole class.

23a Tell students to work in small groups. Each group should choose either the pilot situation or the ATCO situation. They should discuss the situations in detail and come up with contingency plans and strategies. Allow plenty of time for groups to prepare their analyses. If some groups finish before the others, tell them to analyse the other situation (i.e. either the pilot or ATCO situation). Afterwards, discuss the situations in detail with the class. Make sure you discuss both situations, as this will be important for the role-play in exercise 23b.

> Suggested answers:
> In the air, Air China 2539, an Airbus 330, is at FL 080 approaching Manila with a hydraulic failure, which has impaired its braking capability, and three concussed passengers injured during turbulence. In addition, the crew are on extended duty (at the limit of or beyond their legal length of duty) due to a two-hour delay leaving Beijing. For all these reasons they wish to expedite their approach. They have prepared for an ILS approach to Runway 06, the longer of the two runways at 3,737 metres due to their downgraded braking.
> On the ground at Manila, the weather is bad (low pressure at 992 hectoPascal, wind 15 knots, gusting to 21 knots, visibility at 1,500, but decreasing, low 700-foot ceiling also decreasing, rain showers and a thunderstorm to the south-east).

b Put students into pairs, ideally one person who has analysed the pilot situation and one who has analysed the ATCO situation. Students make dialogues in pairs. Afterwards, they could swap roles and repeat the dialogues. Then ask some groups to act out their dialogues for the class. Finally, discuss the effectiveness of the strategies and contingencies with the class.

If you have an odd number of students you will need to have a group of three, where the third student is a co-pilot.

Putting it together: Approach and landing accident reduction (ALAR)

Quote: Tell students to close their books. Check students understand the meaning of *rushed* (= in a hurry, too fast to do things properly). Then discuss these questions with the class:

- What should a pilot do if he/she is given a clearance that will lead to a rushed approach? [**Suggested answer:** request another more convenient clearance]
- What should a pilot do if he/she has insufficient time for a change in plans during an approach? [**Suggested answer:** request to make a missed approach, enter the hold and prepare the new approach]
- What are the dangers associated with rushed/ unstabilised approaches? [**Suggested answers:** lack of concentration and attention; incomplete tasks; poorly crosschecked actions; flying too high, too low or too fast; being 'behind the aircraft'; ineffective last-minute adjustments to the airspeed and rate of descent; loss of situational awareness]
- What are a pilot's priorities during approach? [**Suggested answers:** being on the localizer and glideslope; maintaining situational awareness; having a contingency plan for a missed approach; having a properly briefed crew; being ready to go around; anticipating (staying ahead of the aircraft)]

Students then read the quote to compare the answers with their own. Discuss with the class whether they agree with all the advice.

24a, b, c, d, e Students discuss the questions in small groups. After a few minutes, open up the discussion to include the whole class.

> Suggested answers:
> a The flight crew are confused; they are studying the charts for an airport they are probably not familiar with; neither pilot is flying the plane; they have to deal with the controller while focusing on another task.
> b The controller is giving them too much information at the same time, complicating the issue with different options and giving them information they do not need at this phase of the flight.

c A stabilised approach is when the aircraft is at the correct airspeed, at the correct rate of descent, on the glideslope and localizer beams, and in the correct flap/gear configuration.

d If the crew do not have enough time, they should take delaying action (hold, orbit) or go around if they are already on the approach.

Preparation

Language focus: Expressing preferences

Tell students to close their books. Read the four questions from the *Language focus* box aloud to elicit suitable responses. Students then compare the answers in the box with their own ideas. Afterwards, students close their books again. Elicit from the class the four questions and five answers onto the board, drawing attention to the use of *to* after *prefer* but not after *rather*. Point out also that negative preferences are formed with *not* before the second verb (*I'd rather not park / I'd prefer not to park*, not *I wouldn't rather park*). Elicit which structures can be followed by either noun phrases or verbs [**Answers:** *I want sth / I want to do*; *I'd prefer sth / I'd prefer to do*] and which can only be followed by a verb [**Answers:** *I wish to do; I'd rather do*].

25 Go through the example with the class. Elicit other ways of asking about and expressing the same preferences (e.g. *Would Runway 28 Left or 21 Right be preferable? I'd rather use Runway 21 Right because it's longer*). Point out that cues are only provided for the questions: students will have to invent their own answers. Students then work in pairs to make dialogues, using structures from the *Language focus* box.

Suggested answers:
Student A
1 I'd prefer Runway 21 Right because it's longer.
2 I'd prefer to make a long final in order to have more time to stabilise.
3 I'd rather divert as I'm afraid we'll be below our minima in 20 minutes.
…

Student B
1 I'd prefer to make a low pass to make sure the gear is properly extended.
2 I think it is preferable to stop on the runway because I am not sure of our nose wheel steering system.
3 I'd prefer not to taxi to the gate as I'd rather the firemen checked our engine first.
…

26a ◉3.33 Go through the examples with the class, focusing especially on the structure *to ask/tell sb to do sth*. Then play the recording, pausing after each transmission for volunteers to report what the controller said. Afterwards, students test each other in pairs using audioscript 3.33 on page 190.

Suggested answers:
1 They told us to report the runway in sight.
2 They asked us to confirm that the gear was down and locked.
3 They said we were cleared to land.
4 They informed us that QNH is 1015 and that we were Number 3.
5 They said that this was a right-hand circuit for Runway 26.
…

b ◉3.33 Students work alone to work out where the stress should be and then listen again to check. Make sure students realise they should mark the stressed syllables on the highlighted words in the script on page 190. When you go through the answers with the class, make sure students are comfortable pronouncing these words.

Answers:
re<u>port</u>   <u>Lo</u>calizer
con<u>firm</u>   re<u>star</u>ted
<u>tra</u>ffic   <u>en</u>gine
<u>run</u>way   <u>air</u>speed
es<u>tab</u>lished   <u>al</u>titude

27a Tell students to work through the eight situations in any order they choose. Make sure they realise that they will need to invent some information, such as call signs. They could either make their dialogues orally or as a writing homework. Afterwards, ask some volunteers to act out their dialogues for the class.

Suggested answers (beginnings only):
Pilot 1
Pilot: Zhengzhou Approach, Korean Air 809, five miles from touchdown on ILS approach to Runway 12. We are experiencing fluctuations in our glideslope indication. Confirm glideslope serviceable, Korean Air 4673.
ATCO: Affirm, glideslope serviceable. No anomalies reported. Say again your position.
Pilot: 4.6 miles DME …

ATCO 1
Pilot: TACA 557, we are a B737 at 3,000 feet heading 240 degrees. We were not able to intercept the localizer from DME arc. Request instructions.
ATCO: TACA 557, I will give you vectoring for visual approach Runway 28.
…

If you have an odd number of students you will need to have a group of three, where the third student is a co-pilot.

Background notes:

- *Amber transit lights* refer to the amber lights which are illuminated when the landing gear is moving between its extended and retracted positions and vice versa.
- *Right green arrow* is the green arrow (or indicator light) which shows that the right-hand main gear is extended and locked down.
- A *base leg* is the part of a conventional landing circuit when the aircraft turns off the downwind leg and flies perpendicular to the extended runway centreline before joining the glidepath.
- The *lateral distance* is related to the aircraft's horizontal movement (heading, course, track) and the localizer part of the ILS.

b **The reports can be oral or written. Ask volunteers from each group to report back to the class. Afterwards, discuss with the class how well they resolved the situations.**

Communication

28a **○3.34 Go through the information in the table, eliciting possible risk factors. Then play the recording, pausing after each part for students to make short dialogues in pairs. Discuss each situation with the class to make sure everyone knows exactly what has happened and to predict what might happen next, before moving on to the next part. Afterwards, you could ask pairs to swap roles and repeat the whole conversation from memory.**

If you have an odd number of students you will need to have a group of three, where the third student is a co-pilot.

Background notes:

- *LT* stands for local time.
- *FMS* (*Flight Management System*) is a computer system that uses a large data base to 1) allow routes to be pre-programmed; 2) interface with the AFCS (Automatic Flight Control System), i.e. autopilot and flight director; 3) memorise and update navigation aids; 4) provide information to the EFIS (Electronic Flight Instrument System) for PFD and ND displays.
- *EGPWS* (*Enhanced Ground Proximity Warning System*) is a system providing crews with forward warning of the risk of collision with terrain in sufficient time for them to take avoiding action. EGPWS or TAWS (Terrain Awareness and Warning System) is combined with a *Global Positioning System* (*GPS*) for greater accuracy in remote areas.

- A *navigation accuracy check* refers to the crew's practice of crosschecking different navigation instruments and sources against each other in order to make sure their data is correct.
- The *Automatic Direction Finder* (*ADF*) is a flight instrument which indicates the direction from which the signal from a non-directional beacon is coming.
- The *Non-Directional Beacon* (*NDB*) is a ground-based beacon with a given Morse identifier used by the pilot in conjunction with the ADF in order to establish his/her position.
- The *Navigation Display* (*ND*) is one of the main pilot instruments which provides compass heading and navigational and weather radar return data.
- An *Air Safety Report* is a report written after an operational incident. Transparent, non-blaming reporting of incidents contributes significantly to improvements in safety, and a better understanding of error chains.

b **Students prepare their reports in small groups, either orally or in writing, and present them to the class. When the reports are ready, ask volunteers to present them to the class. Give and elicit feedback on the effectiveness of the reports.**

> Suggested answer:
> The VOR radial signal started to fluctuate during the final approach, and the information disappeared at about 1,200 feet above ground level. It was quite dark outside. In the absence of any proper visual cues and VOR, we decided to go around and to follow the standard missed approach procedure.
> While we were in the hold after go-around, ATC confirmed that the VOR/DME was functioning correctly as far as they knew. Following that confirmation, we decided to perform a navigation accuracy check. All indications were consistent except the ADF. The FMS showed us we were on course. Only the NDB showed us off track.

Debriefing

29 **Discuss the questions with the class, allowing plenty of time for every student to share his/her experiences.**

Progress check

Students work alone to complete the progress check and then discuss their notes with a partner. Then go through their comments with the class, focusing on how to overcome any remaining weaknesses.

DVD: *NZ60: A free lesson* (Part 2)

Communicative and operational issues

In Unit 9 we looked at the circumstances of the approach of NZ60 and how the crew realised that they were on too steep a glideslope due to a glideslope transmitter anomaly, and decided to conduct a missed approach. This avoided a case of CFIT, flying into the ground several miles short of the runway with all the instruments appearing correct. In this final unit we explore what was involved in the decision-making process from both technical and human factors perspectives.

30 **Tell students to discuss in pairs. Make sure they discuss the causes of the incident and its outcome. Afterwards, elicit as much information from the class as you can. You could use the following questions to check their understanding, and if necessary you could play the Unit 9 clip again.**

a Where were the crew trying to land?
b What was the first suggestion that something was wrong?
c Did the ILS readings indicate that there was a problem?
d What problem did the crew have to deal with?
e When did they realise that there was a more serious problem?
f What action did they take?
g What was the source of the faulty information?
h What was the outcome of the incident?

> **Answers:**
> a At Faleolo International Airport near Apia (/ˈɑːpiːə/), in the Samoan Islands.
> b The glideslope capture was very sudden. The aircraft was going faster than expected.
> c No, they were normal. There were no flags or warnings to indicate that there was a problem.
> d the excessive speed of the aircraft
> e When they looked out of the window and couldn't see the airport lights.
> f They performed a go-around.
> g the glideslope transmitter
> h The crew landed the aircraft safely on the second approach.

31a **Elicit from the class one or two examples of inputs which can guide the crew during approach. Then play Part 1 for students to make notes of the inputs. They compare their answers in pairs before feeding back to the class.**

> **Answers:**
> The crew have the following inputs at their disposal: ILS Localizer and Glideslope; DME (e.g. Faleolo); Vertical Speed Indicator; Airspeed Indicator; Radio Altimeter; airport approach and runway lighting.

Background notes:

◆ *VOR* stands for VHF Omnidirectional Range.
◆ *NDB* stands for Non-Directional Beacon.
◆ *Centreline indications* are the indication of alignment on the runway centreline provided by the localizer.
◆ *LAND 3: Autoland* refers to a Category 3 autopilot mode which was engaged, and which allows the aircraft to be guided automatically down to the runway threshold.
◆ *DME* stands for Distance Measuring Equipment.

Extension activity:

Write the following phrases on the board. Students discuss in pairs what was said about each of them and then watch again to check. When you check with the class, make sure they fully understand all the phrases.

◆ *strengthen our defences*
◆ *cautious, diligent and well-prepared*
◆ *mindset*
◆ *high workload*
◆ *made the picture fit*
◆ *descent rate*
◆ *portrayed*
◆ *interrogated*
◆ *anomalies*
◆ *a feeling of unease*

> **Answers:**
> ◆ The investigators analysed the incident in order to look for opportunities to *strengthen our defences* (= reduce the risk of similar incidents) in the future.
> ◆ It was obvious that this crew were *cautious* (= careful), *diligent* (= they followed the procedures properly) and *well-prepared* for the approach.
> ◆ The crew had a normal *mindset* (= way of thinking) for pilots conducting an ILS approach, i.e. they trusted the most precise information.
> ◆ The crew had a high *workload* (= they were busy).
> ◆ When the Captain didn't see the runway lights, he *made the picture fit* by assuming that there was weather in front of him.
> ◆ They saw a *descent rate* of just over 1,000 feet per minute.
> ◆ The information being *portrayed* (= shown) on the instruments was wrong.
> ◆ The autopilots *interrogated* (=carefully checked) all data and found absolutely no *anomalies* (= problems) with the status of the ILS information.
> ◆ The crew had a feeling of *unease* (= worry) when the glideslope captured.

b, c, d **Make sure students fully understand the questions, especially** *reconcile* **(= find a way of understanding conflicting pieces of information). Tell students to discuss the questions in pairs and then feed back to the class.**

Answers:
b The ILS is both more precise and generally more reliable than the VOR and NDB.
c The crew's initial mindset meant that they concentrated on managing the excessive energy (momentum) of the aircraft and looking for explanations for their impression of being rushed other than the ILS. At first they explained the absence of runway lighting at their altitude by weather ahead and the high energy by their weight and a tailwind.
d their sense of unease even when they had resolved the energy problem

32a **Go through the questions with the class to predict what the answers might be. Then play Part 2 for them to answer the three questions. They discuss their answers in pairs before feeding back to the class.**

Answers:
1 Because the ILS is generally very reliable and precise. It is located on the airport and so can be constantly monitored and quickly corrected.
2 a combination of the discrepancy between their current altitude and their distance from the Faleolo DME transmitter and the unusual closeness of the lights on a nearby island
3 15 seconds

b **Discuss with the class.**

Suggested answer:
Crosschecking takes two forms: 1) comparing Captain and First Officer data, e.g. System 1 and System 2, and 2) comparing data from two external sources, e.g. altitude / radio altitude and distance from a DME transmitter. In both cases, crosschecking enables the crew to know if one source of data is incorrect.

Extension activity:

Write the following words and phrases in two columns on the board. Students work in pairs to match the beginnings with the endings to make phrases from the clip. Note that the word information appears twice. Point out that they should do the easiest ones first and then come back to the more difficult ones. When you check with the class, make sure they all understand all the phrases.

1 the distance/ altitude ...
2 the apparent ...
3 the adjacent ...
4 to examine ...
5 compelling ...
6 to remain ...
7 to validate ...
8 to violate ...

a closeness of the lights
b your trust in sth
c information
d anomaly
e island
f their options
g vigilant
h information

Answers:
1 d   2 a   3 e   4 f   5 c/h   6 g
7 c/h   8 b

Background notes:

- An *anomaly* is a conflict between different sources of information.
- *Apparent* comes from the verb to appear: *The lights appeared to be close.*
- If something is *adjacent* to something else, it is right next to it.
- If something is *compelling*, it is very strong and persuasive.
- If you remain *vigilant*, you stay alert to possible problems.
- If you *validate* information, you check it to make sure that it is accurate.
- If your trust is *violated*, it is broken.

33a **Tell students to read the instructions carefully. Discuss with the class if they know, or can guess anything about, the Swiss Cheese model (see** *Background note***). It may help to point out that Swiss cheese is characterised by having many large holes.**

Tell students to watch Part 3 and to note the five defences that were breached. They compare their answers in pairs before feeding back to the class.

Answers:
The five defences were:
1 the NOTAM which informed the crew of an unmonitored landing aid;
2 the ILS ident (identifier), i.e. the radio frequency of the ILS transmitters;
3 the ILS warning flags on the aircraft instruments;
4 the glideslope intercept check and;
5 the GPWS (Ground Proximity Warning System).

Background notes:

♦ James Reason, author of *Human Error, Managing the risks of institutional error* and *The human contribution*, created the famous **Swiss cheese model of human error**; his thought is behind much aviation human factors research and training. The best way to picture the Swiss Cheese model is to imagine a light source (e.g. a torch), representing potential risks, being blocked by a slice of cheese, representing precautions. With normal cheese, all the light will be blocked by a single slice. But the holes in Swiss cheese would allow some light to get through. A second slice of Swiss cheese would block some of this light, but it might take five or six slices to completely block the light. In other words, no single precaution is sufficient, because all precautions have holes. Therefore, it is necessary to have several back-up precautions. See http://sustainability.bhpbilliton.com/2005/repository/health/ourapproach/employeehealth.asp for a visual representation of this model in a different context. There is a similar visual representation in the DVD clip.

♦ A *unanimous* /juːˈnænɪməs/ decision is agreed by all members.

♦ An *ident* /ˈaɪdent/ is the radio frequency which identifies a particular navaid transmitter.

♦ *NOTAM terminology* refers to the formulation of the NOTAM message.

♦ *Unmonitored or not-ATS monitored approach and landing aids* refers to the ILS transmitters not being either automatically self-monitored, or monitored by the air navigation service provider.

♦ If a system is *degraded*, it is operating with only part of its capability.

♦ *Proximity* is another name for closeness.

♦ If sth is *reinforced*, it is made stronger.

b, c, d **Students discuss the three questions in pairs and then feed back to the class.**

Answers:
b 1 The NOTAM defence was breached by ambiguous language being used in the NOTAM; 2 The ILS identifier, which usually indicates a correct signal, was present throughout the approach; 3 The ILS warning flags were not triggered because the ILS transmitter provided enough information for the aircraft ILS system not to detect a malfunction; 4 The glideslope intercept check was not completed because the crew were busy managing the energy and trying to reconcile the other data; 5 The GPWS was not triggered because the aircraft was in landing configuration (flaps, then gear extended).

c The crew's situational awareness was not breached because it led to them deciding to go around.
d Their situational awareness was formed by their continuing sense of unease, the lights on the nearby island appearing too close, and the discrepancy between their present altitude and the Faleolo DME indication.

34a **Students work in small groups to discuss the question. After a few minutes, open up the discussion to include the whole class. Once the students have fed back, develop the notions of trust and team work as factors which contribute to safety and elicit the students' own experiences.**

Suggested answers:
The other factors which contributed to effective decision-making in the case of NZ60 were: the crew's lack of complacency and ongoing effort to reconcile the data at their disposal; a sense of trust between the team members which had been created before the approach; the ability to exchange their opinions and doubts; good teamwork by focusing on complementary aspects of the approach; and the presence of a third pilot on the jump seat who was able to take part of the workload.

b **Discuss the place of trust, team-building and safety-conscious attitudes in the workplace; how they can be created and threatened. Ask students how management can assist in enhancing these factors. Talk about the role of effective communication and language proficiency in promoting these factors.**

PART C
Review

Pronunciation

1a **3.35** Make sure students understand which words they should underline. Then play the recording for students to complete the task. When you check with the class, ask volunteers to read each sentence aloud with the same urgency.

> Answers:
> 1 immediately
> 2 armed man
> 3 left
> 4 unable
> 5 decreased; 300 feet
> 6 seems; vehicle
> 7 nose gear; extended
> 8 windshear
> 9 Go around; go around; Right
> 10 severely concussed; divert

b **3.35** Play the recording again, pausing after each sentence for students to repeat, either individually or as a class. Make sure they use the correct stress. Afterwards, students practise in pairs using audioscript 3.35 on page 190.

c **3.36** Go through the words briefly with the class to make sure they know how the words are pronounced. Note that they will have a chance to practise the pronunciation in exercise 1d, but at this stage it is important to make sure they can hear and understand the differences. Then play the recording for students to complete the task. They check in pairs before feeding back to the class. Afterwards, students practise in pairs using audioscript 3.36 on page 190.

> Answers:
> 1 walking   7 clearing
> 2 against   8 quiet
> 3 watch   9 old
> 4 we'll   10 height
> 5 wet   11 thanks
> 6 had   12 past

d **3.37** Play the recording, pausing after each pair of words for students to repeat, either individually or as a class. Afterwards, students practise in pairs using audioscript 3.37 on page 190.

Structure

2a **3.38** Write the eight question words/phrases on the board (so that students don't have to look in their books while listening). Then play the recording, pausing after each sentence for a volunteer to make a question using one of the question words/phrases. Discuss with the class the suitability and grammatical accuracy of each question before moving on to the next sentence. Afterwards, students can test each other in pairs using audioscript 3.38 on page 190.

> Suggested answers:
> 1 Which runway is in use?
> 2 Why are you returning to land?
> 3 How many passengers have you got on board?
> 4 When do you expect to be crossing Bratislava?
> 5 How much fuel do you have in reserve?
> 6 What is your problem?
> 7 Who told you to expect delays? / How long a delay were you told to expect?
> 8 Why do we need to take delaying action?
> 9 How much should we reduce our speed (by)?
> 10 Which level should we expect?
> 11 Which runway is closed?
> 12 What is our new ETA?
> 13 Who will meet our sick passenger?
> 14 How much more time do you need? / How long do you need?
> 15 Which automation have you lost?

b Students work alone to match the events with the actions. They check in pairs before feeding back to the class.

> Answers:
> 1 e   3 h   5 d   7 b
> 2 g   4 a   6 c   8 f

Extension activity:

Students test each other in pairs by reading one of the beginnings (1–8) to elicit a suitable ending from their partner, whose book is closed.

c Students work alone to choose the correct option and then check in pairs. When you go through the answers with the class, elicit why the incorrect answers are wrong.

> Answers:
> 1 b   3 b   5 c   7 b
> 2 a   4 a   6 c   8 c

Vocabulary

3a Students work alone to complete the sentences. They check in pairs before feeding back to the class.

Answers:
1 descent	5 glare
2 vectors	6 slippery
3 veering	7 stabilised
4 beam	8 confusing

Extension activity:

Students test each other in pairs by reading one of the sentences aloud, substituting the work 'blank' for the gapped word. Their partners, whose books are closed, have to supply a suitable word for each blank.

b ◉**3.39** Go through the eight technical problems briefly with the class to make sure all students understand what they mean. Then play the recording for students to complete the task. They check in pairs before feeding back to the class.

Answers:
1 c	3 e	5 d	7 f
2 g	4 a	6 h	8 b

Background notes:

- A *flame-out* is a loss of combustion in a gas turbine engine.
- *Radar clutter* refers to the fact that too many aircraft are displayed in the same part of the radar screen and so have become indistinguishable from each other.

Extension activity:

Students work in pairs to try to remember as much as they can about each sentence in the recording, using only the list of technical problems to help them. Afterwards, discuss with the class what the sentences were about and then play the recording again to check.

c Students work alone to complete the sentences. They check in pairs before feeding back to the class.

Answers:
1 at	5 for
2 in	6 on
3 from	7 long
4 between	8 inbound

Extension activity:

Students test each other in pairs by reading one of the sentences aloud, substituting the work 'blank' for the gapped word. Their partners, whose books are closed, have to supply a suitable word for each blank.

Background note:

NHL is a navaid identifier in Australia.

d Students complete the sentences and then check in pairs before feeding back to the class. As a follow-up, you could ask students to test each other in pairs by reading out one of the sentences and pausing after the gapped word (e.g. *The pilots confused …*) to elicit from their partner a suitable ending.

Answers:
1 confused	5 reported
2 distracted	6 decided
3 expected	7 called out
4 experienced	8 managed

Fluency

4a ◉**3.40** Go through the instructions with the class. Make sure they also understand and can pronounce all the words in the cues, including *manoeuvrability* /mənuːvrəˈbɪlɪtɪ/ and *epileptic fit* (= a seizure, sometimes characterised by uncontrolled body movements, associated with the medical condition epilepsy). Then play the recording, pausing after the first communication for a volunteer to suggest an appropriate way of expressing concern, using the cue. Discuss the best answer with the class before moving on to the next communication. Afterwards, students repeat the exercise in pairs, using audioscript 3.40 on page 190.

Possible answers:
1 We are worried because we are running short of fuel and only have 45 minutes fuel endurance.
2 I am concerned as we have human organs on board for the local hospital and cannot be delayed any longer.
3 We have a heavy load and our braking is downgraded, so I am afraid that Runway 08 Left with 2,100 metres landing distance available will not be sufficient.
4 I'm worried that we may be below our minima for a VFR approach.
5 I'm concerned about the vectors you have given us to capture the ILS and a step-down approach: we have limited roll control and reduced manoeuvrability.
6 We are very worried about one of our passengers who has suffered an epileptic fit, and requires urgent medical assistance.

Comprehension

5 ◉3.41 Go through the introduction and the ten sentences with the class to make sure students fully understand the situation and the vocabulary. Then play the recording for students to complete the task. Students discuss their answers in pairs, including trying to remember as much as they can about the incident. They listen again if necessary before feeding back to the class.

Answers:
1 T
2 F – it is landing on Runway 19 Left
3 F – he intends to stop as soon as the runway is vacated
4 T
5 T
6 F – the fire service is on Ground frequency
7 F – in the tailpipe
8 T
9 F – the right-hand engine is shut down; the left-hand engine is running at idle
10 T

Background notes:

◆ The aircraft's call sign is Etihad 339 Heavy. The word *Heavy* is added because it is a wide-body aircraft such as a B747, B777, B767, A330, A340, A380 or MD-11.
◆ If somebody has *fired a bottle*, it means that the fire-extinguishing bottle has been discharged.

Interaction

6 Go through the instructions with the class. Students then work in pairs to conduct the dialogue. Students could swap roles and repeat the activity. Afterwards, ask volunteers to act out their dialogues for the class. Give and elicit feedback on the effectiveness of the communication.

Possible answers:
Pilot: Ankara ACC, Indonesia 088. We are a Boeing triple seven Extended Range at Flight Level 390 en route to Amsterdam from Jakarta. Our Engine Number 1 oil level is decreasing. We are monitoring engine performance, but request lower level to start APU, and wish to consider a diversion for a precautionary landing, Indonesia 088.

ATCO: Indonesia 088, descend Flight Level 210. Report on reaching. Keep us advised of the situation on board. Kayseri, Ankara and Istanbul are all possible alternates en route.

Pilot: Indonesia 088, Flight Level 210. The APU is running and Engine Number 1 is on reduced thrust, Indonesia 088.

ATCO: Indonesia 088, advise intentions

Pilot: We prefer to continue to Istanbul to connect with code-sharing partners, Indonesia 088.

...

Pilot: Ankara, Indonesia 088, We have an Engine Number 1 low oil pressure warning. The engine is at flight idle. Request diversion for precautionary landing at nearest alternate. We have 214 passengers on board, Indonesia 088.

ATCO: Indonesia 088, precautionary landing. Ankara Esenboga is at 68 nautical miles.

Pilot: Request coordinates of Esenboga International Airport, Ankara, Indonesia 088

ATCO: The coordinates are: 40 degrees 07 minutes 41 seconds North, 32 degrees, 59 minutes, 42 seconds East.

Pilot: 40 degrees 07 minutes 41 seconds North, 32 degrees, 59 minutes, 42 seconds East. Request weather, Indonesia 088

ATCO: Ankara Esenboga International Airport, Information Hotel at 03:00 Zulu: wind 050 degrees, four knots; visibility six kilometres; cloud scattered 2,800 feet, overcast 4,200 feet; temperature nine degrees, dewpoint six degrees, QNH 1007, ILS approach Runway 03 Right

Pilot: wind 050 degrees, four knots; visibility six kilometres; cloud scattered 2,800 feet, overcast 4,200 feet; temperature nine degrees, dewpoint six degrees, QNH 1007, ILS approach Runway 03 Right, Indonesia 088

ATCO: Indonesia 088, contact Ankara Approach 118 decimal 2

Pilot: Indonesia 088, we have a passenger who is very agitated at the prospect of landing in Turkey. He is causing quite a disturbance in the cabin, Indonesia 088.

ATCO: Do you require police or medical assistance on arrival?

Pilot: Negative. The passenger will be in transit only. I have reassured him that he will not have to pass immigration, Indonesia 088.

...

Pilot: Indonesia 088, we are at 8,000 feet. Request ILS approach Runway 03 Right

ATCO: Indonesia 088, cleared ILS approach Runway 03 Right

ATCO: Indonesia 088, confirm established Localizer and Glideslope

Pilot: Localizer captured. We are stabilised and have the runway in sight, Indonesia 088.

INDEX

H

I

J

K

L

M

ACKNOWLEDGEMENTS

The publishers would like to thank the following:
Design and page make-up: eMC Design Ltd.
Freelance editor: Ben Gardiner
Index: Linda Hardcastle

Jeremy Day would like to thank Bożena Sławińska for teaching him so much about the needs of pilots and Air Traffic Controllers and for arranging a tour of the Warsaw control tower. He would also like to thank the Warsaw controllers who gave of their time and provided insights into their work. Thanks to co-author Philip for his patience and expertise, and to editors Ben Gardiner and Keith Sands. As always, thanks to Ania, Emilka and Tomek for their patience and support.